I0125443

FROM IDOLS TO ANTIQUITY

THE MEXICAN EXPERIENCE

William H. Beezley, series editor

FROM IDOLS TO ANTIQUITY

Forging the National Museum of Mexico

MIRUNA ACHIM

University of Nebraska Press | Lincoln and London

© 2017 by the Board of Regents of the University
of Nebraska

Portions of the introduction and chapters 2, 4, and
5 previously appeared in "The National Museum of
Mexico, 1825–1867," *Museum History Journal* 9, no.
1 (2016): 13–28, http://www.tandfonline.com. Used
with permission.

Portions of chapter 3 previously appeared in "The
Art of the Deal, 1828: How Isidro Icaza Traded
Pre-Columbian Antiquities to Henri Baradère for
Mounted Birds and Built a National Museum in
Mexico City in the Process," *West 86th* 18, no. 2
(September 2011): 214–31. Published by the Univer-
sity of Chicago Press.

All rights reserved. Manufactured in the United
States of America. ∞

Library of Congress Control Number: 2017953893

Set in Scala by Rachel Gould.

For Constanza and Julian

CONTENTS

ILLUSTRATIONS

ACKNOWLEDGMENTS

In the summer of 2009 I came upon Irina Podgorny's book on the Museum of Natural History in La Plata, Argentina. Contrary to other works on nineteenth-century museums that I was familiar with, this book had relinquished grand narratives of nationalism and national identity to focus on the more mundane aspects of everyday practice. It made for a compelling account, where contingency, shortage, and ambition played as big a role if not bigger than abstract ideas of nation building. I began searching for an equivalent of Irina's book that would tell the story of Mexico's national museum, founded in 1825, only to run, again, into stories of national identity. Moreover, for the first five decades of the National Museum of Mexico, I could probably have fit all the available literature in five pages. I was often told that there was nothing else to say or a longer history would have been written already. Intrigued, I turned to the archives, at first tentatively, then increasingly convinced that there was enough material to tell a longer and richer story about Mexico's first national museum. By the time my desk was crowded with files about different aspects of the museum, I realized I was writing this story.

Irina has been an inspiration, an intellectual companion, and an irreverent friend over these years. I was lucky enough to receive encouragement and support from many other people along the way. I am especially grateful to the following colleagues and friends: Esther Acevedo, Akuavi Adonon, Alejandro Araujo, Violeta Aréchiga, Paulina Aroch, Bernardo Bolaños, Mario Barbosa Cruz, Mario Casanueva, John Charles, Laura Cházaro García, Natalia Coloballes Soto, Susan Deans-Smith, Jean Baptiste Fressoz, Will Fowler, Alicia García Bergua, Roger Gathman, Stefanie Gänger, Nicholas Jardine, Enrique Krauze, Carlos López Beltrán, Leonardo López Luján, Andrea Martínez Baracs, Rodrigo Martínez Baracs, Yolanda Mirón

Río, Iris Montero Sobrevilla, Bertina Olmedo, José Pardo Tomás, Matthew Robb, Estela Roselló Soberón, Sandra Rozental, Antonio Saborit, Simon Schaffer, Silvia Sebastiani, Nuria Valverde, Jennifer Varnes, Jude Webber, Martina Will de Chaparro, and Zenia Yébenes.

I have presented different aspects of this book at different moments, and I would like to thank audiences at Cambridge University, Imperial College, University College of London, CNRS (France), CSIC (Spain), UCLA, UNAM, and especially the Foro del Mediodía at the Universidad Autónoma Metropolitana–Cuajimalpa for their stimulating questions, which have encouraged me to nuance and sharpen my arguments.

In the course of my research, I have benefitted from the generosity and erudition of librarians and archivists at different institutions: Biblioteca Nacional de Antroplogía e Historia and the Archivo Histórico del Museo Nacional in Mexico City; the Nettie Lee Benson at the University of Texas at Austin; the Bibliothèque Nationale, the Archives des Musées Nationaux, the Archives Nationales, and the library of the Musèe du Quay Branly in Paris; the British Library and the library of the British Museum in London; the Newberry Library in Chicago; the Latin American Library at Tulane University; and the Pennsylvania Historical Society. Special thanks are due to David Grossman at the American Philosophical Society in Philadelphia.

Researching and writing this book would not have been possible without generous financial support by the Universidad Autónoma Metropolitana–Cuajimalpa and by Conacyt. For the last stages of this book, I am particularly indebted to the two anonymous reviewers for their comments and suggestions, to my editor Bridget Barry, and to the dedicated staff at the University of Nebraska Press, whose high professionalism and encouragement have proved crucial to the completion of this project.

Rodrigo Martínez Baracs was an indefatigable and receptive listener and critic from the beginning to the end of this project.

Arturo Ramírez arrived late in the process of my writing this book, to renew once more my belief in coincidence and my attraction to chaos theory.

This book is dedicated to Constanza and Julian, who have been the best of companions while I carried on research in archives and libraries on both sides of the Atlantic. They have taken our various relocations with good stride. Their wisdom, understanding, sense of humor, and impatience with my long working hours have brought joy to my life and have given me a much-needed balance in the course of the past six years.

FROM IDOLS TO ANTIQUITY

INTRODUCTION

The Uses of a National Museum

A Cabinet of Curiosities

The National Museum of Mexico was founded in 1825 by presidential decree, participating in the generational tide that brought forth
museums in Brazil (1818), Chile (1822), Argentina and Colom-
bia (1823), Peru (1826), and Bolivia (1838). The transition from
colony to independent state in these countries—with the exception of Brazil—seems to have been closely followed by plans for
a national museum, as though to show that nationhood meant
cultural as well as political independence. Implicit in these acts
was the expectation that museums would become repositories of
national objects—whatever they might be—and somehow forge
the kind of stories around these objects that would give meaning
to the nation and teach its people to become citizens. In this sense,
a museum is a constitutional institution; if the paper constitution
bears the burden of defining a nation's legal framework, the objects
of a national museum bear the burden of constituting a nation's
cultural framework. As Lucas Alamán (1792–1853), the powerful
minister of internal and external relations who was behind the
creation of the National Museum of Mexico, declared before Congress in 1825, the genuineness of Mexico's independence would
be consummated by such institutions of public instruction as a
national museum. The state would, in essence, produce its citizens
by educating them in what it meant to belong to the nation; they
would, in turn, reproduce the state.

Despite the elevated rhetoric with which its foundation was her-
alded, the reality is that during the first four decades of its existence,
the National Museum of Mexico was neglected by the state. The
museum did not occupy a space especially built for it but eked out
its existence in the very cramped quarters granted to it at the uni-

versity in the center of Mexico City. And the museum's first curators complained of lack of space; of the government's habit of using the museum as a military barracks when the occasion presented itself, which happened all too frequently given the internecine power plays and wars that marked the tumultuous history of the young country; and of the perennial lack of money, which prevented the museum from pursuing an ambitious agenda of acquisition, exploration, and research.[1] During this period, the museum collected taxonomically diverse things: preconquest antiquities, colonial documents and paintings, mummies, shells, insects, fossils, silver ores, meteorites, engravings of the French imperial family and of U.S. presidents, armors, stuffed animals—and some live ones as well. These all existed in such close proximity one with the other that one of the museum's early visitors exclaimed that the national collection was merely "a jumble of fragments," a far cry from the embodiment of a unified image of the nation, even if it was, perhaps, an appropriate correlate and metaphor for the political conflicts that defined Mexico's barely contained anarchy during these decades.[2]

As much as they speak of material and logistical issues, the problems that bedeviled the National Museum of Mexico during its first decades are tied up with a profound crisis of meaning: What defined and gave meaning to a national museum in the early nineteenth century? Were legislative or presidential decrees enough to ensure a museum's existence? Was a museum an assemblage of concrete objects? Or was it a coupling together of some instituted form and institutionally prescribed content, marked by the public recognition of the social and symbolic uses of that pairing? More generally, how should a national museum construct the cultural authority to claim exclusive rights to collect certain objects and to control the production of knowledge about them?[3] The answers to these questions are not self-evident today, and they certainly were not in Mexico's postindependence years. Beginning in the 1870s, relative peace and stability would allow all the elements associated with a successful museum to come together during the so-called Porfirian Era (1876–1910): adequate space; a program; a policy for

acquisitions, exhibits, and admissions; and a quantitatively significant collection that was backed by the government and recognized
as such by Mexico's governing classes, followed, perhaps a little less
certainly, by the Mexican public at large. This glorious ending has
served to obscure the deeper contingency of the historical process
of the museum's coming into being. Renouncing the temptation of
teleological certainties, this book reconstructs the museum's early
history, between its foundation in 1825 and the end of the Second
Empire in 1867, when it was far from evident it would become
today's world-class National Museum of Anthropology.

Histories of the Museum

The historiography of the National Museum during the institution's first half century is scant, particularly when compared with
the solid scholarship both on the history of collecting in the late
Enlightenment and on the construction, collection, and display of
Mexico's national patrimony during the last decades of the nineteenth century.[4] The historiographical gap that corresponds to the
early museum is not an exception; we know little about most of
Mexico's institutions during the first few decades postindependence,
which have revealingly been called Mexico's "forgotten years."[5]
This neglect, it has been convincingly suggested, is not a matter
of pure chance. Rather, it reflects a mindset that began in the late
nineteenth century, when Mexico's liberal elites, in an attempt to
legitimate their own claims to power, began constructing the history of what had come before, through evolutionary metaphors that
accounted for the consolidation of the Porfirian state. In this grand
narrative, the disagreements, conflicts, and detours that marked
the nation's travails over fifty years were flattened and simplified,
and Mexican history came to be written through an agonistic perspective, as a series of oppositions that brought liberals against
conservatives, republicans against monarchists, and nationalists
against traitors—those, that is, who supported foreign interven-
tions. According to the late nineteenth-century liberal credo, it was
in the aftermath of these prolonged conflicts—concentrated, ultimately, in the battle pitting the reactionaries and foreigners rep-

resented by Maximilian I (1832–67) and the truly Mexican forces led by Benito Juarez (1806–72)—that the Mexican nation came to express its true republican essence. As Timothy Anna pointed out, by assuming the existence of a coherent entity called Mexico, "uninterrupted since the time of ancient civilization," historians have missed the process of its being created.[6]

These observations concerning the course of Mexico's politics in the nineteenth century can be useful to understanding the historiography of the National Museum. As the late nineteenth-century museum came to embody the alliance between the Mexican state, state-sponsored archaeology, and the search for narratives that would endow the liberal state with illustrious genealogies stretching back to preconquest civilization, its curators began looking back on the museum's early history to create a legitimating narrative that mirrored the Porfirian discourse about Mexico itself. The waste and chaos of the first fifty years were redeemed by the advent of a new breed of liberal scholars and policy makers who understood what the museum's essence and mission were about and set the floundering institution on the right course. Nineteenth-century liberal ideologies have exercised a tremendous influence on the way the history of the museum has been told ever since, through the "linearity of a singular narrative," which sees the museum as a coherent entity with intrinsic qualities, launched on a recognizably progressive trajectory, which would culminate in a national institution that functioned in the same way national museums functioned in Europe and the United States.[7] Especially influential in this story line have been theoretical arguments, espoused by cultural historians since the 1980s, that connect the birth of national museums in Europe and America with the construction of national identities. From the perspective of this reading, the museum is a *dispositif* for educating the taste and the gaze of the public in the spirit of national unity, a platform for the creation of "imagined communities" of citizens, while the visit to the museum enacts the ultimate "civilizing ritual."[8]

It becomes immediately clear that when viewed against this frame, the history of the early years of the National Museum of Mexico is nothing but a history of negations of these essences. The museum, more frequently closed than open to the public and unable to display its collection around a legible narrative, was hardly a space for the production of national imaginaries. More critically, it failed to create consensus, among the governments in turn, that its collection could become a valuable agent for building up much-needed national unity. Confronted by these contradictions with respect to the standard museum narrative, historians have tended either to dismiss the museum during these early years as a pitiful attempt at trial and error or to vindicate it as a seed imprinted from the very beginning with the genetic information it would need to develop into a mature museum. In either case, what Anna has concluded with regards to the political history of Mexico's forgotten years holds true for the museum as well: historians have missed the process of its emergence. To reconstruct this process is to reconstruct its contingencies and ambiguities, a dimension that is eclipsed when one views the museum teleologically, from the vantage of its renown today. The effort is well worth it, as the story that begins to take shape is relevant, not only for the particular case of the National Museum of Mexico, but for the history of collecting and museums in Latin America and in general. There is nothing essential or obvious about the coming into being of the institutions of modernity; there is improvisation and uncertainty, conveniently forgotten and overwritten by stories of success.[9]

Forgetting, as Friedrich Nietzsche pointed out, is the privilege of the strong, who know how to forget. Perhaps as a reflection of those shocks that have shaken Mexico's political order since Carlos Salinas's presidency (1988–94), and put into doubt the establishment and its conventional wisdoms, the Mexican past is being remembered differently.[10] The museum's early history, as part of those forgotten decades, has begun to attract a number of topical studies: reassessments of its natural history collection; reconstructions of episodes in the history of Mexican antiquarianism; reviews of legislation, as related to the museum and more broadly to the definition and management of collectibles, especially antiquities; and accounts of the museum during the Second Empire.[11]

These piecemeal approaches correspond to contemporary disciplinary notions of how museums specialize—in natural history and archaeology, for instance—but unfortunately they do little to advance our understanding of the total cabinet-like nature of the museum itself. We require a truly comprehensive history of the museum's first half century, one which would give an account of its activities as they were executed (or more often, aborted) within the cultures of early nineteenth-century collecting, which were in turn defined by even broader political and cultural (national and international) contexts.

In part, the lack of easily accessible archival material helps explain why scholarship so often compresses the early years of the National Museum of Mexico into a relatively short and unanalyzed episode of a larger history. A summary search at the Archivo Histórico del Museo Nacional (AHMN), housed at the National Museum of Anthropology, yields 472 volumes related to administrative and operational aspects in the museum's history between 1831 and 1964. Of these, only half of volume 1 covers the forty-year period I study in this book. This half volume is far from being the only source that would allow us to reconstruct the early history of the museum, but other sources are scattered across the archives and libraries belonging to the different government departments that were directly responsible for the museum at different moments in its early history: the Secretary of Internal and External Relations, the School of Mines, the Secretary of Public Instruction, and the Second Empire, whose archives are all held by Mexico's Archivo General de la Nación (AGN). Another considerable portion of documents related to the museum's early history can be found in a rather nondescript section at the AGN that bears the telltale name Sin Sección (literarily, "sectionless"). Here we find materials that have apparently daunted the classificatory intentions and criteria of the archivist. The difficulty faced by government officials when it came to giving the museum a place within the state bureaucracy reflects larger organizational issues faced by the museum: its difficulties in securing the necessary financial support and an adequate material space for its collection. As for the documents themselves, they cover a broad and variegated terrain of topics, themes, and concerns. They include the museum's operating protocols; appointments and dismissals of personnel; contracts with taxidermists, bricklayers, carpenters, and architects; correspondence with other museums and collectors; acknowledgements of donations; petitions for objects; proofs of objects leaving the museum; inventories; drafts for expedition and excavation projects; and requests for money from various government agencies.

Together, these records yield the protean contours of a fluctuating social and material space, which challenges our modern sense of the museum's mission. Things did not just go to the museum to be embalmed and explained but were just as often in transit as they orbited uncertainly between curators, collectors, adventurers, and amateur scholars. Inventory control was lax and depended on the personalities doing the overseeing. The rules for collecting, organizing, and displaying the collection confound our sense of logical and ethical museum practice. How can we explain that a museum curator exchanged Mexican antiquities for stuffed birds or that, in those crowded quarters, another would have built a cabinet to house objects, knowing they were fakes? Indeed, these are puzzles that we will attempt to explain in this book. The more daunting task is what to make of what is so often not there in the archival record. Reflecting on the dispersal of Mexican archives during the nineteenth century, the early biography of the museum thickens and ebbs out, offering little certainty as to the day-to-day operations of the museum and challenging the presumptions of institutional history. How can we then tell a meaningful story of the museum's emergence by patching together scattered fragments and incomplete records?

In the early stages of my research on the museum, I came upon a project on the history of the Pitt Rivers Museum at Oxford University in the nineteenth century, coordinated by Chris Gosden, the curator of archaeology at the Pitt Rivers between 1994 and 2006.[12] Though the archival record of the Pitt Rivers is considerably more abundant than that of the National Museum of Mexico, to write about the English museum, the historian was brought face-to-face with the challenge of making sense of a heterogeneous assemblage of things, which continues to bear testimony today to how a bygone age thought and organized the material world. Taking his departure from material and object studies, Gosden and his team proposed to study the Pitt Rivers as a "relational museum," by reconstructing the relations that were improvised and rehearsed around objects or collections of objects that entered the Pitt Rivers during the nineteenth century. People collect objects, wrote Gosden, Larson, and Petch, though they considered the reverse to be just as true: objects collect people, implicating them in different forms of interaction, etiquettes of exchange, and hierarchies. Without offering an exhaustive history of the Pitt Rivers, this account condenses around moments in the museum's history, presenting them as the interplay of social, cultural, and material trajectories. Taking archival "records [as] historical paths" allowed Gosden, Larson, and Petch to trace the profile of the museum "beyond [its] immediate, physical confines."[13]

Gosden's notion of the relational museum struck me as a way to reckon with the unity of the museum on a theoretical level. Institutional approaches, with their assumptions about how institutions think, would simply write off the National Museum of Mexico in the period I am examining as a false start, a blip on the timeline that we can skip over, confident that the real starting point of the museum was when it began to matter, institutionally, to the Mexican government—that is, sometime in the early years of the Porfiriato, in the 1870s. By contrast, the patterns intrinsic to the museum's first fifty years opened up for me when I gave up looking for an incipient institutional rationality and began following the historical paths of people and objects associated with the museum beyond the cramped spaces of the institution to places as far off as the mines of Chihuahua, the desserts of Durango, and the selva of Yucatán; Egypt and China; the Louvre in Paris; the British Museum in London; the American Philosophical Society in Philadelphia; and private cabinets in Mexico City, Campeche, and Potsdam, to name but a few. Tracking the trajectories of people and things presents us with a messy and entangled story that is not the broad and sweeping story we might want, with a state-founded institution finding its way after some initial and inevitable failures. Instead, the story, and the museum itself, takes shape painstakingly, through small-scale interactions spread across space and time. The picture that begins to emerge here shows that, far from following previously scripted protocols, the museum's strategies for collecting, preserving, displaying, and studying objects developed improvisationally, in practice, and were mediated by interpersonal relationships, private greed, competition for collectibles, imperialist claims on certain kinds of objects, market, and intellectual ambitions, all of which were projected on the museum as often as they derived from its personnel and its supposed mission. The fortunes of the museum were determined as much by material conditions—such as bad or difficult roads, blockades imposed by foreign powers, the fragility or weight of certain objects, and the availability of printing presses and of trained technicians to operate them—as by any evolving master plan.

Throughout this book, the National Museum of Mexico emerges as one of the nodes, where local, national, and international politics of collecting were being played out. It is not common for a Mexican museum—or a Latin American one, for that matter—to become a unit for analyzing the production, organization, and display of knowledge about human and natural history in the early nineteenth century. In the "Century of the Empire," it has been often assumed that Latin America provided vast fields for the collection of specimens, which would be accumulated, assembled, studied, and exhibited elsewhere, in Europe and the United States.[14] What is missing from the otherwise rich and detailed accounts of the politics of imperial collecting in Latin America is the recognition that local actors—from statesmen to scientists, from cultural elites to Indian guides—were not simply passive transition points, or mere transactional costs, but pursued their own strategies for collecting, exchanging, studying, or impeding the exportation of objects. This blind spot is akin to a larger, paradigmatic blind spot in the historiography of Latin American science, which only understands science in Latin America as an exogenous variable.[15] This book strives to recover the story of Mexican collecting as it emerged at different sites as both exchangers and intermediaries in the trans-Atlantic traffic of objects, ideas, and representations that took place in this period. Ultimately, as historians have persuasively argued in other colonialist or imperialist contexts, Mexican intellectual claims to know certain objects or classes of objects were used to legitimate the nation's rightful material claims on them, as forms of positioning against outside competition for collectibles.[16]

Idols, Antiquities, Artifacts

The story of the museum's long beginnings, as I tell it here, is inseparable from the mixed commodification of preconquest antiquities, with their value set by science and politics as well as rarity and fashion. There is no intrinsic property that made Mexican antiquities compelling and interesting to scholars and grave robbers alike in the nineteenth century. During the previous two and a half centuries of colonial rule, Spanish policies toward the vestiges of Mexico's ancient past were complicated, veering—mostly in the years immediately following the conquest—between the missionary zeal to destroy the vestiges of an idolatrous age and the humanist urge to collect and study them as clues to the history of mankind. Sometimes, the two impulses were only two sides of the same coin. Franciscan friar Bernardino de Sahagún (1499–1590) was one among many early evangelizers who gathered detailed accounts of life in preconquest Mexico, with minute descriptions of the objects at the heart of everyday practice, in an effort to understand the social and religious rituals of the Indians, in order to all the more effectively extirpate them. The Spanish Crown also took an active interest in the material vestiges of ancient Mexico. Starting in 1536, "treasures" found in tombs, temples, and ancient burials became property of the king. Though some of these objects were incorporated into princely cabinets of wonders, many others, especially those made of metal, were melted for coinage.[17] As for carved stones, after undergoing an initial wave of destruction and defacement, many were transposed from the sacred to the profane sphere, where they became now a doorjamb, now the base of a column or the strut supporting a construction, lending

Mexico City the air of an outdoor museum to those blessed with an antiquarian imagination, while those unblessed, the majority of urban dwellers, simply accepted them as symbolically neuter parts of the cityscape.[18]

After the frenzy of the first period of the conquest passed, there were those who, in the seventeenth and eighteenth centuries, studied and, to some extent, collected preconquest or postconquest objects and manuscripts. Among these, the baroque polymath Carlos de Sigüenza y Góngora (1645–1700) stands out for his excavations at the Pyramid of the Sun in Teotihuacan and for his hypotheses, which, taking a cue from the Jesuit scholar Athanasius Kircher (1602–80), suggested an Egyptian origin for the ancient Mexican civilizations.[19] Half a century after Sigüenza y Góngora's death, in the mid-eighteenth century, the ill-fated Italian cavalier Lorenzo Boturini (1702–53) amassed a rich collection of codices and manuscripts, before his papers were seized and he himself was expelled from New Spain for his involvement with the cult of the Virgin of Guadalupe.[20]

The meaning of Mexican antiquities among the new class of intellectuals—who identified, to a greater or lesser extent, with the Enlightenment—became a topic of consideration in the transatlantic discourse of the second half of the eighteenth century. This went hand in hand with an ongoing program of exploration, collection, and study of all aspects of human and natural history of the colonies, sponsored by Carlos III. This program intended to convert the latent intellectual assets of the worldwide empire into real utilitarian functions, making Spain competitive again against other emerging imperial powers. The foundation of metropolitan and colonial institutions, such as the Royal Natural History Cabinet in Madrid or the School of Mines in Mexico City, and the organization of a number of scientific expeditions to the New World were all parts of this program. However, there were also outside impulses at work, a particularly important one being the stimulus from the antiquarian interest in another part of the far-flung Spanish Empire, the spectacular discoveries at Pompey and Herculaneum in the Spanish viceroyalty of Naples.[21] Imperial policy changed from pious hostility or indifference nurtured by the Habsburgs of the late seventeenth century to important support for finding and studying archaeological sites throughout the empire under the Bourbons. This was not only a question of a change of dynasties; it was also an event in intellectual history, as the Enlightenment problematic of history came to replace universal sacred history, while at the same time borrowing motifs from the latter.

The old neglect of preconquest vestiges began to seem like a vestige itself. In Mexico, Antonio María de Bucareli y Ursúa, viceroy of New Spain between 1771 and 1779, disposed that antiquities scattered around Mexico City and its environs be gathered together in a museum, to be installed provisionally at the Royal University, where he founded the first chair devoted to the study of preconquest antiquities. There is not much evidence of the work carried out either by the museum or by the chair, which were, in any case, short lived.[22] The following decades ushered in important studies of preconquest antiquities, many of them by Mexico's Creole elites. In the 1780s José Antonio Alzate y Ramírez (1733–99) visited the ruins of Xochicalco, south of Mexico City; he published detailed, illustrated descriptions of the site.[23] Farther afield, in the Audiencia de Guatemala, the Crown was sponsoring expeditions to the ruins of Palenque.[24]

In this context of growing antiquarian interest, some very big monoliths were unearthed in Mexico City's central plaza as a result of an urban improvement project ordered by Viceroy Revillagigedo in the early 1790s: the so-called Calendar Stone; the Teoyamiqui, or Coatlicue; and the Stone of Tízoc. They immediately became objects of study and contention among Mexican scholars, including Alzate; José Ignacio Borunda (1740–1800), a lawyer at the Real Audiencia; and the astronomer and mathematician Antonio de León y Gama (1735–1802), who offered conflicting hypotheses about the iconography and the uses of the monoliths.[25] Beyond their disagreements, in the writings of these Creole intellectuals, preconquest vestiges were a source of pride and the basis for vindicating Mexico's ancient past besides the ancient civilizations of the Old World. These sentiments were not devoid of ambivalence: the recognition of Mexico's advances in the past induced comparison with the state of Mexico in the present, particularly of the majority of its putatively ignorant and backward Indian population. Views like these led religious authorities to rebury the Coatlicue in the patio of the university, in an effort to stem what were perceived to be newfound expressions of idolatry toward her.[26]

The Crown's support of a piecemeal approach to the study of Mexican antiquities was a stage in the development of a more ambitious exploration program, codified in the Royal Antiquarian Expeditions (1805–8), which were tasked with "producing exact drawings of the buildings and other monuments and thus perfecting the ancient history of the country, to give an idea of the taste and perfection which its naturals achieved in the country."[27] Guillermo Dupaix (1746–1818), the captain of a dragoon regiment who arrived in Mexico just as the dust was settling on the debates surrounding the monoliths unearthed in Mexico City and who had done some antiquarian work around the Mediterranean, was placed in charge of the expeditions. During three years, Dupaix, in the company of Luciano Castañeda, an artist trained at the Royal Academy of Fine Arts of San Carlos, undertook three trips to study ruins scattered around New Spain: first, to Orizaba, Cholula, and Xochicalco; second, to Xochimilco, Chalco, Ozumba, and Oaxaca; and third, to the Tehuantepec Isthmus, Guiengola, Ocosingo, and Palenque. Dupaix returned to Mexico City with antiquities and objects of natural history and with a large number of descriptions and travel diaries, maps, plans, and drawings of antiquities.[28] Some of this material began to be published in the 1830s and would form quintessential references for the study of Mexico's ancient past.

Two other factors contributed to stimulate scholarly interest in Mexican antiquities in the early 1800s. One was Alexander von Humboldt's *Vues des cordilleres et monuments des peuples indigènes de l'Amérique* (1816), an opulent, folio-sized book that placed images and descriptions of ruins and antiquities alongside monumental volcanoes and gorges, produced in the wake of Humboldt's travels though the Americas in the early 1800s. The other was the deluge of information about ancient Egypt, following Napoleon's ill-fated

military expedition there—an expedition that, in true Enlightenment fashion, deployed a team of 167 scholars. By the time Mexico
gained independence in 1821, Napoleon was gone, but the fashion
for antiquity was stronger than ever.

In opening the country to commerce and investment by European
countries that had long been excluded by the Spanish monopoly
on the New World, the Mexican government made Mexican antiquities attractive to the international market as well as to intellectuals working in the various fields of history, archaeology, and art.
Even when they did not always guarantee financial gain for their
collectors, Mexican antiquities, thought to resemble Egyptian ones,
reinvigorated scholarly conjecture about the nature of the relationship between the Old and the New Worlds and, less innocently,
between Mexico's glorious ancient past and its miserable present.
In turn, speculations like these sparked questions and debates, as
they did in newly independent Greece, about the ownership of goods
that were deemed the heritage of "mankind."[29] Who could be best
trusted to study and preserve them, and therefore, who should own
them? Neither the Mexican government nor the North Americans
and Europeans considered for a moment that antiquities should be
the property of the Indians on whose lands many of these objects
were found. But could Mexico's cultural authorities be trusted with
them? Did antiquities belong, as the Mexican government began
to claim by prohibiting the exportation of preconquest objects as
early as 1827, to the Mexican nation, as its cultural property? Or
were they fragments of the past of all mankind, and as such, should
they be gathered together in European and U.S. museums that had
the material and intellectual resources to house and study them?

From Idols to Antiquity explores the spaces, agents, and literary
and material technologies that contributed to shaping these debates
and thereby to defining the (economic, cultural, and symbolic) uses
of Mexican antiquities in the first half of the nineteenth century. As
Mexican antiquities—as well as their images and descriptions—
circulated between adventurers, collectors, cabinets, academies,
and museums on both sides of the Atlantic, their meanings were
constantly at play in the different story lines in which they figured.

These story lines were, as well, lines of intellectual and material property in which contending claims to own objects were linked to contending claims to know them. In turn, intellectual positioning in the competitive terrain of Mexican antiquarianism sustained forms of positioning in broader national and international political contexts. By the end of the period I study here, Mexican antiquities had become both the objects of a science of antiquity and the objects around which stories of Mexico's triumphant republicanism began to be written. The alliance between the Mexican nation and state-sponsored archaeology had grown so powerful that it is easy to overlook that it took decades for the state to recognize the advantages it would entail and decades more before it became apparent that, in embracing a Mexico that extended back before the conquest, the state had developed a populist ideology.

Overview

While the story I tell here follows closely the chronology of the National Museum of Mexico between 1825 and 1867, each chapter is structured around specific theoretical and thematic concerns. Chapter 1, "Genealogies," provides a thick description of the museum's foundation by following closely the early biography of one of its staunchest allies, Lucas Alamán (1792–1853), as he transited from member of the viceroyal elites to minister of internal and external relations in an independent country. Technically signed into existence by Mexico's first president, Guadalupe Victoria (1786–1843), it is easy to think of the museum strictly as a creation of the new republic, one among the first and most representative institutions of independence and nationhood. But contrary to this commonly held view, the legacy of Spain's colonial regime to independent Mexico would play an important role in the making of the museum. This came in the form of habits of collecting and studying antiquities and natural history, developed under the Bourbons—after all, the personnel who directed the museum had been educated in the finer institutions of learning in viceroyal Mexico—and in the form physical objects that were discovered and gathered together in the late eighteenth century. One of the more important questions for the museum was how to adapt (and override) these models of collecting to the new formations of economic and social power both in Mexico and in the transatlantic world. Could Mexico collect and exchange objects in the name of an abstract entity called "the nation"?

In chapter 2, "Measures of Worth," I explore this question through the career of Isidro Icaza (1783–1834), the museum's curator between 1826 and 1834. Unfortunately for Icaza's ambition to build up a strong institution, the inaugural years of the museum were years of considerable turmoil in Mexico in which various fundamental issues of governance were thrashed out. The 1824 Constitution had granted individual states great autonomy with respects to the federal government, and the following decades experienced instability as the forces of centralization versus those of federalism often abandoned the precincts of debate to take up arms against each other. In this context, a national museum was hardly a priority for the Mexican government. For the eight years he was at the head of the museum, Icaza struggled to make the museum matter to the authorities and to the public. First, he sought to do so by giving it a solid legal foundation. He created a set of norms for the museum that included a fixed budget; protocols for the collection, display, and handling of objects; and regular opening hours for the public. As a reflection of the gap between law and practice, these norms were ignored more often than not, even after they were approved in Congress in 1831. Second, Icaza sought to educate the more enlightened members of the public about the importance of the museum through a monthly publication, the *Colección de antigüedades*, which came out in 1827. The *Colección* paired lithographs and explanations of antiquities and made a strong case for Mexico's ancient past as comparable, in its arts and in its political, social, and religious institutions, to the ancient civilizations of the Old World, while presenting the museum as both keeper and interpreter of the nation's past. In the face of political and social unrest, the *Colección* failed to make an impression and was suspended after only three issues. By the early 1830s the museum, unable to prove its exclusive claim over both objects of antiquity and natural history, was vying with other competitors, both locals and foreigners, for collectibles.

Chapter 3, "Collecting the Ruins of Palenque," gauges the museum's capacity to collect in a shift of the area of analysis to the comparatively distant ruins of Palenque, some eight hundred kilometers from the capital. Starting at the end of the eighteenth century and increasingly during the first half of the nineteenth, Palenque became one of the rare Mexican places fabled for its ruins not only among antiquarians but in the popular press as well. Touted as the vestiges of America's most enlightened ancient civilization, Palenque set in motion a race to uncover mysteries shrouding the origins of the New World and its ties with the ancient civilizations of the Old World. In an attempt to claim both material and intellectual ownership over the site, the museum sought to enter the race by forging expeditionary projects in collaboration with foreign explorers between the late 1820s and the mid 1830s. These expeditions showcase the museum's difficulties with collecting objects. The museum's problems with Palenque were logistic (the absence of reliable roads and means of communication made the place mostly inaccessible), political (the right to the ruins were claimed both by the local villagers and by the state government of Chiapas), and cultural (local villagers, who invested the ruins with cultural and economic meanings quite different from the museum's, could not understand the museum's intentions there or the intentions of the explorers who came to the ruins in the museum's name). For the next decades, the ruins of Palenque would be collected abroad, which contributed to the sense that Mexico had lost control of the vestiges of the more advanced ancient civilizations in its territory. To overturn these impressions, the museum had to find a way to prove Mexicans were legitimate heirs to their antiquity that went beyond the passage of toothless and easily flouted laws concerning cultural properties.

Rising to meet this challenge was a key motif in the consolidation of antiquarian studies in the years between two disasters for Mexico, the Texan War of Independence (1835–36) and the U.S.-Mexican War (1846–48). This is the substance of chapter 4, "Modes of Display." Here, paper proved to be an important ally for the museum. Because the crowded spaces at the museum offered little opportunity for scripted and coherent exhibits, it was in the form of drawings, lithographs, photographs, descriptions, newspaper articles, letters, and molds that knowledge about antiquities was produced and circulated. While the study of the American past was happening in many places at once—from London to Philadelphia, from Paris to Cincinnati—the emergence of independent presses in Mexico and the increasing availability of printing expertise gave the National Museum an opportunity to curate Mexico's ancient past—that is, to select objects; to name them; to make them legible to the Mexican public through images, descriptions, and explanations; to make sense of them scientifically and even morally; and to deploy them, intellectually and politically. Paper, in other words, contributed to the emergence of Mexican antiquarianism.

Chapter 5, "José Fernando Ramírez, Keeper of the Archive," reconstructs the history of the National Museum through the intellectual and political biography of José Fernando Ramírez (1804–71), who was at the helm of the museum, with some interruptions, between 1852 and 1865. A multifaceted man who reached the highest echelons of Mexican politics, having served as a cabinet member under various governments, he was, at the same time, one of Mexico's finest intellectuals, a member of scholarly academies, a bibliophile, and an accomplished antiquarian, responsible for a new turn in the study of Mexican antiquity. Having had the opportunity to compare firsthand archaeological vestiges of the New World with those of other civilizations, Ramírez was critical of the teleological narratives that presented Mexican antiquity as an imitation of the ancient civilizations of the Old World. In the cases where Mexican antiquities resembled those of Egypt, China, or Babylon, these were no more than coincidences, insisted Ramírez, analogies that arose in separate places under similar conditions that determined the form of archaic societies. Rather than postulate emissaries who might have imported civilization to America, Ramírez believed Mexican antiquities had to be examined in their own right. He proposed a method of study that, while echoing the historicist ideals of contemporary scholars, harkened back at the same time to the eighteenth-century writings of Mexican antiquarians like León y

Gama and Alzate. Ramírez argued that the science of Mexico's past was contingent on the creation of a very large archive, which would permit careful and judicious comparisons between a vast array of sources, including colonial chronicles, codices, toponymics, and cartographical, chronological, astronomical, and linguistic material. Ramírez dedicated most of his life to building up that archive.

By the early 1860s the so-called Guerra de Reforma (1857–61) would give an excuse for a French invasion and for the creation of Mexico's Second Empire. The fierce competition for Mexico's natural and cultural properties, which was arguably marginal to the main developments during the country's first decades of independence, was about to assume center stage. The history of the museum in this context is the topic of chapter 6. Following in the footsteps of the successful military campaign that dispersed Juárez's Mexican troops, Napoleon III created the Commission scientifique du Mexique. The aim was to gather as much information on the invaded territory as possible, in order to satisfy both French utilitarian needs for markets, colonies, raw materials, and strategic positions, and appetites for objects of scholarly curiosity, such as antiquities, natural history, and anthropological data. It was in this mise-en-scène that Emperor Maximilian arrived in Mexico in 1864. Deflating the expectations both of the Mexican monarchists who had offered him the "Mexican crown" and of the French who supported his empire, Maximilian surrounded himself at first with moderate Mexican intellectuals of a liberal bent and pursued his own scientific program meant to produce (natural, historical, and antiquarian) knowledge about the country. At the same time, Maximilian understood how the museum could be fashioned into a source of cultural, political, and symbolic legitimacy for a government that was undoubtedly an outsider, and he made efforts to strengthen the institution and to make his relationship with it visible. We all know Maximilian's fate—Édouard Manet's famous picture of his execution has burned the scene into the consciousness of the modern world. What is less appreciated is that during the Second Empire, the museum began its transformation from a storeroom of objects at the university to a symbolically charged space in the National Palace appropriate for displaying Mexico's natural and antiquarian treasures. At the time of Maximilian's death in 1867, the museum's antiquities were still packed in boxes. It was up to the officials of the liberal republic to unpack the boxes, set the objects up in their new spaces, and make the mute stones speak to the Mexican public and to the scientific world, proclaiming Mexico's identity over time. The alliance between archaeology and state power finally took the shape that, perhaps, Icaza was envisioning. The museum, increasingly identified with its antiquities, would become "one of the principal stages where the rituals of political autonomy were re-enacted through public commemoration ceremonies and special exhibits."[30]

These dazzling certainties make it hard to imagine today a time when it was not so. There is hardly room for the museum's first fifty years in the story of its ulterior success. Only when we understand this epoch in terms of its own certainties and ambiguities can we approach the "event" of the National Museum, which struggled to assert its agency by accomplishing a double task: forging preconquest antiquities into the objects of a science of Mexico's past and using that process to make the case that they belonged exclusively to something called the "Mexican nation." This, the museum's curators felt, would give the institution the seriousness and privilege that would realize the rhetorical promise embedded in the decree that founded it. But the path to this accomplishment was full of detours, frustrations, and dead ends. During its first half century all aspects of the museum, from its contents to its site, were subject to an institutionally wounding uncertainty.

1 GENEALOGIES

Enlightenment Legacies and the Education
of Don Lucas Alamán

From a strictly formal point of view, the history of the National Museum of Mexico began on March 18, 1825, when President Guadalupe Victoria signed it into existence, at the behest of his young and dynamic minister of internal and external relations, Lucas Alamán.[1] Inasmuch as it endowed the new nation with one of the staple institutions of nineteenth-century independence movements, the foundation of the museum entailed at the same time a gesture of recognition, a taking hold of the social spaces, the intellectual resources, and the material properties independent Mexico had inherited from the viceroyalty of New Spain. As it began to take shape between 1823 and 1825, during Alamán's time in office, the museum was, to a large degree, Alamán's creation; its coming into being bears testimony to Alamán's own coming of age in colonial New Spain, to the cosmopolitan interests and relations he acquired during the War of Independence, and to his ability to reconfigure viceregal legacies to establish the foundations of a national institution.

Lucas Alamán was born in 1792 into a silver-mining family in Guanajuato. He received his early training in Latin and mathematics. Just as important was the autodidact part of his education, in the enlightened salons of Guanajuato's intendant Juan Antonio de Riaño (1757–1810), bishop Manuel Abad y Queipo (1751–1825), and Miguel Hidalgo (1753–1811).[2] Soon, these men would be pitted against one another in one of the most infamous moments of Mexico's War of Independence. On September 28, 1810, Hidalgo's rebel forces laid siege to the Alhóndiga de Granaditas, a grain storage and marketplace in Guanajuato, where royalist troops under Riaño's command and well-to-do Creoles had retreated and were holding out. The insurgents set fire to the door, invaded the building, and, overriding Hidalgo's orders, pillaged the stores and massacred loyalists. "That afternoon and night and the following night," wrote Alamán years later in his *Historia de México* (1844–49), "they sacked all the shops and houses in the city belonging to Europeans. On that fatal night the scene was lighted by great numbers of torches, and nothing was heard but the noise of blows crashing against doors and the ferocious howling of the rabble applauding their fall and rushing in triumph to remove goods, furniture and everything else."[3] These early images of a rabble just waiting to pillage the "Europeans" not only remained with Alamán the rest of his life as a political motif but also probably had something to do with his notion of how precarious a culture and its objects could be.

By the end of 1810 Alamán moved to Mexico City to escape the ravages of war and to complete his education. There are no surviving descriptions of Mexico City when Alamán lived there in the 1810s, but Alexander von Humboldt depicted the city some years earlier, at the time of his visit in 1803. Humboldt found the medium-sized city, with its population of over 130,000, not lacking in grandeur.[4] He was impressed with "the imposing character of its natural surroundings": the Chapultepec Forest to the west; the sanctuary of Our Lady of Guadalupe to the north; San Ángel and San Agustín de las Cuevas (Tlalpan), with their enormous orchards, to the south; and Texcoco Lake, as "beautiful as the most beautiful Swiss mountain lakes," to the east.[5] Organized orthogonally, the city grew around the cathedral, the mint, and the viceregal palace. In equal measure, Humboldt's attention was drawn to the Botanical Garden, the Royal Academy of San Carlos, and the Seminario de Minería (School of Mines) in "a building [that] could adorn any main plaza in Paris or London."[6] All these institutions were newcomers on the urban scene, the result of the Bourbon reforms aimed, on one hand, at increasing productivity and commercial efficiency in the colonies and, on the other, at filling out the educational void left by the expulsion of the Jesuits in 1767, with the further intent of making the colonial elites loyal to the Crown.

After his arrival in Mexico City, Alamán took classes at all these institutions. He studied first at the School of Mines. Founded in 1792, its mission was to impose the latest technical developments in the modern sciences of chemistry and mineralogy on mining activities in New Spain, which had taken the lead in silver production among Spain's American possessions. The school boasted prestigious faculty like Fausto de Elhuyar (1755–1833), who had taught at Uppsala and Freiberg before becoming the first director of the School of Mines in Mexico, and Andrés del Río (1764–1849), author of the celebrated mineralogical treatise *Elementos de oritognosia o del conocimiento de los fósiles* (1795). The education of mining engineers, it was hoped, would revive tapped-out mines by finding lower-grade ore and would improve proven moneymakers, like the Valenciana mine in Alamán's native Guanajuato.[7] Alamán graduated from the School of Mines in 1813.

The same year, he attended lectures by Vicente Cervantes (1755–1829) at the Botanical Garden in the viceregal palace. Trained in Madrid, Cervantes had arrived in New Spain with the express mandate to establish a botanical garden and a chair of botany in Mexico City. His botanical lectures, inaugurated in 1788, were aimed at introducing Linnaean taxonomies and the most current European botanical knowledge into a modern curriculum. At first, this provoked serious polemic in Mexico City by confronting supporters of universal classifications against those of local, use-based categories.[8] By the time Alamán attended Cervantes's lectures, an entire generation of young botanists had become adept at the Linnaean system. Thus, Alamán's education, like those of his fellow Creoles, was the product of Enlightenment reforms that liquidated an older paradigm that tolerated a crossover view of natural phenomena, ultimately guided by analogies and teleological reasoning, in favor of arranging knowledge about the natural world according to some ultimately reduced set of universal principles. In retrospect, this training would be of immense use as Alamán carried out an extensive and fruitful correspondence with Mexican and foreign scholars in various sciences. Besides training in the sciences, Alamán cultivated the arts, learning to play the guitar and studying drawing and painting at the Royal Academy of San Carlos, founded in 1781 and aimed at developing a young Creole's *buen gusto*—that is, his taste for the forms of classical antiquity and his capacity to recognize and reproduce them.[9]

Around these formal institutions for learning, Alamán would have encountered a vibrant semipublic sphere that brought together the city's political and scientific elites. There were periodicals—such as the *Diario de México*, founded in 1805 by law-trained Carlos María de Bustamante (1774–1848) and by Jacobo de Villaurrutia (1754–1833), a magistrate at the Real Audiencia, and the socially and politically critical *El Pensador Mexicano*, founded in 1812 by José Joaquín Fernández de Lizardi (1776–1827). At the same time, the late eighteenth century saw the emergence of collections and private cabinets. In 1790 an article in the *Gazeta de México* described various collections of "curiosities" around Mexico City. Those amassed by José Antonio Alzate y Ramírez, Mexico's foremost Creole intellectual, and by José Longinos Martínez (1756–1802), one of the naturalists on the Royal Botanical Expedition to New Spain led by Martín Sessé and José Mariano Mociño, stand out for their abundance in "objects from the three reigns" of nature.[10] Stimulated by scientific expeditions to the New World in the last decades of the eighteenth century, private collecting was increasingly modeled on instructions produced specifically for the expeditions in an effort to define collectibles (rocks, taxidermies, pressed plants, and, increasingly, antiquities) and to discipline collecting practices.[11] Although many of the collectors mentioned in the *Gazeta* in 1790 were no longer around when Alamán lived in Mexico City, their collections had survived, passed on to other hands; Longinos's cabinet, for instance, was transferred to the Colegio de San Ildefonso after his death in 1802.[12] Besides, new collections had emerged on the urban scene. Humboldt lavished special praises on the beautiful collections of physics, mechanics, and mineralogy at the School of Mines.[13] He found the Botanical Garden "small but extremely rich in rare natural productions" of "much interest for commerce or industry."[14] He took note of the collection of ancient casts at the Royal Academy of San Carlos.[15] And he was especially impressed with the private cabinet of Ciriaco González de Carbajal

(1745–181?), a magistrate at the Real Audiencia, who owned "very remarkable oryctognosic and geological collections" and a "superb cabinet of shells, formed during his stay in the Philippines, where he deployed the same zeal for the natural sciences, which distinguished him in Mexico."[16]

González de Carbajal's interests were not limited to the natural sciences. Having served as a member of the Comisión de Antigüedades of the Academia de la Historia in Madrid, he was instrumental in promoting the Royal Antiquarian Expeditions (1805–8), which deployed Guillermo Dupaix and his draftsman Luciano Castañeda to study the ruins of New Spain, as far as Palenque, Oaxaca, and the Isthmus of Tehuantepec. The expeditioners returned with detailed notes and descriptions, drawings, antiquities, and natural history samples. Viceroy José de Iturrigaray founded the Junta de Antigüedades and commissioned González de Carbajal, Dupaix, Ignacio Cubas (178?–1844), a secretary in the viceregal archives, and José Mariano Beristáin y Souza (1756–1817), an eminent theologian and bibliographer (author of the celebrated *Biblioteca Hispano-Americana Septentrional*, 1816–21), to study preconquest manuscripts and monuments—among them, the manuscripts produced by Dupaix's expeditions.[17] Though the Junta was beginning to feel the shortages of war by the time Alamán arrived in Mexico City, it is hard to imagine that the young Creole would not have become acquainted with its work and with some of its members, especially considering that Dupaix had close ties with Fausto de Elhuyar, the director of the School of Mines, where Alamán was a student.

Such was then Alamán's education during the three and a half years he spent in the capital of New Spain. He acquired solid training in the sciences, some education in the arts, especially in the classical arts, and probably some very basic idea of the fledgling field of Mexican antiquarianism. In 1814 he traveled across the Atlantic, to study, by his own account, the great artistic monuments of Europe. His itinerary was modeled on that of Antonio Ponz (1725–92), a member of the Royal Academy of San Fernando in Madrid who had published the eighteen-volume *Viage* [sic] *de España o Cartas en que se da noticia de las cosas más apreciables y dignas de saberse que hay en ella* (1772–94), partially in response to foreign disparagement toward the Spanish arts as backward and of little value. Ponz traveled around the peninsula, compiling detailed information on Spain's architectural and artistic patrimony, which he complemented with illustrations. It is not difficult to understand how the *Viage* would have resonated with Mexican readers at a moment when Creole scholars like Beristáin, Alzate, and León y Gama were similarly engaged in vindicating New Spain against foreign detractors or how Ponz's descriptions and illustrations would have inspired the artistically inclined Alamán.

Alamán's five-year journey through the continent amounted to something of a grand tour—that quintessential eighteenth-century institution, as exercised by Goethe and by English aristocrats, meant to bring about the young traveler's greater *Bildung*. To see with his own eyes the legacies of ancient Rome and Greece, to sharpen his artistic sensibilities in front of the products of the Renaissance and Humanist periods, and to acquaint himself with an international circle of like-minded cognoscenti was a way of complementing the text-based learning of the classroom with the experiential weight of the senses and the sociability of the man of the world. During his five years abroad, Alamán frequented the Royal Cabinet for Natural History in Madrid, the Muséum d'Histoire Naturelle and the Louvre in Paris, the British Museum in London, as well as smaller museums and cabinets. He arrived at an especially interesting moment, when national museums were formed and art sacked by Napoleon was being repatriated from Paris to countries of origin, following Napoleon's defeat.[18] This must have had some effect on the future founder of the National Museum of Mexico.

At the same time, for Alamán, the tour led to the formation of long-lasting ties with scholars and future business partners. Alamán first landed in Spain, where he met Casimiro Gómez Ortega (1741–1818), director of the Royal Botanical Garden, and fellow Mexican Pablo de la Llave (1773–1833), who was at the time organizing the natural history specimens in the Royal Cabinet. De la Llave would later return to Mexico to take charge of the natural history specimens at the National Museum. On his next stop, in France, Alamán made some of his most interesting acquaintances. There he met the controversial Servando Teresa de Mier (1765–1827), who had been exiled from New Spain for his 1794 sermon conflating the Mexican deity Quetzalcóatl with the apostle Saint Thomas; abbé Henri Grégoire (1750–1831), the French bishop turned revolutionary, constitutionalist, and suffragist; and Humboldt, with whom Alamán would correspond after his return to Mexico and whom he tried to interest in a new visit to the young republic.

From France, Alamán continued on his tour, going to England and Scotland and then on to Italy, Switzerland, Germany, and Holland, with "the avowed intention to study the nature and effects of the governments on their respective countries."[19] In Berlin he met the celebrated geologist and paleontologist Leopold von Buch (1774–1853), and he stopped for almost two months in Saxony to observe methods of extraction and the new machinery employed at the Freiberg mines and to forge long-term friendships with engineers. In Switzerland he struck a fruitful friendship with botanist Auguste Pyrame de Candolle (1778–1841), as reflected by the letters exchanged between the two in the following years. When Alamán sent de Candolle dried plants from his native Guanajuato, the latter obliged by naming a new species after Alamán, And when de Candolle sent one of his more promising students, Jean-Louis Berlandier (1805–51), to act as botanist to the Mexican-sponsored geographical expedition to Northern Mexico in the late 1820s, Alamán facilitated Berlandier's integration and provided de Candolle with reports on the progress of the expedition.[20]

Alamán returned to Mexico in 1820 and published a paper on the causes of the decline in the production of the mines in New Spain, showing his intentions to return to the family business of mining.[21] Events throughout the Spanish Empire dictated otherwise. By May of 1821, Alamán began to dabble in politics when he attended the Cortes of Spain, to which, under the reestablished Constitution of 1812, he had been elected as the deputy from Guanajuato. This was the short period in which many of the former Spanish colonies in Spanish America were considering stepping back from full independence in favor of a commonwealth arrangement, with each of them having federal power. In the Cortes, Alamán promoted mineralogical matters dear to the hearts of the Guanajuato mine owners, and he took a side in the debate about the Crown's American subjects, presenting a strong case for autonomy. He pointed out that the citizens of New Spain were free and had the same rights as the Spanish under the new Constitution, but in fact they were being subjected by Spain to the ancient order. Spain's attempt to repress American autonomy was failing, at the cost of much bloodshed; its one chance was to accept some kind of federalism, with Americans having the right to choose their own governors, a system of political administration that had been proved viable in the United States.[22]

Alamán was in Madrid when Mexico declared independence from Spain in 1821, followed by Agustín de Iturbide's (1783–1824) self-proclamation as emperor, which doomed the federalist project. Alamán made recourse to all his "brilliant eloquence, undaunted courage, and unanswerable arguments, to vindicate the cause and conduct of his self-delivered country: he showed that Mexico was independent because the very events had dissolved her dependence; that Spain had long left Mexico to her own resources and was confessedly unable to protect her from aggression; that with most affectionate and dutiful perseverance, Mexico had continued faithful to the mother country." And he hoped that the fidelity between Mexico and Spain would turn to friendship, allegiance, and affection.[23] These arguments made little difference to the Spanish. While the viceroy of New Spain, Juan O'Donojú, surrendered to the forces of independence by signing the Treaty of Córdoba on August 24, 1821, the Spanish monarchy made a retrograde attempt to reconquer Mexico, besieging the fort of San Juan de Ulúa in Veracruz, which would hamper Mexico's commercial relations into 1826. All boats arriving to Mexico would have to pass through the Isla de Sacrificios. Other countries recognized Mexican independence sooner, de facto if not de jure.

After short stops in France and England, where he set up mining associations, with an eye toward reestablishing the Mexican mining industry, Alamán returned to Mexico in March of 1823, with a certain reputation brought about by his address in the Cortes. He brought with him Mexico's first lithographic press and a host of other objects of curiosity and of "use to the country's progress," such as a collection of old master paintings, ancient and modern coins, twelve cinnamon plants from Martinique, mango from China, guinea fowl, and a beautiful pheasant.[24] He arrived amid political unrest that resulted in the ousting of emperor Iturbide on March 19, and on March 27 a provisional government was established and placed in the charge of Nicolás Bravo (1786–1854), Guadalupe Victoria, and Celestino Negrete (1777–1846).[25] The celerity of these changes prefigured a pattern of coups, countercoups, sudden elevations, and sudden downfalls that would take hold in Mexican politics up to the 1870s. Alamán was named minister of internal and external relations on April 16.

Alamán was then thirty years old. Born under Mexico's colonial rule, he had come of age during its War of Independence. Having received his education in some of the empire's most prestigious institutions, which were aimed at shaping a political and intellectual class capable of solving Spain's challenges into the nineteenth century, Alamán explored scientific and artistic interests that brought him into contact with a network of international scholars and their institutional patrons, so that he had acquired more knowledge about state-of-the-art standards in administering politics and cultural goods than perhaps anyone else in Mexico. Alamán's education and experience and the ties he had built with the Mexican and European elites made him an excellent choice for minister of internal and external relations, a post that demanded the accommodation of the young country's needs with international ambitions and interests. He brought to it a special talent to act as broker between peoples and places, to make projects and institutions happen.

"Without Instruction, There Is No Liberty"

One of the more formidable tasks that faced Alamán in 1823 was to obtain a close understanding regarding of the state of the country after a ten-year-long War of Independence, a one-year monarchy that culminated in political turbulence, and a sustained attack on the port of Veracruz by the Spanish. To this end, a week after he was signed in, on April 23, reactivating the old bureaucratic forms of the empire in a new republican guise, Alamán sent out letters to the political leaders of the different Mexican states, to inquire about a wide range of issues concerning demographics, commerce, industry, mining, and roads. He was equally preoccupied with the country's educational establishments and dispatched letters to deans of colleges and universities, including the directors of the School of Mines, the Botanical Garden, and the School of Surgery, asking for information about the functions and practices of each of those institutions; for reports on the subjects that were being taught there; and for inventories of the books, manuscripts, machines and other instruments, and "monuments" of antiquity they might possess. This letter was prefaced by a kind of cultural manifesto, where Alamán equated Enlightenment with the adoption of a code of political norms mediated through knowledge of rights and responsibilities.[26]

Most of Alamán's correspondents had remained in place during and after the war—as was the case with Elhuyar at the School of Mines and Cervantes at the Botanical Garden—and were well positioned to report on their particular institution. Among those who answered the minister's call was José María Bustamante (1786–1829), a professor at the School of Mines who offered to turn in objects, drawings, and papers from the Dupaix expeditions and thereby contribute to Alamán's goal of "bringing together Mexican antiquities."[27] After his third expedition, Dupaix had settled in Mexico City to revise his notes, but he died in 1818 before completing the task. The bulk of his objects, manuscripts, and personal effects were then passed on to his will executor and friend Fausto de Elhuyar.[28] Elhuyar deposited Dupaix's papers in the School of Mines.

Throughout the summer of 1823 Alamán also corresponded with Cervantes, his old botany teacher, to ask his opinion about creating a museum that would house "curiosities," such as Dupaix's papers, manuscripts, and antiquities, and would optimally be adjoined to the Botanical Garden.[29] Cervantes concluded his task of reconnaissance quickly, though he hardly had Dupaix's manuscripts or antiquities in mind as he did so. He suggested instead the formation of a Museum of Medicine, Surgery, Pharmacy, and Natural History in the Hospital de los Naturales.[30] In this plan, Cervantes called for the demolition of the hospital's chapel and for the evacuation of its cemetery, in order to provide enough space to plant three thousand species of "the most rare and curious" specimens. Other rooms in the old hospital would become classrooms for teaching useful sciences, such as surgery and practical medicine.[31] What Cervantes had in mind was the revival of a tradition of observation and experimentation in the natural sciences, which he had helped build as the director of the Botanical Garden and which had suffered drastically during the war years. Clearly, Alamán's more cosmopolitan idea of a complex serving the arts and sciences that would house antiquities and natural history for the wider public was not on Cervantes's horizon.

While exchanging letters with Cervantes, Alamán also corresponded with Ignacio Cubas, who had important experience in the viceregal archives—he had participated in the Junta de Antigüedades set up in 1808 to examine Dupaix's findings—and had in the meantime held posts as Emperor Iturbide's archivist in 1822 and as member of a short-lived Conservatorio de Antigüedades, which Iturbide had established at the university.[32] Alamán entrusted Cubas to continue gathering and organizing the manuscripts and antiquities that were housed in the Ministry of Internal and External Relations.[33] Cubas's preliminary survey revealed a significant loss of papers, symptomatic of the scattering of archives that characterized most independence movements in Spanish America. Especially worrisome was the state of the Boturini collection, which Cubas himself had inventoried twenty years earlier, in 1804. To avoid future destruction and extraction, Cubas recommended that Boturini's "museum" be incorporated into a national museum.[34] For the time being, Alamán created the Archivo General y Público de la Nación on August 23.

By the end of the summer of 1823, Alamán had been presented with two very different ideas for a museum, both of them legacies of Mexico's colonial past: a practical museum for students of medicine and botany, modeled on the natural history cabinets that flourished at the end of the eighteenth century, and a museum meant to house the antiquities and manuscripts that the government held unsystematically in various locations, despite efforts and intentions by various colonial officials to bring them together as a collection. While the latter idea was, in one way, merely a bureaucratic convenience, it also provided a platform for a grander vision. Yet besides the obvious differences between these two models, it is useful to put them in their context, where we can see their commonalities. By the end of the eighteenth century, both natural history objects and antiquities had acquired value that was both cognitive and connoisseurial. They were objects, in other words, that were valuable to study in their own physical being, but they were also paradoxical commodities, the exchange value of which—especially in the case of antiquities—depended on their authenticity and uniqueness. These objects began to be collected and written about for these different motives, and while many were sent abroad, many also remained in Mexico. After independence was won from Spain, the caretakers of these objects were summoned by Alamán to share their enormous expertise and insider knowledge. Cervantes, Cubas, and Elhuyar were, in this sense, transitional figures, whose suggestions were half in the past, even as they attempted to anticipate the new institutions of the future.

On November 8, 1823, with the answers to his inquiries in hand, Alamán was ready to report back to the Mexican Congress on the state of the republic and on his activities during his first months as minister of internal and external relations.[35] It speaks to the interest generated in Mexican affairs abroad that his report was quickly translated into English and incorporated into Joel R. Poinsett's (1779–1851) *Notes on Mexico* (1825), together with Poinsett's account of his own experiences as member of the U.S. Legation in Mexico, with translations of official Mexican documents, such as a project for the Mexican Constitution, and with reports on commerce. A year later, Alamán's 1825 report to Congress was again almost immediately translated and published, this time by the future British prime minister Benjamin Disraeli (1804–81), under the title *The Present State of Mexico*. The revolutions in Spanish America had collapsed the traditional imperial embargo on information about the colonies, which had been applied defensively by both the Habsburg and Bourbon regimes, always fearful of land grabs by the non-Spanish world. Mexico's independence, coinciding with the stabilization of post-Napoleonic Europe, was seen by the transatlantic business community in the 1820s as a favorable condition for investment.

Alamán's 1823 *Memoria* presented the image of Mexico in a state of such "deplorable ruin," so broken politically, socially, and economically, that Alamán acknowledged that it "ha[d] been impossible to remedy, in a few months, the evils produced by many years of desolation, and by one year of errors."[36] Among the more serious plights visited on Mexico was the threat of political unrest, perpetrated by "turbulent men, who sought to promote their own interest in the general confusion," and of social dissolution, rooted in the increasing insensitivity to pain and death among "people who had grown accustomed to violence and assassinations."[37] Also of grave concern was the damage suffered by the country's infrastructure: roads and bridges lay in shambles making transit and commerce impossible; farms lay abandoned; and even the mines that had proved most productive under the colonial regime, such as the fabled Valenciana mine, had fallen into disuse and were for the most part flooded. Mexico was thus "poor in the midst of riches."

Alamán also informed on the state of Mexico's cultural properties. Lack of funds had forced the Academy of San Carlos to close, while the Botanical Garden had become a ruin of its former self. At the same time, he reported that "precious monuments of Mexican antiquities" and "others, relating to the earliest period of the Spanish conquest, [collected] in a great measure, due to the efforts of the enlightened and celebrated traveler Boturini," had suffered the "same disorders"; several of them had disappeared altogether, while others were incomplete or had been partially destroyed.[38] He reassured Congress that those "monuments" that remained were being indexed carefully, and he urged that they be gathered together to form the basis for a museum.

Alamán's proposal for a museum was part of a larger heading on public instruction. The museum would be—together with schools, libraries, and establishments of higher training like the School of Mines or the Botanical Garden—a house of learning. "Without instruction, there is no liberty," declared Alamán, echoing a view to which many of his more enlightened contemporaries subscribed.[39] He called on Congress to "look beyond pecuniary difficulties and to use all means at its disposal to promote education," which he understood in a broad sense—not just as a prerequisite of all cultural enterprises, but as basis of a wide array of undertakings, from agriculture to commerce and navigation.[40] He believed and hoped that "education [would] mold the habits and character of [the] people, dissipating their religious and political preoccupations."[41] Did Alamán think that education would bring Mexicans together, beyond the factions and frictions that were becoming visible in Mexican politics and would haunt the country for the next half century? Did he mean that liberty, as promoted through public instruction, more than just independence from a foreign power, was liberty from internal dissensions? Would he have thought of liberty as the privilege of the enlightened man, a kind of liberty of the spirit that came with access to culture and its objects? Or did he think all Mexicans would be free?

If the rhetoric of state-funded educational advancement might have been accepted in the higher circles, so that a museum would have been seen as an instrument for education, there was hardly a consensus as to what it would mean to teach Mexicans about their freedom or as to how a museum would go about teaching it. For instance, the writer and political pamphleteer José Joaquín Fernández de Lizardi saw liberty in terms of freedom from the Spanish colonial regime. His rejection of the three hundred years of Spanish rule was so strong that Lizardi's "patriotic calendars" in the 1810s and early 1820s, which familiarized the reader with the heroes of Mexico's history, skipped completely over the period between 1521, the fall of Tenochtitlan, and 1821.[42] Likewise, Carlos María de Bustamante—journalist, historian, participant in the War of Independence, and an active politician in the postindependence years—took an exclusive interest in Mexico's preconquest history, to which he devoted his antiquarian energies, both in the form of collecting and writing.[43]

Alamán, by contrast, did not share this rejection of the Spanish past, for which he quickly earned a characterization as a conservative. Indeed, after his return to Mexico in 1823, his writings reflect an increasing engagement with the totality of Mexico's history, including the colonial regime and the consequences of that legacy for independent Mexico.[44] During his early years as minister, that attitude could be summed up in one gesture—his defense of one of the most symbolically charged legacies among those of the Spanish regime in Mexico, Hernán Cortés's tomb in the Hospital de Jesús, which became the butt of satires and inflammatory literature over the summer of 1823. Getting word that the tomb was about to be desecrated by self-proclaimed patriots on Independence Day, September 16, Alamán arrived there early, exhumed the bones, and buried them in an undisclosed location.[45] In his political life, he defended reconciliation and encouraged Spanish immigration. He opposed expressions of nationalism that called for the destruction of objects or for the expulsion of all Spaniards, as was the case with an 1827 bill. He saw with alarm the brain drain that ensued as foreigners were subject to persecution. He knew many of the emigrants, for instance his old mineralogy professor, Andrés del Río, who left for the United States.

As he called for the foundation of a museum before the 1823 Congress, Alamán probably hoped differences of ideology and politics would work themselves out with proper education. Unfortunately, time would prove him wrong. There were other pressing matters, as well. Archives and cultural properties had been scattered and lost during the War of Independence, and the republic was not proving vigilant enough to avoid further destruction. And soon, foreigners looking for investment opportunities in the newly independent country began showing an increasing interest in these same properties. All this convinced Alamán that Mexico needed a cultural policy that would begin by bringing together for safekeeping those things Mexico had inherited from colonial times—antiquities, manuscripts, and objects of natural history—even before it was worked out where or how they would be studied or displayed.

"Our Most Innovating Countryman Was Allowed to Ransack the Superb Capital of Mexico"

Alamán would soon have his first experience with a foreign prospector. William Bullock (1773–1849) was one of the first non-Spanish Europeans to visit Mexico in 1823, after the three-century-old Spanish system of vetting travelers collapsed.[46] Bullock was, above all else, a showman. The child of a traveling waxworks exhibitor from Sheffield, he opened a museum of curiosities in Liverpool in 1801.[47] In 1809 he went to London and commissioned the building of a new museum site in Piccadilly Circus from Peter F. Robinson. Robinson chose to model the façade on the Temple of Hathor at Dendera, and Bullock's museum soon became known as Egyptian Hall.[48] There, he mounted increasingly popular exhibits, with his antiquities and curiosities "rivaling" the British Museum, which acquired the Rosetta Stone and the Parthenon Marbles, while Bullock was displaying such prize crowd bait as the military carriage that Napoleon had been forced to abandon at Genappe, after his debacle at Waterloo.[49]

Among Bullock's most successful shows was the *Pantherion*, on display throughout 1812. Advertised as containing "upwards of fifteen thousand natural and foreign curiosities, antiquities, and productions of the fine arts," it professed to display "the whole of known quadrupeds," many of which had been preserved by Bullock according to the latest taxidermy techniques, "in a manner which will convey the perfect idea of their haunts and mode of life."[50] It is not unlikely that at some point in his travels in England, Alamán would have paid for a ticket to see the wonders of Egyptian Hall. Would he have recognized the differences between the full-immersion, public-pandering display of natural history and the more sober display at the Muséum in Paris? Would he have appreciated the imperialist sweep and insouciance of Bullock's show?

For most of his collection, Bullock depended on travelers and the trades he could make at the docks in Liverpool and London. In 1823 he widened his sphere of exhibitions by going to Mexico. Bullock documented his travels in his *Six Months' Residence and Travels in Mexico* (1824), which was enough of a success for the author to publish a revised edition the following year, which included maps and plates and medical "instructions for the preservation of health" against tropical-climate diseases like cholera and dysentery. The book was translated into French, German, and Dutch in the following years and soon achieved a citational status in the subgenre of books about Mexico that began to appear across the Atlantic. Other travelers would take their cue from the Englishman's account and compare their own impressions to Bullock's marveled descriptions of Mexico's wonders, from miniature hummingbirds to imposing volcanoes. Bullock's book owed its success not just to its utility as a travel guide to Mexican places but rather to the way Bullock represented postcolonial Mexico as a terrain of possibility and opportunity for Europeans. Written under the sign of a contagious optimism, *Six Months' Residence* advertised itself as a compendium of "remarks on the present state of New Spain, its natural productions, state of society, manufactures, trade, agriculture, antiquities, etc."[51]

As a visual counterpart to his book, back in London, Bullock organized the first-ever and hugely successful exhibit on Mexico. *Modern and Ancient Mexico* opened at Egyptian Hall at the beginning of 1824 amid enthusiastic reviews by the press and attracted record numbers of visitors. As he had done in his previous exhibits, Bullock printed out descriptions and illustrated catalogues of the exhibit, which meant that its audience was not restricted to those who physically went to see the shows but instead included the large public for the visual culture of curiosities and exotica. In one of the rooms in Egyptian Hall, Bullock captured the "atmosphere" of "Modern Mexico" (fig. 1).[52] Against the landscape of the central valley—with its distant volcanoes, ample view of the Texcoco lake, the church of Guadalupe in the distance, and the cathedral close up—he reproduced a hut and a "native" garden, which brought together cacti, gigantic calabash, and the curious "árbol de mani-

1. William Bullock, exhibition of modern Mexico at the Egyptian Hall, London, 1824. Lithograph, drawn and printed by A. Aglio. Beinecke Rare Book and Manuscript Library, Yale University.

tas" (*Chiranthodendron pentadactylon*), which so many travelers would continue to admire at the Botanical Garden in Mexico City. In the foreground, he placed cases that displayed models of plants, fruit, mounted animals, and samples of the country's minerals. In other words, the visitor was given a preview of the wealth one could expect to encounter when traveling to Mexico or investing in one of the speculative schemes that were beginning to appear in London touting Mexican mining wealth.

In the room destined to "Ancient Mexico" (fig. 2), Bullock took advantage of the recent remodeling of Egyptian Hall as an Egyptian Temple to re-create (or rather, to freely imagine) the "Temple of Mexico." In so doing, Bullock made explicit the scholarly hypothesis that there was some diffusionist tie between the civilizations of ancient Egypt and ancient Mexico—a thesis that was defended by various archaeologists and anthropologists up to the beginning of the twentieth century and that would tie in with larger controversies

2. William Bullock, exhibition of ancient Mexico at the Egyptian Hall, London, 1824. Lithograph, drawn and printed by A. Aglio. Beinecke Rare Book and Manuscript Library, Yale University.

about race and civilization, which shaped the imperialist politics and culture of the era. The walls of the "temple" were covered over with codices, both copies and originals from the Boturini collection, which Bullock professed to have consulted in the School of Mines. The codex-papered walls served as setting to a great number of preconquest objects, original antiquities, and molds of very big pieces. A practiced and talented showman, Bullock played with scale and display to produce strong sensations. The sacrificial rituals of ancient Mexicans made an enormous impression. A huge cast of a snake with its jaws open allowed a view of a hapless man about to be swallowed; the poor victim's last sight of this world was the replica of a sacrificial altar, the so-called Stone of Tízoc, and of the monstrous Teoyamiqui, the bloodthirsty goddess, clothed in a skirt festooned with human skulls. Along with the objects, Bullock had imported from Mexico a native Indian, José Cayetano Ponce de León, who moved liberally around the salons of the Egyptian Hall. Visitors found him docile, intelligent, and well informed on the history and affairs of his country; in his rudimentary English, José Cayetano explained the uses of the objects displayed and ventured interpretations of the codices on the walls.[53]

How did Bullock manage to amass the Mexican antiquities and

the manuscripts listed in his catalogue? As he made it clear on the title page of his catalogue, most of the objects were "collected on the spot, with the assistance of the Mexican government." Bullock's enterprise must have seemed to Alamán like a good opportunity to drum up interest in Mexico in the financial center of the world, London. Bullock surely had an inkling of his place in the plan to publicize Mexico, and he dedicated the 1825 edition of his book to Alamán, writing that the minister's "valuable assistance" had enabled Bullock to "acquire the information contained in these volumes [. . .] and to collect and transmit to his native country those articles of antiquity and curiosity which have given the English nation their first insight into the manners and customs of the depressed but powerful people, with whom [the English] are about to enter into close alliance."[54]

Alamán's assistance consisted mainly in securing good will and allies for the English traveler by recommending him to people who would be of use. Many of the same people who had welcomed Humboldt to New Spain almost twenty years earlier received Bullock into their professional spaces and into their homes in 1823. Cervantes guided Bullock around the Botanical Garden and furnished him with lengthy explanations on local flora and with plant and seed samples. In the School of Mines, Bullock copied manuscripts pertaining to Dupaix's antiquarian expeditions. Castañeda showed him drawings still in his possession. At the same time, Alamán enabled Bullock to make casts of some of the more emblematic Mexican antiquities: the Calendar Stone, the sacrificial altar of Tízoc, and the statue of the goddess Teoyamiqui. Because the Calendar Stone was fixed at the time against the northwest wall of the cathedral in Mexico City, Alamán intervened with the clergy to allow Bullock "to erect a scaffold against the cathedral and take an impression of it in plaster, which was afterwards carefully packed up and with some difficulty conveyed to Vera Cruz [sic], [whence] it arrived safely in England."[55] The Calendar, testimony to the "striking perfection" achieved by the Aztecs in the sciences of astronomy and stonework, would take central place in Bullock's exhibit on ancient Mexico.

The casts for the massive nine-feet-high basalt-hewn goddess

Teoyamiqui required more work. In the late 1790s the statue was buried in the patio of the university, supposedly to prevent its veneration by the Indians. It was temporarily dug out in 1803 during Humboldt's visit to Mexico City. Humboldt included a short essay and drawings of it in his *Vues des cordillères*. The Teoyamiqui was buried one more time and was underground at the time of Bullock's visit. "With some difficulty the spot was ascertained," and following intervention by Alamán and by Andrés del Río, authorities at the university had the statue disinterred. "It was the labour of a few hours only," wrote Bullock, "and I had the pleasure of witnessing the resurrection of the horrible deity, the colossal monster [. . .] before whom tens of thousands of human victims had been sacrificed."[56] While he was making casts of the Teoyamiqui, Bullock claimed to have witnessed firsthand the revival of the Indians' reverence toward their ancient goddess. An old Indian apparently ventured so far as to complain, "It is true that we have three very good Spanish gods, but we might still have been allowed to keep a few of those of our ancestors."[57] Others placed "chaplets of flowers" on the figure. Bullock, who professed to be well acquainted with the "black legend" of the cruelty of the Spaniards and their wanton destruction of the vestiges of the ancient Mexican civilization, gathered up some sympathy for "the extreme diligence of the Spanish clergy" who, after three hundred years, had not managed to banish the last "taint of heathen superstition among the descendants of the original inhabitants."[58] So, it made perfect sense to Bullock when "the goddess was again committed to her place of interment, and hidden from the profane gaze of the vulgar."[59] The Teoyamiqui would finally be disinterred and placed on exhibit in the National Museum in 1833.[60]

One of the more interesting episodes in Bullock's book found the protagonist at work on a cast of the sacrificial altar of Tízoc. This cylindrical stone, twenty-six feet in diameter, lay buried in the square of the cathedral, one hundred yards from the Calendar Stone, "with only the upper surface exposed to view, which seemed to have been done designedly, to impress upon the populace an abhorrence of the horrible and sanguinary rites once performed on this altar."[61] When he learned that the cylinder's sides were covered with carvings, Bullock asked the clergy for permission to have the earth removed around it, which the latter not only agreed to but also paid for. Over the next few days, Bullock and his son, their bodies half submerged in water, made casts of the stone, causing quite a stir among the populace, who "would frequently express their surprise as to the motives that could induce [Bullock] to take so much pain in copying the stones; and several wished to be informed whether the English, whom they did not consider to be Christians, worshipped the same Gods as the Mexicans before conversion."[62] Bullock took advantage of the attention to ask his onlookers if they had come across similar idols, and he was thus able to purchase many other rarities. There were no regulations in place to hinder the commerce in Mexican antiquities; in Bullock's account, all of Mexico City was an outdoor fair of antiquities. He found idols on every corner: incrusted in the façades or foundations of buildings, under the gateway of houses, in the cloisters of churches. Collecting had a limit, however. Most pieces were too heavy, and he had to make do with casts.

Bullock did not find the Mexican manuscript business quite so free and easy. Manuscripts, drawn on deer skin or "upon some species of paper made of the fibers of the great American aloe," were held in such high esteem by the Mexican government that "no offers could induce [Mexican authorities] to part with these manuscripts until [Bullock] had given them an assurance that, after they had been copied in England, [he] would transmit them again to Mexico."[63] In the catalogue of his exhibit, Bullock remembers that it was through the support and liberality of the Mexican authorities that he returned to London with originals from the Boturini collection. But this story is questionable. Alamán for one seemed to remember differently, and he responded to the news that Bullock was displaying Mexican manuscripts in London by writing to José Michelena (1772–1852), representative of the Mexican government in Britain, urging him to pursue the repatriation of the codices in Boturini's collection. Under circumstances that have not been elucidated, these manuscripts did return to Mexico, and we can speculate that Bullock returned them in order to capitalize on his investment in a silver mine, on which he staked the next phase of his career.[64] Bullock's silver-mine investment, like the majority of the British investments in Mexican mining at the time, went bankrupt.[65] Disillusioned with Mexico, he traveled to the United States in 1827, where he founded a utopian community, Hygeia, in Ohio. Like his mining enterprises, Hygeia proved to be no success. Bullock returned to England, where he died in 1849.

Though it lasted only a few years, Bullock's Mexican adventure was a milestone in the relationship between the Mexican government and that increasingly stock character in nineteenth-century Mexico, the foreign traveler turned speculator and collector. Bullock's 1823 residence in Mexico coincided with Alamán's first months as minister of internal and external relations and with the latter's efforts to arrive at a thorough understanding of the Mexican state's properties and power, as well as the economic status of Mexico. With Alamán's help, Bullock gained access to people, information, and objects, which consecrated him as an insider on Mexico, a country few in England knew about. On his part, Alamán most probably believed Mexico would profit from the publicity that portrayed it as an investment opportunity for Europeans.

Publicity proved to be a double-edged sword. It gave the impression back in England that Mexico offered unlimited prospects. As one reviewer of the exhibit in Piccadilly Square put it,

Mr. Bullock spent six months in Mexico [visiting] the capital and many principal cities and, with the usual zeal and assiduity, climbed volcanoes and pyramids, drew landscapes and temples, exhumed ancient images and unniched (sic) long established gods; collected minerals, birds, natural productions, costumes, works of native arts, and manuscripts, and beyond all, availing himself of the political situation of the country, which opened channels jealously damned up since conquest by the Spaniards, obtained possession of early manuscripts and other records of the most remarkable kind, and apparently, of the highest antiquarian value.[66]

This reviewer goes on to suggest, "Mr. Bullock arrived when the floodgates were open for the first time during centuries and his only difficulty seems to have been to collect the best and carry out the most. Revolution had changed the feelings of the governors and our most innovating countryman was allowed to ransack the superb capital of Mexico."[67]

In Mexico, enterprising foreigners would find mines, raw materials of all sorts, foodstuffs, dyes, medical remedies, and collectables in the form of natural productions and antiquities. Under the Spanish imperial rule, these items had been jealously protected, but after independence they entered circulation under the same regimes of free trade as commodities. When Bullock arrived in Mexico, there was hardly any protocol in place to limit the ambition of the collector or to prepare the state to intervene in cases of cultural property. The dialogue between Alamán and Bullock was inscribed in the norms that had been developed among the collectors and amateurs of the eighteenth century. And Alamán was able to exercise political leverage in order to insure that certain properties were returned to Mexico. But it was becoming clear that trust and the kind of leverage exchanged between Bullock and the personable and powerful minister would turn out to be an exception rather than the rule in nineteenth-century Mexico's deals with profit-bent foreigners.

Coupled with the perception of an immense wealth of natural resources and antiquities was the idea that Mexicans (and other Spanish Americans) could not be trusted to exploit their country's resources. The flooded mines that had fallen into disuse were commonly brought up as example of mismanagement, sloth, and decadence, in the same way Bullock's descriptions of idols scattered around Mexico City became a measure of local disinterest and neglect toward Mexico's ancient past, or of what remained of it, in the wake of what were commonly perceived to have been three centuries of secrecy and fanatic destruction perpetrated by the Spanish. To pluck out Mexico's inexhaustible riches from its soils and to extract antiquities were, in Bullock's logic, acts of retribution, which would awaken Mexico from its slumber and restore it to its future. Thus, one reviewer cast Bullock as a rescuer in a thematic that would be varied with the occasion but would always involve an object endangered by its very discovery in Mexico and rescued by its transfer to the safety of Europe:

> The Revolution, besides giving ingress to foreigners, had, as always is the case in times of general commotion, unbarred and thrown open many offices of records and other places of security; and those things which had perhaps been stored up for ages, during which space of time they might never have seen the light, on a sudden were found in the possession of the multitude, from whose destroying hands each work that was obtained might attribute to the person so fortunate as to recover it, its preservation. At a time precisely like this, Mr. Bullock arrived in Mexico; and from hands like these, many most valuable antiquities were by him rescued, which are now safely brought over to England.[68]

In this way, discovery, rescue, and transfer were conflated into one legitimate event, for which the acquisition of the Parthenon Marbles by Lord Elgin two decades earlier was a powerful precedent. In 1823 the terms of rescue were ephemeral. Bullock's extraction and transfer of antiquities to England were measures that would, eventually, be reversed as the Mexican "multitude" and their dangerous hands were calmed down and educated. And the "safety" of England would secure Mexico's treasures in the same way that the safe accumulation of capital in England allowed the English to loan to Mexico and invest in Mexican mines for a fair return. According to a familiar colonial logic, the absolute nature of property rights proclaimed in the liberal era was superseded by the older law of the treasure seeker when it was a question of rights inhering to a non-European group that did not have the power to assert them.

During Alamán's first year in office, it was becoming increasingly urgent to pass laws stating the state's claims over specific objects and to envision protocols for collecting and preserving them, both against Mexican mobs bent on the kind of destruction Alamán had witnessed firsthand and against "rescuers" like Bullock. In his 1823 address to Congress, Alamán—making moves that were being made elsewhere in Europe, the United States, and Latin America—had insisted on the need to "centralize" Mexico's "monuments." This would establish a division between the domain of commercial properties, which could be subjected to the marketplace and, under state regulation, could accommodate foreign investors, and the domain of cultural property, where the private market not only would be regulated by the state but would be limited in the property it could claim, as the state's claim would come first. In his next address to Congress, a year later, Alamán made it clear that the issue could wait no longer.

Museum by Decree

Alamán gave his second report as minister of internal and external relations on January 11, 1825. He had some progress to report. A number of steam engines had been imported, and mines were being worked. Many roads had been repaired, and a commission had been sent to the Isthmus of Tehuantepec to assess the possibilities for opening an interoceanic canal there. Alamán trusted this would improve commerce, although internal transactions were hampered by presence on the market, at any given time, of moneys and weights that had been coined differently. The country had not yet achieved the abundance and prosperity it presented before the war, but the minister hoped, overoptimistically, that "prudent politics, enlightened governing, tranquility, time, and political confidence would take care of the rest."[69] Public instruction suffered due to lack of funds, but there were a few signs of improvement. The Botanical Garden had resumed classes. Some young talents at the Academy of San Carlos had been sent to Rome to study painting, sculpture, and architecture.[70] For his part, Cubas reported substantial advances in his classification of the country's archives.[71] His work had brought to light many "curious documents of ancient history that the viceroyalty had hidden or forgotten."[72] The Dupaix manuscripts were being incorporated into the archives Cubas was curating at the time. All this progress encouraged Alamán to appeal to Congress to form a museum "by a junction of all the remains of

Mexican antiquity, with an addition of all the natural productions of the country."[73] The minister's petition came with a caveat; Congress would have to commit infrastructure, money, and work to the museum. Even if a physical and an institutional space for Mexico's cultural and natural properties could be achieved, a museum would be more than that space. Its success would be "the work of time and of continued diligence [. . .] aided by funds disposable for the purpose, of which there is yet an insufficiency."[74] There would be no lack of diligence among the museum's personnel over the next decades, though funding proved to be perennially short.

Two months after his report to Congress, on March 18 Alamán wrote to the dean of the university to inform him that President Guadalupe Victoria had decided to found a museum:

His Excellency, the President of the Republic, has resolved to form, with the antiquities collected in the Isla de Sacrificios and with others that exist, a National Museum,[75] for which has been destined one room ("salón") at the University; all necessary expenses, for shelves, locks, Museum guards, etc. will be erogated by the Supreme Government. Therefore, His Excellency would like you to assign the space to be allotted to this object of national utility and luster, letting this Ministry know [your decision], so it can commission a person and proceed [with the formation of the Museum].[76]

We should take a moment to reflect on what this modest announcement meant and how it shaped the future of the museum.

First of all, the step taken to found the museum at that specific moment has to do with a very concrete need for space to bring together antiquities, those that had been safeguarded at different institutions, as well as the recently collected ones from the Isla de Sacrificios. An island off the coast of Veracruz, the Isla de Sacrificios functioned as a makeshift port in the 1820s, while the port of San Juan de Ulúa was under Spanish occupation until 1826. Even before they set foot in mainland Mexico, foreigners took advantage of their layover at the Isla de Sacrificios to survey the island

and collect preconquest objects scattered all over. Alamán sought to curb the practice and ordered the soldiers stationed there to collect "furniture, idols, and antiquities" and to transport them to the capital.[77] A box of objects was sent to Mexico City on March 1 and would have arrived there some days later.[78] Faced with the decision of where to deposit these objects, Alamán probably thought the museum could no longer be postponed. This helps explain why, if we were expecting some formal and high-sounding edict, all we have to attest to the foundation of the National Museum is a matter-of-fact letter from one government official to another. Yielding most likely to time considerations, the museum was produced through an administrative act by the executive branch and was not the result of legislative action. The distinction is important because, rather than achieving status as a legal entity, the museum would depend for the next eight years on the whims of elected federal officials who did not always agree that the nation actually needed this object of utility and luster or, for that matter, on how to make it useful or illustrious.[79]

Second, the museum would be housed at the university, which flanked the National Palace on the southern side. In a sense, the university was a logical space for the museum. At the university, the museum would join *El caballito*, the fine equestrian statue of Carlos IV cast by Manuel Tolsá in 1802 for Mexico City's central plaza, where it remained until 1823, when "patriotic" mobs threatened to destroy it. In 1824 Alamán had it transferred to the central patio of the university, a less public but much smaller space where it always seemed disproportionately big to visitors.[80] Like Cortés's bones—and ultimately like the museum—the statue was one of Alamán's symbolic rescues. Under the patio of the university, newly interred again after Bullock's visit, lay the goddess Teoyamiqui, who would thus become the literal foundation for the future collection of Mexican antiquities.

These symbolic associations between the museum and the university turned out to be deceptive, belied by the concrete condition of the museum there. By March 20 the dean of the university had found a space for the museum: the mathematics classroom. This was a miserably undersized space; over the next forty years, it became a serious problem for the conservation and the display of objects, compelling successive conservators to look for space elsewhere. Moreover, though we might be induced to believe that locating the museum at the university would have promoted scholarly collaboration between the two institutions, such did not turn out to be the case. Unlike the School of Mines or the Botanical Garden, the university, dating to the sixteenth century, was a bastion of conservatism, steeped in scholastic reasoning and averse to the Enlightenment legacies that shaped the collection, organization, and study of natural and manmade objects by the museum. A thorn in the flank of more liberal regimes, the university was often closed down, to be reopened by conservative governments.

A few days after the mathematics classroom was ceded over, Ignacio Cubas, the dedicated antiquarian and archivist, was put in charge of the museum. The problems Cubas faced as the museum's first director were immense. He had to set up an infrastructure, and he hired carpenters, bricklayers, glassblowers, locksmiths, and other craftsmen to build shelves and cabinets where the museum's first specimens would go.[81] At the same time, he confronted an even more daunting task: that of filling up shelves and museum spaces with objects. It is impossible to know what objects Cubas had in mind when he ordered the cabinets. Unfortunately, as is the case with most museums and collections, these early cabinets have not survived the destruction wrought by modernization, and no visual records exist of the museum at this stage. We do have acquisition records, though, and they reflect a lack of guidelines for the collection of objects. Rather than follow a preestablished plan, Cubas tried to bring together as many things as possible. Some arrived at the museum through official channels. On March 20, for example, Cubas inventoried natural history objects collected by the government-sponsored expedition to the Isthmus of Tehuantepec: forty-four samples of rocks; thirty-three packages with shells gathered from both coasts and two lithophytes; various samples of wood and four plugs of tobacco; and fifty-three named seeds and eighty-two unnamed seeds.[82] Other objects were purchased, as was the case with "two stones [. . .], sculpted in the ancient style, one of them, a cylinder with a flower in the center, the other, a human figure, a little bigger than half a vara," for which he paid 6 pesos with 4 reals to one Andrés Estrada.[83]

The vast majority of objects that arrived at the museum in 1825 did so through donations. On May 9 Cubas received "seated dolls" from Santiago Tlatelolco; a lizard sculpted on top of a square stone from under the bridge of Alvarado; a human figure (*muñeco*), one vara (a little under a meter) tall, and coiling plumed serpents of different diameters, disinterred from the chapel of San Salvador. Cubas thought the snakes coiled around the moon represented an ancient belief that the moon waned because it was eaten by a snake.[84] Two months later the conservator recorded the donation of the statue of a seated Indian, a coiled snake, a coyote sitting on its tail, and a toad, all made of stone, as well as four skulls and bones made of the volcanic stone tezontle. The seated Indian merited further explanation by Cubas, who thought the statue seemed sad and dejected at "seeing his country invaded by barbarian Spaniards"—a politically charged interpretation that reversed the usual descriptive, with the Spaniards becoming the barbarians in Cubas's inventory. Cubas went on to say he believed that it was this statue that gave its name to one of the streets in the city center, the so-called Calle del Indio Triste.[85] Some of the objects received by the museum during 1825 were, as recorded by Cubas, very heavy, which makes one wonder what techniques were employed to bring them into the museum. Cubas did not say.

Weight and transportation proved to be impediments for collecting some objects. During the summer of 1825 Carlos María de Bustamante sent the museum notices of antiquities he had come upon in Mexico City and its environs. Demolition work in the southwestern corner of the National Palace had revealed a red stone engraved with cactus "leaves," which Bustamante took for the Mexican Empire coat of arms. He presumed that the relief had been among those that were torn down when Cortés ordered the building of the cathedral and that it was later recycled, like so many other pieces of preconquest stonework, to build the viceregal palace. In any case, he insisted that it was important to examine the relief and to bring it to the museum. Cubas responded that it was not possible, not only because of the size of the piece, but because extracting it from the wall would have compromised the stability of the building.[86] Farther afield, amid the ancient ruins of Texcoco, Bustamante found "beauties that would marvel Europe," which were beginning to attract foreign travelers. He advised Cubas to send for some of the objects, particularly for a sculpted snake in the process of devouring the head of a woman—a symbol of the moon, Bustamante believed. It would have been easy to place them in a canoe and carry them across the Texcoco Lake to the capital, but Bustamante thought they might be too heavy, so he suggested transportation by carriage. It was urgent, Bustamante insisted, that Mexican authorities excavate these sites, and he advised that Castañeda be sent there to survey the place and make drawings of the ruins. Apparently, Castañeda was sent to the ruins, though there are no records of his drawings.[87]

Over the following years, Bustamante proved undaunted in his search for Mexican antiquities. His casual disregard for local customs and claims shows the other side of the norms of treasure hunting that ruled notions of cultural property in Mexico at this period; for if the foreign collector felt justified in taking rarities if he could, the museum was receiving suggestions, which it sometimes acted on, that simply disregarded the local context of finds, their use and value to the community, in favor of their seizure by the central cultural institution of the state. One of the great problems of the museum was that, like the Mexican state itself, the balance between the central state apparatus in Mexico City and the variegated forms of local, district, and regional authority were far from being worked out.

The first months of the museum were characterized by a state of urgency, to create material conditions for collecting while building up a collection at the same time. In retrospect, this state, exacerbated in part by the fact that objects were beginning to be carried away by foreigners, would stretch on for decades. The museum needed to lay claim to things quickly, to bring them into its space; as minister, Alamán proved to be a powerful ally, acting beyond his official duties, such as those of authorizing expenses, to ensure strong beginnings for the museum. At the center of a prolific correspondence with friends and associates, he fielded demands for local natural history specimens in exchange for collections built in Europe.[88] He traded letters concerning the nature and scientific properties of objects collected by the members of the Tehuantepec commission.[89] And he intervened before local state governments to ensure they did not cede antiquities and manuscripts to unscrupulous foreigners.[90]

Alamán's involvement with the museum reflected just how strongly he felt that the success of the institution depended on him for protection and promotion. As Benjamin Disraeli wrote in his preface to the English translation of Alamán's 1825 report to Congress, "new institutions, in theory however powerful, in their nature however beneficial, possess, for a considerable period after their adoption, but a nominal existence."[91] Disraeli romantically claimed that only genius could transform this nominal existence into a concrete reality and flatteringly professed to have recognized that genius in Alamán. Although Disraeli was not speaking specifically of the museum, but of the entire "infant state" of Mexico, and his mining speculations cannot be separated from the praises he lavished on Alamán, it is not difficult to see that Disraeli's dictum can be applied to Alamán's relationship with the museum. To the extent that the museum existed at all and that an inchoate framework had been set up in Mexico to define cultural properties and to defend the state's title to them, it was owing to Alamán's efforts.

The question, not rhetorical, was what to expect when the museum lost its powerful advocate, when a strongman like Alamán was no longer there. Following a series of meetings with the U.S. representative Joel R. Poinsett, who was playing an increasingly influential role Mexico's internal politics, Alamán, who was defending the formation of a Spanish American commercial alliance against a bilateral (and asymmetrical) treaty with the United States, saw himself losing ground and resigned from his post on September

26, 1825. Poinsett would go on to sign the treaty with Sebastián Camacho (1791–1847), Alamán's successor. Alamán left behind a politically fragmented country gripped by intensifying debates between centralist and federalist factions, where the possibilities for economic and social restoration seemed unattainable. As for the museum, Alamán had endowed it with a physical space, albeit insufficient, which presupposed the formalization of the Creole, eighteenth-century practices of collecting and studying natural history and antiquities. The museum thus represented a potentially powerful newcomer into the complex of institutions—including the School of Mines, the Botanical Garden, the viceregal archives, and the libraries and archives of the various religious orders, each of which had their own collections—that had been generated during the colonial period. It inherited, by way of complex legacies, both objects from these older collections (and from those of private individuals) and the personal expertise that went with caring for them.

The challenge for a national museum was to adapt the collecting culture of the eighteenth century to the new claims of the republic, claims that invested the property of those things owned by "nobody" in "everybody"—every citizen of the nation. These were not problems unique to Mexico; they were problems being sorted out in England, Prussia, France, Spain, and the United States as well. What was specific to Mexico was that the divides about cultural property and practices—the role of church, of state, of different states, of citizens, of foreigners—had not been resolved by independence. As minister, Alamán had decided on these questions on an ad hoc basis, providing funds to facilitate purchases on behalf of the museum or exerting leverage with foreigners like Bullock to ensure the repatriation of manuscripts. But Alamán's larger-than-life presence in the museum did little to ensure the institution's legal or financial autonomy from the whims of politicians who might be less generous, more caught up with different emergencies, or less convinced of the importance of a national museum for the young republic. The museum's allotted space, money, and relationship with government officials, with the Mexican public, or with foreign visitors were, after all, measures of its worth, matters of recognition and visibility. During its first half century, the history of the National Museum of Mexico is a struggle for recognition, as its conservators mobilized different political, commercial, and intellectual strategies to exert the kind of civil pressure, internally and externally, to prove the museum's exclusive right to collect, display, and speak in the name of an assemblage of objects; to establish continuities between these objects and the Mexican public; and ultimately, to make what initially seemed like a heterogeneous assemblage of things tell stories in the name of that abstract entity, the Mexican nation.

2 MEASURES OF WORTH

First Inventory, Gains and Losses

After Lucas Alamán left his post at the Ministry of Internal and External Relations, Ignacio Cubas stayed on as head of the National Museum of Mexico for a few months before he was named director of the National Archive. On November 29, 1825, the new minister of internal and external relations, Sebastián Camacho, placed Isidro Ignacio Icaza (1783–1834) in charge of the museum. A member of a powerful merchant family at the center of an extensive trade network within Spanish America, Icaza studied theology before he taught philosophy at the Colegio de San Ildefonso and served as dean of the university during the last years of the viceroyalty. His name appears among those who signed Mexico's act of independence on September 28, 1821. Under Emperor Agustín de Iturbide, he participated in a commission on education reform. Icaza's ties with the church and with the university and his associations with Mexico's economic and political elites made him a strong candidate for the conservatorship at the museum, to which he would bring both his experience with various institutions of learning and instruction and his social and political clout—which Cubas, whose background was more humble, lacked.

A week after his appointment at the museum, Icaza wrote Minister Camacho to say that he was grateful for the nomination, which corresponded to his "literary inclinations," though he admitted that he had no idea what the job entailed. In his letter, he demanded an inventory of the collection and a list of the responsibilities and limitations of his post as well as a declaration of the kind of support—financial and institutional—he could expect from the government.[1] In other words, Icaza did not, at this point, have a sense of what the museum was about or of the extent to which it mattered to the authorities. Icaza did not receive a reply from the minister's office, which he could interpret as meaning that the museum was not a priority for the politicians and ideologues in Congress or as a sign that he would be given a free hand to run the museum as he wished.

Perhaps Camacho did not reply to Icaza's letter asking for specifics about the collection because he did not have anything to say. The decree that had founded the museum made abstract reference to its utility for the nation. And yet, examined a little more closely, the sense of the phrase disappears in a cloud of rhetoric. How was the museum to be useful, and what power would it have to satisfy this mandate? In any case, by the time Icaza was appointed conservator, there existed a physical space and a collection of objects that ostensibly defined the museum. What the museum lacked was any solid definition of its internal functions (concerning the collection, preservation, study, and display of objects) and of its external relations with government authorities, donors, other museums and collectors, and a more general public. As the failure to acknowledge Icaza's letter of acceptance shows, it also lacked a sense of the kind of commitment it could expect from the upper echelons of the government.

Icaza quickly understood that it was up to him to come up with an inventory and with a protocol for the operation of the museum, which would frame its day-to-day activities, while, more ambitiously, fashioning it into a recognizable protagonist both in the life of the newly independent nation and among the international circuits that collected and gave meaning to Mexico's natural history and to the objects of its past. This chapter focuses on Icaza's eight-year conservatorship, between 1825 and his death in 1834, and reconstructs Icaza's multifold strategies as he struggled to lay a firm foundation for the museum. The degree of his success was intimately entangled with legal, political, and cultural processes well beyond the control of the museum.

By the end of December, Icaza, in collaboration with Ignacio Cubas, produced an inventory of the collection.[2] In keeping with the two men's respective literary and antiquarian interests, rather than being a comprehensive register of the museum's objects, the inventory focuses exclusively on those objects related to Mexico prior to its conquest and, to some extent, to its colonial past, allowing us a rare glimpse into the state of the antiquarian collection soon after the museum's foundation. Listed are such things as documents on palm bark, maguey, deer skin, and parchment; maps or plans of towns and villages, produced in the decades following the conquest; codices; genealogies; books of tributes; and land titles, many of which had been part of Lorenzo Boturini's collection.

The inventory also lists the preconquest objects in the museum's collection. Some had been housed by the university since their excavation in the 1790s, including a sacrificial altar and the "colossal simulacrum" of the goddess Teoyamiqui, still buried under the patio of the university. Most of the objects had entered the museum during Cubas's first year in charge of the institution, and the inventory organizes them by provenance, whether they came into the collection by purchase or donation, in accordance with the conservator's belief that by giving recognition to the donor, others would come forward with objects. Other than that, things are identified quite summarily by appearance, material, size, and the place where they were found. Yet while admitting that theirs was not a rich or detailed inventory, in his cover letter to Camacho, Icaza highlighted the fact that cataloguing objects had been a time-consuming task, which had kept the two men away from other tasks for weeks. This meant there was a pressing need for an assistant to help with future inventories and correspondence. In addition, Icaza indicated that it was imperative for the museum to be able to count on a fixed budget, rather than continue to operate on an ad hoc basis, subject to the whims and timings of Congress. A fixed budget, explained Icaza, would ensure that the museum would become a "formalized" space; in turn, the knowledge that the museum had been "formalized" would allow it to deal as an equal with various collectors who had all offered "appreciable donations" for the museum but wanted first assurances that the state was fully backing the museum. Otherwise, Icaza warned, these "patriots" would change their minds about donating objects, and the fledgling institution would risk "missing some of the more interesting and appreciated objects, which enlightened foreigners are in a hurry to take out of the country."[3]

Icaza soon experienced the consequences of those risks. On the last day of 1825, he wrote a note to Camacho to inform him that he had received a "most interesting" proposal, to transfer the collection of the "celebrated antiquarian" Antonio de León y Gama to the museum.[4] This was indeed a coup; as Camacho would have probably known, in the last decade of the eighteenth century, León y Gama had produced studies on Mexican antiquities that continued to be touchstone antiquarian works in the postindependence years. Besides being a scholar of antiquities, León y Gama had collected manuscripts and books that were produced by the intellectuals of New Spain, including, among others, writings by seventeenth-century polymath Carlos de Sigüenza y Góngora; he also possessed many manuscripts and codices from Boturini's collection. When León y Gama died in 1802, his archive came to rest in the hands of his executor, José Antonio Pichardo (1748–1812), from the Oratory of San Felipe. From his Jesuit friend Andrés Cavo (1739–1803), who was exiled in Rome, Pichardo received letters entreating him to do everything in his power to retain the archive in Mexico and avoid having it follow other "precious" documents to their "sepulchers" in libraries in Madrid or fall into the hands of Napoleon, who was amassing, in the early 1800s, a "library of ancient things." As Cavo wrote on March 1, 1803, "if Napoleon comes to know what [León y Gama] possessed, he is capable of asking for it; and our country would lose such precious monuments. [. . .] This evil is irremediable, for it seems everyone is bent on extracting from this kingdom many monuments [. . .] of the ancient Mexicans."[5] Pichardo, like Cavo, belonged to a liberal priestly cast within the Catholic clergy and to a distinct Creole intellectual culture with a sense of its own vulnerability to European ambitions, and he kept the collection in Mexico until his death, in 1812, when it passed on to Pichardo's own testamentary executor, José Vicente Sánchez.

So it certainly looked like an early victory for the museum, that it should be named the final repository of the archives of León y Gama. Icaza and Sánchez arranged for the transfer to take place on January 19, 1826. But on January 14 Icaza informed Camacho that the transfer had been called off because the museum lacked the infrastructure necessary to safeguard the León y Gama collection. Not one single shelf was available to store the archives, and the museum did not have a watchman to ensure the integrity of the materials.[6] It is hard to know, in retrospect, if it was Sánchez who refused to make the donation due to the impoverished condition of the museum or if it was Icaza who, for the same reasons, decided it was best to await a better moment.

That moment never arrived. A few years later, in his preface to the edition of the *Descripción histórica y cronológica de las dos piedras* (1832), which compiled previously published and unpublished antiquarian material by León y Gama, Carlos María de Bustamante complained that Sánchez refused to allow anyone to see the collection of manuscripts. "I do not know the cause," he added, and he publicly exhorted Alamán, who was by then minister of internal and external relations again, to use all his influence to persuade Sánchez to turn over both León y Gama's manuscripts and the ancient documents the former had used in his studies. Bustamante—who, as we have seen in the previous chapter, had an exalted sense of the nation's claims to cultural properties like antiquities and documents—insisted that these documents belonged by right to the Mexican government and that they should be edited and published.[7] His plea might not have been picked up by Alamán, but it seems to have tipped Sánchez off that the archive had a palpable and exploitable worth. After the collection disappeared from public view, it eventually ended up in the Bibliothèque Nationale in Paris.

Two months later, Icaza found out that an English merchant had exported "fifteen or sixteen loads" of ancient monuments, while Colonel Mariano Villaurrutia was selling some of the choicest antiquities of Texcoco to private collectors, right behind Icaza's back in Mexico City.[8] Surprisingly, there is no mention in Icaza's letters and records of an even more worrisome loss: the purchase and export in 1824 by Latour Allard, a native of New Orleans, of an impressive collection of antiquities and manuscripts that included 180 "idols," statues of serpents and other animals, and some reliefs pertaining to the Royal

Antiquarian Expeditions; 120 drawings by Dupaix and Castañeda; and a notebook that had belonged to Boturini. In this case, the seller was the expedition's very draftsman, Luciano Castañeda, who, having fallen on hard times, was looking to make a living.[9]

This loss of antiquities led Icaza to write Camacho a biting letter protesting against the extraction of Mexican antiquities and of other types of objects by foreigners interested in this "branch of literature" and in "commercial speculation." Again, Icaza insisted that once these objects left the country, there was no hope of retrieving them, which would result in irreparable loss to the Mexican people who would thus be stripped of the "original titles to [their] history." For Icaza, Mexican "monuments" (antiquities) had both epistemic and symbolic value. They formed, on the one hand, the vestiges on which Mexico's foundations would be written—to allow antiquities to be exported out of the country would leave all future scholars of Mexico's past no choice but to reconstruct Mexican history in foreign archives and museums or to content themselves with mere copies. On the other hand, Icaza thought that the nation's engagement with its antiquities was an important part of the process that would consecrate it as a civilized nation equal to any other.[10]

Although to our contemporary ears Icaza's arguments might sound wholly convincing, as they employ the type of rhetoric that is now taken for granted in the self-presentation of a national museum, these were not agreed upon conventions in 1826. Icaza was claiming that in some way, the essence of Mexico's past and present depended on the national ownership, conservation, and study of preconquest objects. But contrary to Icaza's convictions, antiquities participated in different regimes of value at once—Icaza hinted at scholarly and commercial interests by foreigners, though the uses of antiquities were also locally determined, at village or state levels. To bring them into the museum, all other meanings of antiquities would have had to be neutralized in favor of a series of inferences: that antiquities held the key to Mexico's history and the state's claim to them measured the country's status as a civilized nation, that they belonged in the museum, and that the museum belonged in the capital of the republic.

For these claims to be realized, Icaza insisted again, the government first needed to formalize the existence of the museum by investing it with a budget and with a comprehensive set of laws. In the absence of postindependence legislation to regulate the activities of the museum, he asked the Mexican government to consider enforcing a royal decree of 1804, which had arranged for the collection and study of antiquities by putting Guillermo Dupaix in charge of the Royal Antiquarian Expeditions. Like many laws ratified before independence, this decree was not expressly abolished and continued to be operative; in fact, Luciano Castañeda still received a wage, as specified in the decree. In the legal framework of the expeditions, Icaza saw useful precedents for the collection and protection of objects related to Mexico's natural and civil history. Although he acknowledged that motivations of the court in Madrid may have been more avaricious than altruistic, since in the end the court had ordered many of the objects to be exported to the metropolis, Icaza pointed out the fact that, contrary to Mexico's independent government, even Mexico's "oppressors" had not let the country's ancient history fall into oblivion.[11] Icaza's letter seemed to have no effect on Camacho, who neither initiated a sweeping set of new norms nor acknowledged the viceregal precedent. It was not entirely up to the federal government to emulate viceregal policy toward antiquities. The 1824 Constitution gave great autonomy to the states and little to the federal government. This meant also a very reduced budget, which in turn affected how much could be given to the museum. Still, Icaza would keep on lobbying for the government to support the museum and institute protocols to claim and save Mexico's antiquities.

In Need of Laws

By May of 1826 Icaza had been in his post for just a few months, but he already realized that Congress was not going to act on its own to create a legal protocol that would empower the National Museum to function in the way he envisioned. Undeterred, on May 3 Icaza submitted his own "Proyecto de reglamento para el Museo Nacional" for consideration by Congress.[12] The project began by stating the museum's objective in terms of collecting on the grand scale: the museum would be empowered to collect, for public use, everything that could give the most exact and up-to-date knowledge of Mexico's "primitive population"; it would gather expressions of the origin and the progress of the sciences and the arts (among both Mexicans and other peoples); and finally, it would collect instructive samples of the country's natural productions and of the properties of its soil and climate. This mandated the acquisition of the following classes of objects: statues, paintings, and hieroglyphs produced prior to or at the time of the Spanish invasion, together with the vestiges of the ancient peoples of other American nations and of other continents; coins, lapidary inscriptions, and tokens relative to notable events and people of all regions; paintings, sculptures, and other products of the fine arts; scientific machines and useful inventions; complete collections of the three branches (plants, animals, and minerals) that make up natural history; rare and curious productions of nature, especially those of the Mexican soil; and finally, antiquarian works and natural histories, in manuscript or printed form, that could produce knowledge about Mexico, its revolutions, and the analogy of its inhabitants with those of the rest of the world.

Icaza's project included specifications of the museum's employees. At the top of the museum's personnel was the director, who would no longer be stuck with the kind of inventory work Icaza had been doing. Instead, his more elevated responsibilities included the acquisition of objects and the liaison between the museum and Mexican authorities and private correspondents. He would coordinate his duties with those of two conservators—of antiquities and of natural history—who would be responsible for preserving, classifying, and studying the objects in their respective collections. An illustrator and an assistant, two secretaries, and two watchmen would complete the staff of the museum. There is a curious disjunction between the museum's universal scope and the humbleness of its staffing requirements. Either Icaza was deficient in organizational vision, or, more likely, he pushed for what he hoped he could get from Congress.

The remainder of Icaza's project concerned more-practical rec-ommendations, such as the museum's open hours—Tuesdays, Thursdays, and Saturdays, between ten and two—and a strict pro-tocol for the extraction of objects and books from the collection. In a separate note, Icaza suggested that the museum should expand beyond the room it had been granted at the university to occupy four main spaces: the bottom floor at the university would be reserved for ancient monuments, both Mexican and foreign; a room on the first floor would display coins and modern models of machines of all types; another would hold the cabinet of natural history; and a third room would serve as the administration's offices. Icaza's phys-ical plan for the museum was the first of a long series of proposals whereby he unsuccessfully sought to accommodate the growing collections either within the university or in nearby buildings.[13] He saved his financial considerations for last. The museum's budget would have to guarantee staff wages—he left the amounts to the discretion of his "superiors"—and day-to-day maintenance of the grounds. A more substantial sum would allow for acquisitions, and Icaza stipulated that this sum could be augmented as needed, pending approval by Congress. To temper the effect of this request on Congress, Icaza promised that all purchases would reconcile economic considerations with estimates of the grandness and importance of the object to be bought.

Once again Congress seemed to have other business to deal with than ratifying Icaza's project for the museum. So on June 15, antic-ipating that Congressmen would soon adjourn their sessions for summer recess, Icaza wrote again to impress on Congress that the "Reglamento" should be urgently approved.[14] Over the previous months, Icaza explained, the museum had been refurbished and cleaned, and from government announcements in the press, there was a popular expectation that it would soon open. Mexicans and foreign travelers were curious to examine the antiquities gathered there by the government. But the museum would run too great a risk if it were opened without an approved set of rules for operation. Failure to ratify even a provisional protocol would send a message to possible donors that the Mexican state was not serious about the museum, which could only have the disastrous consequence of discouraging them. Instead, the flow of objects out of Mexico would increase, and the proofs of America's past inventions and discoveries would be lost or put in the hands of foreigners. With his letter, Icaza included modifications, obviously designed to make the museum less costly, to the project he had presented a month earlier. He reduced the number of employees from a total of nine to five—a primary and a secondary "conservator," a draftsman, a secretary, and a watchman. And he suggested annual wages for each employee: 1,500 and 800 pesos for each conservator respectively, 800 for the draftsman, 400 for the secretary, and 300 for the watchman. And 100 pesos would cover office needs.[15]

Just as Icaza had feared, Congress left for the summer before approving his protocol. It would be another five tumultuous years before it was finally signed into effect on November 21, 1831, with Alamán's support. In the meantime, the museum operated on an ad-hoc basis, submitting all its acquisition requests to Congress, which was slow in dispensing money. Lack of funding, coupled with political instability, was also responsible for the museum only being open on a sporadic basis. Writing in 1828, the English traveler Mark Beaufoy claimed that he had "a soldier break open the door" to the museum, "the key having been lost."[16] Although Beaufoy's anecdote seems doubtful, given what we know from archival documents that show important activity in the museum during that year, it is plausible that Beaufoy might find the museum closed to the public for long periods of time. Still, when open, it did receive a steady flow of visitors, as it became an obligatory stop for foreigners on tours of Mexico City.

At the same time, though not officially approved, Icaza's protocol served as a guide to structuring both the collection and the personnel of the museum. Over the years, the collection grew along the lines traced by his project even though, due to the cramped quarters, which necessitated the promiscuous juxtaposition of objects, the different categories may not have been explicit to visitors. The organizational collaboration between antiquarians and naturalists was a prominent feature of the museum into the early 1900s.

Letters, Loops, and Loopholes

Icaza's letters to various government agencies eventually led to an official dispatch, dated October 6, 1826, from Camacho to the "political leaders" of the different states of the republic, asking them to inform his ministry about objects that could be of interest to the museum. Alluding to the 1804 royal decree that Icaza had brought to his attention, Camacho vowed that the Mexican government would not fall short of its colonial predecessors but would also put its full support behind the production of knowledge about antiquities and natural history.[17] At the same time, the minister of justice and ecclesiastical and secular affairs, Miguel Ramos Arizpe, sent out missives to bishops and archbishops in which he denounced the loss of antiquities and of "some curious specimens of natural or artificial production" at the hand of ecclesiastical corporations. He asked his correspondents to put "national glory" above all other considerations and send valuable objects to the government, which would dispatch them to the national cabinet.[18]

For the most part, political and ecclesiastical officials simply acknowledged receipt of Camacho's letter. Even when the circulars reached people with a greater degree of expertise, like the botanist Pablo de la Llave, who was then canon at the cathedral in Valladolid (today Morelia), the answer could have used a little more detail: de la Llave sent in some "ancient chiseled pyrite," a "clay pipe, a copper turtle, a tiger's head, obsidian stones and a natural snail," without providing further information as to the origin or the possible meanings of these objects.[19] This was a reflection of the state of the art in the fledgling field of Mexican antiquarianism.

The governor of Chihuahua penned a promising answer, writing that his state possessed interesting samples of silver ore. Icaza followed up and asked Camacho to purchase "four stones of virgin silver, with little extraneous matter in them," from Batopilas, Chihuahua, for the price of 1,418 pesos and 2 reals, insisting that "curious examples of the mineral kingdom deserve singular appreciation in all well-organized cabinets." Considering that Mexico owed its fame to the richness of its mines, Icaza deemed the absence of "such productions" in the museum unpardonable.[20] Although I have not been able to find out if the request was granted, the project of building up a mineralogical collection was well under way by the 1830s, and the museum would boast a comprehensive mineralogical collection as well as specimens with mostly a curiosity value—such as dendrites, diamonds, and oysters with pearls.[21]

State officials in California took Camacho's pleas most seriously. On March 22, 1829, Juan Manuel Riesgo, general commissioner for the Occident, sent the museum "curiosities" obtained through the trade along the Pacific Northwest: a feather-lined tunic, manufactured by the "Coriakas" (referring perhaps to the inhabitants of Kodiak Island), and an "exquisite" leather belt; the model of a canoe with rowers and huntsman, a harpoon handle, and an impermeable shirt of bear intestine, all used for hunting sea otters; a bow strung with nerve fibers and arrows used by the Indians of California; and a paddle from the Society Islands, made of flint, since, Riesgo noted, the Russians do not allow the use of iron or steel.[22] The commissioner also sent a certain Luis Bringas to Mexico City along with the objects to answer any questions about the artifacts.

Just as indicative of the state of cooperation in Mexico—as the struggle between the federalists and the centralizers became a larger issue for the new state—were the unenthusiastic responses to the circulars by state governors in Yucatán and Tlaxcala. On February 16, 1827, José Tiburcio López (1790–1858) of Yucatán wrote that no preconquest objects were left there because the Spanish invaders—soldiers "possessed by the grossest ignorance," on one hand, and missionaries seeking to extirpate "idolatry and necromancy," on the other—"threw into indifferent flames, statues, paintings, ciphers, and characters [codices?]."[23] Nor did López send in naturalia, though he admitted his state abounded in interesting objects from the animal and plant kingdoms; he suggested that the central government hire an "instructed" person to conduct surveys and collect objects.[24] López's diagnosis respecting the absence of antiquities in Yucatán is especially ironic at a moment when foreign travelers were beginning to visit the peninsula in search of antiquities. Because he knew the peasants in Yucatán rather well,

López must have been aware of the presence of preconquest vestiges throughout his state.[25] For his part, the governor of Tlaxcala, Cristóbal González Angulo, made an explicit appeal to local politics when he denied Icaza the banner brandished by Hernán Cortés when he entered the city of Tlaxcala in September of 1519 on his way to Tenochtiltan, the capital of the Mexican Empire—the banner belonged to the City Hall, which would not part with the banner or with ancient manuscripts, even in the midst of dire financial difficulties.[26]

Finally, the governor of the state of Mexico, Lorenzo Zavala, adamantly opposed relinquishing objects from his state to the museum. Throughout 1826 a certain Saturnino Islas had worked as Icaza's contact in Teotihuacan, Otumba, Atlixco, and Texcoco, whence he remitted antiquities to the museum.[27] In July of 1827 Islas delivered "three sackfuls of bones" of "an unknown animal" unearthed from the properties in the Texcoco region.[28] Zavala accused the parties engaged in the transaction of illegality but agreed to cede the skeleton in the name of "the good harmony that should be conserved with the Federation." In fact, Zavala had his own ideas about what the good harmony of the federation entailed, being a staunch federalist who defended the rights of individual states over those of the central government. Camacho responded that the donation would have been illegal only if the skeleton had been seized against the will of the owners on whose property it had been found. He concluded his letter by asking Zavala to turn in the rest of the skeleton, which he had in his possession.[29] Even when, as in this case, the museum obtained the skeleton it desired, the curator was left to deal with the problem of paying Islas for his expenses, the 93 pesos and 7 reals incurred in transporting the bones and other objects. To Islas's petition, Icaza could only give the humiliating answer that, as of August of 1828, the museum had not received any money since January.[30] As Icaza was warding off Islas, he was being rebuffed by the government on his request for 300 pesos for a "fine mineralogical collection" and 4,000 pesos to buy Buffon's *Histoire naturelle*—useful, he claimed, for the classification of the natural history cabinet.[31] Instead, he was instructed to find a cheaper reference book and to pay the museum's debts to Islas before considering new purchases.[32] There is no record as to how the conflict was resolved.

As the eclectic responses to the circulars indicate, government officials were not sure what was considered valuable enough to be taken out of circulation and put on display in a national museum. Antiquities? Silver ores? Northwestern furs? Stuffed birds? Curious skeletons? Zavala, for instance, made no objections to antiquities leaving his state but considered the bones of an unknown animal valuable enough to have wanted to keep them. This incident further highlights another ambiguity: to whom did collectibles belong? There was no consensus around an answer, especially as the issue was entangled in the fierce debates between federalists and centralizers, which led to full-fledged civil wars during the first half century of Mexico's independent existence. Nor was it simply a matter of choice between sending an object to the National Museum or keeping it for a fledgling local one. As certain objects began to gain commercial or symbolic value in the international market for curiosities, they were sold to the wealthiest buyers, who often happened to be foreign collectors. The chronically underfunded National Museum was at a disadvantage in this rivalry; for even when it obtained an object, the agent who arranged discovery and transport of the object was often left to pay his own bills.

Still, despite difficulties of all kinds, the collection of the National Museum grew, through government intervention and private donations. In his February 1828 address to Congress, the minister of internal and external relations, Juan José Espinosa de los Monteros (1768–1840), boasted about the museum by highlighting some of the holdings: six hundred paintings and drawings on the history of indigenous peoples; two hundred stone and four hundred clay monuments; sixty manuscripts; forty-two paintings by Mexican artists; two hundred kinds of shells and minerals; wood samples; maritime productions; and extraordinary bones.[33] The museum's eclecticism was an expression of Icaza's encyclopedic ambition—to bring together antiquities, natural history, objects of ethnographic interest, and industrial productions—which shared an ethos with other museums both in the Americas and in Europe during that era.[34] Like his contemporaries, Icaza was striving to achieve a museum of universal knowledge, even in the context of a slowly developing crisis concerning the logical possibility of universal knowledge.[35] But while the more established museums could go on accommodating an infinity of disparate things, the National Museum in Mexico did not have adequate space to sort its hodgepodge of objects. Although on paper, in his project for the museum, Icaza developed a division by species according to the classical model, the physical space he commanded did not correspond to that mental space. In November of 1827 a caustic review of the museum, which appeared in the periodical *El sol,* scoffed at how Icaza had arranged, "on the same shelf, a little idol, a stuffed parrot, a crystallization, a plant, a doll, a wax bird, a shell. Such a shelf is no longer fit for a cabinet but for a showcase, of the kind our grandmothers used to decorate their sitting rooms." The reviewer, seeing no pattern among these juxtapositions, seemed especially irritated by the presence of "superfluous" stuff and by the absence of the more "exquisite productions" of the natural realm. Finally, he drew attention to another major defect of the museum: the exhibits lacked explanations, so visitors left the place in the same state of ignorance with which they came in. "Such establishments are for instruction: but there's darned little [instruction] to be obtained here." The reviewer expressed hopes that the approval of a set of norms for the museum would improve its situation and signed off as Rosa Isidica.[36]

Although women, like the Marquesa de la Selva Nevada, were patrons of the arts and built notable collections, "Rosa Isidica" is likely an anagram for Isidro Icaza. It is hard to imagine that the conservator would have heaped so much verbal abuse on himself, so it is more likely that some detractor was playing a prank on him. In essence, Icaza and the critic agreed: beyond the numbers that Minister Espinosa de los Monteros boasted of in his report to Congress, the only way that the museum could have signaled its relevance in the life of the new nation as a place for learning was by being given space, funds, and organization. Since his arrival at the museum, Icaza had made every effort to convince the federal government to commit to a legal framework and financial independence for the museum. In 1827 Icaza opted for another tactic than that of appealing, memo by memo, to the political hierarchy: he decided to educate the public directly about the importance of the museum.

A "Literature" for the Museum

On August 25, 1827, Icaza and Isidro Rafael Gondra (1788–1861) published the announcement of an upcoming publication, the *Colección de antigüedades que ecsisten en el Museo Nacional*.[37] The two men had known each other since Gondra had studied theology at the university under Icaza. Now Gondra was Mexico City's deputy in Congress, but he had continued to follow his mentor's career, taking up the cause of the museum to such an extent that after Icaza's death in 1834, Gondra was chosen as his successor. The *Colección*, they explained, would gather together, on paper, objects from the collection of the museum. Icaza and Gondra claimed that the peoples who lived in Mexico at the time of the Spanish conquest had been largely forgotten, both unintentionally and through deliberate acts of destruction of their material records. Of course, Icaza and Gondra acknowledged that their project was built on the viceregal policies of collecting and studying the vestiges of America's preconquest past. But the rhetoric of "burial" and "forgetting" was probably meant to prod "the enlightened government of the Republic" to see the museum as the best way of studying the country's past through the antiquities it had gathered together for a general audience. Icaza and Gondra hoped that the *Colección* would achieve what the museum itself was struggling to do. Affording the theoretically endless space of drawing on paper plus text, the paper collection would educate through images and descriptions to compensate for the difficulty of making the objects speak for themselves. Maybe Icaza and Gondra were also hoping that the *Colección*, by gaining the museum a sympathetic audience among influential people, would expand its authority and pressure the government to support more consistently the institution and its activities.[38]

The periodical would be published monthly and sold by sub-scription, at 4 pesos per issue. Each issue would be made up of four pages of illustrations of objects chosen from among the muse-um's broadly defined antiquities—sculpture, hieroglyphs, historical scenes, and drawings from the Dupaix and Castañeda manuscripts—with explanations of each object. The *Colección* would make use of lithography, a relatively new medium that, compared to engraving, enabled a higher degree of technical detail and allowed an image to be reproduced thousands of times without sacrificing quality. Icaza and Gondra hired the French lithographer Pedro Robert and the French illustrator Jean-Frédéric Waldeck (1776–1875) to work on the *Colección*.

Waldeck has not received the full-scale biography his long and eventful life certainly deserves, not least to shed a steady factual light on certain of the more Munchausenian episodes Waldeck liked to tell about himself. For instance, is it true, as Waldeck liked to claim, that he had received artistic training under Jacques Louis David? Or that he had participated in Napoleon's campaign in Egypt?[39] His passage through and involvement with Mexico are easier to track down, both in his own writings—interestingly, as historian Pablo Diener points out, most of Waldeck's writing is about Mexico—and in the writings of those with whom he came in contact.[40] Waldeck first became aware of Mexico in London in 1822 when he illustrated the book that turned Palenque into an object of European fascination: Antonio del Río's *Description of the Ruins of an Ancient City Discovered Near Palenque*, which had remained unpublished since it was originally written in Spanish, in 1787. Perhaps for the purposes of research, Waldeck also vis-ited Bullock's exhibition *Ancient and Modern Mexico*, which was showing in London a year later. By his own account, the book and the exhibit motivated him to want to see the originals in Mexico.[41] The occasion presented itself in 1825, when Waldeck filled a post as engineer with the English mining companies in the district of Tlalpujahua. His stint as mining engineer lasted less than a year, and by 1826 he was in Mexico City, where his hand as a society portraitist brought him to Icaza's attention. Why Icaza would have chosen Waldeck for the *Colección*—when he could have employed Castañeda, the museum's salaried draftsman, who had the merit of having participated in antiquarian expeditions—deserves some reflection. By the late 1820s Castañeda's antiquarian drawings had come under attack as untrustworthy by Waldeck, among others.[42] On the other hand, Waldeck's work as an illustrator for the *Description of an Ancient City*, which preceded his arrival in Mexico City, probably brought him to Icaza's attention in the first place, while it was the artist's familiarity with the lithographic process that might have tipped the scales in Waldeck's favor.[43]

By September 26, 1827, Waldeck had finished the first set of four plates, and the first issue of the *Colección* came out shortly after. An ambitious publication, 49 x 38 cm, it consisted of four lithographs preceded by two pages of explanations written by Waldeck. The first image is of a somewhat odd "historical" scene (see fig. 3). Waldeck had chosen to depict a gathering of five seemingly indigenous men with incongruous beards and Roman-looking togas, set off against a space reminiscent of classical architecture. Through the background arches, a telltale palm tree locates the viewer in the tropics. One of the men, to whom the attention of the spectator is directed, sits on what appears to be a stone throne, in the center of the composition; the other four appear to be dressing him. A feather crown on the ground will probably complete the dressing ceremony. The scene—freely based on a description Waldeck claims to have found among Boturini's manuscripts—depicts Huitzíhuitl's coronation in 1403. Waldeck's plate imagines the council of elders as they gathered together to choose a successor after the death of the first Mexican king, Huitzíhuitl's father, Acamapichtli, in 1402. The chief priest coveted the title for himself but, in what Waldeck interpreted as respect for a peaceful and orderly transfer of power, acquiesced to recognize Huitzíhuitl as the new monarch. The scene probably represents the moment when the young king is anointed with the insignia of power.

This episode, wrote Waldeck, gives a clear idea of how, by the dawn of the fifteenth century, Mexican civilization had achieved a high degree of ceremony, refinement, and decorum; it had become

3. Jean-Frédéric Waldeck, Huitzíhuitl's coronation. *Colección de antigüedades,* no. 1, 1827. Beinecke Rare Book and Manuscript Library, Yale University.

4. Jean-Frédéric Waldeck, Mexican soldier. Sepia drawing. Courtesy of the New-berry Library, Chicago. Call no. Ayer Art Waldeck, box B3, plate 48.

5. Jean-Frédéric Waldeck, comparison between Mexican and Greek female heads. Pencil drawing, sketchbook. Courtesy of the Newberry Library, Chicago. Call no. Ayer MS 2188, p. 51.

"a nation at the pinnacle of prosperity and order in all aspects of government." Waldeck's choice of a balanced, neoclassical composition reinforces the political and moral messages of the scene by insisting on composure, equanimity, and self-control. Thus, Waldeck put forth his ideas about ancient Mexico by fitting, as Esther Pasztory has observed, exotic-looking characters from Mexican history into European imaginary with respects to classical antiquity.[44] This is a persistent pattern in his oeuvre, as reflected by his series of color plates of rather fantastic types from ancient Mexican history (see fig. 4) or by a quite striking comparison he drew in his sketchbook between the profile of an indigenous woman and that of a classical Greek one (see fig. 5). To envision ancient Mexican history, something for which he had very few visual references, Waldeck translated it through Greek, Roman, and Egyptian iconographic and narrative elements he was familiar with. His neoclassical inclinations fit perfectly with the intellectual expectations and the political necessities of the fledgling Mexican Republic and aligned Waldeck's visual production with the textual ambitions of authors like Carlos María de Bustamante who also sought to understand modern Mexico with a hermeneutic forged out of the classical past, as he did in his *Mañanas de la Alameda de México* (1835–36). Compositions such as Waldeck's reconstructions of "historical" scenes for the *Colección* stand at the origin of the genre of historical painting in nineteenth-century Mexico.

In the second plate, Waldeck copied some of the drawings produced by Castañeda in the context of the Royal Antiquarian Expeditions (see fig. 6). They represent, as Waldeck wrote, a stone with two concentric circles on one of its faces and the sculpture of a lizard, originally from Xochimilco, the canal-crossed town to the south of Mexico City. These monuments, wrote Waldeck, gave credit to the knowledge and perfection achieved by Mexicans in geometry, architecture, and sculpture. A "sign of ancient Mexicans' munificence," these stones were distant "from the crude simplicity which characterizes the miserable huts of savage and uncultured peoples" and were "worthy of comparison in design and execution with the remains of ruins in Asia and Europe." Waldeck concluded that an

6. Jean-Frédéric Waldeck, antiquities from Xochimilco. *Colección de antigüe-dades*, no. 1, 1827. Beinecke Rare Book and Manuscript Library, Yale University.

abyss separated contemporary Indians who lived in those "miserable huts" and had barbarian customs, from those who, before the arrival of the Spanish, had reached a pinnacle of sophistication in their arts and politics. This conclusion associated itself with the question of the origin of American civilizations, which had been repeatedly asked by Europeans since the discovery of the New World. By the nineteenth century, however, explanations to that puzzle, increasingly entangled with the issue of the gap between Mexico's glorious past and Mexico's poor present, gave birth to a very lively discourse.

For the third plate, Waldeck reproduced a scene from a codex on maguey (see fig. 7). For Waldeck, it represents the trial of a man; the accusers, their arms stretched out as a sign of the veracity of their oath, stand above the accused, while below, a fourth woman, shedding tears, implores for forgiveness, to no avail. The man's fate has been cast—the accused will be burnt, as confirmed by the burning logs under his arms. The manuscript from which this scene is taken has been lost since the nineteenth century, and Waldeck's plate has been considered the only extant copy of it.[45] Yet knowing that Waldeck seldom shied away from fanciful interpretations, we can question the lithograph's degree of fidelity to the lost original. How much did the artist's notions of classical justice influence the way he read this and other scenes or objects? Did he introduce new pictorial elements or eliminate details in conformance with these notions? In other words, far from being merely passive representations, Waldeck's images were more often than not interpretations, constitutive of knowledge production.

The question of fidelity must also be raised concerning Waldeck's exclusive authorship of the pictorial representations and the written descriptions of the *Colección*. Some historians have seen the hand of Ignacio Cubas in the wording of the descriptions.[46] Though Waldeck made no mention of Cubas in his meticulously kept diaries, he did record encounters with collectors and scholars of Mexican antiquities and made references to visits to the private museums of José Justo Gómez, Conde de la Cortina (1799–1860); of José Mariano Sánchez Mora, Conde de Peñasco (1777–1845); and of the

7. Jean-Frédéric Waldeck, fragment of a codex. *Colección de antigüedades*, no. 1, 1827. Beinecke Rare Book and Manuscript Library, Yale University.

Marquesa de la Selva Nevada. No doubt he met and talked to members of those circles that were interested in antiquities, imbibing fashionable theories about the Mexican past current among them. Again, his representation and interpretation of this codex reflected his own expectations about the classical content of ancient Mexican institutions and played into postindependence anxieties of Mexico's subordination by offering a compromise—a "national romance" that posited as the origin for the Mexican nation one that was neither Spanish nor indigenous but that put it into the line of inheritance of some great and now-fallen civilization.

Finally, the fourth plate presents an inside view and the cross section of a three-legged clay container (see fig. 8). The artist declared himself baffled by the animal form in the center and

8. Jean-Frédéric Waldeck, three-legged clay vessel. *Colección de antigüedades*, no. 1, 1827. Beinecke Rare Book and Manuscript Library, Yale University.

by the "hieroglyphic frieze" around its rim and admitted that he could not determine if the vessel had been used for religious or domestic purposes. Unable to explain the meanings and uses of the bowl, Waldeck classed it with the large collection of "Etruscan-style" vases at the museum, a stylistic homology that confirmed his and others' speculations about the Old World origins of ancient Mexican civilization. To make up for the little certainty he had regarding ancient Mexican objects (for as with his previous stint as a mining engineer, Waldeck was adept at improvising knowledge he did not possess by training or experience), Waldeck tried to establish comparisons with other art forms, drawing on what he knew of antiquities of the Old World. Using this method, he was able to produce a typology of the museum's collection of ancient vases and even went so far as to propose a theory of the evolution of this art form. Some of the vases, wrote Waldeck, pertained to an era "when art was in its infancy," as observed in the arts of all ancient nations. During the second phase, to which the vase he drew belongs, Waldeck recognized the influence of the "Etruscan or Egyptian genius." Finally, for the third stage, Waldeck referred to two alabaster vases excavated on the Isla de Sacrificios, which reflected a "mutation in style," evidently affected by the influence of the Japanese arts.

In this manner, the first issue of the *Colección* introduced the public to a sample of the antiquities held by the National Museum. While in the actual space of the museum, the objects put in close and incongruous proximity to each other failed to convey their significance to visitors like "Rosa Isidica," the *Colección* gave the artist and the editors an opportunity to rethink the collection, to separate, for special notice, a few choice things, to display and explain them, and to enlist them into a system of knowledge that made them available for theory and explanation among collectors, scholars, and a wider public. Yet the first issue of the *Colección* hardly caused a stir among its intended audience. I have come across only one review of the *Colección*, which appeared in the newspaper *El repertorio mexicano*: "We have before us the first number of the Mexican Antiquities [. . .] and cannot but applaud the patriotic undertaking of its editors," wrote the anonymous reviewer.[47] Taking cues from Waldeck's descriptions, the reviewer drew attention to the similarities between the Mexican monuments reproduced in the *Colección* and those of the Egyptians and the Carthaginians, concluding that these felicitous similarities gave "luminous amplitude to the history of the country, revealing progress in the arts of the nation, which, for many years, had been believed to be in a state of ignorance and barbarity." The reviewer obviously had insider knowledge of the printing of this first issue of the *Colección*, having referred to some of the setbacks experienced by the editors, such as the scarcity of suitable paper, which forced them to undertake various trial runs in order not to waste the paper they had. The reviewer found cause for optimism for the second installment, which would be printed on a whiter, thicker, and stronger paper. In turn, a more attractive publication would attract more subscribers and help recuperate the costs of production.

Yet by mid-October, Waldeck noted that Icaza had decided not to continue the *Colección* unless it could pay for itself. In the end, Icaza commissioned the second issue, and on November 6 Waldeck turned in the plates with their glosses. The third issue was scheduled for December, but growing tensions between Waldeck and Robert, along with the impingement of political and social turmoil from the outside, pushed back the publication date to February of the following year.

The second and the third issues followed the structure of the first, beginning with Waldeck's reconstructions of "historical" episodes at the Mexican court: the election of a general for Huitzíhuitl's army and the arrival of ambassadors at the court of neighboring King Tezozomoc, to ask for the king's daughter as wife for Huitzíhuitl, in 1403. The scenes bolster Waldeck's hypothesis that the ancient people of America and those of the Old World shared a common origin, as supported by similar religious and political practices, which resulted, Waldeck thought, from (albeit infrequent) commerce between continents. The other illustrations were also aligned with his theory. It is hard to escape the feeling that Waldeck specifically chose scenes that he believed shared similarities with

9. Jean-Frédéric Waldeck, antiquities. Waldeck points out that the temple model identified by number 3 shows a markedly Japanese style; he thinks the small carving, number 5, resembles carvings on the Temple of Dendera. *Colección de antigüedades*, no. 2, 1827. Beinecke Rare Book and Manuscript Library, Yale University.

10. Jean-Frédéric Waldeck, clay seals. *Colección de antigüedades*, no. 3, 1827. Beinecke Rare Book and Manuscript Library, Yale University.

Old World antiquities. A number of objects, originally from the neighborhood Santiago Tlatelolco, that Waldeck depicted in the second issue struck him as stylistically similar to images of the household deities the Romans called Penates. In one object, he saw a distinctly Japanese touch, while he thought another showed a notable and curious resemblance to sculptures from the Dendera Temple in Egypt (see fig. 9). For the last plate in the second issue of the *Colección*, Waldeck depicted, among other objects, two clay seals that proved that the ancient Mexicans, like the ancient cultures of the Old World, knew the arts of printing—that is, they had found a way to "multiply and perpetuate a drawing, a portrait, and consequently, any sign representative of interesting events or objects" (see fig. 10).

The *Colección* became an early casualty of the political strife in Mexico when it was suspended after the third issue, having published a total of twelve plates and six pages of text. Icaza had originally envisioned the creation of a paper collection as a way of circumventing the obstacles he faced in building up and displaying the physical collection. But in the end, the *Colección* could not escape the institutional political and financial problems already besetting the museum. A quarter of a century would pass before the museum sponsored another publication, the *Catálogo de la colección mineralógica* (1852) by Joaquín Velázquez de León; it would be half a century before it began publishing the monthly scholarly journal *Anales del Museo Nacional* in 1877. The museum's collections—especially its antiquities—continued to appear in print in other venues, and many of its objects were the topic of scholarly discussion and interpretation. But private initiatives, not the museum, were what enabled the publications.

Artists, Brokers, Smugglers

After the *Colección* ended, Waldeck continued to draw objects in the museum's collection and began preparing an exploration trip to the ruins of Palenque. Icaza often allowed Waldeck to take home certain objects: on February 22, 1828, he borrowed a *teponaztli* (a type of drum) to complete a sheet on musical instruments; on February 26 he began work on the relief of a "Tartar-looking head"; on March 4, on a relief of Quetzalcóatl found in Tula; on March 31 the museum sent someone to his house to retrieve an obsidian mask. This kind of coming and going of objects in and out of the museum might strike us as odd; in fact, Icaza's protocol made provisions for the removal of objects from the museum, likely to continue a custom of borrowing that relied on trust between gentlemen collectors. At the same time, it is very likely that Icaza would have wanted to keep a man of talent, like Waldeck, close by, for future collaboration. The director had not given up entirely on the idea of making the museum's collection visible through illustrations and studies of its objects. If Waldeck were to publish his drawings, then, without the museum spending a peso, he would be fulfilling the desire for publicity that was part of Icaza's plan.

In fact, Waldeck was not the only artist to work in the museum. Toward the end of 1829 Carl Nebel (1805–55), a young architect originally from Hamburg, joined Waldeck in a project that aimed to complete an album of illustrations of considerable size, modeled on the albums of Egyptian and Greek antiquities that were, at that time, enjoying great popularity in Europe.[48] The publication would include objects not only from the museum but also from archaeological sites around Mexico City and from some of the more notable private collections at the time, such as those of the Swiss merchant Lukas Vischer (1780–1840), of the German merchant Carl Uhde (1792–1856), and of Mexico's own Conde de Peñasco, the owner of a greatly admired collection of antiquities, coins, and natural history objects, especially minerals. Most of Waldeck's and Nebel's work in the museum was fated to remain unpublished, in part due to a serious falling-out between the two; still, in 1836 Nebel published his *Voyage pittoresque et archéologique dans la partie la plus intéressante du Mexique*, giving European readers the opportunity to enjoy its fifty lithographs of museum objects, city views, rural scenery, ancient ruins, and Mexican costumes.

Sometime after Waldeck and Nebel began working in the museum, on a recommendation by U.S. representative Joel R. Poinsett, Icaza granted Bohemian artist Maximilien Franck (179?–

1838) similar privileges. Since Poinsett also introduced Franck to collectors in the English and U.S. communities in Mexico City, he was able to draw a large number of antiquities from both the museum and private collections between 1829 and 1830. In all, his visit resulted in eighty-one plates, with illustrations of over six hundred distinct objects. The majority of Franck's drawings are of objects from the National Museum, making his album our most complete visual archive of the antiquity collection in the museum as it was in 1830.[49] In March of 1830 Franck left Mexico for Paris, via Philadelphia and New York, taking with him the album as well as a collection of more than five hundred objects. After being profusely admired at the American Philosophical Society, his album reached Paris. While Franck's collection of antiquities was bought for 8,000 francs by the Louvre, where it formed the nucleus of the ancient American collection, his drawings, though enthusiastically praised by the members of the American Philosophical Society, did not turn out to be a sure investment. Franck had hoped to sell the drawings to the Louvre, but with a price set at 30,000 francs, the album did not attract buyers until years later.[50] It is now at the British Museum; the drawings, carefully secured in a large blue box, still await publication.[51]

Franck's album, however, is of rare artistic merit. On large sheets, 55 x 43 cm, Franck drew a great diversity of objects, from clay vessels and musical instruments to masks and statues. On some plates, a few objects stand out, dramatically; on others, he gathered together up to thirty figurines, heads, and fragments (see figs. 11 and 12). Some objects are represented in full size; others, reduced. In some cases, he drew more than one perspective of the same object, though most of the time, just one. He used graphite to draw attention to details and to model, with great subtlety, transitions of light and shadow, in such a way that objects achieve volume and weight. Next to each object, Franck noted down—in his small and uniform handwriting—its size, material, and provenance (meaning, mostly, the collection name). For some objects, Franck wrote down, as well, his interpretations of their meaning and style, with his choice skewed to those that appeared to testify

11. Maximilien Franck, drawings of Mexican antiquities. Graphite on paper.
Plate 2. © Trustees of the British Museum. All rights reserved.

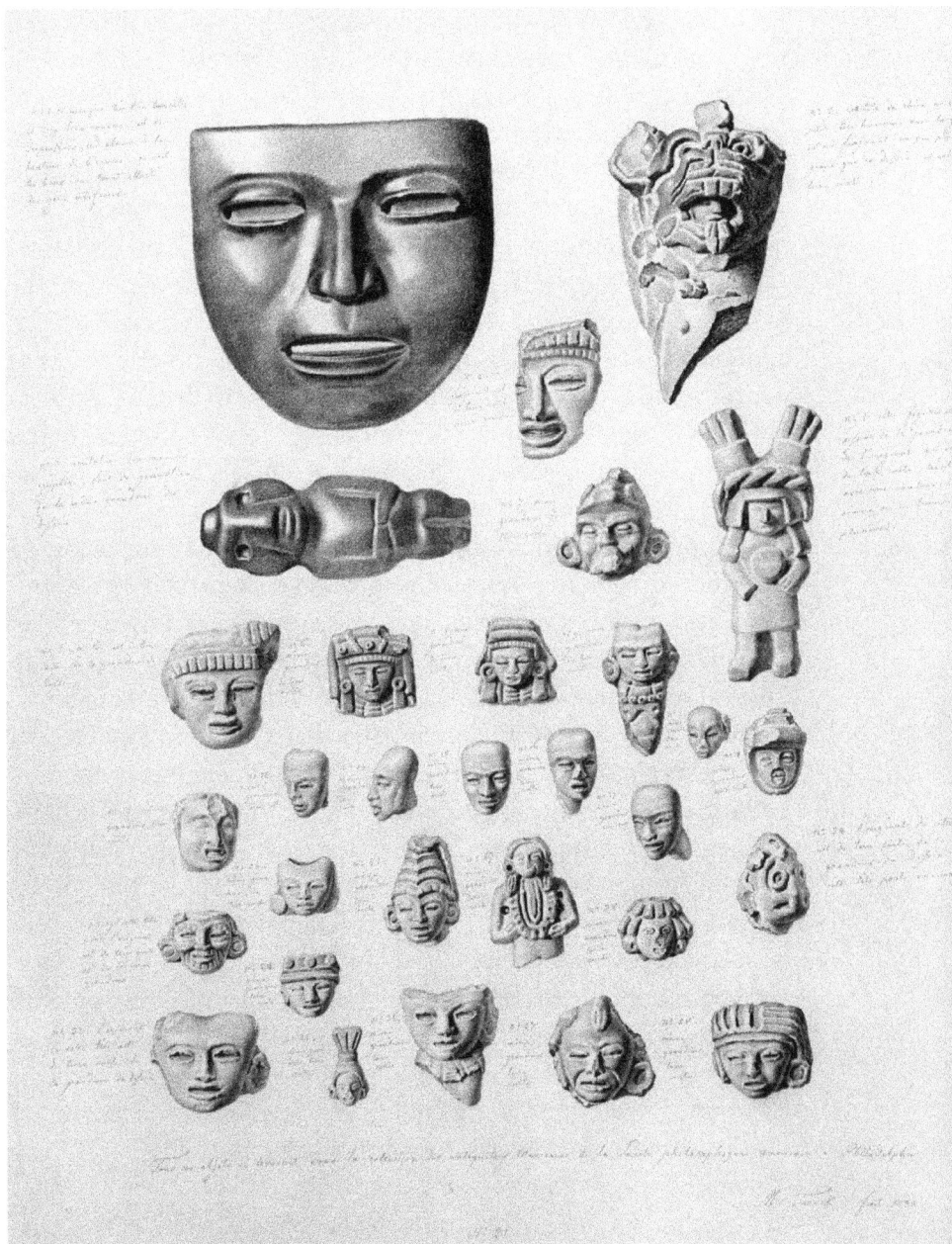

12. Maximilien Franck, drawings of Mexican antiquities. Graphite on paper.
Plate 20. © Trustees of the British Museum. All rights reserved.

to links between Mexican civilization and those of the Old World. His comparisons are mostly to Egyptian, Chinese, and Etruscan antiquities. All in all, the effect of the eighty-one plates is one of extraordinary beauty and plasticity.

Taken together, Waldeck's, Nebel's, and Franck's drawings present a rich register of the antiquities circulating among various spaces of collecting in the early 1830s. Waldeck's diaries from this period complement the visual record with abundant information on the kinds of dealings and exchanges that went on around Mexican antiquities.[52] His diaries offer a rare glimpse into the activities of an antiquities aficionado, collector, and dealer in the late 1820s in Mexico City and illuminate the worlds he moved between—those of the museum, of Mexican government officials, of artists, of brokers, and of unnamed peddlers, to mention just a few.

His practices, undoubtedly colorful, were no more so than those of other foreigners turned collectors and dealers who made Mexico City a major contact zone for an increasingly buoyant market in collectables. Foreigners rarely went to Mexico in the 1820s with the express intention to collect or traffic with antiquities or natural history. They went as diplomats, speculators, and investors, bent on making a profit, whether by establishing colonies or by mining, manufacturing, agriculture, banking, or commercial scheming of one kind or another. Once in Mexico, they began collecting objects, in part because they moved in social and political circles where collections were a form of socializing and in part because certain objects, like Mexican antiquities, were becoming interesting both to Mexicans and to foreigners. It was easy to start a collection. Many foreigners had money and ties with Mexican elites who were collectors themselves. Poinsett, for example, occupied a prominent place in Mexican politics and acted as patron and donor to the museum, recommending artists like Franck to draw the collection and engaging in what seems like unfavorable exchanges for the museum. Thus, in return for a "good" copy of the U.S. Declaration of Independence and six portraits of U.S. presidents (two of them framed), Poinsett obtained from Icaza "three basalt sculptures, two vessels, a mask and a clay salver from Palenque."[53]

Although amassing objects was a licit activity both for Mexicans and for foreigners, by late 1827 exporting antiquities out of the country no longer was. On November 15 Congress ratified a law that prohibited the expatriation of monuments and antiquities, of cochineal, and of gold and silver, in the form of powder or ingots. (The law exempted the removal of small amounts of gold and silver powder and ore for scientific purposes.)[54] This law was the Mexican government's response to the unregulated traffic in precious metals and antiquities. But rather than serving as a deterrent to the exportation of antiquities (or of gold and silver, for that matter), it seemed to have the opposite effect; it worked as an incentive for foreigners to gather up as many collectibles as possible and to devise ingenious ways of smuggling things out before the government could rigorously enforce the law. Collectors and sellers appealed to the 1827 law in order to drive up the value of Mexican antiquities abroad. Collector William Bullock, for example, offered Mexican artifacts to the British Museum, saying, "It may be fairly inferred that these are the only specimens that will find their way to Europe."[55] Whether Bullock truly believed this or whether he hoped to sell as many of his objects as possible is hard to know. But his prediction, if it was made in good faith, could not have been less on target, as the following decades saw the intensification of trafficking with Mexican antiquities.

Social and professional standing—which aided foreigners in forming collections—also proved to be an advantage when it came to exporting collections out of the country. Commercial and consular involvements familiarized collectors with the workings and the failings of the evolving Mexican political and justice systems, with the border and port controls at points of exit from Mexico and with the contraband routes that successfully evaded the Mexican customs officials.[56] Bribery of customs officials may have accounted for some illicit export, as did smuggling skills, the most infamous example of which is probably provided by the Frenchman J. M. A. Aubin (1802–91), the most determined buyer of the Boturini collection. When Aubin left Mexico in 1839 with a fabulous collection of preconquest and early colonial manuscripts, which would come to form part of the Bibliothèque Nationale in Paris, he disguised ancient manuscripts by tearing their pages apart and mixing them with his own notes, thus evading customs officials.[57] Waldeck himself made recourse to an age-old method for smuggling out his collection of antiquities before he left Mexico City in April of 1832 to conduct explorations in Palenque: a double-bottomed suitcase covered in horse leather. In the hidden compartment, he placed his drawings together with antiquities of various sorts. He made a list of these objects in his journal entry on January 15; among the most valuable items on the list were ten manuscripts on agave paper, including "a 52-year calendar," a "theological-astronomical" manuscript, genealogies of several Indian villages, and documents related to the conquest of Azcapotzalco. Without giving further details, Waldeck also listed six boxes full of "terracottas" and a tobacco box with a golden idol "of great value because of its rarity." He calculated the value of the objects he sent to London at 5,295 pounds, 14 shillings.

Both collectors and traffickers of antiquities were bound together with the museum during the institution's first decades. Private and official collectors participated in the same culture articulated around forms of socialization among gentlemen amateurs. The National Museum depended on its alliance with collectors, as collectors were the ones who made preconquest Mexican history fashionable and were most interested in what the museum had to offer. So it comes as no surprise that it was often people tied to the museum, like Waldeck, Franck, or Poinsett, who managed to amass some of the more interesting collections. Still, there are essential differences between collecting by the museum and collecting by private individuals. Dependent as it was on the support of an (often) indifferent state, subject to bureaucratic scrutiny and government authorizations, the museum was far less nimble and adept than private agents at acquiring objects in a fluid and fast-moving market.

When private collectors began to export their collections out of Mexico, it is understandable why Icaza began looking at foreign collectors with suspicion, even as he sought alliances with them, and why he was so insistent on making the museum a primary player in the market for collectibles and in the imaginary of the Mexican people. By 1831 Icaza had become convinced that foreign would-be collaborators could not be trusted, because they put their private interest above the needs of the museum. He went so far as to petition Alamán, who was again holding the office of minister of internal and external relations, to desist from engaging in deals with them on behalf of the museum, writing, "Since the foundation of the Museum, many foreigners have asked for and obtained permits to explore ruins. But they have ended up taking more liberties than those stipulated in their contracts, and the results are little favorable for the Museum and for the nation."[58] Icaza's list of culprits included Franck, who, after being allowed to draw as many objects in the collection as he wanted to, "with great annoyance to the Museum staff," offered nothing to the museum in return. Most vexingly, he sold a plate he had offered as a gift to the museum and then departed for France, taking his album with him. Waldeck had disappointed Icaza more than any other foreigner, for Icaza's collaboration with Waldeck had been deeper, making Waldeck's betrayal that much more resented. To Alamán, Icaza accused the artist of never mentioning the provenance of the objects he drew and of refusing to allow the museum to make copies of his drawings. None of the publicity Icaza was looking for materialized.

Abandoned by authorities and at the mercy of foreigners, the National Museum might have looked to Icaza like it was in such precarious shape that it might dissolve, a not uncommon fate for Latin American museums in the postindependence decades of the nineteenth century. Icaza must, then, have felt some relief when Alamán pushed through legislation that finally ratified the existence of the museum as a legal entity. On November 21, 1831, Congress decreed the formation of a scientific establishment composed of three branches—antiquities, industrial productions, and natural history—and of the Botanical Garden.[59] The director of the museum would be the caretaker of antiquities and industrial productions, while a natural history professor would oversee the Botanical Garden and natural history section in the National Museum. Furthermore, the decree put the establishment in charge of a board of directors, seven men (including the conservator and the natural history professor) of "high reputation and erudition," to be named by the federal government.[60] A Sociedad del Museo Mexicano, made up of men of equally high credentials, would have the task of promoting the progress of the museum inside and outside the capital. The decree, based on Icaza's protocol, was an important step forward for the institution. One of Icaza's most important points, however, was neglected; Congress failed to provide the museum with its own operating budget. In consequence, it would remain subject to the caprice of politicians and to the turbulence of Mexican history for decades, which seriously hampered its efforts to collect specimens and lay exclusive claims to the "titles" of Mexico's past.

Icaza died on February 17, 1834. After provisional conservatorships by Ignacio Cubas and by Joaquín Oteiza, Isidro Rafael Gondra—who had gained some degree of reputation for his participation in the edition of the *Colección de antigüedades*—was named conservator of the museum in February of 1835.[61] He took over a ten-year-old institution that was still struggling to come to grips with a fundamental challenge: how to measure its worth as a national museum to a country that was still in the process of asking what it meant to be a nation.

3 COLLECTING THE RUINS OF PALENQUE

The Race to the Ruins and the Palenque Prize

In 1847 Arthur Morelet (1809–92), a French naturalist traveling through Central America and southern Mexico, sojourned for fifteen days in Palenque, in the state of Chiapas. Morelet had few ambitions as an antiquarian, and he spent most of his time there collecting birds and snakes for the Muséum d'histoire naturelle in Paris, as well as discovering new species that would bear his name. Still, the ruins of Palenque left an indelible impression on him; he felt an "inexpressible agitation of the spirit" in the midst of all that "nameless debris." "There was no tradition attached to that monument and none explained its origin," and Morelet feared that the "dumb stones" would disappear without a trace, back into the jungle, before they would yield up their secrets. More than the encroachment of vegetation was erasing the ruins, though. Ironically, as travelers like Morelet became interested in Palenque, their interest hastened the demise of the ruins. Morelet mused, "Where are those stucco reliefs that excited Dupaix's imagination? [. . .] Some have disappeared forever, others have been mutilated or removed from the walls where they were embedded; if a few vestiges still survive, it is thanks to the wreckage of time, that has saved them from that perpetrated by travelers. It is true that, to make up for it, they have inscribed their names in the place of the old souvenirs."[1] Time, nature, and man were conspiring to deepen the mysteries of the ruins at Palenque. Although Morelet had not arrived there with the intention of unlocking those mysteries, the mixture of fascination and nostalgia they exerted on him helps explain the urgency with which others tried to do so before these remains crumbled into nothingness.

Attempts to unveil the enigmas of Palenque had been going on since the late eighteenth century, although it was in the late 1820s when, spurred by a competition organized by the Société de géographie in Paris, the race to Palenque began in earnest. The National Museum of Mexico struggled to become a protagonist or at least a partner in the explorations. Instead, as this chapter will show, the ruins of Palenque, eight hundred kilometers from the capital, in the remote state of Chiapas, the last to join the Mexican republic, would become a showcase for the museum's incapacity to organize and control antiquarian research and for the extent to which such research was traversed by all kinds of broader interests and agendas.

The first explorations of Palenque had begun in the eighteenth century as part of an ambitious program by the Spanish Crown to study ancient vestiges throughout the empire.[2] Palenque came to the notice of Spanish officials in 1773, when Fray Ramón de Ordoñez y Aguiar (?–1825), canon at the cathedral of Ciudad Real de Chiapas, sent a report on Palenque to the president of the Real Audiencia de Guatemala, who eventually ordered a preliminary survey of the ruins by the architect Antonio Bernsaconi (?–1785) a decade later, in 1784. Ordoñez y Aguiar had, in the meantime, been busy writing his "Historia de la creación del cielo y de la tierra," in which he postulated that the ancient cities had been constructed by a race of builders led by a certain "Votan." In 1787 Captain Antonio del Río (1745–89) used Bernasconi's survey as the basis for a more in-depth exploration of Palenque, which bore fruit in a report containing detailed descriptions and drawings of reliefs and plans. This report, too, was not published until 1822, when a translation with engravings by Jean-Frédéric Waldeck appeared in London under the title *Description of the Ruins of an Ancient City, Discovered near Palenque*. A few years before the start of the War of Independence, Guillermo Dupaix and his draftsman Luciano Castañeda visited Palenque in 1808, in the context of the Royal Antiquarian Expeditions. Dupaix and Castañeda returned to Mexico City to prepare reports of their explorations. But once the war started, antiquarian study was hardly a priority for the viceregal government, and Dupaix died leaving his work unfinished. As a result, while Palenque was becoming an object of fascination among antiquarian circles, facts about the ruins reached the savant world at a trickle. When the National Museum was founded in Mexico City, it appeared that it would become a logical depository of the objects and information gathered at the ruins.

Antiquities from Palenque began reaching the museum in the mid-1820s. This was, firstly, the result of a political event; Chiapas, which had been part of the Audiencia of Guatemala during colonial times, opted for incorporation into the Mexican Empire and later into the Mexican Republic in 1822, instead of the newly formed Central American Republic, as its location and culture might have suggested. Mexican generals Javier Bustamante and Juan Pablo Anaya led a federal mission to Chiapas, between 1824 and 1827, to ensure its process of "Mexicanization."[3] In the course of his mission, Anaya visited Palenque and extracted a small collection of antiquities and objects of natural history, which, he trusted, "would present sufficient material for the observations and useful research of national professors." Of special interest are the 570 pages, including eighteen drawings, of Ordoñez y Aguiar's *Historia de la creación del cielo y de la tierra*, a relief inscribed with hieroglyphic writings, a mask, a "stone which seems to have formed a ring," two "martinets," and "five flutes of enormous size, made of wood," which—contradicting Ordoñez y Aguiar's hypothesis of the origin of Palenque—Anaya believed had been sent by Americans to "Naerit, the king of Babylon, thus called by the Americans, who was from these lands [which were known as] Culhuacan."[4] In other words, the Mexican general believed, as did a number of Central American antiquarians, that the Old World had been peopled by emigrants from America. Among the objects of natural history that went to the Botanical Garden in Mexico City, Anaya sent live animals: five bitterns and a royal eagle. He wanted Mexicans to be able to see this symbol of Mexico that appeared in its flag.[5]

Some months later, conservator Icaza registered the donation by Castañeda of objects he and Dupaix collected during their expeditions twenty years earlier. Besides "bundles" of descriptions and drawings of Palenque, Monte Albán, Mitla, Zaachila, Tehuantepec, Tepeji el Viejo, Tonila, Papantla, Tlacolula, Texcoco, and San Juan Teotihuacan, Castañeda turned in objects from Palenque: stone heads; eight human figures of different sizes and in different postures; masks; stone "idols"; sculptures of animals; a polished, green, tear-shaped stone; a small knife of the same green stone; lance heads and arrow heads; many clay figures representing dogs, foxes, and human heads; forty fragments of stucco from ancient buildings; and a wooden *teponaztli*.[6]

The donation by Castañeda would be the last Palenque relics to arrive at the museum for a long time. This was not because of disinterest in Palenque, but quite the opposite. Starting in the late 1820s, the ruins in the distant state of Chiapas—so elusive, so hard to reach, so different from those of central Mexico—became the object of fascination in Europe and the United States, sparked by the publication of del Río's *Description*. Del Rio's text left enough tantalizing gaps to fascinate scholars who were still absorbing the influx of Egyptian antiquities on the heels of Napoleon's expedition. Here were more archaeological mysteries: Who built Palenque? Where did its ancient inhabitants come from, and how did they "vanish"? What esoteric knowledge did their hieroglyphs hide? What was the nature of the link, if any, between the ancient civilizations of the Old and the New Worlds? What relationship did contemporary Indians have to those noble and civilized ancestors?

Questions such as these were taken up by the Société de géographie in Paris, founded in 1821 with the express mandate of collecting "geographical" knowledge from around the ancient and contemporary world—and here, "geography" was given an ample and eclectic scope, extended to but not limited by politics, economy, commerce, and the search for mineral and agricultural riches. In March of 1826 the Société set up a 2,400-franc prize, the so-called Prix Palenque, for the most thorough study of the ruins at Palenque, Copan (in modern Honduras), and Utatlan (in modern Guatemala), to be turned in by December 31, 1829. The prize called for the production of plans and descriptions of the sites; observations on the customs of contemporary and ancient Indians; vocabularies of ancient languages; and information about the local character "Votan," who had assumed a status, in the eyes of the Société, comparable to that of Buddha.[7] It was an ambitious program that showed a fine, metropolitan ignorance of real conditions for exploration in Chiapas and Central America. The Société began receiving reports on Palenque in 1828; during the following decade, the *Bulletin de la Société de Géographie* became the primary space in which information and theories about the ruins of Chiapas, Yucatán, and Central America were aired and debated. The region became an arena of fierce antiquarian competition in the 1830s.

The museum, theoretically, should have been the central Mexican partner in the exploration of Palenque, since, at a minimum, most would-be competitors needed the support and permission of the Mexican government to travel to the ruins and carry out excavations. As well, the museum should have aggregated information that had already been turned up in Mexico, by New Spain's antiquaries and collectors, for instance. Between the late 1820s and the mid-1830s, records show a considerable number of foreign travelers requesting permissions for archaeological exploration; when these requests were granted—which in most cases they were—it was with the express clause that the antiquarian reports be filed with the museum and that a portion of the objects excavated be deposited there. The obvious advantage for the perennially underfunded museum was that it would gain from the de facto outsourcing of exploration and the collecting of antiquities by foreigners. These were at least the expectations by the likes of Icaza and Gondra; they would prove difficult to enforce.

A Notoriously Advantageous Deal

On November 5, 1828, Icaza asked the Ministry of Internal and External Relations to authorize a deal he had negotiated with the French abbot Henri Baradère (1792–1839?). Baradère would give the museum seventy "African" birds and eighteen Mexican birds, "dissected and mounted," and a collection of butterflies and insects in their glass frames, in exchange for 145 drawings of preconquest ruins produced by the Royal Antiquarian Expeditions. Besides manuscripts, Baradère was asking for letters of safe conduct to several archaeological sites, Palenque among them, and for permissions to excavate and collect objects; in return, he pledged to donate to the museum half the objects he found and to give the museum "duplicates" of the other half.[8] The ministry agreed to the deal. In retrospect, it is hard not to think that Icaza was either a dupe or had some hidden, discreditable reason for making this deal. How could he have imagined that the drawings and antiquities were equal in value to stuffed birds? And yet Icaza believed that he had done well and went as far as to boast that the deal had been "notoriously advantageous."[9] Why? What were Icaza's calculations and expectations as he signed the contract? And how, given the values at play here, can we assess how the deal played out?[10]

Baradère was, like other contemporary travelers to Mexico, a jack of many trades. Having completed his theological studies, he went as a cleric on an evangelizing mission in Senegal (1820–22) and returned to France to act as canon of Tarbes. The administration of the spiritual life in Tarbes apparently failed to satisfy his desire for adventure, however. In 1828 he voyaged to Mexico with a plan, devised by the French and the Mexican governments jointly, to establish a French colony in Coatzacoalcos, in the Isthmus of Tehuantepec, deemed at the time to hold great strategic and economic promise.[11] Baradère was to act as prospector and informer on the scheme, which quickly proved to be a fiasco, as the French colonizers wilted under the heat, illness, and insolvency in mosquito-infested and humid Coatzacoalcos. Their plight was notorious enough that Balzac referenced it at the beginning of his novel *Peau de chagrin*, and it led to a stream of firsthand testimonies that denounced conditions in the colony and repudiated Baradère's optimistic outlook on the place.[12] As the French fled Coatzacoalcos, Baradère turned to other tasks, like stuffing birds and catching butterflies, and finally made his way to the capital. The lure of the Palenque Prize brought him in contact with Icaza, who gave him access to the Dupaix and Castañeda manuscripts and negotiated his permission to explore the ruins of Palenque.

But if Baradère could well imagine the advantages he would reap from the deal with Icaza, we have to make an effort to imagine what advantages Icaza thought he would reap. First, Icaza was excited about the prospect of obtaining the collection of stuffed birds for the museum. By the early nineteenth century, taxidermy had become popular among the nascent middle class in Europe, and museums on both sides of the Atlantic displayed such collections as part of their sense of their function.[13] It was also a moment when the science of preservation was quickly changing—improvement in taxidermy techniques, popularized by a spate of manuals, made the manipulation and conservation of animals and plants increasingly feasible to lay people. In his "Manuel de taxidermie à l'usage des marins" (1819), René-Primevère Lesson, a marine botanist in Rochefort, instructed mariners and officials in the French colonies on how to make good use of their leisure hours by preparing valuable or unknown specimens, for which collectors were willing to pay high prices. It is a knowledge that will "open a career," quipped Lesson.[14] When Henri Baradère lived in Senegal, he may well have received his instruction in taxidermy from this book, which would explain his having spent his spare time collecting African, and later Mexican, birds, some of which were later traded to the museum in Mexico.

By contrast, as an unfriendly review had suggested in 1827, the National Museum in Mexico had little to show for a country so rich in birds and butterflies.[15] During viceregal times, especially in the latter part of the eighteenth century, the Spanish Crown had placed great value on the scientific exploration of its colonial domains and on the collection and preservation of natural history specimens.[16] The National Museum of Mexico was a product of some of the collections amassed during those late colonial times and was put under the management of people educated and trained under the monarchical policies that saw the production of natural objects as having both scientific and economic interest. Such was the case with naturalist Pablo de la Llave, who finished his training at the Madrid Royal Cabinet of Natural History before taking over the natural history branch at the National Museum in Mexico, as well as with his successor, the botanist Miguel Bustamante. But though the museum could count these highly capable men among its personnel, it lacked the employees that would perform the more mundane tasks of going out into the field to collect and conserve natural history specimens.

Moreover, as was also the case with antiquities, the museum lacked a policy for the collection and display of natural history. There were attempts to compensate for these shortages by training and engaging amateur naturalists; with this purpose in mind, Bustamante published in 1839 a small taxidermy manual, *Memoria instructiva para colectar y preparar para su transporte los objetos de historia natural*. It is difficult to gauge the influence of this book— just as it is hard to assess the tacit influence of popular magazines, which spread the fad for natural history—on the expansion of the museum's natural history collection. In any case, with the exceptions of objects acquired though exchanges with foreign museums and cabinets, most of the specimens of natural history, especially taxidermies, that entered the museum until the 1860s were donations by private individuals. Oftentimes, they did not match the higher standards of conservation; in fact, there were often complaints to the contrary.[17] In this context, Baradère's offer of a collection of exotic African birds must have appeared enticing to Icaza.

Baradère's offer to collect antiquities on behalf of the museum, even considering that the institution would have to part with half of them, was just as attractive; Icaza, as we have seen, was not in any position to mount an expedition on his own. Baradère's offer seemed to have little cost. The canon did not ask for any public funding for his travels and excavations, so the museum would not have to give money on spec. True, the museum agreed to pay for the transportation of antiquities, but Icaza calculated that the expenses would be moderate, because Baradère would send back to Mexico City only objects lighter than two arrobas (approximately fifty pounds). In special cases, the museum would be called on to authorize the shipment of heavier objects if the value of the piece compensated for its transportation costs.[18] Perhaps most importantly, the symbolic elements were favorable. The deal gave the museum a prima facie guarantee that it exercised control over the collecting of antiquities. In theory, the museum would have the last word as to what would be brought back from the field. Ultimately, it would decide what to keep and what to relinquish to the French traveler to take back to Europe.

One of the more important items involved in the transaction between Icaza and Baradère was the publication of the Dupaix and Castañeda manuscripts in France. Here, again, Icaza thought he was operating in the museum's interest; he considered that the publication of these materials in Europe would yield high returns by "ensuring the visibility of the Mexican nation among a constellation of enlightened nations."[19] By contrast, not to act on Baradère's proposal would have resulted in the loss of these "most precious monuments" and in the "discredit of the [Mexican] Republic among the other cultivated nations."[20] What one reads behind Icaza's decision is the eagerness to create discussions around objects and documents housed by the museum and thereby fashion the institution into a protagonist in an emerging context for the study, exchange, and interpretation of antiquities. Icaza, then, was bargaining for visibility and symbolic capital, which he needed in order to make the museum count in the collecting cultures of the nineteenth century.

The story, however, turned out quite differently. Baradère went only as far as Mitla, Oaxaca, and returned to France before making it to Palenque. By June 1829 Baradère was back in Paris, writing to the Société de géographie to claim, incongruously, the Palenque Prize. He defended his decision to leave Palenque out of his explorations by saying that "only a government or maybe a company would be able, after much spending and fatigue, to disentangle, amidst the chaos of Palenque, [its] marvels and maybe riches."[21] To make up for his "omission," Baradère was returning to France with the manuscripts of the Royal Antiquarian Expeditions, which, he claimed, the Mexican government was jealously hiding from the English. (In reality, the English already had access to these documents, which had been imported to Europe by Latour Allard.) To take them out of the country, Baradère described how he had negotiated a special treatise with the government. These manuscripts, together with a number of antiquities, were what the traveler presented before the Société.

Baradère's collection of documents and objects had a positive reception among the French antiquarian circles. A few weeks after Baradère had sent in his claim, David Baillie Warden (1778–1845), the former U.S. consul in France, himself a collector of American antiquities, read a report on Baradère's collection before the Royal Society of Antiquarians of France.[22] Warden called attention to the fact that the objects brought back by Baradère formed the largest collection of Mexican antiquities in Europe, after that of Latour Allard, but Latour Allard's collection was by then in England, after the Louvre had refused to purchase it. Furthermore, continued Warden, while Latour Allard had built his collection by purchasing objects one by one from vendors, Baradère was the only European who had been granted the right to carry out excavations by the Mexican government—a claim that, although true, avoided the tricky topic of whether any of the objects Baradère took back to France had been obtained through personal excavations.

Warden described Baradère's collection carefully, drawing attention to objects the latter had collected "on site": a marble relief of a skull, a stone sculpture of a rabbit, bells made of hide, and fifty clay "idols" of more or less "bizarre" shapes. Mixed among the genuine antiquities were exotic bric-a-brac, such as a coconut carved in the shape of a sepulcher and decorated like the palace at Mitla (most likely made and sold at the site by local artisans). There were also several manuscripts: the scene of a human sacrifice painted by the Aztecs on agave paper; a map of Texcoco and one of Mexico City, both from the Boturini collection; a tax table, in hieroglyphics, dating to the sixteenth century, also from the Boturini collection; the copy of a genealogy of Aztec kings; and a putative Christian doctrine manual, which Cortés's spies had supposedly given Moctezuma.

For Warden, the most valuable element of Baradère's collection, however, was the portfolio of 145 illustrations produced by Dupaix's expeditions, representing temples, houses, fortifications, pyramids, aqueducts, divinities, coins, and hieroglyphs. The drawings, explained Warden, had been found lying covered up in dust in some corner of the natural history cabinet in Mexico City, when Baradère exhumed and rescued them for the sake of the arts.[23] With slight variations, Warden's story employed a common trope in European archaeological discourses: the schematic fantasy of the intrepid and clairvoyant European scholar who uncovered archaeological treasures that Americans (south of the U.S. border) were too benighted to recognize and too lazy to maintain. It is not hard to imagine, therefore, that the arrival of Baradère's collection in Europe was seen, not as part of a deliberate policy by the museum, as Icaza would have hoped, but as the work of an adventurous foreigner rescuing a forgotten history. In turn, this would have contributed to the growing perception in Europe that Mexican cultural policy was negligent and run by the ignorant, thus creating an image of the museum in Mexico City as a weak cultural agent that could not be treated as an equal with European agents and entities.

Despite Warden's positive appraisal of Baradère's antiquarian achievements in Mexico, the Société did not award him the prize. By then, the Société had received word that other travelers were preparing reports on Palenque, so it announced that it would postpone its decision on the Palenque Prize until 1832, while awaiting firsthand accounts of the ruins.[24]

"Mexican Champollion" in Palenque

By November 1829, Mexican papers also began publishing notices about the Palenque Prize, urging scholars to undertake expeditions to the ruins. It was in this atmosphere that a number of foreigners living in Mexico sought government permissions to explore the site. In a letter dated October 30, 1830, the French consul Adrian Cochelet informed the Société de géographie that the German architect Carl Nebel was about to leave for Palenque. Cochelet was confident that Nebel, "a talented young man" with a good knowledge of ancient Mexican history, would win the prize.[25] However, Nebel's trip to Palenque never materialized, because the Mexican government refused his proposal and he failed to find private backers.[26] Nebel went instead to explore ruins in the state of Veracruz and would publish his descriptions and beautiful lithographs of them in his *Voyage pittoresque et archéologique dans la partie la plus intéressante du Mexique*.

Nebel's petition to travel to Palenque had caused a serious rift between him and his collaborator Jean-Frédéric Waldeck, who also had his heart set on the ruins since his participation in the English publication of del Río's *Description of the Ruins of an Ancient City*. In the fall of 1831 Waldeck proposed his own exploration project to Alamán, then minister of internal and external relations. On the basis of the questionnaires produced by the Société de géographie for the Palenque Prize, Waldeck defined the purpose of his expedition to be the discovery of the origin of the Mexican people, which was still "an enigma to be solved." Waldeck hoped that the ruins of Palenque would provide answers to this genealogical puzzle.[27]

Despite the incontestable importance of these ruins to understanding Mexico's ancient origins, Waldeck wrote that Palenque had been studied little and poorly. He considered del Río's illustrations of the ruins defective and Castañeda's even more so. Only a "master drawer," such as himself, equipped with instruments adequate for topographical and astronomical studies of the site and for producing maps and plans, could accomplish something better. He also proposed to make molds of the reliefs that covered Palenque. In particular, he wanted to make molds of the relief that represented, Waldeck thought, the Adoration of the Cross by "Tlaloc or Vishnu" on one side and by "Jupiter or Brahma" on the other and, as such, revealed the twofold origin of the Mexican people. Waldeck would exhibit the molds in London and Paris, before donating them to the National Museum in Mexico City.

Where others had insisted that only an expedition of numerous specialists could penetrate the jungle in Palenque, Waldeck claimed that he could venture there by himself. All he requested from the Mexican government was protection for two years. Specifically, he asked Alamán for letters of recommendation to state and local officials, who would have to allow him transit, grant him permissions to carry out explorations, and supply him with laborers that would perform the practical tasks of the excavations. To finance the expedition, Waldeck calculated that he would need 10,000 pesos, which he thought he could raise by selling forty subscriptions, at 250 pesos each, for the book based on his exploration. Two-thirds of the profits of his book would go to the subscribers, and one-third to the author. Alamán took to Waldeck's proposal with enthusiasm. He sent letters to state governors and other high-placed officials and to members of Mexico's cultural elites, detailing Waldeck's project as a viable way to promote "knowledge about the precious antiquities and monuments that illustrate the history of the country" and to satisfy the desire of antiquarians in Europe to compare Mexican antiquities from Palenque with those of Egypt. He invited them to buy subscriptions and asked state governors to protect and aid Waldeck along on his way to the ruins.[28]

It is worth remarking here that it was Minister Alamán, not the museum, who was involved in helping Waldeck, even though the museum would be the final repository of Waldeck's work at Palenque. One reason is Alamán's personal interest in the museum, which often led to his involvement in its administrative affairs. In addition, by the 1830s, Icaza had grown wary of the promises of most foreign travelers, since he had been burned previously by the likes of Waldeck and Baradère. Icaza advised prudence before outsourcing antiquarian expeditions until Mexico had some kind of official protocol that would force the traveler to abide by Mexican laws prohibiting the extraction of antiquities and to fulfill his commitments with the museum.[29] Icaza's misgivings apparently did not matter to Alamán.

In November 1831, government authorities in Tabasco, Chiapas, and Yucatán committed their support to Waldeck's project. By April 1832 Waldeck was on his way to Palenque, after obtaining half the money he had aimed for.[30] By then, the Société, in expectation of the results of more explorations, had postponed once again its decision on the Palenque Prize until 1834; it would continue to postpone the prize until 1839.[31] Before arriving at Palenque, Waldeck stopped in Villahermosa, Tabasco, just as a cholera epidemic was reaching Mexico and in the midst of an insurrection led by Santa Anna that would topple Mexico's government. In Tabasco, Waldeck met a fellow countryman, the French physician Francisco Corroy (?–1836), who had done some exploring at the ruins of Palenque and produced literature about the site; by the time he met Waldeck, Corroy was already sending his observations to various learned societies, including the Société de géographie. He shared with Waldeck both his antiquarian and practical knowledge, such as itineraries and road conditions, and put the traveler in contact with people who would be of help to Waldeck during his time in Palenque, where Waldeck arrived in May of 1832. A few days later, Waldeck sent out letters to various officials, describing the state of affairs at the ruins.

To the governor of Chiapas, Ignacio Gutiérrez (1792–1851), Waldeck complained that the mayor of the village of Palenque, a few kilometers from the ruins, had denied him the right to visit the site unless he accepted two local people as guards to accompany him. When Waldeck tried "to resist this imposition [by] showing the letter from the Supreme Government, the mayor [claimed he] did not know the ministers and asked who Alamán was." More-over, the mayor informed Waldeck that "he should not count on Indian workers for the excavations because they were needed to start work on the new church"; this, the traveler thought, "was a pretext occasioned by bad will." Waldeck was also shocked by the condition of the ruins; they were "in a state of dilapidation, caused by the stupid ignorance and carelessness of the mayor," who had allowed strangers and a certain Señora Irene from the village to remove reliefs from the site. As a result, only five reliefs were still intact since Dupaix's explorations twenty-five years earlier. Waldeck concluded his letter by asking the governor of Chiapas to order the local authorities to facilitate his mission at the ruins.[32] We have no record that the governor complied with Waldeck's request.

In a letter to Icaza, Waldeck expanded on his previous complaint about the conditions of the ruins. Waldeck's first visit to the site had, naturally, corroborated his hypothesis that the origin of the Mexican people could be linked to both Egypt and Asia. But he was disconsolate to report that the relief of the so-called Adoration of the Cross, the most important proof for his theory, had been removed from its place by the malign Señora Irene, who was, as well, unpa-triotically selling antiquities to North American collectors. The central relief of the Adoration of the Cross, the one representing the "cross" proper, had been separated from the two side reliefs representing "Yupiter-Brahma" and "Vishnu-Tlaloc," respectively, and lay on rollers, awaiting transportation to the coast, whence it would embark for a museum in Philadelphia. Other reliefs had been removed and hidden by village folk in their houses. Waldeck had taken possession of the ruins in the name of the Mexican nation, but the mayor informed him that they belonged to the people, who could do as they wanted with them. Since the village was at some distance from any federal military force, the question of ownership could not be solved by physical coercion.

Instead, Waldeck had come up with the plan, with which he hoped Icaza would agree, to remove the remaining reliefs "from the hands of those who, lacking intellect, mishandled them and rendered them useless to history" and to place them in the custody of the museum. Since Palenque was only eight leagues from the gulf, to which it was connected by a serviceable road, Waldeck proposed hiring carriers to bear the reliefs on their shoulders to boats, of which there were plenty travelling up and down the estuary in Tabasco. From there, the reliefs would presumably be shipped to Veracruz. Waldeck was silent about the second, necessary leg of the journey over the long and mountainous road from Veracruz to Mexico City. He calculated the total cost of the freight at 1,500 pesos—a small price for the museum to pay for antiquities that were selling at 30,000 pesos on the market.[33] Waldeck's letter did arouse authorities in Mexico City to direct Governor Gutiérrez to check on the state of the ruins.[34] Gutiérrez, who was a federalist, was opposed to President Anastasio Bustamente's centralist regime, and he took some months to respond to these letters. In any case, there were more urgent events to attend to in Mexico City; Santa Anna's rebel army arrived in Mexico City in August of 1832, ousting Bustamante and Alamán, the museum's ally.

Waldeck's correspondence with state and federal authorities allows us a glimpse of just how far, geographically and politically, Mexico City was from the small village of Palenque. Local officials felt comfortable claiming not to recognize the names or the powers of members of the federal government. The mayor of Palenque had judged shrewdly that governments in Mexico City came and went.

After all, Waldeck had barely arrived when the government signatories to his agreement were ousted, and who knew how long the ousters themselves would last? On the other hand, as the mayor knew, Señora Irene wasn't going anywhere. This put Waldeck in a rather ludicrous position. He wasn't, after all, either Mexican or from Chiapas. His rhetoric, with its phrases about claiming antiquities on behalf of the nation, must have sounded preposterous. The villagers in Palenque were not impressed; the mayor was merely stating the common feeling when he told Waldeck that the ruins belonged to the local people and were theirs to remove or to sell to the highest bidder if they so desired. At that moment, the top bidder appeared to have been a museum in Philadelphia, if Waldeck is to be believed. It was not just a matter of price; Philadelphia was actually closer to Palenque, from a logistics point of view, than Mexico City. Shipping antiquities—heavy, fragile, and unwieldy—to the North American port by water required a simple, short trip over land from Palenque to Villahermosa, Tabasco, while shipping to Mexico City, in the absence of railways, required massive overland portage through areas that were both trackless and almost invariably politically unstable.

Ignored by the federal government, Waldeck, like the villagers of Palenque, began to think of himself as being on his own. He set up house on the top platform of a pyramid for the following eight months, creating an informal claim to the ruin. After his initial letters to Mexico City, Waldeck's correspondence with (newly installed) government officials was at best sporadic, tending to be closely connected to his various crises with local authorities. Instead, he began writing extensively to European scholars and scholarly societies and to Corroy. The eleven letters he dispatched to Corroy capture Waldeck's day-to-day struggle for food, authority, and physical well-being as he stubbornly persisted in the ruins. But domestic details aside, mostly he reported he was busy at work. His letters to Corroy describe him discovering several ruined complexes; clearing out the vegetation to the river Chacamaz, four leagues south of the ruins, where he discovered an ancient road that ran north to south; and taking topographic and geographic measurements of the roads, rivers, forests, and ruins, four leagues to the west and four to the east.³⁵ He drew reliefs and was ready to start making molds. For this, he pleaded with Corroy to send him gypsum and aqua fortis, essential for dissolving the calcareous deposits on the reliefs, which would reveal the hieroglyphs and enable him to take molds of them. He was sure exhibiting the molds in London and Paris would meet with consummate success. Moreover, making molds would save him the time he would have spent copying hieroglyphs; instead, he could concentrate on drawing plans and picturesque vistas, which would, he was sure, help him market his writings in Europe when it was time to put together his book. The "savage majesty of the ruins," with their strikingly exotic contrast to the comparatively domesticated landscapes of Europe, would appeal to the European public's taste for the exotic and inscribe Palenque into the list of iconic ruins.³⁶

The emotional toll of isolation left its mark on Waldeck, who in the course of his eight months in Palenque became increasingly distrustful, difficult, vain, and overbearing. The rude jolt he had received when he arrived in Palenque and found ruins being boxed up for Philadelphia made him aware, on an almost paranoid level, of potential competitors at the ruins, who he suspected were spreading false rumors in the capital that belittled his own accomplishments. He complained to Corroy that there seemed to be a general perception in Mexico City that he had not done much in Palenque. To defend himself against alleged ill will, Waldeck asked Corroy to publish an article in a newspaper in Veracruz, *El censor*, testifying to Waldeck's productivity, having completed one hundred drawings and five hundred pages of text by mid-March. "It is always necessary to draw the attention of the public to the object one means to exploit," explained Waldeck.³⁷ It was against Americans, who were showing a growing interest in the ruins, that Waldeck unleashed his unmitigated loathing, which he combined with anti-Semitism: "My collection is more important than those that can be gathered by Americans, who are largely ignorant of natural history and of all the sciences, with the exception of the industrial and the mechanical arts. [. . .] A commercial people can never be scientific but can be Jewish to the excess, even when baptized by the first lunatic."[38]

But while Waldeck was playing defense in Mexico, he was also securing new allies in Europe, beginning fruitful correspondences with the Royal Society in London and with the Société de géographie, both of which started publishing his letters. He found a new and powerful ally in the Irish antiquarian and publisher Lord Kingsborough (1795–1837), the eccentric scion of a rich family, who was at the time publishing a multivolume series of documents on Mexican antiquities. Kingsborough bought five subscriptions to Waldeck's project and, Waldeck claimed, was persuading other members of his set to do the same.[39] Waldeck bragged to Corroy that Kingsborough had honored him with the title of "Mexican Champollion," which fed Waldeck's already-elevated sense of his own importance: "My name, my commission, and the little I am worth is known by the letters I have written to scientists."[40] He told Corroy that he was going to appeal to General Santa Anna in Mexico City to impede all would-be explorers from arriving at the ruins before Waldeck himself had finished his studies there.

Corroy could hardly have been delighted by Waldeck's claims of exclusive rights to the ruins. They were, after all, competitors for the Palenque Prize, and both were zealously corresponding with the Société de géographie. The prize was much more than just a matter of money. It was, preeminently, about prestige, about who had truly explored Palenque first and most thoroughly, who was bringing the most detailed and truthful knowledge back to the metropole, all at a time when enthusiasm for ruins was running high. And the ruins of Palenque were commanding curiosity and interest not only among scholars but also among an educated public that could read popularized accounts of archaeological discoveries in papers and magazines. In the overlap of scholarship, popular media, and commerce in antiquities, a culture that combined the spectacular and the scientific was being formed. Furthermore, the older networks for the production and exchange of antiquities and of information about them, which were based on the culture of curiosity collector, were being supplanted by, or at least competed with, new nation-based institutions. In this setting, the protocols for studying and reporting from Palenque were fluid at best.

To ensure a stake in the exploration, both Waldeck and Corroy were busy expanding and diversifying their connections and correspondents. Waldeck kept up his correspondence with the National Museum in Mexico City and with government officials at first, but he evidently wanted to make a name for himself across the Atlantic and went looking for more-powerful patrons, like Kingsborough and the Société, who could aid him in this quest. Corroy, on the other hand, capitalized on relations he developed as a doctor in Tabasco—where, in the busy port, he came in contact with Americans—to send in reports on Palenque alongside writings on more strictly medical matters to the Lyceum of Natural History in New York.[41] He also used his correspondents as go-betweens in shipping the artifacts first to the United States and then to the Société in Paris. Via members of the Lyceum, Edmé François Jomard (1777–1862), the president of the Société, received Corroy's "idols" and his reports on Palenque. Waldeck's letters to Corroy reached the Société by the same conduit.

Waldeck left Palenque by July 1, 1833, after he ran out of money and food.[42] His departure seems to have been hastened by accusations that he had been stealing antiquities. In April of 1833, in a letter to Governor Gutiérrez, Waldeck renewed his charges that village people had been removing antiquities and called for the state government to take simple steps toward the conservation of the monuments: inspect the ruins each month and keep them clean of vegetation. These, Waldeck insisted, would be temporary measures, since the publication of his book would attract the curious and the scholarly, which, in turn, would guarantee the preservation of the ruins, as was the case in Syria and Egypt.[43] In response to Waldeck's accusations, Gutiérrez wrote to Mexico City, claiming that Waldeck was the one wanting to buy antiquities. The governor also pledged to inquire about the costs of placing the reliefs back into their original places at the ruins or of transporting them to the museum in Mexico City. Yet he also made it clear that he would not recognize the central government's claims to own those monuments;

echoing arguments that had been made before by state governors, he wrote that antiquities belonged rightfully and unequivocally to individual states (in this case, to the state of Chiapas) where they were located.[44] There is no paper record that shows that Gutiérrez followed up on his promises, and it does not seem that the reliefs in question were restored to their original place, let alone shipped to Mexico City. But even if concrete measures might have been taken in this case, it is not difficult to see how antiquities were lost sight of in the tangle of conflict that pitted states' rights and agendas against those of the federal government and travelers' personal interests and ambitions as collectors against the claims of villagers, about whose uses for antiquities in this period we know little.

Waldeck's flight from Palenque took him first to Campeche and then to Mérida, where he managed once again to arouse the suspicion of the authorities and the common people. General Francisco de Paula Toro, the interim governor of Yucatán and Santa Anna's brother-in-law, made a pretense of being sympathetic enough to Waldeck's expedition in order to discover Waldeck's secrets. Toro assumed Waldeck was spying for the British Crown, because Waldeck was receiving funds from England (presumably through subscriptions by Kingsborough) to study monuments in Mexico.[45] Waldeck's problems with the authorities began in earnest in the fall of 1835, after his visits to Uxmal, Mayapán, Chichén Itza, and Cozumel contributed to mounting misgivings that he might have been stealing antiquities.[46] Waldeck's former friend, Corroy, added to the poisonous atmosphere that began to surround Waldeck in Mexico by portraying the old man as a greedy, self-centered trafficker of antiquities. In July 1835 Waldeck had resourcefully managed to return to Palenque, which so disturbed Corroy that he wrote to the Ministry of Internal and External Affairs in Mexico City, to remind them that Waldeck had not fulfilled any of the contractual terms that he signed off on with Alamán, who had now been ousted long ago. Corroy claimed Waldeck was abusing his special permits and protections to buy antiquities for his own use. These objects, and the fruit of his research, he was sending to London. Corroy insisted that Waldeck's authorizations to carry out antiquarian work at the

ruins be revoked immediately and that the objects in his possession be seized. Foreigners, Corroy maintained, had been the great
perpetrators of the destruction of the ruins, which was against the
law and the spirit of the law, which rightfully reserved the ruins
and their exploration for the Mexican government itself. After
this windup, Corroy concluded with a pitch to be commissioned
as one of the leading members of a new antiquarian expedition
to Palenque that was being organized in Mexico City. He claimed
that given his proximity to and knowledge of the ruins, he was
especially equipped to ensure their conservation.[47]

The interim president Miguel Barragán (1789–1836) thanked
Corroy for his letter and obliged him by assigning him to the commission post.[48] At the same time, officials in Mexico City warned
customs officials in Campeche, Sisal, Tabasco, and Laguna de Térmi-
nos that Waldeck had hidden a cache of antiquities somewhere in
the vicinity of Mérida and asked them to act in accordance with
national laws and remain vigilant against the exportation of these
objects.[49] By order of Governor Toro, Waldeck's house in Mérida
was searched on January 16, 1836; though no antiquities were
found, the inspectors did confiscate a box with sixteen of Waldeck's
drawings of antiquities. Were the accusations, after all, false? Had
the objects already been shipped off? Incensed, Waldeck tried to
recover the drawings by calling on past connections in Mexico
City. A letter to Francisco Fagoaga, one of the original subscribers
to Waldeck's antiquarian expedition, led to the disclosure by Fagoaga that Toro had acted on his own when he seized the drawings.
They had been sent to Mexico City and were in the possession of
the museum. There they would be copied before being returned
to Waldeck; or else if he were so inclined, Waldeck was invited
to go to Mexico City to make the copies himself.[50] The museum
had by then run out of patience with Waldeck. Rather than face
the wrath of officials and subscribers, Waldeck decided to cut his
losses, sacrificing those sixteen drawings to "filibusters." He left
Mexico on March 24, 1836, eleven years after his arrival, embarking
undercover on the English boat *Lyre*.[51] There is no record of how
Waldeck smuggled out antiquities, if indeed he possessed any. As

for the museum, there is a sad irony in the fact that its returns, five years after Alamán had signed the agreement with Waldeck, amounted to sixteen drawings. Even so, it fared better than most subscribers to the project, who saw no returns on their shares whatsoever. Kingsborough's recompense was more substantial. Once in Europe, Waldeck published his *Voyage pittoresque et archéologique dans la province d'Yucatán* (1838), which bore a fervent dedication to Kingsborough.

As Waldeck explained in his introduction to the *Voyage*, he meant for this book to be the last in a series of three books. The first book was to be on Mexico's ancient history, based on documentation acquired on site; the second would have offered a specific study of Palenque in which he would put to use his explorations at the ruins, where, it was true, he had remained longer than any previous explorer. He had begun the series with the last book, which included detailed descriptions of the ruins at Uxmal, because everything he had gathered on Uxmal had been confiscated by governmental order. Here, Waldeck was presumably speaking of the sixteen drawings that were sent to Mexico City by Governor Toro. Fortunately, he had made copies of these materials, but knowing that "the barbarians in Mexico" had his originals, he feared that if he postponed the publication of his voyage to Uxmal, "any speculator, capable of profiting from the loot perpetrated by the chiefs of the republic, would beat him to it and publish his work under some supposed name."[52] In France, Waldeck's book contributed to creating a climate of animosity toward Mexico, by echoing a common sentiment that foreigners were being swindled by Mexicans; this perception was only amplified by the Pastry War (November 1838–March 1839) between France and Mexico, which had as its starting point the Mexican government's failure to honor its debt to a French pastry chef whose store had been destroyed by street mobs during a mutiny in 1828.[53]

As with so many of Waldeck's grandiose projects, the first two volumes of his series were never published. Over the following years, there is a sense that his opinions and expertise were quickly rendered obsolete after the ruins were explored by more Europeans and Americans. Not until the 1860s, which marked the height of renewed French interest in Mexican antiquities, in the context of the French intervention in Mexico, was Waldeck's name remembered to the extent that the Ministry of Public Instruction in France put together a commission to determine the merits of the drawings he had made during his explorations in Palenque and Yucatán. The commission, led by Léonce Angrand (1808–86), a scholar of Peruvian antiquities, expressed the caution that Waldeck's meticulousness might have led him to "restore" ruins arbitrarily; this, rather than helping interpretation, could be a source of confusion for future students of these ruins.[54] In the end, it was decided that the drawings were good enough to illustrate Charles Étienne Brasseur de Beaubourg's *Monuments anciens du Mexique, Palenque, Ocosingo et autres ruines de l'ancienne civilization du Mexique* (1866).

The Sociedad de Anticuarios de Palenque

Waldeck had nothing to fear from Mexican "barbarians" and "freebooters." The museum did not publish his drawings; eventually, on Lord Kingsborough's insistence, the Mexican government returned them to Waldeck.[55] In fact, even before Waldeck left Mexico, by the summer of 1835 the museum was ready to put Waldeck behind and attend to the serious business of uncovering Mexico's preconquest past by planning a new expedition to Palenque with Baron René de Perdreauville. Perdreauville seems like an odd choice to lead an expedition for a museum that had been burnt before by its relationship with adventure-minded foreigners. A member of the old French noblesse, Perdreauville, after Napoleon's fall, emigrated to New Orleans, where he became a member of the Grand Lodge of the State of Louisiana.[56] Little is known of what took him south of the border, where, like so many others, he became interested in Mexico's ruins and explored various sites in central Mexico. Of particular interest is his short survey of the ruins of Xochicalco and the caves at Cacahuamilpa, south of Mexico City in 1835, a joint venture between Perdreauville; the National Museum; and the minister of internal and external relations, José María Gutiérrez de Estrada (1800–1867). Perdreauville and his team spent two weeks at the ruins and returned to Mexico City with measurements, plans, and drawings of Xochicalco. But the mapping of Cacahuamilpa had to be aborted, in part because bad weather had thwarted the men's intention to penetrate deeper into the cave and in part because their Indian guides refused to go any farther once they caught sight of human skeletons on the ground. Still, Perdreauville reported, the commission had discovered new interiors of the cave and produced a plan and drawings of the cave. It is not clear if the expedition brought back any objects, either specimens of natural history or antiquities. Upon his return, Perdreauville published a description of his visit to Xochicalco and Cacahuamilpa in the *Revista mexicana*.[57] By all accounts, his expedition was a hearteningly visible success for the museum, especially in comparison to previous ventures that had born few fruits within Mexico.

It might have been the Xochicalco expedition that made the museum realize that it had at last found an explorer who was dedicated, competent, and responsible, making him perfect to head the more audacious expedition to Palenque. By 1835 the museum had long given up hope that Waldeck's expedition to Palenque would produce any tangible benefits for the institution.[58] Lack of results wore onerously on the museum's reputation; for as far as the Mexican public could see, scholars in France and England— Baradère and his collaborators on the one hand, Kingsborough on the other—dominated the exploration of Mexico's past, publishing multivolume works on the remnants of Mexico's ancient past and circling in particularly on the ruins of Palenque. If Mexico was to play a role in telling its own history, it was crucial to capitalize on the enthusiasm and expertise that placed the country at the center of international attention and to demonstrate its capacity to generate knowledge about its past. In this context of both anxiety and interest, the Instituto de Geografía y Estadística (later the Sociedad Mexicana de Geografía y Estadística) was founded in 1833, with participation by many of the same scholars that formed the museum's administrative board. The Instituto, like its Parisian counterpart, had a broad understanding of "geography" and "statistics" and aimed to produce scientific studies about as many aspects of the young country as possible, including its geography, population, languages, and history.[59]

It is also at this historical conjuncture that the Mexican Sociedad de Anticuarios de Palenque was formed, to foster the development of a program of archaeological research led by Mexican scholars. On July 22, 1835, members of the museum's administrative board, jointly with René de Perdreauville, presented their proposal for the Sociedad to the new minister of internal and external relations, Manuel Díez de Bonilla (1800–1864), for approval. The proposal began by describing the motivations that had led them to form the organization: despite all the explorations on Palenque that had been undertaken, there was still no methodical and detailed study of the ruins. There were as many hypotheses on the origins of Palenque as there were authors to hypothesize about them, meaning that there was no consensus about what the evidence meant. No exploration of Palenque had yet resulted in any definite benefit to the country's understanding of its past. On the contrary, all such explorations had been produced by violating the laws concerning Mexican antiquities and, as part of the process, illegally exported precious objects to Europe. All these arguments were marshaled implicitly and explicitly against Waldeck, with the conclusion being that his privileges needed to be revoked and that the museum needed to take control over research expeditions.[60]

Evidently, the argument being made was to persuade the state to give the Sociedad de Anticuarios de Palenque a special position, commissioning an official exploration party that would produce positive evidence using scientific methods to faithfully catalogue and detail the features of Palenque and other "interesting monuments." An additional benefit to such a commission was that the Sociedad could set the rules for the study of Mexican ruins and attain its place as an equal to other societies, such as the Société de géographie, in the world of antiquarian studies and the race to explore Mexico's archaeological riches. Though the Sociedad de Anticuarios de Palenque was inviting foreigners to participate, the project sought to attract primarily Mexican scholars.

The nationalistic overtone had political implications for a Mexican state that had still not fully solved its political problems: whether it would be a federal republic or a centralized state, whether it would be ruled by democratic elections or by military strongmen, whether it had the ability to defend its territory from the aggressor to the north and other imperialist powers. Palenque, the "American Thebes," proved that America had known civilization before Europe did; claiming this past was as much a part of Mexican sovereignty and unity as dealing with the powers that threatened it in the present. The writers of the proposal explicitly aligned themselves with Mexico's liberal present, even as the "new, repairing government" they were petitioning, Santa Anna's government, was busy tearing apart liberal reforms put in place by previous administrations. Behind the rhetoric, the founding members of the society offered Mexico's government a pact—in return for an interest in the ruins, the government would gain prestige as the bearer of the ancient values of civilization, enlightenment, glory, and maybe the capacity to prevail over the ravages of time and adversity.

Even though Perdreauville's group presented themselves as the anti-Waldeck project, they also borrowed from Waldeck's model. Their activities, too, would be financed by subscriptions (seventy in all), each being given a share in the management of the project and a share of the products of the exploration. Unlike all previous agreements for the study of Palenque, the Sociedad de Anticuarios de Palenque, though an autonomous organization, had strong ties with the National Museum. Three of the five members in charge of the society were from the museum: Gondra, the museum's conservator; Bustamante, the head of the natural history section at the museum; and the Conde de la Cortina, chair of the museum board. The other two members were Perdreauville and Corroy. The statutes of the Sociedad, agreed upon in the course of an exchange of letters between the society and the government, reflected commitment and deference to the museum. Thus, the second statute stipulated that all the antiquities collected by the expedition would be inventoried and that the "doubles" (similar-looking objects) would be given to the government, which would deposit them in the museum. The rest of them belonged to the Sociedad and would be distributed among the shareholders. Of equal interest was another statute that called for the members of the expedition to collect—on the margins of their archaeological research—birds, reptiles, insects, plants, and mineralogical samples, which were to be turned in to the Sociedad and to the National Museum. The expeditioners had a deadline of six months after the explorations to turn in a detailed topographical description of Palenque, along with descriptions of the monuments, statues, reliefs, and antiquities. They would have an extra six months to submit visual documents like plans and drawings.

Baron de Perdreauville would lead the expedition to the ruins, while Corroy would act as representative of the Sociedad on site. Corroy's antiquarian knowledge and practical experience, it was argued, would be vital for the success of the expedition. After his approval by Minister Díez de Bonilla, Corroy sealed his association with the project by sending the museum antiquities from Palenque (various idols; reliefs; and a jasper and a clay mask, which he had probably collected on his previous trips to Palenque) and some natural history specimens (a petrified starfish and the petrified bark of a tree).[61]

The proposal by the Sociedad was published in the *Diario del Gobierno* on October 5, 1835. By late November the governors of Chiapas, Yucatán, and Tabasco sent letters of support, promising to safeguard the explorers. And yet after this promising start, the Sociedad disappears from history. We have no details concerning Perdreauville's expedition. Its existence was positively denied forty years later by Chiapas-born historian and politician Manuel Larrainzar (1809–84), who, in a study on American antiquities, wrote, "Even though this project attempted to bring together public and private interest [. . .] and though the names associated [with it] boded well for the fulfillment of such a laudable enterprise, several adverse circumstances obstructed its happening and after that, nothing serious or formal has been [undertaken]."[62] Larrainzar did not explain what he meant by "adverse circumstances." Perhaps, after Waldeck had burned his investors, there was no support in wealthy circles for yet another promise of wealth from Palenque. There was, after all, only a limited circle within the Mexican elite who would be interested, and they were probably the same people who had divvied up for Waldeck.

It is very possible that the Sociedad was simply the victim of political circumstances. In October 1835, the same month that the Sociedad announced itself, U.S. settlers in the Mexican state of Texas declared war on Mexico. The events of the war, culminating in the defeat at San Jacinto of April 12, 1836, and the ignominious treaty recognizing Mexico's loss of Texas on May 14, surely lowered the confidence of potential shareholders. In addition, the same year, Corroy, the society's would-be representative in Palenque, died. But if the Sociedad had effectively died with Corroy, it had a surprising posthumous existence in France. In its 1836 issue, the *Journal de L'Institut Historique* published a translation of the constitution of the Sociedad de Anticuarios de Palenque.[63] This was the last time the society would enter the news on either side of the Atlantic. During the following decades, the study of Palenque would be organized exclusively from abroad.

"All Eyes Are on Your Country"

On April 5, 1836, the Société de géographie met again to discuss the Palenque Prize and to put out a long review of the state of explorations in Palenque.[64] The prize committee declared itself gratified to see that the prize had elicited fieldwork and opulent publications in Europe. On-site studies included those by Corroy, Waldeck, and Juan Galindo (1802–39), the governor of the Petén region in Guatemala. The reviewers gave Corroy high marks for "ardor and enthusiasm," though they judged the ten reports on Palenque he had sent to the Société between 1827 and 1832 to be lacking in precision. The commission praised Waldeck for the sheer volume of his explorations at sites in Chiapas and Yucatán, which had resulted in topographical elevations; plans; drawings of sculptures, buildings, and symbolic characters; research on natural history; portraits of the local Mayas and Lacandones; and studies of their customs. And they commended him for bringing Uxmal to the attention of the scholarly world. Still, the commission judged

Waldeck's conjectures regarding the history and language of America's ancient builders as "chancy." Juan Galindo's hypotheses, especially his suggestion that the American race was the oldest one on earth, were not taken up by the judges. They simply commended him for his map of Palenque and for filing the first reports on the site at Copán in Central America.

As for the studies published in Europe, the commission singled out Kingsborough's *Mexican Antiquities* and Baradère's *Antiquités mexicaines*. Kingsborough had published seven volumes of his magnum opus since 1830—the eighth and ninth volumes would come out posthumously in the following years. The fourth, fifth, and sixth volumes consisted of the Dupaix and Castañeda material that had been brought to Europe by Latour Allard. Baradère had begun publishing the same material in 1834 in installments; by the time the commission read its resolution, most of the two-volume *Antiquités mexicaines* had come out.

In the Société's review of these various reports, Palenque begins to take on the features of a standard site of study; produced by the interaction between human and nonhuman agents—explorers, government officials, scientific societies, roads, forests, snakes, technologies of representation, images, and texts—the ruins in the jungle of Palenque became the "mobile object of antiquarian research."[65] Although the Société was evidently pleased with its role in promoting Palenque as a topic of interest to the scholarly world, it was not entirely satisfied with the research produced up until that point. The commission reminded the public that it had initially asked for "facts [and] positive observations made at [different] sites" throughout Central America—geographical "discoveries," topographical plans, exact maps, excavations, studies of ancient monuments and language, in tandem with reports on harbors and on river courses, on the presence of minerals and on the fertility of the soil—suggesting that economic and commercial agendas were intricately tied with archaeological interest. In the archaeological terrain, most of the competitors, however, had produced more conjectures than facts, which did not resolve the enigma of these ancient civilizations; almost all had neglected to furnish commercial and economic data. So despite prolonged attention on Palenque, the Société did not consider the world considerably richer in information that could help it make sense of the region. In other words, nobody deserved the prize![66] To mitigate the blow, or to prolong the suspense, the commission decreed that the award would be postponed for another three years, until 1839. In the meantime, the Société conferred silver medals on Kingsborough, Baradère, and Galindo; Waldeck and Corroy tied for bronze medals. This anticlimax was, as it turned out, the commission's final word on the prize. When the Société met again in 1839 to discuss the prize, no award was conferred because no new competitors had come forward.[67]

By then, both the players and the vectors of archaeological interest were shifting, as the ruins of Yucatán were beginning to attract the attention of travelers and explorers. In 1841 clamoring for the reestablishment of the Constitution of 1824 and the return to federalism, Yucatán seceded from the Mexican Federation; it remained independent until 1848. These years saw the flourishing of a local press, the *Museo yucateco* and the *Registro yucateco*, and of local interest in the new republic's history.[68] At the same time, Yucatán was becoming the object of antiquarian interest in the United States, where the stakes were rhetorically commingled with the reigning notions of manifest destiny. Writing in 1845, Benjamin Moore Norman (1809–60) urged his fellow Americans to take advantage of the purported Mexican lack of interest in antiquities and to undertake the exploration of these "wonders," which belonged appropriately to Americans (one assumes, from the United States).[69] By then, John Lloyd Stephens and Frederick Catherwood had already been exploring ruins in the region in the two trips (in 1839 and in 1842) that they detailed in two immensely popular books—*Incidents of Travel in Central America, Chiapas, and Yucatán* (1841) and *Incidents of Travel in Yucatán* (1843). In addition, a lavish album of color lithographs by Catherwood—*Views of Ancient Monuments in Central America, Chiapas, and Yucatán*—was published in 1844. As a result of their journey, Stephens and Catherwood oversaw the shipment of an important number of antiquities to New York.

Then, in 1844, exploiting the conflicts between the runaway state of Yucatán and Mexico City—with Mexico refusing to recognize the independence of Yucatán and banning practically all trade with the peninsula—a group of French and English scholars vowed to uphold Yucatán's claims for independence in return for permission to explore Yucatán's ruins. A letter to this effect—signed in the name of the "scientific commission for the exploration of Mexican antiquities" on January 29, 1844, by St.-Priest, who had participated in the publication of *Antiquités mexicaines*, and addressed to the "governor of Yucatán"—was published a year later in the *Registro yucateco*.[70] St.-Priest reported on a meeting at the Royal Society in London, attended by such grandees as Prince Albert and Prime Minister Robert Peel, that was concerned with Baradère's *Antiquités mexicaines*. The discussion had centered on the origin of American civilization, and it was decided that only an expedition to the ruins could bring resolution. The project, which had been taken up enthusiastically by European scientific societies, held a particular and exclusive interest for Yucatán, explained St.-Priest: "Nobody ignores that Yucatán is an inexhaustible mine of historical and archaeological wonders, and that there are more monuments to see and study in this country than in the rest of America. It is for these reasons that the exploration of Yucatán, carried out in great detail, is the object of a transatlantic expedition."[71]

It would be difficult to separate the political implications of this proposal from its antiquarian prospects. The promise of political recognition, which was desperately sought by Yucatán's government, was obviously displayed here as a decoy for foreign intervention, archaeological and otherwise. The proposed expedition, however, was not carried through. In 1848, in the face of the Caste War—which pitted Creoles against the indigenous population of Yucatán—the autonomous republic of Yucatán asked Mexico for help to quench the rebellion; in return, Mexico delivered on terms that forced Yucatán to return to the federation. Reunion with Yucatán was not followed by any new National Museum–sponsored expeditions to Yucatán. Mexico in the 1850s was recovering from its disastrous war with the United States, which, for the government, put any antiquarian expeditions on the back burner.

During the first decades following its foundation, the National Museum of Mexico made several attempts to overcome its perennial lack of money and personnel by contracting with would-be explorers, invariably foreigners, at moments when ruins in Chiapas and, increasingly, in Yucatán exercised a special lure on antiquarians and adventurers on both sides of the Atlantic. The museum was banking on this method to amass artifacts and become a cultural entrepreneur in American antiquities exploration and collecting. One of the more curious effects of the story of the museum's relationship with foreign collectors is the sense of the museum as a vanishing object, one that moves out of focus as one gets closer to it, that most of the time seems to be offstage. The drama of exploring and collecting Palenque was happening elsewhere—at the ruins and in New York, Philadelphia, London, and Paris, where political, commercial, and antiquarian alliances were forged; objects, shipped; letters, exchanged; books, published; and prizes, meted out.

The question I have tried to answer here, by reconstructing a series of attempts by the museum to collect and study ancient vestiges in Palenque, is why, in this period, it always failed to do so. We could point out that the museum was on the periphery of most of the networks that led in and out of Palenque, but in terms of sheer distance, of course, Mexico City was closer to the ruins than New York, Paris, London, or Philadelphia. Periphery is more than a geographical place. Rather than a given, a network is an achievement. Networks require work. Distance needs to be controlled and managed at every stage along the way. To say that a place lies at the periphery means that it does not have the power to organize action at a distance, to turn itself into a center, and to ensure that people and objects make their way to it.[72] In this chapter, we have examined the many different ways in which the museum had trouble managing the tentative networks it tried to build to the ruins in Chiapas and, later, in Yucatán.

To understand where the museum went wrong, we have to imagine that Palenque was bound to the museum by a series of weak links. First, as we have seen in the previous chapter, the museum did not operate as an autonomous institution but had to consult the government and obtain approval for even its most mundane transactions. But governments in Mexico succeeded each other at a vertiginous pace, and the museum mattered differently to different officials. When deals were struck between would-be explorers and government representatives, who were not only often swept from office but whose acts were institutionally forgotten, it was easy for the former to ignore the contractual protocols that the museum had imposed on them. The farther away a traveler journeyed from Mexico City, the weaker the links with officials in the capital, and the less the traveler had to fear from violating the law and his promises. Certainly, this had to do with geographical distance, but it had more to do with the kind of recognition or influence exerted by the federal government throughout the republic. Other sets of rules, assumptions, and practical realities were at play in different states, regions, or villages, which meant that the farther away from the capital they found themselves, the more it became impracticable for travelers to rely on expectations they (or the museum) had formed in Mexico City. Successful exploration required learning to become actors in local power plays. Transactions here were mediated by local alliances, rivalries, and friendships, not by the state or by protocols the museum might have been trying to establish or impose. Tolerance or sensitivity to local ways and customs could prove important tactical assets to deal with indifferent or, worse, hostile local authorities, competitors in the race for the ruins, rough roads, unreliable sources of food or shelter, tropical illnesses, or venomous snakes.

But it was not only that the conditions of explorations changed as one traveled away from the capital; the meanings and use of objects changed within the circle of other contexts. Simply put, few people whom explorers met seemed to believe that antiquities belonged in the museum simply because the government in Mexico City had ordered their collection and transportation there. Antiquities were a showcase for greater tensions between federalist and centralist projects for the nation. It was not always a matter of ideological resistance, although this was not unheard of: witness the touchy correspondence between the governor of Chiapas and officials in

Mexico City. At times, it was the promise of economic gain that explained the opposition to relinquishing objects for free to the government when they sold well to others. At other times, there was religious or cultural resistance: antiquities were at the center of community life in villages where such objects held significance, testifying to syncretism and idiosyncratic forms of Christian worship. To procure sacred objects, or even objects in which other outsiders showed a curious interest, a combination of skill, charisma, and economic inducements was necessary on the part of travelers.

At the same time, archaeological sites—most notably Palenque but over time other similar sites in Yucatán as well—became arenas for the display of international interests. This mirrors a political dynamic wielded also in Egypt and Greece, where imperialist powers intent on being gatekeepers of the past founded their legitimacy not simply on physical force but also on the claim to be the intellectual inheritors of ancient civilizations.[73] This was not a trivial matter, since it allowed for extensive intrusion in the subordinate polities. The struggle for antiquities reflected issues other than the scholarly one of unlocking the enigma of Mexico's ancient past.[74]

Finally, the personal ambition of travelers was also an important factor to take into account when assessing the outcome of deals between explorers and the museum. Many foreign travelers saw Mexico as a place with less rule, where they could make a fortune. Others came hoping for fame, and others combined the two motives. These persons encountered a museum that could make promises but did not have the ready funding to pay for the objects secured by adventurers. It was also evident early on that the museum did not have the capital, financial or cultural, to put out publications that would place it at the vanguard of antiquarian studies. It made sense for travelers, therefore, to multiply their chances of becoming known and read by collaborating with institutions that were more firmly established, like the Société de géographie in Paris or the Royal Society in London. The museum could do little to impose norms or protocols on travelers or to punish them for violating laws against the export of antiquities.

Thus, the deals signed by museum directors and travelers-turned-antiquarians should not be seen as cases of swindlers descending on a weak state in the throes of developing its institution and taking maximum advantage, although it may appear that way upon a superficial first reading. Rather, the network we have tried to reconstruct was wholly enclosed within the emergent relations between postcolonial Mexico and representatives of colonial powers who were claiming stakes in the country's wealth and were applying a double standard of behavior—on the one side, insisting that Mexico abide punctiliously to its agreements and, on the other side, making foreign nationals quasi-immune to the rules of property and honesty adhering in Mexico.

For the museum, this set of circumstances resulted in a vicious circle. While struggling to turn itself into a significant agent in the cultures of nineteenth-century collecting (the value of which it implicitly recognized), the museum remained on the margins of those cultures precisely because it was not recognized as an important center for collecting objects. It was obvious to the museum's officials that they needed new strategies for recognition. By the late 1830s, the museum turned again, as it had ten years earlier, to paper.

4 MODES OF DISPLAY

A Jumble of Fragments

Until 1877 the National Museum of Mexico produced no guides to its collections. We have to rely on inventories and purchase reports to find out what things were brought into the museum; even this record is one-sided, in that the institution archives contain no records of how these things were exhibited for public view for its first fifty years. Luckily, we do have numerous descriptions of visits to the museum, mostly by foreign visitors and a few by Mexican nationals, during this half century.[1] Frances "Fanny" Calderón de la Barca (1804–82), the wife of the Spanish ambassador, visited Mexico City in 1842. Her reaction to the museum speaks for how most visitors perceived it: "The Museum [. . .], owing to the want of arrangement and classification in the antiquities, and the manner in which they are crowded together in different rooms of the university, appears at first undeserving of attention." But after a closer look, she discovers the presence of some valuable objects.[2]

Crowding was a big problem for the museum, and this became apparent from the very moment the institution was founded at the university. Twenty years later, objects forced together in unlikely juxtapositions made it impossible for curators to propose an overall narrative for the national collection or to highlight what was valuable about it. This was an impression shared even by visitors who did take the time to describe in detail those objects and the way they were displayed, as was the case with Brantz Mayer (1809–79), the secretary to the U.S. legation in Mexico between 1841 and 1843, our most complete guide to the museum during those years. After visiting the museum through Mayer's account of it, the next two chapters turn away from the physical museum to focus on strategies adopted by its directors in the 1840s and 1850s to make sense of the collection and its specific objects on paper.

Mayer's description of the museum was published in his *Mexico, as It Was and as It Is*, which came out upon his return to the United States in 1843. By his own account, the book, written in the wake of Texan Independence and in the context of escalating tensions between Mexico and the United States, strove to present its U.S. audience with a well-balanced account of Mexico, with judicious descriptions of Mexican commerce, manufacture, and politics. Mayer was especially drawn to the country's pre-Hispanic past. In fact, his short stay in Mexico planted the seed of a long-term interest in American antiquities—and in his search for ancient monuments, he visited "every spot of interest," from the ruins at Texcoco, Texcotzingo, and Teotihuacan to the "remarkable remains at Cholula and Xochicalco" and the cabinets of private collectors like the Conde de Peñasco. "Whenever it was convenient, [Mayer] spent much of [his] time in the Museum, where [he] made accurate drawings of almost every striking and important object," many of which he included in the book. He deeply regretted that his other duties "limited [him] to but a brief inspection and study of these relics."[3]

Let us follow Mayer on one of his visits to the museum in the "fine old monastic building" of the university, as he steals time away from other duties. There is a relic of recent violence that he notes as he enters the building: marks of stray bullets that "pierced and injured" the facade of the university, which were fired during the 1841 coup d'état engineered by Santa Anna to make himself the head of the Mexican government. In the large interior patio, he confronts a scene that we can envision from the finely rendered contemporary painting by the Italian painter and lithographer Pietro Gualdi (1808–57) (fig. 13).[4] The courtyard, surrounded by a two-story arcade, is dominated by a "colossal bronze statue of Charles IV," which Mayer thought was too large for the space it took up here, even as he judged it to be "of great majesty and worthy of most judicious praise" and comparable only with the "famous statue of Marcus Aurelius at Rome."[5] From the statue in the center, Mayer makes for the entrance on the left-hand side of the courtyard, where Gualdi's painting shows a fenced structure beyond which we can glimpse some monumental preconquest statuary.

13. Pietro Gualdi, interior of the university. *Monumentos de Mejico, tomados del natural y litografiados por Pedro Gualdi* (Ciudad de México: Massé y Decaen, 1841). Some of the larger monoliths of the museum—probably the Coatlicue—are visible in the left corner. Beinecke Rare Book and Manuscript Library, Yale University.

One real to the porter admits Mayer into the enclosure, where a first glance elicits conflicted impressions: amid the "mass of filth, dirt, and refuse furniture," next to a "mimic tree, with a stuffed bear climbing up it, a bleached and hairless tiger skin dangling from the ceiling, and half-a-dozen Indian dresses made of snake-skins, fluttering on the wall," he comes upon the "relics of antiquity for which thousands would be gladly paid by the British Museum, the Louvre, the Glyptotheca of Munich, or, indeed, by any enlightened Sovereign, who possessed the taste to acquire and the money to purchase."[6] What we identify nowadays as the most noteworthy Mexican antiquities are all there: "the grand and hideous idol of Teoyaomiqui" towering above the "confusion"; the great Stone of Tízoc ("with a stone cross now erected in the middle to sanctify it"); a colossal head of serpentine, in the Egyptian style of sculpture; carvings of feathered serpents; and the statue of the so-called Sad Indian (Indio Triste), in whom some saw a destitute witness to the Spanish conquest. For Mayer, a contemporary of the Indian Wars in the United States, the statue is a figure of moroseness—brows "drawn together with anger," eyes "wide and glaring," tongue "slightly protruded from the mouth," "a fixed, stony gaze of imperturbable surliness and impudence in the face."[7] Scattered over the floor lie numberless figures of dogs, monkeys, lizards, birds, serpents, "all in seemingly inextricable confusion and utter neglect," all of them "deformed and hideous" manifestations of "the dawn of religious ideas," when men "personified every evil which assailed them under the shape in which it became annoying, [to] appease [it] by worship and offerings."[8]

Leaving the enclosure on the ground floor of the university, Mayer climbs up the flight of steps to the first floor, where the rest of the collection is divided between three rooms corresponding to objects from colonial history, antiquities, and natural history. In the first one—a large hall that, "like everything in the republic, is neglected and lumbered"—hang the portraits of Mexico's viceroys, "in the stiff and formal guise of their several periods," some "in military costume, some in monkish, some in civil, and some in the outlandish frills, furbelows and finery of the last century." Among the portraits, Mayer singles out those of Isabella and Ferdinand as "worthy of the point of Velazquez."[9] In a corner of the same room, Mayer is surprised to see a throne, next to an unfinished relief of a trophy of liberty, above which, inexplicably, "in a rude coffin of rough pine boards, [lies] a mummy, dug up on the fields of Tlatelolco north of the city."[10]

The adjoining room holds together "a jumble of fragments of the past and present." Its center is graced by "a Castle and Fortification, made of wood and straw, with mimic guns and all the array of military power." This crude model was "the work of a poor prisoner, the labor of years of solitude and misery."[11] If this seems like an unworthy object to command such an important position, the museum's board of directors had a justification for its purchase, claiming that the model was a genuinely Mexican artistic production and thus fell under the museum's writ.[12] In itself, the decision speaks of just how underdetermined the category of "artistic productions" was. Next, Mayer pauses before a numismatic cabinet, "tolerably rich in Spanish specimen" and in Roman coins, "which promises, under the care of Mr. Gondra, to become exceedingly rare and valuable"; he then turns to a cabinet that displays, "among gimcrackery, some beautiful specimens of rag and wax work."[13] The statuettes, "admirably executed" in the precarious sleeping-quarters-turned-ateliers of poor families, represent "Mexican types, with their costumes and trades." Mayer finds them to be "most faithful to reality" and recommends purchasing them because they would "adorn any collection" and "command a couple of doubloons each in Europe."[14] In another corner, he is drawn to "a plain, unornamented suit of steel," purportedly Cortés's armor.

Nearby, encased in a glass frame, hangs one of Cortés's banners, with the Virgin Mary "painted on crimson silk, surrounded with stars and an inscription." Below the banner is an old Indian painting, "an authentic record of some of the cruelties practiced by Spaniards in subduing the chiefs of the country, and striking terror in the minds of the artless Indians."[15] It shows Doña Marina, the translator and ambiguous instrument in Cortés's conquest, holding a rosary necklace and Cortés giving orders that are presumably being executed in the scene underneath, where a guileless Indian is being attacked by a bloodhound. Is there a dialogue or a critique implied by the conservators who placed the banner above the painting? An attempt to show abuses perpetrated in the name of religion? Mayer does not say, and given the haphazard cast of the assembly of artifacts, it is difficult to say if the juxtaposition is accidental or meaningful. It is true, however, that the cruelty of the Spanish was a common topic in the writings of both foreign travelers and Mexican liberals at the time. Under this image hangs a picture of the last of the kings of Texcoco; beneath that, on a stand, "in the midst of hideous stone idols," are two funeral vases—the "most beautiful relics in the Museum," which had been found full of human bones in Tlatelolco.

In the same room, there are cases with "valuable" Mexican antiquities "gathered together by the labor of many years and arranged with some attention to system."[16] One displays tools and ornaments: hatchets, which Mayer finds to be strikingly similar to those of native North American Indians, unearthed around Mayer's native Baltimore; bows, arrows, and obsidian arrowheads, "some of them so small and beautifully cut, that the smallest bird might be killed without injuring the plumage"; and obsidian beads and mirrors. Another case exhibits vases and cups discovered in 1827 in the "subterranean chambers" of the Isla de Sacrificios, which, due to what Mayer calls the "inertness of the Mexican government," had been liberally exported to European museums by ship captains.[17] Next, he turns to a cabinet with "household gods" and musical instruments, such as rattles, whistles, and *teponaztli*.

On the westward-facing side of the room are models of Mexican mines, each made of stones from the mineral regions of Mexico. They portray, "most faithfully," "the various parts of the mines, the modes of obtaining the ore, of freeing [mines] from water, of sinking shafts," as well as the dress, appearance, and labor of the workmen, represented as silver figurines. Hung about the walls of the room are copies of Mexican codices depicting aspects of Mexican history, genealogies, and calendar systems. The originals, informs Mayer, "had been taken to England shortly after the establishment of Independence and have not been returned."[18] Given the disorganization of the museum, Mayer thinks that "they are perhaps better there than they would have been in Mexico, where the existing remains of antiquity excite no curiosity and hang, from year to year, covered with dust, and unexplored, on the walls of the University." Indeed, Mayer considered that, with the exception of Carlos María de Bustamante, there were no other scholars that took an interest in the antiquities in Mexico. A "disappointing" glance at the room dedicated to natural history, where the "present fares no better than the past," ends Mayer's visit.[19]

Although his description of the museum stands out for its richness of detail and its genuine interest in the objects on display there, Mayer shared the sense conveyed by other visitors that the museum, far from being a crown jewel of Mexican scholarship, was instead an indictment of Mexican indifference. Objects had been grouped together in disparate lumps, "with some attention to system"—whistles with drums, small idols with small altars, arrows with arrowheads and obsidian blades—but on the whole, there was no palpable thread in this labyrinth, no overall order of things, no organizing metaphor behind the collection. It was evident that the museum was more the nation's storeroom—a product of seemingly unplanned accumulation—than its educator. Even if the museum experience was relatively new in the first half of the nineteenth century, when the collector mentality competed with the exuberant spirit of the fair in the "science" of organizing the museum, the Mexican national collection fell short of the organization and exhibition that characterized some of its European contemporaries. As a result, picking one's way through the collection, with its inexplicable juxtapositions, did not produce the edifying experience that normally justified the endowment of museums in other lands.[20] Mayer drolly remarked, "Gondra [then in charge of the museum] did no more than open the door of these saloons on stated days and smoke his cigar quietly in a corner, while the ladies, gentlemen, loafers, and *léperos*, wander[ed] from case to case, and lift[ed] up their hands in astonishment at the grotesque forms. What those forms and figures [meant]; what was represented by such an idol, or by another—receive[d] the unfailing Mexican answer, '*Quién sabe?*'—'who knows, who can tell?'"[21]

Instead of inspiring the visitor with a citizen's pride in Mexico, the museum gave the loafers who wandered into it an excuse for time wasting. As for the more interested scholar, the dearth of scholarly material on Mexican antiquities compounded the bewilderment most visitors experienced in front of these objects. Among the more important students of Mexican antiquities, Mayer listed León y Gama, Humboldt, and Kingsborough, but he pointed out that their works were not easily available. As a result, "a stranger [like himself] who had other occupations" would have a hard time receiving "an accurate or connected idea of Mexican art."[22] Mayer hoped his book would provide guidance for such a stranger. At the same time, by putting into circulation descriptions and drawings of Mexican antiquities, he strove to make them available for comparison with the objects drawn and studied by others.

Though Mayer's assessment of the state of Mexican antiquarianism was basically correct, Gondra did, in fairness, do more than sit in a corner and lethargically smoke his cigar. The museum's conservator shared with a handful of Mexicans a genuine interest in the study of Mexican antiquities, although their efforts became more visible in the years after Mayer left the country. There was, on the one hand, the suggestion that the museum, brought under the jurisdiction of the School of Mines in August of 1843, become more directly involved with public instruction, by organizing public lectures on archaeology, mineralogy, zoology, and botany.[23] But it was found that such a program required more funding than the museum was able to advance. In any case, Mexico City already hosted several literary and scientific associations loosely connected with the museum, which dedicated themselves, along the lines of societies for the advancement of learning that flourished in other countries, to public instruction. Their topics, whether literary or scientific in nature, were increasingly local, revealing a new commitment to discovering Mexico at a critical moment in the young nation's life. Mexico's "tragic decade"—between the war with Texas (1836) and the war with the United States (1846–48), both resulting in massive territorial losses for Mexico—was also a decade of introspection and soul-searching, when intellectuals and politicians alike sought to define what Mexico was about.[24] Their privileged medium for reflection was print—mostly periodicals but also books—which received an important impulse with the consolidation of several printing houses and with the manifest improvement in printing technology by the late 1830s. Print would turn out to be one of the museum's strongest allies.

Paper, Ink, and Communities of Print

In 1827 Icaza and Gondra had tried to make the museum's collection of antiquities visible through the *Colección de antigüedades*, but the publication was subject to the same limitations experienced by the museum itself. Over the next decade, the museum's conservators, taking another path, engaged foreign artists to produce albums of Mexican antiquities, but these experiments ended in frustration and even loss to Mexico's reputation for guarding its culture. Objects from the museum figured from time to time in the local press, in the late twenties and in the early thirties, for instance, in *El Iris* and in the *Registro trimestre*; however, these periodicals were ephemeral, as was the case with most periodical literature in Mexico in the first half of the nineteenth century.[25]

The consolidation of more-stable printing enterprises in Mexico did not happen until the late 1830s, in response to the same economic and technological currents that were expanding media in Europe and North America.[26] Often backed by wealthy editors, the print media took advantage of the specialized technical base and of a larger pool of experienced editors and writers. This could rightly be seen as the emergence of a Mexican "Republic of Letters," increasingly made up of members of the postindependence generation, who did not look back on imperial models.[27] In this context, there arose a demand for subjects of interest, and what suited this demand best was the exploration of a country that had long existed as a collectivity of separate regions, in a population that was lacking in literacy. Within these forums, ideas were communicated and debated; a public, albeit very small, that was avid both for facts about Mexico and for news from abroad felt itself part of a larger cultural endeavor.

Ignacio Cumplido (1811–87) was one of the more representative members of the new generation of editors who dominated the printing industry in mid-nineteenth-century Mexico. After holding a few jobs in his early twenties—apparently, he did some work as naturalist for the museum while training as an editor—Cumplido published his first periodical paper, *El fénix de la libertad*, which ran between December of 1831 and June of 1834 and which identified him strongly with the liberal cause and even earned him a certain martyrdom when the paper was shut down by Santa Anna under a law promulgated in May 1834.[28] A year later, Cumplido began publishing the *Calendario de México*, which he would put out almost every year for the rest of his life. In March 1837 Cumplido took over *El Mosaico mexicano*, which Isidro Gondra had launched in October of 1836.[29] This literary magazine would soon become a showcase for the members of a literary association, the Academia de Letrán, founded in 1836, which became a place of encounter between some of the more established cultural authorities of the moment, like José María Tornel (1787–1853), and a generation of emerging young writers, of liberal tendencies, who came to maturity in the postindependence years, including Guillermo Prieto (1818–97) and Ignacio Ramírez (1818–79). Many of them held public posts and met in the arena of politics as well. Years later, in his *Memoria de mis tiempos*, Prieto credited the Academia de Letrán for being the first association of this kind in Mexico and for having "emancipated" Mexican literature "from all other [literatures]" by giving it its "peculiar character."[30]

A common commitment to explore Mexico in writing brought members of the Academia de Letrán together with Cumplido, who, upon taking over *El Mosaico*, vowed to "nationalize" it—that is, to give precedence to Mexican poetic and scientific collaborations and to topics of national interest over translations of foreign articles. He envisioned an ample use of lithography, which was "appropriate for the representation of fields, rivers, mountains, and forests [. . .], portraits, and other expositions."[31] For this purpose, Cumplido imported into Mexico the first steam-driven Stanhope-type flatiron presses, which would enable him to print chromolithographs.[32] When *El Mosaico* came to an end in 1842, Cumplido started a new literary magazine, *El Museo mexicano*, with the collaboration of Agustín Massé and José Decaen, who were well known for the quality of their work and their expertise in the use of chromolithography.[33] Prieto and Manuel Payno (1810–94) were the editors in charge of *El Museo mexicano*, which, like its predecessor, continued to publish contributions by the members of the Academia de Letrán, in addition to those of the Conde de la Cortina and Mariano Otero (1817–50).

Though the Academia de Letrán was the first of its kind, it was not the only one. In 1840 a group of intellectuals—including the

Spanish ambassador in Mexico Angel Calderón de la Barca (1790–1861) and José Gómez de la Cortina—founded the Ateneo Mexicano, a name that put in a neat shorthand the ideology of Mexican liberal circles, who saw themselves and Mexico as being in the historical line of civilization going back to Greece. The Ateneo, which identified itself with the aim of "promoting useful knowledge," met in the Colegio de Santa María de Todos los Santos, where it held public lectures on a variety of topics.[34] In 1844 the organization founded the eponymous literary magazine *El Ateneo Mexicano*, published by Vicente García Torres (1811–93) between 1844 and 1845. Thus, the years between the late 1830s and the early 1840s saw the emergence of a political and cultural elite that promoted nationalism in literature and chose periodicals as an optimal medium for the exploration, discussion, and exchange of a broad range of topics of specifically national interest. The editors of *El Museo mexicano* expressed a commitment shared by other periodicals when they wrote in their introduction to the first issue:

We offer scholars and the literary-minded a light and agreeable review of a multitude of objects, all of them interesting and some of great importance. [. . .] No nation needs [journals] as much as we do. Without a literature of our own, the history of our origins still unpublished, the number of persons who cultivate the sciences reduced, a Mexican bibliography will not match up with those of countries set in the course of civilization for a long time to come. But the memory of past people, the recollection of the important events we have witnessed, the conservation of astonishing discoveries in the arts and the sciences, all the precious facts about the mysterious antiquities of our country, about its ancient and present state, about its natural history, so rich and surprising in all three branches of nature, all these monuments, we insist, all these facts collected until now, deserve to be conserved in a *Museum* [. . .]. Such is the purpose of a paper that hopes to be worthy of being called Mexican for the important articles it will publish in mineralogy, botany, zoology, antiquities, bibliography, and the history of our country.[35]

In other words, for its editors, *El Museo mexicano* would function as a counterpart to the National Museum by opening up more-accessible paper galleries to offer their joint audience objects pertaining to different categories: natural history, antiquities, and scientific and artistic "discoveries."[36]

It is here, on paper, rather than in the precincts of the financially destitute museum, that a "connected idea" of Mexican history could be encompassed. Here we can find explanations and interpretations that were so sadly lacking for a visitor like Brantz Mayer, who had to invent his own stories to piece the museum together. Like Mayer, Gondra and his contemporaries took to paper to give the public "guidance" to the museum and to answer questions about the Mexican past that were being posed by the antiquities dispersed over the Mexican landscape. What conventions for choosing, representing, and viewing them were being shaped both in Mexican and in international antiquarian circles? And what relevance did more or less "connected" histories told of Mexico's past have for envisioning Mexico's present? These questions, while the museum still lingered on as a dependent of the university's space, seemed easier to answer in print.

Paper Antiquities

In the course of the 1830s and 1840s, among the objects on display in print, those pertaining to Mexico's ancient past came to occupy an increasingly important space.[37] When Gondra started *El Mosaico mexicano* in October of 1836, he included a section for the study of antiquities, both from Mexico and from other parts of the world. When Cumplido took over the publication of the journal, he continued this section, supplying it with illustrations, and put Carlos María de Bustamante in charge of a new series, "Documentos inéditos y curiosos para la historia de Mexico." The goal of the section on antiquities, as Gondra defined it in his article "Arqueología," was to show "the most delectable and representative monuments of different civilizations": the pyramids, obelisks, and colossi of the Egyptians and the Persians; the hippodromes of the Greeks; the baths, amphitheaters, and triumphal arches of the

Romans; the pyramids and *teocalli* (temples) erected on mountain tops by the Mexicans.[38] The Mexicans' claim to a history as rich and ancient as any European one was illustrated by putting side by side Theban mummies and Cretan sarcophagi; fragments of del Río's expedition to Palenque in 1787; descriptions of the ruins of Mitla and Huatuzco by Dupaix; reports on the ruins of Monte-Real and Misantla, unearthed in the 1830s; and interpretations of a sculpture of the goddess Centeotl, donated by the convent of Santa Teresa to the National Museum. In *El Museo mexicano* Cumplido continued publishing articles on antiquities. Throughout 1844 the paper ran a series of articles under the title "Un Viejo Mundo en el Nuevo"; here, in his reviews of antiquarian literature, José María Tornel proclaimed that the antiquity of the New World was comparable to that of European civilization: "The authors of the *Antiquités mexicaines* have just operated a revolution in the sciences; Columbus discovered a new America and they have discovered an ancient America."[39]

A number of the articles on Mexican antiquities that came out in Mexican literary venues during these years were translations. Several books were published within a few years of one another and became obligatory references on Mexican antiquities: Baradère's *Antiquités mexicaines* (1834–36), Kingsborough's *Mexican Antiquities* (1830–48), and Stephens and Catherwood's *Incidents of Travel in Central America, Chiapas and Yucatán* (1841) and *Incidents of Travel in the Yucatán* (1843). And the international acclaim of these works did not go unnoticed in Mexico. Mexican students of antiquities responded to these books with an ambivalent mixture of admiration, gratitude, criticism, and, to some degree, patriotic resentment that it was foreigners and not Mexicans who were carrying out the more important research on Mexico's past. For Gondra, it was urgent to make "rectified" translations of these books available in Mexico, in order to put Mexican scholars "on the level of archaeological knowledge that was being disseminated in civilized countries" and to keep them informed about the "resolution of grand questions [. . .] of interest to the entire orb."[40] Gondra took a first step and published a translation of Charles Farcy's "Preliminary Discourse" from *Antiquités mexicaines*.

He had more than strictly antiquarian reasons for doing so—he hoped to set straight what he perceived to be widely circulating untruths about the exchange, years before, of Dupaix's manuscripts on Palenque for Baradère's stuffed birds, which we examined in a previous chapter. First, he wrote, the documents were not abandoned or forgotten by the time of Baradère's visit, as Farcy had implied; it had been Icaza and Gondra himself who had brought them to the attention of the Frenchman hot in pursuit of the Palenque Prize. Second, against accusations that "the inexactness of the drawings was equal to the fictitious beauty of the birds," Gondra insisted that Castañeda's drawings were indeed faithful to the objects they represented.[41] He abstained from commenting on Baradère's bird-stuffing expertise, perhaps viewing an apologetic on this topic as a dead loss, since Baradère's birds had disintegrated by the 1840s. Instead, Gondra criticized the illustrators of the *Antiquités mexicaines* for not rendering Castañeda's drawings truthfully; while on the topic, he charged Kingsborough's images as guilty of exaggeration. And he settled accounts with Waldeck, whom he accused of having defrauded the government on multiple fronts, including the way he spent the money that was meant for the study of Palenque.[42]

Over the course of almost a decade, articles on Mexican antiquities amounted to a handful of essays and a few images. Among the disparate topics broached in these magazines, where the articles covered volcanoes, bird nests, perfumery, advice for the education of girls, and hymns to the moon, Mexican antiquities were never a central focus. Still, they formed a constant and recognizable feature in the periodical literature between the late 1830s and the mid-1840s. In this context, such articles raised the question as to what editors, artists, and writers—including the museum's director, Gondra—achieved or aspired to achieve by putting into circulation descriptions and images of antiquities. On a basic level, as Gondra explained, he intended to make Mexican antiquities visible for a wider audience—in a way that antiquities in the museum were not—and to forge public interest in them.[43] In this way, "constant comparisons" between antiquities would "form the taste and excite the curiosity for [antiquities] with as much vivacity and enthusiasm as these objects are worthy of" and would attract collaborators to the field.[44]

Above all, Gondra hoped he would attract the attention and funding of the federal government. Funding would not only allow the museum to transform itself from the mere storeroom of historically interesting bric-a-brac that Mayer described, but it could also be used for the excavation and study of antiquities. Gondra's tactics came with some knowledge of the state apparatus he was trying to pressure, since he had held, after all, various posts in government. In spite of this, his connections never gave him the leverage to move his fellow legislators on behalf of antiquities. However, he did find some echo outside the government. Other writers also demanded government commitment to antiquities. As "L.E.," who signed one of the articles in the series "Monumentos mexicanos" that appeared in *El Museo mexicano*, maintained, the study of antiquities by Mexicans was more urgent than ever; the Spanish government had invested more effort and money into the study of preconquest ruins than postindependence governments did. As a result, foreigners explored and extracted monuments and mocked Mexicans, as they mocked the Arabs, for permitting the removal of these objects.[45] Since the foundation of the National Museum, its conservators had insisted that unless Mexicans proved they could claim, physically and intellectually, the vestiges of Mexico's ancient past, they risked falling into the same category as "other savages." To "lift the obscure veil that covered the history of [the] country," as Gondra persuaded his contemporaries to do, was at the same time a way to reveal the state of its present civilization.[46]

Print would become a fitting medium for the advancement of antiquarian studies in Mexico; unlike other objects, antiquities often had a singularity, fragility, or cumbersomeness that made them too delicate or too heavy to be easily transported. Paper brought both people and things together, as it circulated in ways that the objects themselves could not, making them available, through representations and descriptions, to collectors and scholars and allowing for the kind of "collaborative" and "constant" work that Gondra thought was fundamental for the progress of antiquarian studies. More than the physical objects themselves, then, it was traveling paper collections—as they exchanged hands between museums and learned societies, between scholars and interested laymen—that set the terms for the meanings of antiquities within the circles of the various disciplines (anthropology, history, and archaeology) throughout the nineteenth century. Paper gave relevance to certain objects or types of objects; allowed for the discussion of (moral, political, and aesthetic) criteria for the selection and organization of antiquities into canons; determined the grounds for their comparison between one another; disciplined ways of seeing, of representing, and of talking about them; created agendas for future archaeological expeditions; and influenced collecting trends and strategies both among amateurs and museums.[47] In other words, paper collections of antiquities, whose production and circulation was crucially accelerated by the increasing use of lithography, helped bring about what archaeological historian Alain Schnapp has described as the nineteenth-century transformation of antiquities into the objects of study and proof of the fledgling science of archaeology.[48]

Finally, paper, especially periodicals, with their ad hoc editing structures and relatively quick rhythms—rhythms that were related to the contract between the periodical and the subscriber, rather than to the scholar and his or her object of study—provided the contemporaneity within which opinion and agendas vied for notice. This is especially important in the Mexican case; for during this period, it is difficult to imagine a book by a Mexican author that could comprehensively explain the country's ancient past. A book-length publication would have represented a risky financial enterprise for a publishing house and would have called for a kind of permanent positioning that few writers would have embraced at a moment when the value—financial, intellectual, historical, and symbolic—of Mexican antiquities was undetermined and when the study of antiquities produced more questions than answers.

Heirs to Antiquity

Among these questions, few were as consuming, in both the popular and antiquarian circles of the 1840s, as those concerning the origin and identity of America's preconquest peoples. If antiquarian studies attested to the formidable accomplishments of ancient American civilizations, questions inevitably followed regarding who America's ancient dwellers were, what had happened to them, and who their descendants were. In turn, the answers to these inquiries led to charged questions about ownership: Who were the true heirs of Mexico's ancient past? And consequently, who could rightly own the vestiges of antiquity?

Shared wisdom among contemporary antiquarian circles was that the enlightened and cultured ancient peoples who had left behind spectacular antiquities were Toltecs. But this only postponed the answer; in fact, Mexican papers bore testimony to the lack of any central consensus concerning the identity of the Toltecs, reporting now one, now another theory indiscriminately. It was a field in which the unknowns, far from enforcing intellectual modesty, became the base for vast and fantastic intellectual superstructures. Kingsborough proposed an unconventional hypothesis—rejected by most of his contemporaries, although finding a distinct echo among American Mormons—that American civilization had been the work of the lost thirteenth tribe of Israel.[49] The collaborators to the *Antiquités mexicaines* posited that America's ancient civilization had an Egyptian, an Indian, or a Phoenician origin, but they acknowledged that there was no firm explanation for how the links between the continents took place.

> What a new abyss to fill for the historian, the geologist, the antiquarian, all avid for the science of the past! What became of the supposed submersion of that Atlantis, of which certain proofs still signal its existence, albeit in an uncertain manner? What becomes of that brilliant theory of the recent emergence of the double American continent, theory based on its young human races and on its young volcanoes, not yet extinct? Where did the first inhabitants come from? Is it from Asia or Africa that, before Europe had any pretensions, they carried their arts and the other fruits of their civilization? How many centuries did they thrive for?[50]

This line of questioning led many to speculate about what had happened to the ancient builders of America's ancient civilization; or as the editors of *Antiquités mexicaines* wondered, "What catastrophe could have changed the face of those lands, to the point of effacing from the memory of men their ancient splendor?"[51] There was some agreement that the ancient dwellers had been effaced by a combination of human and natural causes. Kingsborough and the team of writers who participated in the *Antiquités mexicaines* opined that the Toltecs had suffered a massive die-off sometime between the sixth and the eleventh centuries AD, with a remnant retreating south toward Peru—leaving vestiges like Teotihuacan, Cholula, Mitla, and Palenque on the way—in the face of famine, pestilence, natural calamity, or invasions of barbarous tribes, which included the Chichimecs and the Aztecs. But whether those first civilizations had died by natural catastrophes or at the hands of barbarians, one thing was certain: the enlightened builders of ancient America had long perished by the time of the Spanish conquest. There were, in other words, few links between the ancient dwellers and the peoples of the New World encountered there by the Spanish in the sixteenth century and, by extension, the American Indians, who continued to make up most of Mexico's "ignorant" and "superstitious" population in the nineteenth century.

Evidence from other disciplines seemed to bear out these conclusions. By the nineteenth century, a range of fields of inquiry—from chemistry, comparative anatomy, and geology to history, geography, paleography, and philology—were called on to supply "positive truths" (like those produced by the natural sciences) for the study of archaeology.[52] Among the natural "facts" that enjoyed great popularity in the Mexican papers of the moment were those produced by phrenology and incipient racial studies. It was popular, for instance, to compare the heads of criminals and contemporary Indians.[53] Along less tendentious lines, comparisons were made between American races and those of other continents, which were backed up by correlations between the profiles and facial angles of different human "species" (Caucasians, Mongols, Ethiopians, Americans, Malays, and Africans).[54] Illustrations were often taken from pieces of sculpture, with, for instance, the superposition of the profile of the Greek Ariadna with the Venus of the Hottentots. Deep conclusions were drawn about the respective moral traits one could infer from noses, lips, and jaws.[55] It is not surprising that this practice would be used to frame such purely fantastic speculations such as that positing the existence of "giant races" in America.[56] The exchanges between the pseudosciences of the character of races and peoples and the discipline of antiquities ran deep; reports about American antiquities and articles on phrenological and character archetypes often appeared side by side in the same journal.

Together, ruins, carved stones, clay figurines, profiles, skulls, giant bones, and rocks demarcated a fraught and crowded space where answers about the origins of America's first enlightened dwellers and, correlatively, speculation about their disappearance, or about the causes that led to the degradation of their descendants, were beginning to take shape.[57] The questions, posed in the "scientific" domain, were not alien to issues that moved within the larger public domain, for these epistemological questions came with politically and culturally charged motives. The social context in which anatomical, geological, and archaeological "facts" were debated was one that was touched at every point by conflicts of ethnicity, nationality, and institutions themselves. The conclusion that contemporary Indians and the enlightened dwellers of the past had little in common with one another could be used, with a good conscience, to dispossess the present-day Indian from the lands, natural resources, and ruins they must have usurped in some distant past.[58]

But even as it was clear to certain speculative scholars that antiquities could not possibly belong to contemporary Indians, it was still not necessarily the case that the heirs of the Toltecs were the coterie around, for instance, Santa Anna. Men like Gondra and Cumplido advocated the National Museum to show that the country was worthy of its civilizational mission; until they really had a museum, it would seem—especially to Europeans and North Americans— that the country was not a worthy guardian of civilizations that had preceded it. Hence, the country's antiquities would be better placed elsewhere. The turn to print seemed a cheap way to escape this double bind. It would, in one blow, make Mexican antiquities public and provide the space for scholars to engage with Mexican antiquities in light of the topical questions of contemporary antiquarianism. Ironically, this nationalistic effort culminated with a translation project: the publication of two different translations of U.S. historian William H. Prescott's *History of the Conquest of Mexico* (1843), which offered new opportunities for showcasing materials from Mexico's ancient past.

Prescott's *History of the Conquest of Mexico*

After publishing, to international acclaim, his *History of the Reign of Ferdinand and Isabella* (1837), Boston-based historian William H. Prescott (1796–1859) began work on a history of the conquest of Mexico. What Prescott had in mind, as he pored over documents that Spanish imperial policy had kept under wraps for over three centuries, was a balanced view of the conquest, somewhere between Antonio de Solís's *Historia de la Conquista de México* (1684), which sang "an undiluted panegyric" to Cortés, and William Robertson's *History of America* (1777), which focused on the errors and the excesses of the conquerors. By contrast, Prescott strove to "expose in strongest colors the excesses of the Conquerors [while giving] them the benefit of such mitigating reflections as might be suggested by the circumstances and the period in which they lived." In other words, Prescott "endeavored to present not only a picture in itself, but true to its proper light, [. . .] to the spirit of the times."[59]

As he made inroads in his readings, Prescott realized that, to capture the "truth" about Cortés's enterprise in its full context, he needed to understand as much as possible about the vanquished. The story of the "discovery" and conquest proper begin in book 2, preceded by a sweeping view of Aztec civilization, meant to "enable the reader to understand the difficulties which the Spaniards encountered in their subjugation."[60] Prescott's history is based primarily on two types of sources, preconquest and colonial, even as the historian declared repeatedly to have held little faith in either. He found Mexican hieroglyphic sources—as reproduced in Kingsborough's

Mexican Antiquities—to be inferior to those of the Chinese and the Egyptians; for Prescott, Mexican hieroglyphs were little more than "clumsy [. . .], grotesque caricatures of the human figure."[61] Above all, he shunned Mexican hieroglyphs for the "arbitrary" interpretations to which they gave rise. "A Mexican text looks often like a collection of pictures, each of them [. . .] having to be made out separately,"[62] he wrote. Though he conceded that in ancient times Mexican hieroglyphs were "read" by individuals trained in their meaning, Prescott claimed that the art of "reading" ancient "texts" had been lost; hence, these sources were of little help to the historian. He applauded, on the other hand, efforts to find the "literary relics of Toltec predecessors," which he expected would prove to be more legible than those of the Mexicans.[63] Colonial works dealing with preconquest Mexico, written overwhelmingly by missionaries and men of the church, had a little more merit for Prescott, though he warned against the Catholic "bigotry" of a chronicler like Torquemada and the tendency to "load" histories with profane and biblical examples, in the case of Clavigero. Prescott saw value in Sahagún and Boturini and blamed Spanish imperial policy for the fact that their manuscripts remained unpublished through colonial times.[64]

So having used philological criticism to sort through his sources, Prescott began his *History of the Conquest of Mexico* with a discussion of the nature of the "primitive races" that settled central Mexico. Prescott built on the view he attributed to Humboldt, that this territory had been inhabited by Toltecs, a people well instructed in architecture, agriculture, metalwork, and in many of the most useful mechanic arts, who "disappeared from the land as silently and mysteriously as they had entered it."[65] On came "numerous and rude tribes," like the Chichimecs, followed by the Aztecs and the Acolhuas. Prescott followed the fate of these latter two tribes, as they settled in Tenochtitlan and Texcoco, respectively, to acquaint the reader with their legislature, politics, mythology, religion, agriculture, mechanical arts, arithmetic, astronomy, chronology, and hieroglyphic system of writing. Overall, he had a difficult time reconciling the more gruesome aspects of Mexican civilization—the practice of human sacrifice and cannibalism, for instance—with

Mexican refined forms of monarchic succession and "great proficiency in [. . .] the social and mechanic arts"; to reconcile these customs, he made recourse to the mythical Toltecs, reminding his reader that "all that deserved the name of science in Mexico came" from the Toltecs, "who never stained their altars and still less their banquets, with the blood of man."[66] Prescott had an equally hard time envisioning modern Mexicans as capable of devising enlightened polities, but he asked his public to think of them as

only a conquered race, as different from their ancestors as are the modern Egyptians from those who built [. . .] the temples and palaces, whose magnificent wrecks strew the borders of the Nile, at Luxor and Karnac. The difference is not so great as between the ancient Greek and his degenerate descendant, lounging among the masterpieces of art which he has scarcely taste enough to admire [though] he breathes the same atmosphere, is warmed by the same sun, nourished by the same scenes, as those who fell at Marathon and who won trophies at Olympic Pisa. The same blood flows in his veins that flowed in theirs. But ages of tyranny have passed over him.[67]

Prescott returned to the topic of the origin and nature of ancient Mexican civilization in an appendix to the second volume of his *History of the Conquest of Mexico*, meaning that he continued to think about it as the first volume was being published. Although Prescott agreed that there were important similarities between the ancient civilizations of the Old and New Worlds—the memory of a universal deluge preserved in the material and written vestiges of several peoples; the purported similarities between the pyramid at Cholula and the Tower of Babel; the presence of crosses and references to the baptism in the monuments of the New World—he, like his fellow American John Lloyd Stephens, believed that students of Mexico's ancient past might have chosen to stress coincidences over differences. So he invited the reader to consider also discrepancies between the Old and the New Worlds. Ancient Mexicans, for instance, did not make use of iron and did not drink milk, and their tools, sculptures, and hieroglyphs looked nothing like those of the Old World. This emphasis led him to postulate an autochthonous origin of Mexican civilization. If Indians derived from an emigration from Asia, that preceded the discovery of iron, at the very least.[68]

The *History of the Conquest of Mexico* was published in New York in December of 1843. On January 9, 1844, Prescott sent a copy of the book to Lucas Alamán. The *History* received positive reviews in various North American papers, though it would be nine months before it was mentioned in the Mexican press.[69] On September 4, 1844, the conservative-leaning paper *El Defensor de la integridad nacional* reported that the American edition had sold four thousand copies of the book and that all one thousand copies of the British edition had sold out. A new British edition was being prepared. Once news of the *History* reached the Mexican press, the book continued to make headlines. On September 19 Cumplido's *Siglo XIX* published a translation of Prescott's prologue. Two days later, *El Defensor* announced that the editor García Torres was selling subscriptions to a translation of the *History*, which would include notes by Alamán, prints supplied by the Conde de la Cortina, and drawings of antiquities supplied by Gondra; the book would be issued in installments of thirty-two pages, at 2 reals each, and would consist of two five-hundred-page volumes. A month and a half later, on November 5, Cumplido announced that he would publish a different translation, with contributions by several authors, many of whom had been collaborating on Cumplido's periodicals for some years: Bustamante would review pre-Hispanic names; Gómez de la Cortina would supply documents; Gondra, prints of objects from the National Museum; Juan de Orbegoso and Pedro García Conde, maps and plans; Andrés de Quintana Roo, additions to Prescott's text; and José María Tornel would write a "critical and explanatory note" on Cortés's resting place, shrouded in mystery ever since Alamán had removed the conquistador's remains from the tomb in the Hospital de Jesús.

How can we account for the fact that at a time when the Mexican press had shown little urgency to translate some of the more celebrated recent books on the topic of Mexico's ancient history, such as Baradère's and Kingsborough's, two separate translations of Prescott's book were underwritten and completed? There are several possible reasons, although none of them seems decisive. There are financial considerations in which the two editors might have wanted to capitalize on the book's immediate popularity in the United States and Britain. In fact, in the "Advertencia" in his edition of Prescott's *History*, García Torres made note of the book's celebrity in the United States and of the fact that a new edition of fifty thousand copies was being prepared there. Against this, one must place the fact that other best-selling books with a Mexican focus were also popular at the time; for example, Stephens's *Incidents of Travel in Central America, Chiapas, and Yucatán* sold twenty thousand copies in the first three months after publication.[70] Here, a different rationale might have accounted for the preference of Prescott's *History* over Stephens's *Incidents*; for editors in Mexico City, Prescott's book narrated a history that was, in a way, local, part of their city's very history. Stephens's, on the other hand, spoke of events in the far-off peninsula, which was, between 1841 and 1848, the independent Republic of Yucatán. The regional import of each of these books was not lost on their contemporaries; writing in the *Registro yucateco* in 1845, Justo Sierra O'Reilly praised the translation of Prescott's book into Spanish and expressed the hope that someone would translate Stephens's work, for the glory of Yucatán.[71] Eventually, Sierra decided to do the job himself, with a translation issued in 1848.

Additionally, there might have been ideological differences between the two Prescott translations, which took different stances on Mexico's ancient and colonial history. This would be consistent with, on the one hand, the participation of Alamán, who identified the birth of the nation with the conquest, and with, on the other, Cumplido's initial engagement of writers like Bustamante, who thought it was in the country's ancient history where one had to seek a national past. Still, we should refrain from thinking of the García Torres edition as lacking antiquarian interest. Both Cumplido and García Torres asked Gondra to provide images of antiquities from the National Museum, and he embraced the opportunity to display objects from the collection.

Finally, the two translations of Prescott's *History* entailed different editorial projects. García Torres saw his edition as a milestone between the recent translation of Francisco Javier Clavigero's *Historia antigua de México* (1844), with a focus on Mexico's ancient past, and Lucas Alamán's *Disertaciones sobre la historia nacional* (1844–49), which began where Prescott ended, with the years after the Spanish conquest, to tell a story of Mexico's three centuries of Spanish rule. For García Torres, the three books constituted an indispensable course in Mexican history. Cumplido, on the other hand, was probably imagining an ambitious collaborative project, along the lines of Baradère's *Antiquités mexicaines*, that would bring together the most interesting scientific studies on Mexico's past by Mexican scholars, providing them with a showcase for their work.

The García Torres translation came out first, with the first installments of the *Historia de la conquista de Méjico, con un bosquejo preliminar de la civilización de los antiguos mejicanos y la vida del conquistador Hernán Cortés* going on sale on October 2, 1844. The last installments came out four years later, in 1848. García Torres's *Historia* included a series of footnotes by Alamán, where the latter took issue with facts in Prescott's narrative. His most important critiques were not factual, though; they concerned some of Prescott's interpretations. He disapproved of Prescott's offensive habit of calling the Aztecs "barbarous," affirming that a nation that had achieved the form of government, legislature, and arts that the Mexicans had was far from barbarous.[72] Alamán's most important objection to Prescott's *History* addressed the latter's thinly veiled disdain for Catholic historians as generally untrustworthy:

The reader might have noted the acrimony with which Mr. Prescott treats all the missionaries who have written the history of America [. . .] in all those cases in which their writings touch on matters related with their pious opinions. Generally guilty of these defects are Protestant authors, especially those from the US who conserve their grandfathers' persecuting zeal, much abated among European Protestants. This zeal manifests itself in this constant carping, and [in the failure to] quote any of the opinions of those who follow a different creed without treating them to a burlesque or satirical epithet.[73]

Alamán's footnotes to Prescott's text were not the only thing that made the text a different experience for Mexican readers than for the American and British audiences; visually, the García Torres edition outdid in copiousness and splendor the Harper and Brothers edition of the *History*. The latter included a handful of images (three different portraits of Cortés, his coat of arms, and some maps and plans); by contrast, García Torres's edition incorporated forty-three lithographs by Hipólito Salazar that roughly followed Prescott's narrative. We shall be addressing them later.

Cumplido's edition, the three-volume *Historia de la Conquista de México*, translated by Joaquín Navarro, came out between late 1844 and 1846. It included substantial additions to Prescott's original text, though it was not the collaborative enterprise Cumplido had originally envisioned. By the time the second volume was ready for publication, none of Cumplido's would-be collaborators, with the exception of Gondra, had followed through on their promises. In itself, this is indicative of just how difficult it was to accomplish collaborative work, of the kind Baradère and St.-Priest had achieved in their *Antiquités*, in Mexico, where the cultural circles interested in Mexican history were still dispersed, lax, and unorganized. Still, Cumplido believed that subscribers to the book would not be disappointed; in the end, one of the subscribers had come forth with "comprehensive notes, some critical, others explicative," which, Cumplido believed, would contribute to a better understanding of the book.[74] That subscriber was José Fernando Ramírez (1804–71), a senator for the state of Durango, whose rise to eminence as an antiquarian and historian would involve him deeply and, ultimately, tragically in the history of the National Museum and the politics of Mexico.

There is something deeply interesting about approaching Ramírez's footnotes in a chapter devoted to the paper museum; for if those articles and essays on antiquities to which we have referred above could be thought of as the equivalent of galleries exposing the National Museum's treasures, Ramírez's 125-page "Notas y esclarecimientos," appended to the second volume of the Cumplido edition, could be thought of as the workshop in the basement under the public galleries, where scholars contemplate the fragmentary state of the relics they have gathered and attempt to correct biases and legends with hard fact and reason. To put it another way, Ramírez began his career by carefully digging under and subverting Prescott's text, thereby presaging the standard of ethnographic neutrality, rigorous historical methodology, and freedom from what we would now call Orientalist assumptions that would eventually consign the great romantic vision of ancient Mexican civilization to belles lettres rather than social science.

Ramírez began his "Notas and esclarecimientos" with a historiographical review of the literature on the conquest of Mexico. For Ramírez, Prescott's book on the conquest was crucial because, if for no other reason, it was the first one in over half a century. The last wave of works on conquest history happened between 1770 and 1780: Mariano de Echeverría y Veytia's *Historia antigua de México*, Robertson's *History of America*, Andrés Cavo's *Historia civil y política de México*, and Francisco Xavier Clavijero's *Storia antica del Messico*.[75] But since, Ramírez thought, "exuberance tends to be precursor to poverty," it would be a long time before any of these writings would appear in Spanish and circulate in Mexico. Robertson's book ended up on the Inquisition index, and the Spanish government forbade the translation of Clavijero's book into Spanish. Not until the late 1830s did Mexican readers begin to have access to some of these books. So while antiquarian studies were taking important strides forward—with works by León y Gama, Dupaix, Humboldt, Kingsborough, and Stephens and Catherwood—the "civil part" of Mexican history was "languishing," declared Ramírez. In this context, the importance of Prescott's book was hard to overstate; the U.S. historian put an end to the dry spell in the history of Mexico's conquest, by producing what Ramírez thought was an erudite book of rare diligence, beauty, and luxury of ideas.

Ramírez balanced enthusiastic praise for Prescott's accomplishment with acute criticism for what he considered to be Prescott's most blatant fault—an error of judgment, attributable to the U.S. historian's "instinctive racial distancing" from Cortés's adversaries. This inclined Prescott to see history through the lens of an intellectually damaging partisanship that exalted the figure of the conquistador while heaping "immoderate criticism" on the Mexicans. In one of the more eloquent and more frequently quoted passages, Ramírez summarized his critique in the following terms:

> Mr Prescott has taken up the pen to write the history of *barbarians*: word which, when alternated with that of *savages*, dominates the entire course of his history [. . .]. Since it is an army of *barbarians* that fights off the invaders, their battle cries could not be called by the same name as those of a civilized people; consequently, Mexicans *howled*, and their forces did not *withdraw*, but *fled*. By reason of the same technical language, [Prescott] calls their indomitable valor *rabid furor*, and explains those innumerable and stupendous examples [. . .] of heroism and abnegation not as the voluntary immolation inspired by the holy fire of liberty and of the motherland, but as the brutal effects of rancor, hatred, and irrational ferocity. It is strange that a great historian would lower his majestic pace to the dust of futile criticisms—reserved for feminine affectations and squeamishness—to amuse himself by assessing the melodiousness or harshness of certain Mexican words, of which someone accustomed to Yankee Doodle harmonies, by the way, cannot be a competent judge.[76]

For Ramírez, Prescott's rhetoric was symptomatic of a profound misunderstanding of the state of Mexican civilization at the time of the conquest, as evidenced in Prescott's faulty assertions concerning the alleged simplicity of the Mexican arithmetical and chronological systems, the unintelligibility of the Mexican glyph system, and the incompatibility between the practice of human sacrifice and intellectual and moral progress. Ramírez answered Prescott's claims one by one, dedicating most of his 125 densely argued pages to two topics in particular: human sacrifice and hieroglyphic writing.[77] Regarding sacrifice, Ramírez pointed out that Old World civilizations also engaged in human sacrifice, though Prescott did not seem to think it had led to their degeneration. As for Prescott's disdain for Mexican hieroglyphs, Ramírez blamed Enlightenment historians, with their penchant for filtering the pattern of fact disclosed by events through their philosophical schemas; for disqualifying, misinterpreting, and deriding ancient Mexican records; and for claiming that they all-too-irretrievably mixed fact and fable to be of any use in the search for the truth. However, as Ramírez pointed out, the high standard disqualifying ancient Mexican accounts was lowered considerably when it came to Europe's own history—Marco Polo could have been accused of mythmaking too. Ramírez vindicated hieroglyphs and ancient texts as reliable sources for the scholar who exercised caution and method. He himself would make the search for a dependable method for reading Mexican hieroglyphs a steadfast pursuit during his life.

For Ramírez, this search had to begin with building up an archive. Considering the dearth of historical sources to be a serious obstacle for the study of ancient Mexican history, he assessed the availability and reliability of sources and approved of Humboldt's and Kingsborough's efforts to rehabilitate preconquest documents as serious scholarly material. In his "Notas y esclarecimientos," Ramírez turned to Kingsborough's reproductions of Mexican codices to introduce his reader to Mexican hieroglyphs. These, he explained, were not phonetic—though early missionaries had made phonetic use of them to transmit Christian messages—but were conventional symbols, representing names, ideas, directions, and movements; as such, they proved suitable for recording places and events. Mexican codices were, in this regard, more reliable than Herodotus, who had left few chronological references. By contrast, by making use of their hieroglyphs, Mexicans had commemorated moments in human history alongside earthquakes and eclipses; as a result, historical events could be deciphered and dated by comparing different sources with one another and with other independent systems of timekeeping, such as astronomical events. Therefore, Ramírez insisted, "it was imperative to write a detailed history of the sky in order to write that of the earth."[78]

Ramírez concluded his essay with a lesson in hieroglyphic reading that was a deliberate tour de force, interpreting four stone monuments at the National Museum that had been deemed undecipherable even by authorities in Mexican antiquities like León y Gama and Gondra. We will consider Ramírez's first explanation, of a "basalt cylinder, made up of sticks tied up, in the style of a Roman fascies," which, in ancient Mexico, referred to the "tying up of the years," the end of a fifty-two-year cycle (fig. 14). That moment, Ramírez explained, could have corresponded to any of the years 1402, 1454, 1507, for instance. If the "fascies" represented the end of an era and the beginning of another, the symbol on the front of the bundle, 2 *Acatl* (2 Reed), did not correspond to the first year of the new cycle among the Mexicans, which normally began with 1 *Tochtli* (1 Rabbit). The sign *Tochtli*, however, proved to be a calamitous one, associated with hunger and pestilence: 1454 was the year of the "great hunger" that decimated Mexican people, as recorded in the codex *Telleriano Remensis*. When the cycle began anew, in 1506, the year of the rabbit brought hunger again, as registered again in the *Telleriano Remensis* and in the *Vatican Codex*. So rather than begin the cycle with an accursed year, Moctezuma II reformed the calendar and postponed the tying of the years until the next year, 2 *Acatl*. The reliefs on the bases of the cylinder, noted Ramírez, represented fire and rain gods and denoted—as described by Sahagún and Torquemada—the first day and the first month of the year, respectively. Pursuing his deductions, Ramírez concluded that the basalt monument was both a commemorative monument, the record of the year of calendar reform, and a normative one, dictating Mexican chronology in the years to come. The monument was not undecipherable, after all. Ramírez's lesson in hieroglyphic reading announced an important turning point in the study of Mexico's ancient past: it presaged a new focus almost exclusively on Mexican sources, as opposed to the pursuit of coincidences with objects from other ancient civilizations, and the expansion of those sources to include preconquest and colonial documents, objects and chronological calculations, topography, and philology. Ramírez ended his discussion of the

14. Four monumental stones. Image between pp. 106 and 107. Cumplido edition of *Historia de la conquista de México*, vol. 2. BNAH, Secretary of Culture-INAH-Mex-Photo Library Constantino Reyes Valerio. Reproduction authorized by the National Institute of Anthropology and History.

stone monuments from the National Museum with a plea for the formation of a rich and informed collection of Mexican glyphs.

The third volume of the Cumplido edition bears little relation to Prescott's *History*. It consists of seventy-one plates of reproductions, preceded by lengthy explanations, of objects from the National Museum, codices, colonial manuscripts, and paintings, all of which were chosen by Gondra and executed mostly by Joaquín Heredia, who had worked with Cumplido on *El Mosaico mexicano* and *El Museo mexicano*. Gondra was responsible for the visual material displayed in the García Torres edition as well. Still, there are significant differences in the use of illustrations between the two editions. The main difference can be summed up in the following way: the García Torres edition interpolated images throughout the translation of Prescott's text and, besides summary captions at the bottom of each image, gave the reader no further information about them. In the Cumplido edition, the images, separated from Prescott's history, were gathered together in an album, becoming the protagonists through which Gondra rewrites Mexican history, sometimes parallel to and other times in contradiction with Prescott's narrative. The third volume of the Cumplido edition is practically a museum catalogue—a guided and informed tour of Mexican history on the basis of material from the National Museum.

The plates chronologically follow Prescott's book, with the first group of illustrations related to Mexico's antiquity, the succeeding group related to the encounter between the Aztecs and the Spanish, and the final group related to the conquest proper. Gondra begins by showing codices depicting the Aztec pilgrimage and the foundation of Mexico City. Next come genealogical sheets of the Mexican dynasty; objects related to Mexican mythology and religion, such as sculptures of the gods Huitzilopochtli and Quetzalcóatl, sacrificial instruments and urns, and calendar wheels; and finally weapons, tools used for carving sculptures, and musical instruments, to give a broad sense of the culture and everyday life. Some of the plates group together types of objects, as in the case of sculpting tools, small idols from Yucatán, and musical instruments, as one would display objects in a vitrine (figs. 15, 16, 17, 18). To illustrate the conquest, Gondra selected a series of rare documents produced in Tlaxcala, depicting the meeting between Cortés and the Tlaxcaltecas, and images of "memorable events, ceremonies, sacrifices, and costumes," based on Diego Panes y Abellán's unpublished manuscript (held at the National Museum) "Teatro de Nueva España en su gentilismo y conquista," as well as reproductions of the portraits of Ferdinand, Isabella, and Cortés that Brantz Mayer had admired in the National Museum a few years earlier.[79]

Gondra provided the illustrations with 154 pages of explanations—drawing primarily on Humboldt, Baradère, and Kingsborough—about the origin, physical appearance (size, material, cover, state of preservation), and possible uses of the objects in each plate. In some cases, he included firsthand information. Thus, speaking about naturalistic sculptures of animals, Gondra related the following anecdote: when the chief of a "barbarian tribe from the north" saw a sculpture of the native dogs with hanging bellies, of the kind ancient Mexicans raised for food, he assured the museum curator that, in his travels, he had come upon this race of dogs, which were still fattened up, like pigs, for food.[80] It is a fascinating image, this of a tribal chief from the Sandia Mountains (in present-day New Mexico) touring the museum, but Gondra unfortunately supplies us with no more details about the visit.

In his explanations, Gondra returns repeatedly to the issues of authenticity and autochthonousness, especially concerning those objects that did not look "Mexican." In such cases, Gondra resorted to reconstructing the biography of the object, bringing into play verifiable stories of its "discovery," the credibility of the donor, and comparisons with similar objects. For instance, in the case of a sacrificial urn decorated with a grape leaf pattern, which had been noted by antiquarians such as Waldeck and Franck for its "Chinese" appearance, Gondra insisted that it was Mexican, having formed part of the collection of objects from the Isla de Sacrificios donated to the museum by Antonio López Luna in the late 1820s. But this was not all. The bishop of Puebla had donated a similar vessel found in an excavation in Tepeaca, and Kingsborough and Baradère had referred to the presence of similar vessels in the Mosquito Coast

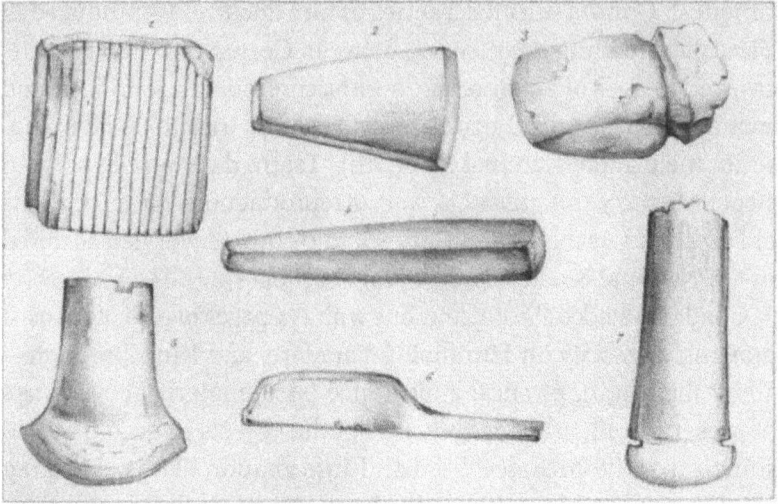

15. Carving instruments of the Aztecs. Lithograph. Plate 20. Cumplido edition of *Historia de la conquista de México*, vol. 3. BNAH, Secretary of Culture-INAH-Mex-Photo Library Constantino Reyes Valerio. Reproduction authorized by the National Institute of Anthropology and History.

region (in eastern Nicaragua). Gondra concluded that urns of this type of ornamentation and design, used to collect the blood of sacrificial victims, belonged to remote American antiquity.

Similarly, Gondra defended the authenticity of a mustached Quetzalcóatl, a relief found originally in Culhuacan; its features, explained Gondra, were similar to those of a Quetzalcóatl statuette recently extracted from the pyramid at Papantla. Javier Echeverría, a collector, possessed a golden version of it. For the museum conservator, the representations of this character, physically different from ancient or contemporary American Indians, were proof that the Toltecs arrived in America sometime in the seventh century, bringing with them "a sweet religion" that offered "flowers and fruit for their gods." The Chichimecs would later invest the vestiges left behind by the Toltecs with the symbols and meanings of their own less elevated beliefs.[81]

At a moment when scholars saw Mexican antiquities through the lens of Etruscan, Chinese, or Egyptian antiquities they were familiar with, Gondra's comparisons ask questions about how to recog-

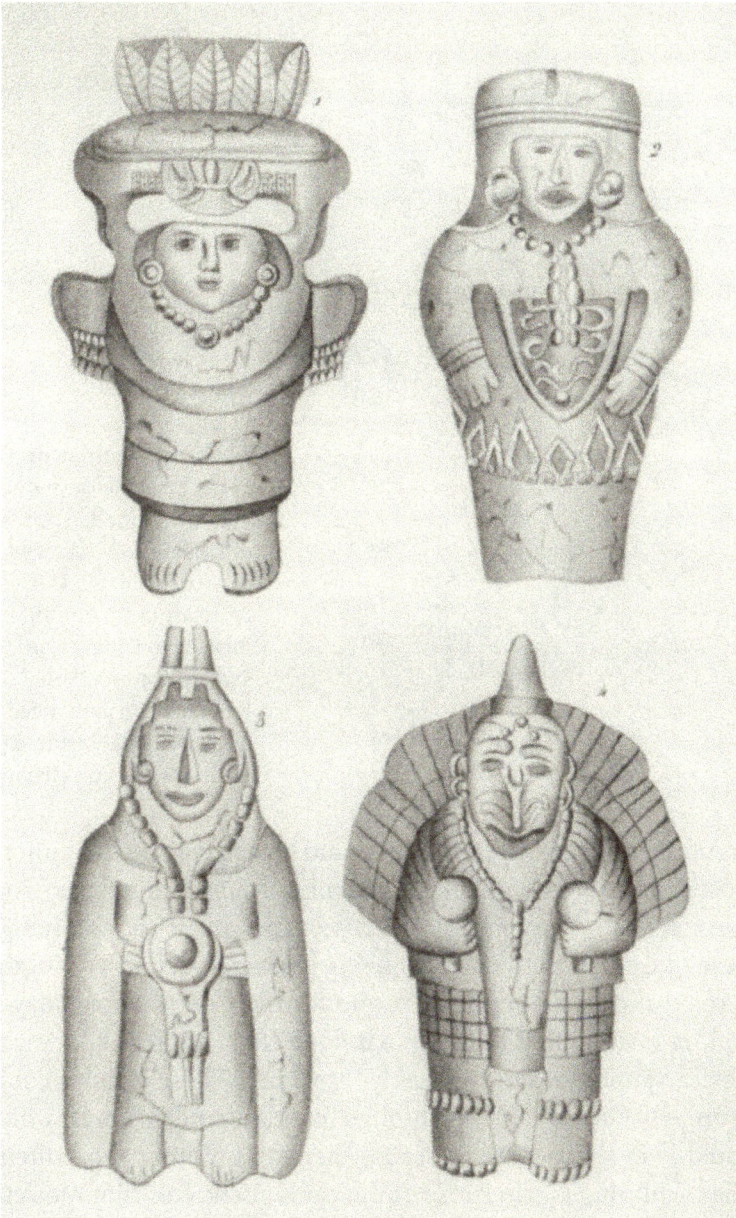

16. Idols from Yucatán. Lithograph. Plate 18. Cumplido edition of *Historia de la conquista de México*, vol. 3. BNAH, Secretary of Culture-INAH-Mex-Photo Library Constantino Reyes Valerio. Reproduction authorized by the National Institute of Anthropology and History.

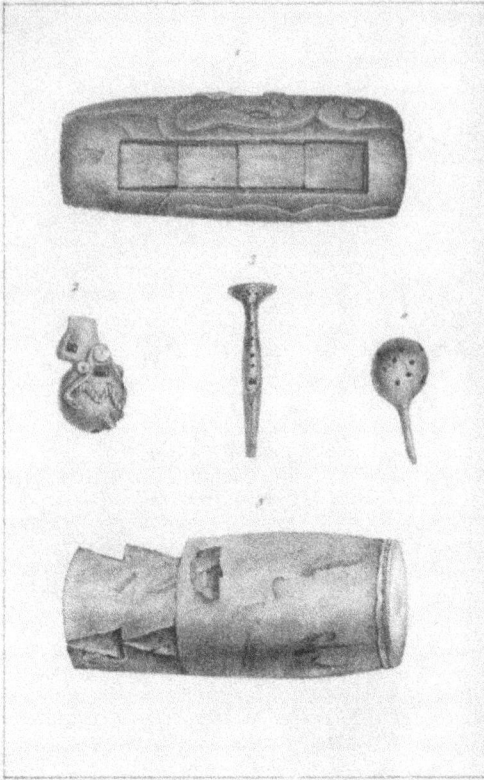

17. Musical instruments of the Aztecs. Lithograph. Plate 21. Cumplido edition of *Historia de la conquista de México*, vol. 3. BNAH, Secretary of Culture-INAH-Mex-Photo Library Constantino Reyes Valerio. Reproduction authorized by the National Institute of Anthropology and History.

nize authentic Mexican antiquities and how to have one's opinions or educated guesses upheld as authoritative by other players in a field constantly disrupted by new discoveries and theories. Though these questions were far from being answered definitively in the 1840s—and one could even argue for their pertinence today—Gondra insisted that there were unique characteristics that made Mexican antiquities recognizably "Mexican." These features could be brought out scientifically through "constant comparisons," which would help shape ways of seeing them and writing about them. After achieving a firm sense of the content and limits of Mexican cultural artifacts, it would be possible to develop criteria for comparing them to the antiquities of other cultures and for considering them in their own right.

The translation of Prescott's *History* into Spanish, especially Cum-

18. Musical instruments of the Aztecs. Lithograph. Plate 22. Cumplido edition of *Historia de la conquista de México*, vol. 3. BNAH, Secretary of Culture-INAH-Mex-Photo Library Constantino Reyes Valerio. Reproduction authorized by the National Institute of Anthropology and History.

plido's edition, put into circulation a fair number of the National Museum's antiquities and presented Mexican antiquarians like Ramírez and Gondra with an opportunity to express hypotheses about them. On the topic of Mexican antiquity, Prescott's *History* had little to offer besides received wisdom about the putative barbarity of the races that peopled America at the time of the encounter between the two worlds. Ramírez and Gondra stripped away these prejudices and showed how they got in the way of a clear view of the historical object—that is, the state of preconquest Mexico. Restoring the Indian antithesis to the telling of a story that otherwise fell into the well-known domain of colonialist epics gave fresh insight into both what was overthrown by the Spanish and the meaning of Cortés's Mexican adversaries. At the same time, besides shaping new ways of understanding the objects and their ancient creators, Cumplido's edition gave visibility to the Mexican curator. To the accusation that vestiges of the nation's past belonged elsewhere because Mexicans showed little interest in them, paper permitted scholars like Gondra and Ramírez to make the case that Mexican antiquities belonged in Mexico because they were being studied there.

Unfortunately, both Mexican editions of Prescott's book passed unnoticed by their contemporaries, receiving almost no acknowledgement, nationally or internationally. Partly, this was due to the timing of these publications, which fell in one of the more tumultuous periods of the Mexican Republic's life. Even as Ramirez was preparing his "Notas and esclarecimientos" in 1845, the United States annexed the independent Republic of Texas, which was perceived by the Mexican government to be a flagrant provocation and the boding of worse things to come. Skirmishes on the Mexico-Texas border served war-bent U.S. president James Polk as a pretext to declare war on Mexico on May 13, 1846; after much debating, Mexico answered by declaring war on the United States on July 7. A year and two months later, on September 8, 1847, General Winfield Scott's army entered Mexico City. U.S. soldiers did so armed with copies of Prescott's *History of the Conquest of Mexico*.[82] This spoke of the book's popularity, of course, but it was not just a matter of being a good read. The similarities between the conquest of Mexico by Cortés, more than three centuries earlier, and its "reconquista" by the United States were not lost on those who took part in this reenactment. As Caleb Cushing, who served in the army that entered Mexico City, wrote, "The second Conquest affords many points of analogy with the first, which strike the observer on the spot. I am posted with five regiments at San Angel, which adjoins Coyoacán, and my rides of duty or recreation in the neighborhood afford me an ample opportunity of noticing these analogies [. . .] the fact that General Scott originally advanced to the City by the causeway of San Antonio, and finally by that of Tacuba, though not certainly because Cortés had done the same."[83] To what extent Prescott's book offered the invading army a promise of victory in the vision of the conquest of a nation fallen into barbarity by a civilized one is only a guess.

As for those twice-vanquished Mexicans, they might have drawn a different conclusion from Prescott's story. The loss of half of the national territory in the course of a decade brought on serious self-questioning and soul-searching. "Why did Mexico lose the war?" asked "Varios Mexicanos" in a pamphlet titled *Consideraciones sobre la situación política y social de la República Mexicana en el año 1847*, which circulated widely throughout 1848. Not because of racial degeneration, as foreigners might have thought, proclaimed the pamphleteers. Rather, just as it had happened in 1521, it was strife and division that had cost them the war: "In Mexico, that which has been called national spirit does not exist nor has it existed, since the nation has not existed either."[84] As the U.S. troops rolled into Mexico City, all Gondra, Ramírez, and Cumplido could do was help safeguard objects from the National Museum, putting them out of the way of the "stiff and tall [. . .] devils."[85] After the peace treaty was signed in February of 1848 and as the U.S. Army began withdrawing, some of these objects slowly returned to take their place in the cramped space of the National Museum.

5 JOSÉ FERNANDO RAMÍREZ, KEEPER OF THE ARCHIVE

Man of State, Man of Letters

In March of 1852 French philologist and historian Jean Jacques Ampère (1800–1864) visited Mexico City, a stop on his extensive journey through North America that he recounted in his book *Promenade en Amérique*. Like his more famous friend, Alexis de Tocqueville (1805–59), Ampère viewed himself not simply as a traveler but as a philosopher of culture. Vividly impressed by the "magnificent spectacle" of sweeping skies and towering volcanoes that formed the natural backdrop of his travels through Mexico, he was at the same time keenly aware that the economic foundation of the country rested on the ill-paid and ill-treated labor of millions of Indians—the majority of whom were indentured and all of whom were exposed, in newly independent Mexico, to forces to which they were partially immune in the colonial era, when they were officially protected by the church and Crown. Crime, Ampère claimed on anecdotal evidence, was rampant, while the institutions of security, the police and the court system, were underdeveloped and eminently bribable. Justice was a matter of individual initiative, which meant taking revenge as one could. Although the Mexican constitution was modeled on that adopted by the United States, Ampère thought, the result was a fundamentally different system, with its patchwork of presidents and military dictators. Ampère was obviously influenced by Tocqueville's observation that laws are adapted to the exigencies of the people, rather than the people being adapted to the exigencies of the law. In Mexico's case, the population did not resemble the hardworking and enthusiastic Americans to the north, as Mexicans did not mix with strangers, their women were luxurious and lazy, and even the country's civilized elites betrayed a "primitive physiognomy."[1]

Ampère showed particular concern for Mexico's most immediate present; in a recent speech, President Mariano Arista (1802–55) had declared the state of the treasury to be "miserable" and had noted that the deficit represented one-fifth of the internal revenue.[2] The financial crisis, Ampère rightly predicted, was a prelude to "the dislocation of the State," and he compared Mexico to "a man condemned to death, who has obtained a respite of undetermined duration," in any case, not for too long.[3] In fact, a year later, in April of 1853, Santa Anna toppled (again) the government. Yet Mexico's elites seemed blind to all imminent dangers and behaved extravagantly, engaging in luxury of all kinds, just as the decadent aristocrats of the Roman Empire had before the barbarian invasions.

Ampère's book is, by turns, a meditation on civilizations and, as the title indicates, a tourist guide. In accordance with the demands of being a tour guide, Ampère does try to explore and describe the sites, such as mines and churches. Inevitably, he turns his eyes on the National Museum, hoping to find "grandeur" in the country's antiquities, just as Brantz Mayer had, among scenes of street violence, ten years earlier. The National Museum Ampère visited in 1852 had expanded considerably since Mayer saw it. In 1848, looking back on some important acquisitions made over the intervening years, Gondra listed three hundred new specimens and some new species of shells; fossil shells from Italy; an entomological collection from China; and more than three hundred stuffed birds, including a bird of paradise and twenty-five hummingbirds.[4] The most important additions to the museum came from the private museum of the Conde de Peñasco, whose collections were auctioned after his death in 1846.[5] These included entomological, ornithological, and zoological specimens and some freaks of nature: a piece of the horn that had grown on the head of customs official Pablo Rodríguez; a human fetus with four legs, displayed in a solution of mercury chloride; and the skeletons of two twins joined together at the sternum. The truly important pieces from the Peñasco collections were Mexican antiquities: serpentine masks, stone figurines of humans and animals, reliefs, manuscripts, chains, and necklaces. Along with these, Gondra was proud of the European antiquities in the collection, such as the ten clay lamps from ancient Roman sepulchers and the ten "facsimiles" of Egyptian mummies.

A decade earlier, Mayer had described the museum as a claustrophobic hoard of jumbled fragments, so we can only imagine how the museum was able to fit its new acquisitions into the same space. Ampère wrote, "The Museum is in such a state of confusion and disorder that it does not permit to study anything fruitfully. It is not that it does not contain very curious objects, but it is difficult to orient oneself there; all is pell-mell, fragments whose Mexican provenance is more than doubtful are confused with authentic monuments."[6]

Ampère, who fancied himself a student of languages and epochs, saw the disarray in the museum as a reflection of the heterogeneity of the material that "evidently belonged to different races and to dissimilar epochs of art." But he also considered it part of a deeper systemic failure: "There is [. . .] a chaos that needs to be handled and it is difficult to do so while the Museum in Mexico is itself in chaos, without a catalogue, without method, without indications that attest to the origin of the monuments."[7] It is in this connection that Ampère mentions José Fernando Ramírez, whom Ampère praises for "dealing with the antiquities of the country" more intelligently than any other person in Mexico. Unfortunately, at the moment of Ampère's visit, Ramírez was Arista's minister of internal and foreign affairs and was not available to converse with the visitor on Mexican antiquities. In lieu of personal explanation, Ampère directed his readers to Ramírez's contributions to the Cumplido edition of Prescott's *History of the Conquest of Mexico*.[8]

Ampère was not alone in being impressed by Ramirez's remarkable erudition or by his passion for the pre-Columbian past. At the time of Ampère's visit, Gondra, who had directed the museum for almost twenty years, resigned.[9] On April 26, 1852, José María Tornel, director of the School of Mines, recommended José Fernando Ramírez as conservator; in Tornel's opinion, Ramírez's archaeological and philological studies, especially in connection to the "problem of the population of the New World," presaged greater "progress in these new sciences" and made Ramírez an ideal candidate for the job.[10] Arista ratified the recommendation in May, and Ramírez took charge of the museum in June of 1852.[11] For the next fifteen years, interrupted by eighteen months he spent in exile, Ramírez had a decisive impact on the institution, which, under his direction, would come to be identified and increasingly recognized as a space for the conservation and study of Mexican antiquities. If the foundation of the museum had been indissolubly linked to the biography of Lucas Alamán, we would have a difficult time understanding the trajectory of the museum in the mid-nineteenth century in the margins of Ramírez's intellectual and political career.

Trained as a lawyer—in the great tradition of generalist Mexican scholars going back to Carlos de Sigüenza y Góngora, José Antonio Alzate y Ramírez, and Antonio de León y Gama in the colonial period and up through the transitional figure of Lucas Alamán—Ramírez was gifted in many disparate departments of learning: a bibliophile, antiquarian, historian, writer, administrator, and editor. During his career, he became one of those larger-than-life figures looming over the history of nineteenth-century Mexico, as was also the case with Melchor Ocampo (1814–61), Ignacio Manuel Altamirano (1834–93), and Vicente Riva Palacio (1832–96). All of them faced battles, both military and political. They signed constitutions and newspaper articles; held political posts; and in the brief moments of quiet, engaged in balanced reflections of their country's past and present. Ramírez published relatively little, leaving behind the drafts of ambitious projects he never had the time to complete. Still, there is something to the judgment of archaeologist Alfredo Chavero (1841–1906), who purchased Ramírez's library posthumously and occupied Ramírez's post at the museum years later: "Ramírez did not write a history of Mexico, yet, he is the foremost of our historians."[12] In the end, Ramírez was undone, and his posthumous reputation was eclipsed, by his collaboration with the Second Empire, which led to his final exile. In the liberal Porfirian Era, he was too controversial to find a secure place in Mexico's liberal pantheon, which ultimately led to his neglect by future generations of historians.[13]

Ramírez was born in 1804 in Parral, Durango, to a provincial mining family.[14] He did not follow in the mining business; in 1837, together with his German brother-in-law, Germán Stahlknecht, he opened a textile factory in El Tunal (Durango). This was an early attempt at industrialization in postindependence Mexico and serves to showcase the obstacles that such ventures could entail, as they had to import both machinery and workers, most of them women, from the United States.[15] For Ramírez, the textile business was a sidetrack from his main interests, which focused, at first, on jurisprudence, the study of which he began in 1819, when he entered the Colegio de San Luis Gonzaga in Zacatecas. In 1823 he enrolled as a law student at the Colegio de San Ildefonso in Mexico City. This gave him a seat from which to witness the political and social agitation that marked the birth of the republic, as Iturbide's brief bid for empire failed and the institutional protocols for republican government were put in place.

Ramírez finished his jurisprudence studies in 1832 and embarked on a career that led him to positions at all levels of government, from local and state politics to national and international arenas. It was a career shaped by the country's inability to hit on a viable form of governance up to the 1870s. Between 1833 and 1842 he served as Durango's deputy to the Federal Congress when its sessions were not interrupted by the dissolutions caused by coups d'état. Combining political assignments with cultural ones, he became a member of the section on legislation and history at the Ateneo Mexicano in 1843, and in 1846 he joined the Sociedad Mexicana de Geografía y Estadística (SMGE). In 1844 he participated in the Cumplido edition of Prescott's *History of the Conquest of Mexico*. Between December of 1845 and January of 1847, he was senator of the republic, with a brief stint as President Gómez Farías's minister of foreign relations at the height of the war with the United States. Caught in occupied Mexico City, he organized the safekeeping of valuables from the National Museum and the National Archive in the wake of the pilfering by American troops and by his Mexican conationals.

After the war, Ramírez became again minister of foreign relations under President Arista and went into exile when Santa Anna came to power. He returned to Mexico in 1856, after the instauration of the liberal regime, and resumed his conservatorship at the National Museum. In June of 1864 Ramírez committed an act that resulted in his ostracism from the official narrative of Mexican history when he accepted Maximilian's invitation to work for the empire. In January of 1867, recognizing that his collaboration had alienated him from the Mexican establishment that was sure to take over after Maximilian, he left Mexico, just a few months before the empire fell, never to return. He died in Bonn in 1871. It is not an easy task to convey the many turns of Ramírez's life through this spare biographical sketch. Confronted with the vagaries of chance and the upheavals of politics, Ramírez found constancy in his engagement with Mexico's past, through objects and books. While his library, his so-called better half (*predilecta mitad*), has been the subject of recent studies, we have no satisfying account of Ramírez's work as museum conservator.[16] The National Museum, like the library, was his refuge, the haven into which he was best able to pour his intellectual ambitions, with a degree of indifference to the tribulations of his everyday life.

Studying Mexican Hieroglyphics

One of the earliest records we have of Ramírez's interest in Mexico's ancient past is a letter he sent Carlos María de Bustamante on June 15, 1838, where he announced the discovery of "precious remains of human antiquity" in a cave in the vicinity of Bolsón de Mapimí, in the Sierra Mojada, Coahuila.[17] The cave held close to one thousand embalmed mummies, wrapped in capes (*tilmas*). They had been placed in the traditional sitting position used by ancient Americans to bury their dead, with the knees bent to the chest and hands placed on the knees. Ramírez thought they had been divided by families, as suggested by groups made up of smaller child bodies and bigger adult ones. Textiles, jewelry, and weapons were also found at the site, and Ramírez sent a sample of objects to Mexico City. He sent along detailed descriptions of them: a band of elastic cloth, 7 varas long, dyed alternately white, red, and black; a flint knife with a wooden handle and an ornament where the sheath joins the handle; a strip of cloth made of twine, torn at both ends, 2½ x ⅓ varas, woven in the style of the sarapes from Saltillo, and marked with bloodstains, which, upon folding, recurred at regular intervals, indicating that the strip could have been used to wrap a wound; an earring made of hollowed bone; a string with small white beads probably made of bone; a snail with a hole drilled through its pyramidal base, which might have been used as an earring.[18]

Ramírez argued that the discoveries in the cave deserved their place in the National Museum in Mexico, where they should be transferred posthaste. A "scrupulous and scientific exam of the bodies" and of the material vestiges in the cave, wrote Ramírez, could yield up important secrets and cast "light upon the ancient history" of the nations that roamed Mexico and founded monarchies there before the arrival of the Aztecs. Specifically, he was interested in determining if the remains pertained to a rich and civilized nation or to the funeral customs of a nomadic and barbarous people. He opted to believe the former was the case, pointing out that embalming entailed technical expertise and social differentiation (only the richer members of a community could afford to be embalmed) as well as religious sophistication (embalming proved some deeper religious belief in the afterlife). Embalming, concluded Ramírez, was a fictitious necessity, a luxury, a matter of pride, the desire for life after death, hardly consistent with the mœurs of barbarous and nomadic peoples. Having inferred this, he probed further, wanting to know if this civilized people had belonged to some autochthonous empire with commercial ties as far as the Pacific—as signaled by the presence of seashells among the remains—or if the cave designated a mere stopover on a peregrination route to the south, where the Mexican Empire would later arise. Ramírez strongly advocated for this last possibility, as referred by a manuscript in the Franciscan convent in Zacatecas, which documented the presence of ruins on an ancient migration route, at 262 degrees longitude and between 26 and 27 degrees latitude.

Ramírez shared the nineteenth-century fascination concerning the origins of the Mexican people with many of the figures we have already discussed—Humboldt, Baradère, and Kingsborough, for example. His letter was not extensive enough to discuss his opinions about international scholarly research in this area, but he does show a firm understanding of the questions asked by his contemporaries and reveals an essentially positivist approach to solving the enigma of the origin of American man, one which combines the evidence of the body read in tandem with the study of antiquities and manuscripts. Ramírez's participation in the Mexican edition of William Prescott's *The History of the Conquest of Mexico* in 1845 strengthened his conviction that ancient monuments, previously considered undecipherable by the likes of Prescott, would yield up their secrets if they were studied together with codices and early colonial chronicles. In fact, as he wrote in his notes to Prescott's book, a rich collection of manuscripts, antiquities, and codices would provide the student of ancient Mexico with a system of references and possibilities for cross-checking, as iconographic, topographic, chronological, and astrological information would reinforce each other to provide evidence for scholarly hypotheses.

After the war with the United States came to an end, Ramírez continued to reflect on the connections between bibliography and antiquarian method. Ramírez's bibliophilia must therefore be understood as the "other side of the coin" of his antiquarian work with objects. A letter to Gondra dated January 1, 1850, is indicative of the integral role he assigned to books and manuscripts in his study of the Mexican past.[19] The pretext of the letter was to inform Gondra about the publication of the last two volumes of Kingsborough's *Antiquities of Mexico*. Even as he praised the publication of valuable colonial material, Ramírez complained that Kingborough had a tendency to truncate the documents, suppressing passages that did not interest him and editing the rest in a biased way toward predetermined conclusions. Furthermore, the illustrations were not very reliable. Ramírez noted that the hieroglyphs in his copy of *Antiquities of Mexico* were often significantly different from those in the museum copy. Reds and greens had been used indiscriminately, and sometimes the order of the figures was not the same in the two copies. Ramírez set out to correct the inconsistencies and "made some discoveries with regards to hieroglyphic writing."[20]

Though he was critical of Kingsborough's editorial decisions, Ramírez was angriest at those who did not publish these valuable materials in the first place, the Spanish libraries that had housed them since the sixteenth century:

It is hard to understand how [. . .] a thousand other treasures of our history could have remained buried under dust and oblivion while scholars in other [non-Spanish-speaking] parts of the world have privileged the study of the history, the archaeology, and the ethnography of the peoples conquered and civilized by the indolent *castellanos*. Do you not feel an undefined sensation of aversion and sadness when forced to read French translations, not always reliable, of the guileless and simple narratives of our elders? Do you not find it shameful that a Spaniard or a Mexican must fish for the disjointed remains of our ancient monuments in this ocean of foreign languages that Kingsborough presents us with?[21]

Ramírez was especially embarrassed when he compared the state of Mexican antiquarianism with what was going on in the United States, where antiquities, though "comparatively miserable," were being collected and studied by the Smithsonian Society.[22] Hence his resolution:

I plan to gather together, in a body as methodical as possible, all the historical traditions, the most ancient and the most authentic, scattered around the good authors of the sixteenth and seventeenth centuries, like Sahagún, Motolinía, Gomara, Herrera, Tezozómoc, Ixtlilxóchitl, Torquemada, Zurita, Acosta, [. . .] to see if, with the help of these records, we can advance the comprehension of hieroglyphic paintings that we owe to Lord Kingsborough's munificence and erudition. This will be the nucleus of my labors [. . .] and my first essay will focus on the famous journey of the Aztecs.[23]

That essay would have to wait eight years.[24] As Ramírez reflected in his letter to Gondra, he could not make use of his time with tranquility: "Party politics [. . .] did not respect the right of scholarship to neutrality."[25] Still, Ramírez did find a solid ally for his endeavors in the nonpartisan SMGE, particularly in the *Boletín de la Sociedad Mexicana de Geografía y Estadística*, which frequently published articles on preconquest history, some of them by Ramírez. Likewise, he prepared a total of twenty-nine articles for the *Diccionario universal de historia y geografía* (1853–56), many of them on pre-Hispanic topics.[26]

Finally, Ramírez's conservatorship in the National Museum gave him a crucial position from which to engage in his bibliographic and antiquarian pursuits. He often relied on networks he had built during his years in politics, at different levels of government, to obtain materials impossible to acquire in Mexico otherwise. Through the Ministry of Foreign Relations, he ordered a copy of Diego Durán's *Historia de las Indias de Nueva España e islas de Tierra Firme* from the Biblioteca Real de Madrid.[27] In Paris, Ramírez had his most solicitous correspondents: Francisco Serapio Mora (1801–80), Mexico's ambassador in France between March of 1851 and June of 1853, and embassy official Andrés Oseguera, with whom he discussed both political affairs and matters of bibliographic concern. Oseguera, whose letters reflect an amateur enthusiasm for the preconquest past, informed Ramírez about the presence of Mexican materials at the Imperial Library in Paris.[28] Both Mora and Oseguera sent him books on various topics, including works on the antiquities of the Old World, such as the ten-volume *Voyages en Perse et autres lieux d'Orient* (1686) by Jean Chardin; *Mémoires sur diverses antiquités de Perse* (1793) by Silvestre de Sacy; and Julius von Klaproth's *Examen critique des traveaux de Champollion, Collection d'antiquités egyptiennes*, and *Description de l'Egypt ou recueil des observations et des recherches* (1809–29), comprehensive descriptions of ancient and modern Egypt on the wake of Napoleon's military campaign there.[29]

A curious thread running through the correspondence between Mora and Ramírez are Mora's reports on his attempts to interest Count Émilien de Nieuwerkerke (1811–92), the director of the Parisian museums, in an exchange of Egyptian mummies in the Louvre for Mexican antiquities. After several frustrated meetings, Mora realized that the count would not part with his mummies.[30] Why the National Museum in Mexico would have wanted an Egyptian mummy is hard to surmise. Perhaps it was simply the desire to own that consummate object of wonder and curiosity that had been drawing museum crowds since the nineteenth century, which would fit the National Museum's position as an institution of amusement and instruction; or perhaps it was, more scientifically, to compare Egyptian mummies with those of ancient Mexico.

Side by side with the books and the objects of Europe's classical past, Ramírez began purchasing books on the Far East, such as the *Description de la Chine* (1839–40) by Agricol-Joseph Fortia d'Urban, which included descriptions of ancient Chinese monuments.[31] Oseguera, who believed in the Mongol origins of the Mexican civilization, also sent Ramírez the *Dictionnaire chinois, français et latin* (1813) by Joseph de Guignes and a Chinese grammar, hoping that it would help the conservator decipher Mexican hieroglyphs by comparing them to Chinese hieroglyphs.[32] These titles give us a sense of Ramírez's wide-ranging historical and bibliographical interests and of his ambition to understand the nature of the relations (if any) between the civilizations of the New and the Old Worlds—through comparative studies of their objects and of their writing systems—and, ultimately, to inscribe the science of Mexico's ancient past in the tradition of scholarly literature on other classical civilizations.[33]

Few objects entered the National Museum during the two years of Ramírez's conservatorship between May of 1852 and October of 1854. It is very likely that the federal budget and, by extension, that of the museum, was too scrimped to allow for any significant purchases. At the same time, Ramírez seemed more concerned with acquiring the materials that would permit him to study and organize the objects already under his custodianship. Ramírez's cares and efforts were devoted exclusively to antiquities, and he remained indifferent, even neglectful, toward the objects of natural history in the museum. This was reflected half a year into his appointment when Ramírez was asked by Pío Bustamante y Rocha, in charge of the natural history section at the museum, to reincorporate bird dissector and taxidermist Manuel Pedrozo, whom Ramírez had recently dismissed. Ramírez bluntly refused Bustamante's plea, alleging that the 1831 museum regulation did not provide for the post of a taxidermist and that the museum had no money to pay for one.[34] Pedrozo answered personally, insisting that he had been working for the museum for ten years, but his explanations were of little avail.[35] Only in the mid-1850s, when Ramírez was purged from the museum by Santa Anna's order, was Pedrozo reinstated.[36] However, with Ramírez in charge of the museum again by the late 1850s, we find the taxidermist pleading for his reincorporation one more time in 1861.[37] Although Ramírez alleged lack of money, it is also tempting to interpret the conservator's decision to do without the taxidermist as an affirmation of his hopes that the museum would become a depository of antiquities and not a cabinet of natural history. Time would endorse his vision.

The Lessons of Exile

Arista was ousted from the presidency in January of 1853, in the midst of a depleted treasury and of internal tumult; Santa Anna came to power on April 20, with the support of, among others, Lucas Alamán, who believed in a strong executive to counter the power of regional caudillos. But after Alamán, the mastermind behind Santa Anna's rule, died of pneumonia on June 2, Santa Anna assumed absolute faculties and the title of "His Most Serene Highness," and his dictatorial regime entered a downward-spiraling course punctuated by cockfights, palace balls, censorship, and persecution.[38] Over forty newspapers were closed.[39] Arista, Benito Juárez (1806–72), and Melchor Ocampo went into exile to New Orleans. Among those who suffered Santa Anna's wrath was José Fernando Ramírez, who was exiled from Mexico City on October 20, 1854, for having served on Arista's cabinet.

Ramírez left for La Noria, in the state of Guanajuato, while his son Lino took charge of the museum. José Fernando Ramírez's correspondence from La Noria reflects a life of study and scholarly exchange, in the midst of perils and precariousness of all sorts. In a letter to Joaquín García Icazbalceta (1824–94) dated February 3, 1855, he wrote that bandits assailed the nearby Hacienda de las Peñuelas that morning and were being expected at La Noria by midnight, so Ramírez was planning to flee. That meant leaving behind material he had been working on, not knowing if he would ever recover it.

What can a man do, when he is dragged from here to there, like a straw blown around by the hurricane? [. . .] Tranquility of the soul and body is the first condition for fruitful study and you can see my situation. In Mexico [City] I had to interrupt and abandon violently a study I had started, which required great and arduous research, lost now with my exile. Here, I have undertaken a more laborious one, on which I had staked flattering expectations. I was hoping I was close to lifting part of the veil that covers the mystery of hieroglyphic writing.[40]

Since retirement in La Noria was turning out to be too stressful, Ramírez asked the minister of the interior, Manuel Díez de Bonilla, to allow him to serve his exile in Europe, where he would advance his research on Mexico's ancient past. "My topic is interesting and could be of benefit to Mexican literature," he wrote to Díez de Bonilla.[41] Following a five-month correspondence—which gives us a sense of how all decisions were subject to the dictator's whims and moods—Ramírez was granted permission to leave the country; in March of 1855 he embarked on a year-long trip to Europe.

His trip was, in a way, an extended grand tour of the museums, collections, and libraries of Western and Central Europe—Oxford, London, Berlin, Potsdam, Vienna, Paris, Bologna, and Torino. At some point, he travelled to Handschuhsheim, where he visited the collection of Mexican antiquities imported there by Carl Uhde.[42] Ramírez did not keep a diary of his travels, at least not one that we know of, but his letters and chronicles give us a strong sense of his encounters with European scholars and a rare glimpse into the reflections of an acute Mexican observer confronting the vanguard of imperial modernity. His train trip from Bremen to Berlin on June 8, 1855, in the company of his brother-in-law, Germán

Stahlknecht, evoked "painful impressions of the inexplicable indifference and even disdain towards people created by train travel."[43] This might have been one of Ramírez's first train journeys, since there was practically no train travel in Mexico until 1880. And his uncomfortableness was aggravated by the fact that he did not speak German: "One experiences the most complete and disagreeable solitude when one ignores completely the language in the midst of an active and boisterous society."[44]

In his visits to libraries and museums, he met scholars interested, like him, in deciphering Mexico's ancient past. Among them, Johann Karl Eduard Buschmann (1805–80), the librarian at the Royal Library in Berlin, had just concluded a study on Aztec place names, *Über die aztekischen Ortsnamen* (1853), a topic of interest to both men.[45] His encounter with Buschmann was probably one of Ramírez's first meetings with a European scholar in his own habitat, and Ramírez observed him closely, as one would a curious specimen: "The community of European savants, properly speaking, forms a particular family of the human species, which is necessary to have met in order to know it because it is not so easy to define it. Generally, they are men entirely withdrawn from society and from boisterousness: simple, ingenuous, enthusiastic, of a palpable frankness, living always in remote times or in the creations of their imaginations, and consequently, without precise notions of those regulated forms and mimicry invented by that which is known as 'Good society.'"[46]

How different the life of a "European savant" seemed to be from the conditions against which the Mexican scholar had to contend in order to produce his own scholarship! For Ramírez, the advancement of knowledge was the fruit of askesis, the withdrawal from that world of politics that ate at Ramírez's soul and time. But this might also be the case of the grass being greener on the other side. Alexander von Humboldt, one of Europe's most celebrated scientists and an obligatory reference for Americanist studies, was a busy man, even in his eighties, in mid-1850s Potsdam, where he served as adviser to the court, and where Ramírez visited him on June 14, with Buschmann's letter of introduction. Ramírez found Humboldt to be a man of "vast knowledge and prodigious memory,"[47] eager for news about Mexico; they talked of many things, from current affairs to the topics most dear to both, archaeology and philology.[48]

By November of 1855, Ramírez was installed in Paris, on rue Sainte Anne, a small street that cuts through the neighborhood behind the Louvre to lead to the Bibliothèque Nationale (then, Bibliothèque Imperiale).[49] Paris in the mid-nineteenth century was a privileged place for anyone interested in the study of Mexican antiquities. In 1851 Adrien de Longpérier (1816–82), the conservator of antiquities at the Louvre, had inaugurated a gallery of Mexican and Peruvian antiquities that brought together various collections of ancient American objects: Maximilien Franck's and Latour Allard's collections of Mexican antiquities, acquired in 1832 and 1850, respectively, and the Peruvian antiquities imported by consul Léonce Angrand. With the exhibit, Longpérier prepared a catalogue, which indicates that the objects were displayed by region—Mexico, Peru, and, in a few cases, Chile—and by what they represented.[50] From the 657 Mexican antiquities, Longpérier first separated and grouped together objects that he termed "sculpture" (ostensibly, human figures), further classifying them by separate categories of animal, mythological, and undetermined figures, which included a "female head with two bullhorns" and an "animal head with bulging eyes surrounded by circles." Next came architectural fragments, vases, baked clay heads, weapons, musical instruments, ornaments (earplugs, pendants), diverse utensils (a mirror, a "desk," and, strangely, a "perfume dispenser" in the shape of a pipe), and seals. Peruvian objects, less numerous than Mexican ones, were classified as figurines, vases, weapons, and "diverse objects." For each entry, Longpérier offered a brief description of the object, specifying its dimensions and the material it was made of; in some cases, he referred the reader to illustrations and descriptions of the object in other sources. There are no equivalent bibliographical references for Peruvian antiquities, although Longpérier compares some of them to objects from Mexico or the Mediterranean.

As evidenced by Longpérier's catalogue, the classification of American antiquities was determined by the categories developed for classical Greek and Roman antiquities. In the preamble to the guide, Longpérier explains why this is so: the few studies on American antiquities published in the nineteenth century did not allow for any certainty about the meaning, usage, or date of the figures, weapons, and utensils or about the mythological concepts or the historical figures represented by the statuettes unearthed at sites like Palenque or Cholula. Longpérier's complaints—that dating methods by checking the soil deposits around the finds were never employed in the case of American archaeology and that there were no serious studies of the Aztec language, indispensable for the classification of Mexican monuments—show a certain provinciality of outlook, since, in fact, eleven different Aztec grammars were in existence at that time.[51] It was as if the French were awaiting an académie for the Aztec language, much like their own for the French language. The advancement of the knowledge of Egyptian antiquities since the decipherment of Egyptian hieroglyphs stood in stark contrast with the backward state of research on American antiquities. Longpérier conceded that ancient Egypt had a more powerful grip on Europeans because of its intimate relation with Europe's own sacred past, that Egyptian antiquities were more available in France, and that American antiquities were bizarre—the negation of the beautiful, which alone could lead to progress—and "not yet classical." But he trusted that his exhibit and catalogue, rudimentary as they were in their explanation of the objects, would be a step in calling scholarly attention to America's ancient past.[52]

There are no written records of Ramírez's impressions of the American gallery at the Louvre, though we know that he did visit the museum from his references to Mexican and other objects there. If he read Longpérier's catalogue, as he most probably did, it is hard to imagine that he would not have shared Longpérier's wish for methodical research on Mexican antiquities, while shunning the Frenchman's more blatant prejudices. In fact, Ramírez spent most of his time in Paris working on his plan to put together a corpus of ancient and colonial Mexican materials, which would form the basis for any systematic study of Mexico's pre-Hispanic past. With this purpose in mind, Ramírez visited Jean Marius Alexis Aubin, the owner of one of the richest collections of Mexican preconquest and colonial manuscripts (384 in all, including codices, maps and plans, drawings, and texts), which Aubin imported with himself to France in 1839, after a ten-year residence in Mexico. Once in Paris, despite his indisputable erudition, Aubin did little to advance the "progress of Mexico's early history." If we believe his fellow anti-quarian Eugène Boban (1834–1908), Aubin's was a typical case of "the secret voluptuousness of the explorer, who, having discovered a treasure, keeps it hidden from all other eyes and saves it for himself alone, with jealous care."[53] It was Ramírez who managed to draw Aubin out of his retreat and to convince him to allow the reproduction by lithography of seven of his choice manuscripts, making them accessible to students of ancient Mexico: the *Mapas Tlotzin, Quinatzin,* and *Tepechpan*; the *Codex Aubin*; the *Codex Ixtlilxóchitl*; the *Historia Tolteca-Chichimeca*; and the so-called *Aubin Tonalámatl*, a twenty-page ritual Mexican calendar of 260 days.[54]

Besides meeting up with the taciturn Aubin, Ramírez spent time poring over Mexican material at the Bibliothèque Nationale, then under the conservatorship of M. Paulin. At Paulin's petition, Ramírez wrote a thoughtful description of the eleven Mexican manuscripts there.[55] These included codices, tribute sheets, Moctezuma's "genealogical tree," and parochial archives. Ramírez's observations regarding "Manuscript #2," the *Paris Codex*, give us a sense of how he went about his descriptions, balancing, in the style of positivist historians, material and iconographic aspects and references to other documents, in this case, the *Dresden Codex*, which Ramírez had studied in Kingsborough's *Antiquities of Mexico*. Ramírez thought the *Paris Codex* resembled the *Dresden Codex* "generically, though not in the detail of its figures":

Manuscript #2: hieroglyphic manuscript, identical in character to the one in Dresden, on vegetal paper, prepared [. . .] by an identical procedure. This consisted in covering the surface [. . .] destined for writing by a layer of plaster or white clay, which was polished and burnished to make it smooth and susceptible to receive the most delicate traces. [. . .] The type of paper used for these manuscripts differed from [that] fabricated by Mexicans. [The paper] is very spongy, thick, and flexible, and, at first sight, looks like ordinary hemp fabric, worn with use; but upon close examination, it is clear that its appearance is due to the thicker plant filaments which have been conserved intact and adhere to the finer and more delicate ones that make up the weft. A papermaker could, maybe, give interesting information about the procedure [...]. I suspect it was [made] by macerating tree bark. Its flexibility is only width-wise; length-wise, it is strong and resistant.

The form or disposition of the manuscript was the one commonly used for important [documents], a band or strip [...] folded like a folding screen ("biombo"). Each screen is a little more than 20 cm tall by 12.5 cm wide, and there are eleven screens total. The total length can thus be estimated at 137.5 cm.[56]

Both the *Dresden* and the *Paris Codices* are of Mayan provenance, and Ramírez thought they represented the "most elevated and perfect civilization in the New World."

The *Paris Codex* had been purchased by the library in 1832, together with many of the other manuscripts he inspected there. The catalogue at the library also listed five Mexican manuscripts that Ramírez could not locate.[57] With help from Ferdinand Denis, the director of the Bibliothèque Sainte-Geneviève, Ramírez found references to the "lost" manuscripts in an issue of the *Bulletin des Sciences Historiques, Antiquités, Philologie* from 1830, which announced the purchase of five Mexican manuscripts in that same year, from the Boturini collection, by the (then) Bibliothèque du Roi. These included such rarities as pictorial reports of the Spanish fleet's arrival in the Gulf of Mexico and of a Spanish camp by Moctezuma's spies and a volume of Mexican parishes in 1580, which paired up glyphs with phonetic writing. This manuscript would have constituted an extraordinary breakthrough in the project of deciphering the writing systems of ancient Mexico, a Rosetta stone holding the key to Mexican glyphs; by looking up the alphabetically written word in a Náhuatl dictionary, one could arrive at the meaning of each hieroglyph.[58] Given the importance of these documents, it is no wonder that Ramírez searched for them all over Paris.

But the manuscripts seem to have vanished into thin air, and Ramírez began suspecting that references to them were no more than concoctions and, as such, a sad reflection of the state of the research on Mexican antiquities:

> When natural propensity, which draws us to run looking for the hidden and the mysterious, is joined by an exalted imagination, a self-absorbed spirit, or personal interest, it is certain that from the pretended revelation of the arcane, one can derive only errors and deliriums, likely to obstruct the revelation of truth. This ill, threatening to science, becomes permanent and turns into a kind of endemic illness when it springs in the midst of an intelligent, spiritual, and lively society, as avid for novelty [. . .] as contemporary society is [. . .]. And for this reason, those who entertain and agitate [society] find themselves always with the difficult need to tell it new things, which forces them sometimes to fabricate stories and discoveries.[59]

This is an index of Ramirez's critique of romantic history. The precision of his own descriptions has a moral and ideological value: history has to be tied to detail rather than to collective emotion or drama. If novelty was the trade coin in Europe, traffic in Mexican archaeology, history, and literature was reaching "colossal proportions"; Ramírez noted with concern that news on Mexico was "being produced daily in the European literary market, and almost everything in false or adulterated species." So while Ramírez appreciated the wealth of antiquities held in Paris, he deplored the fact that Mexico's "ancient traditions and monuments are being disfigured and corrupted by fantastic systems, brilliant in their coloring, but completely empty of reason. Not even drawings, of people and of animals, of palaces and of their ruins have been truthful, and one can imagine what those who trample on truth with a pencil could do [when yielding] a pen." Interestingly, Ramírez thought deceit could be achieved more easily in writing than in drawing.

His list of culprits is vast, and there is a sense that his examples would be funny, were they not so abundant. The catalogue of misrepresentations becomes, in Ramírez's hands, an indictment of prejudice. To start, Ramírez recalled illustrations in the French edition of Bullock's book on Mexico purportedly representing the typical costumes of a military man, a magistrate, and a man and a woman of the "superior classes." But, Ramírez scoffed, the first was decked in the outfit of a Spanish toreador and wore a Napoleonic hat; the second, in the everyday attire of an *arriero*, or a mule driver; the third was dressed like an Indian; while the fourth depicted a woman from the more popular classes. The dress of each of them displayed more or less "fantastic appendages" of different kinds. Turning to the representation of antiquities, Ramírez censured a "Collection of Antiquities from Yucatán" for including Greek-style statues and "monuments of fantastic architecture," models of which could not be found in the country.[60] "An enthusiastic researcher, absorbed in his system, can find whatever he wants in all parts," proclaimed Ramírez; thus, "Dupaix had seen the sun and the zodiac in all religions [. . .] converting the most ignorant people into astronomers. [. . .] Kingsborough [. . .] colonized America with Hindus, just as others sought to people it with Egyptians, Carthaginians, etc., finding proof of their incompatible conjectures in its traditions and monuments." Though Ramírez admitted that "fascination" could generate such deviations from the historical truth, he also thought that more than "fascination" was at stake when an artist, pretending to draw "d'après nature," not only drew what did not exist (hence, kings from Yucatán and Central America riding on elephants) but also "denaturalized and subverted" the originals. The aim was to deceive others. But why? Ramírez concluded that this was done because there was financial gain in delivering novelty to an age avid for news.

So the scholar of Mexican antiquities had to tread with caution, approach all studies with skepticism, and establish a reliable body of materials, which would allow for testing personal hypotheses. And this is precisely what Ramírez did. By the time he resumed his conservatorship in the National Museum, after his return from

Europe, he was one of the few students of ancient Mexico to have travelled east across the Atlantic and to have immersed himself in the current state of antiquarianism. In so doing, he had shed his awe of the seemingly advanced state of European learning. Familiar with Mexicanist scholarship abroad, he could assess the merits of different interpretations, just as he could tell deception from true scholarship and faulty representations from correct ones. He returned to Mexico after having seen practically all there was to see of Mexican antiquities abroad and after taking the opportunity to compare them directly with the vestiges of other ancient civilizations. Most importantly, he took back a considerable trove of manuscripts and books, which would help him corroborate his own theories and give the science of Mexico's past a solid methodological foundation.

Édouard Pingret's "Chamber of Horrors"

Ramírez was back in Mexico by March 1856. The liberal faction led by Ignacio Comonfort (1812–63) and Benito Juárez had toppled Santa Anna and inaugurated a year of debates that resulted in a new constitution. Signed into effect on February 5, the Constitution of 1857 established individual rights, such as the freedom of speech and of assembly, and seriously limited the power of corporations, a measure aimed at the church. The Ley Lerdo (1856) oversaw the sale of church property and the dismantling of convents, which brought to light but also contributed to the loss of many bibliographical treasures that had formed part of their libraries and archives.[61]

By May 1856 Ramírez was back at the head of the National Museum. He had also been offered a magistracy on the Supreme Court, but he turned it down:

When I left this city, to go into confinement, I was busy at one of the more important and necessary assignments in the Museum. [...] This establishment does not have a catalogue, and not even a regular inventory of its objects. In order to create one and the other, it is necessary to bring together information that lies scattered and disorganized in various books and in loose papers. That is arduous work, towards [. . .] the formation of a reasoned scientific catalogue of its objects. [. . .] There is a lot of work to be done at the Museum. I give up a post at the pinnacle of a career in the forum and in the Magistracy, which grants honor, power, influence, and consideration [in favor of] another one, more humble and obscure, which lacks the prestige, while demanding of me more assiduous work and study [. . .] than the Magistracy that I am being offered.[62]

Like some of the scholars he had met and admired abroad, Ramírez would withdraw from the arena of everyday politics and dedicate himself full-time to the museum and principally to its antiquities collection, which for Ramírez was clearly at the heart of the museum's mission. His chance for settling into the tranquil life conducive to study depended to an extent on his ability not to be drawn into the broader political conflicts traversing Mexico. For a few years, he was able to accomplish this.

Among his first accomplishments after his return to the museum, Ramírez published the *Descripción de algunos objetos del Museo Nacional de antigüedades de México*, which came out in 1857 in a limited edition of fifty copies, dedicated to Humboldt. It was included, the same year—and with a slightly different title, "Antigüedades mexicanas que existen en el Museo Nacional de México"—in the album *México y sus alrededores*, which paired up lithographs of "monuments, costumes, and landscapes" with descriptions and chronicles by contemporary writers.[63] The *Descripción*, a first step toward the kind of comprehensive inventory Ramírez had planned on for years as an essential beginning for a true science of preconquest America, is a lithograph of forty-two antiquities from the museum, with long explanations devoted to each one of them. Ramírez begins this text with a straightforward critique of the state of Mexican antiquarian studies, an echo of critical remarks he had penned before: "The terrain of Mexican antiquity remains virgin, notwithstanding the millions of historical volumes that have fallen on it. [. . .] Most of them are no more than verbiage [. . .] awaiting the skillful and patient hand that will accomplish [in the field of antiquarian studies] what God accomplished with chaos."64 An infamous example of the more flippant side of Mexicanist studies, and the direct target of Ramírez's censure was an article by Édouard Pingret (1788–1875) that appeared in the Parisian paper *L'Illustration*.65

Pingret was a painter and a lithographer of considerable reputation in France, a student of Jacques-Louis David, whose subjects included Napoleon Bonaparte. After arriving in Mexico in 1851, Pingret exhibited his work at the Academia de San Carlos, and his pastels produced an immediate sensation.66 A critic hailed him as a painter of modernity: "Pingret is a serialist [*folletista*], full of gala, sparks, animation."67 Another praised the advantages of his pastels for portraiture, particularly for female portraits: "No other kind of painting proffers so many advantages for female portraiture as pastels, whose crayons offer the most delicate and soft colors for rendering the fineness, transparency, whiteness, true coloring, and parchment-like quality of skin; in the same way, it allows M. Pingret to expose the secondary attributes of his sitters with an exactitude that deceives the eye." The author predicted that "many a beautiful Mexican señorita would convert M. Pingret's canvas into a faithful and undestructible mirror."68 Trailing these raves, Pingret became, as Waldeck had decades before, the painter of Mexico's upper classes; most famously, he painted President Arista's portrait, while building up an ample oeuvre of *costumbrista* scenes.

During his five-year residence in Mexico, Pingret developed an interest in antiquities, which, he thought, made him an exception to the rule: "Nobody in the capital busied himself with the souvenirs of the ancient Mexicans; one only thinks of making money and stealing."69 This, at least, was Pingret's story, and it allowed him to present himself as an expert on Mexican antiquities. In this tenor, he contacted the Louvre, offering his services as broker and as artist; if the Parisian museum so agreed, he would buy small pieces and make molds of the bigger ones.70 The Louvre never took up Pingret on these offers—a pity, for he thought he could have counted on all sorts of incredible support for his ventures. He was, he claimed, close to powerful people and had been "an intimate friend of the [National] Museum's conservator, [so] it would have been easy for him to obtain whatever he wished to import." Pingret did not disclose the identity of the all-too-generous conservator, but considering that he arrived in Mexico in 1851 and started to feel the stirrings of antiquarianism sometime later, an obvious suspect would be Ramírez. Pingret confessed that he did not act on the conservator's good will because "a pang of conscience and the fear that the same conservator could have later denounced him [. . .] made him desist from purchasing most of the objects in the Museum, so he took the conservator's daily offers for objects only sometimes." He did acquire an obsidian mask, which he suspected had belonged to the National Museum.[71]

In 1855 Pingret left Mexico definitively, rich in tales and in objects. He arrived in Paris with a collection of 2,400 antiquities—which he claimed to be the largest collection of Mexican antiquities in Europe at the time—and was determined to sell it to the Louvre, where he thought it would significantly enrich Longpèrier's American gallery.[72] At Pingret's request, Longpèrier sent Aubin and Brasseur de Bourbourg, the two most respected experts on Mexican antiquities in Paris at the time, to appraise the collection.[73] Aubin and Brasseur's visits, too brief and desultory for Pingret's liking, produced a shocking conclusion: most of Pingret's "antiquities" were fakes! Pingret attributed the unfavorable verdict to professional jealousy and ignorance.

Snubbed by the Louvre and its experts, Pingret took his case to the arena of public opinion. On September 13, 1856, the weekly *L'Illustration* published Pingret's "Antiquités mexicaines," the article that would provoke Ramírez's ire. To give an idea of his collection, he illustrated the article with a lithograph, where he assembled his objects most worthy of note: the model of the "chapel of a protector-god [. . .] tight-lipped in silence, tongue hanging out in a symbol of speaking" (it is hard to decide if the god was a talking or a silent god); a "Ceres of the Aztecs," one eyebrow raised in distrust, with an ear of corn and a squash in each hand; her counterpart, the "Aztec Bacchus," inebriated or maybe just scowling, in the form of a reclining, rachitic Chac-mool, with swollen belly and skeletal legs, holding a vessel, which Pingret thought must have contained

19. Édouard Pingret, Mexican antiquities. *L'Illustration*, September 13, 1856. Yale University Libraries.

the ritual beverage *pulque*; and the statue of a young man crouching on the ground, sculpted in pink volcanic rock, which Pingret identified as the god of earthquakes (fig. 19).[74]

If Pingret translated Mexican deities into Ceres, Bacchus, and Neptune, Latin gods whom nineteenth-century French readers would know, supplying emotion to the typically expressionless faces of Mexican antiquities, he also knew how to nourish his readers' hunger for the exotic and the unknown, to deliver what Ramírez would call "fantastic systems" to a media system avid for sensationalism and novelty.

Thus, he organized his article around the topic of human sacrifice, on which he offered rather heterodox explanations. In the center of the image, he represented his idea of the sacrificial act: the victim, facedown, lies languidly over a sculpted stone, while the priest stands behind, about to thrust the knife into the victim's back. It is difficult to imagine from this how he would extract the heart. As for the "sacrificial stone," Pingret informed his readers that it was a perfect model of the "enormous stone encrusted in the wall of the Servantes family house in Mexico City," which had served as the very altar on which six thousand victims were sacrificed in celebration of emperor Moctezuma's ascension to the throne. To the left of the victim and executioner duo sits "Mexican Mars, the god of sacrifice," with "bulging eyes, gaping jaws and sharp teeth." Like the sacrificial altar, the flat-faced baked-clay monster was, according to Pingret, a version of a colossal porphyry statue in the National Museum. To the right, a medieval juggler of sorts, in wide-sleeved shirt and feathered legs, sustains a vessel "destined to receive sacrificial blood." Above the juggler, Pingret represented the same vessel; above the sacrificial group in the center is the sacrificial obsidian knife that served to open up the victim's entrails. Pingret thought that the yoke-like object, which is associated today with a pre-Hispanic ballgame, would have been used for catching the head of the victim at the moment of sacrifice. Finally, to conclude his explanations and for added effect, at the bottom of the illustration, Pingret included a relief with what he believed were symbols of death.[75]

Did Pingret actually own a model of the sacrificial pair in the center? Or did he simulate the sacrificial act as a way to show the uses of some of the objects he might have owned, like the model of the "altar," the neck-crushing yoke, the knife, the vessel, the relief, and the clay figurines, much in the way contemporary botanical illustration depicted a plant with flower and fruit simultaneously, as a synoptic vision for the analysis and description of each element? In any case, it is hard not to think of Pingret's lithograph as an intentionally strange assemblage of strange objects, with distortions of the facial expressions and poses of his statues such that Pingret, a respected painter with a keen eye for detail, would not have allowed in his portraiture. Pingret's overenthusiastic imagination may have been to blame in part for having produced fantastic images, but it is also possible that his delusions made him prey to dealers in inauthentic artifacts in Mexico and that Brasseur and Aubin were correct in judging Pingret's collection as riddled with fakes.

Naturally, not wanting to be known as a dupe, Pingret dedicated a good part of his article in *L'Illustration* to insisting that his objects were authentic because they were replicas of larger sculptures on exhibit at the National Museum in Mexico City. In other words, they were originals because they were copies. This is a most surprising conclusion; a copy would have tipped off most buyers of antiquities that somebody was making and selling copies of objects in the museum. This was simply not the case, insisted Pingret, because Mexicans were not interested in their past and in their mythological traditions. With no domestic curiosity for antiquities, there was no market for replicas. Why, he asked, would contemporary Mexican artists make copies of urns, lamps, pipes, flutes, and vessels of domestic use if nobody would buy them or have any kind of use for them? Once out on this limb, Pingret claimed that there was no foreign demand for Mexican antiquities, either. It had been only forty years since Europeans began visiting Mexico, and nobody had thought of bringing back pots and idols. So these objects could not have been created to deceive Europeans, as was being done in Rome and Naples, where the imitation of antiquities was a considerable industry. So, he asked, "wouldn't it be more logical to think of those treasures as recently dragged out from the bottom of the lake, where other treasures awaited to be discovered?"[76]

Pingret's affirmations are hard to take at face value, since the implication is that there were no fakes of Mexican antiquities, which is just the kind of belief that would make a buyer an easy mark for fake antiquities. In fact, as other travelers had written, a market for antiquities—and, by extension, a supply of copies, souvenirs, and fakes—had been burgeoning in Mexico since at least the 1820s; the conservators at the National Museum made a point of showing they knew the difference between antiquities and fakes. Thus, Edward Burnett Tylor (1832–1917), the founder of cultural anthropology, who visited the museum in 1856, described a "particularly instructive shelf" there: a "Chamber of Horrors," which contained "numbers of sham antiquities, the manufacture of which [was] a regular thing in Mexico, as it [was] in Italy."[77] The objects on the shelf had undergone various types of transformations with respects to American physiognomies and to ancient ideals of beauty; by careful examination, Tylor came up with a list of the more common errors committed by forgers. Many of these are immediately apparent in Pingret's lithograph:

> The foreheads of Mexican races are all very low and their paint-ers and sculptors even exaggerated this particularity, to make the faces they depicted more beautiful, so producing an effect which to us Europeans seems hideously ugly, but which is not more natural than the ideal type of beauty we see in the Greek statues. After the era of the Spaniards, we see no more such foreheads; and the eyes, which were drawn in profiles as one sees them in the full face, are put in their natural position [. . .]. Short, squat figures become slim and tall. It is very seldom that the modern counterfeiter can keep clear of these and get back to the old standard. Among the things on the condemned shelf were faces too correctly drawn to be genuine, grotesque animals that no *artista* would [. . .] have designed who had not seen a horse, headdresses and drapery that were European and not Mexican.[78]

Tylor especially warned would-be buyers against earthenware—that is, baked-clay objects of the kind Pingret owned abundantly—because they were easy to fake. Obsidian objects, by contrast, were more likely to be authentic, for "the art of working obsidian is lost and there can be no trickery about that."[79] It is hard to know if the shelf of shams was in place when Pingret visited the museum some-time before Tylor or if Ramírez had it put in place at the beginning of his second conservatorship. Perhaps Pingret simply didn't notice it in the first place. In any case, by the time he returned to France with a collection that looked a bit like the "Chamber of Horrors" in the National Museum of Mexico, he had either been the victim of his own credulity, or he had underestimated the state of Mexican studies and was himself engaging in a swindle.

Toward a Science of the Ancient Past

Whatever the case, Pingret's strategy did not work. After the publica-tion of his article and another ill-fated attempt to sell his collection around 1864, there are practically no records of his antiquities in the French archives. So Ramírez's *Descripción*, which took Pingret directly to task, seems to be a bit of an overreaction. It is possible, however, that Ramírez's censure was a settling of accounts of sorts. Ramírez was museum conservator during a good part of Pingret's residence in Mexico, and the two coincided again in Paris, just as Pingret was unpacking his collection. Though Ramírez did not have access to Pingret's private correspondence, it is not improbable that the Frenchman's blazoning left and right that Mexicans were not interested in these objects and that he had obtained them through the solicitousness of the conservator at the National Museum of Mexico would have reached Ramírez. After all, the Americanist circles in Paris were not that big, and Ramírez did know the key actors in them. But it was not just a matter of getting even personally by pounding on an all-too-easy target. For Ramírez, Pingret's article summarized just what was wrong with Mexicanist studies in Europe: "The incorrectness of drawing competed with the fantasy of the explanations" to deliver news to a mass audience.[80] It was imperative to correct some of these widely circulating errors.

Ramírez published the *Descripción* as a "corrective," a "very small and merely descriptive page taken from that great book that awaits better moments."[81] Ramírez's "descriptive page" is ostensibly modeled on Pingret's still life, in which the same improbable cluster of things—some are drawn out of scale with respect to other objects (the Coatlicue appears smaller than she should, for instance), and some are partially hidden behind others—are collected together in an unidentifiable space that appears to be more a storeroom than a museum (fig. 20). Still, the artist represented each individual object accurately, so much so that the image depicts the passage of time and the weathering of the material.[82] But this is not a scientific illustration, not even to the extent that Franck or Waldeck had attempted by isolating objects as one would specimens of natural history to facilitate their study. Here, the overall impression is one of abundance, meant to put the viewer face to face with the nation's archaeological treasures. In fact, clusters of objects, as represented in this lithograph, became something of a metonym for

20. José Fernando Ramírez, description of antiquities from the National Museum of Mexico. *México y sus alrededores*, 1857. Author's personal collection.

"Mexican antiquities" and would be incorporated as "citations" in later representations of Mexico's past (fig. 21).

But if the visual rendering is not a page in the science of Mexico's past, Ramírez's written descriptions are. To each object, Ramírez has dedicated a separate entry where he assembled information about its formal aspect, size, material, provenance, and circumstances of discovery. There was nothing new in this way of identifying Mexican antiquities; it had become the norm by the mid-nineteenth century, when Adrien de Longpérier published his catalogue of the American antiquities gallery at the Louvre. But in contrast with earlier catalogues, Ramírez's descriptions expanded considerably to include historical, iconographic, and bibliographical notes. More than simple identifications, his entries are case studies where Ramírez sets

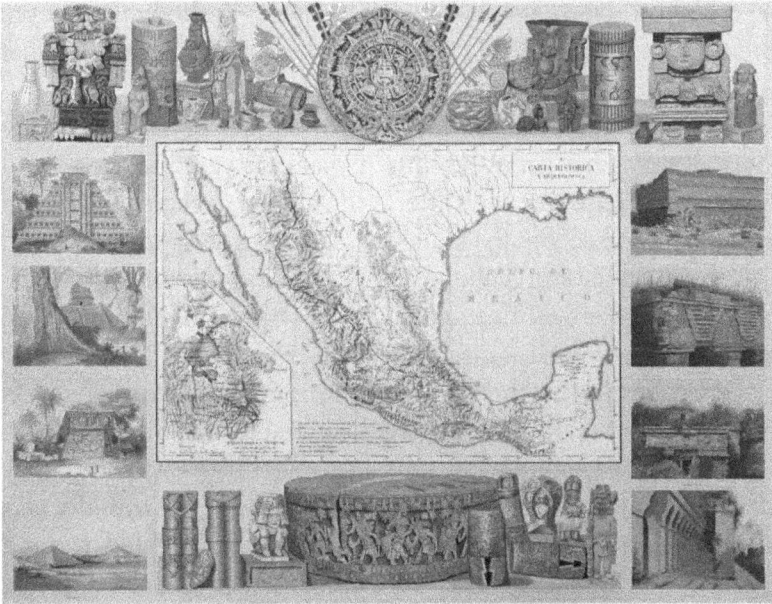

21. Detail of Antonio García Cubas's historical and archaeological map (1885), showing clusters of antiquities represented earlier in the *Descripción*. BNAH, Secretary of Culture-INAH-Mex-Photo Library Constantino Reyes Valerio. Reproduction authorized by the National Institute of Anthropology and History.

forth his hypotheses and makes a call for future scholars to contribute their own findings about each object.[83]

By way of example, we turn to the cylindrical stone to the right, "vulgarly known with the name Piedra de los Sacrificios."[84] Ramírez tells us that the monument of solid basaltic porphyry is 0.53 m tall and 2.67 m in diameter, that the reliefs on the cylindrical faces are 0.021 m deep, and that those on the horizontal face are 0.025 m deep. It was unearthed on December 17, 1791, in Mexico City's central plaza and was reburied in the same place in such a way that its flat surface was level with the ground. It was in this state that William Bullock found it and took molds of it in 1823 for his London exhibit.[85] The stone was transferred to the fledgling National Museum on November 10, 1824; thirty years later Ramírez marked the spot where the sculpture had lain, with an inscription carved on a *chiluca* slab (a porous volcanic stone), "in the hope that the memory of this place might someday be useful for solving what remained unresolved" about the monument.[86]

The statue's intellectual biography was just as exciting as the story of the stone from the time it was discovered to the time it entered the museum. Soon after its discovery, Creole scholar León y Gama theorized that the stone represented a solar calendar, with the symbol of the sun sculpted on the superior side and thirty dancers, standing for the fifteen peoples who venerated the sun, carved around the cylindrical circumference. Humboldt, on the other hand, suggested that the stone had commemorated the conquests of an Aztec king and that it had functioned as a gladiatorial altar.

For Ramírez, neither of the two conjectures was completely acceptable, although they both had some merit. The cylinder was a commemorative and a votive monument, he suggested. It was a historical document that provided information that could not be found in printed or handwritten books about the military campaigns undertaken in 1482 by Tízoc (1481–86), the seventh Aztec king, against the peoples depicted on the circumference. Far from symbolizing dancers, as León y Gama had thought, these figures represented "groups of victors and vanquished, arranged two by two, the one dragging the other by the hair, the vanquished holding a bundle of arrows pointing down, the same way one sees in reliefs of the same genre, in the monuments of Egypt and Assyria."[87] Behind the head of each prisoner, a hieroglyphic symbol gives the phonetic name of his people. At the same time, Ramírez explained that the effigy of the sun, carved in high relief on the flat side of the cylinder, showed the monument's votive associations. Like the Romans, Greeks, and all the famous people of antiquity, ancient Mexicans "understood that all great actions had to refer always to divinity, as the first cause and unique dealer of benefits" and consecrated the monument to the sun, "one of the principal divinities of empire, thus giving thanks for the victory obtained."[88] For an "exact drawing" of the sculpture, Ramirez referred his readers to Carl Nebel's "beautiful collection" of lithographs.

To arrive at his own hypotheses concerning the uses of the stone,

Ramírez sifted through those of earlier scholars. The *Descripción* reads like a procession of authorities, from Clavijero and Fray Servando Teresa de Mier to Humboldt, Franck, Nebel, Dupaix, Mayer, Kingsborough, and the catalogues of various European museums. For each of the objects selected, Ramírez tried to present the reader with the state-of-the-art scholarship specific to the piece and with the opportunity to compare and juxtapose competing hypotheses that had been suggested about its uses or meanings. At the same time, he combined bibliographical erudition with a more concrete sort of knowledge. Such was the case with the small winch-like object to the right of the lithograph, which he identified as a clay instrument, similar to those still used for spinning by indigenous women, who called them "malacates." The National Museum owned many items of this class, of varying form, ornament, or material, "according to the quality of the persons who owned them." Ramírez remembered having seen them also in the Egyptian Museum in Turin, which classified them as "oggeti diversi" and in the British Museum, in cases 29 and 30 of the Ethnographic Rooms. The catalogue of the British Museum described them as "conical, perforated objects, ornamented with native devices, apparently used as BUTTONS or STUDS," a description with which Ramírez disagreed, explaining that the ancient Mexicans did not use buttons and that, in fact, Nahuatl lacked a word for "button." He used the opportunity to take issue with "similar explanations in the catalogues of other collections," which circulated "so many false ideas, so many violent interpretations, so many imaginary analogies and so many fantastical systems, as are present in almost all of the writers on American antiquities."[89]

The *Descripción* is as interesting as an object in the history of archaeological method as it is for the objects it describes. Here, Ramírez begins to set down conventions for studying and representing Mexican antiquities. Against what he rejected as "fantastic systems," Ramírez offered a modest "corrective": description, a deceivingly easy method but one which presupposed the collection of as much information about an object as possible. The science of Mexico's past would begin with building up a very large bibliographical corpus, which lay scattered in libraries, museums, and other repositories across many countries. Through sustained correspondence with collectors, bibliophiles, antiquarians, and editors, Ramírez endeavored to create a database of all that was known of Mexican antiquities in both Europe and America. Just as German historians of the time, beginning with Leopold von Ranke (1795–1886), were emphasizing the crucial importance of finding and applying critical tools to primary documents in order to create scientific histories, Ramírez strove to make Mexico's past the object of a "science of the archive" by collecting, sifting through, and juxtaposing studies, objects, manuscripts, or, in their absence, images of objects and copies of manuscripts.[90]

At the same time, Ramírez brought to bear his understanding of the uses of objects and artisanal procedures in the Mexico of his time, as well as his understanding of the importance of places and place names, of topography and local anecdotes. It is in this sense that he insisted on preserving the knowledge of the exact places from whence an artifact came and that he studied toponymics in relation to myths and traditions about places. "The names of places," he wrote, quoting Leibniz, "preserve the memory of lost languages and the traces of nations that have disappeared."[91] In other words, the use of geographic names could lead to uncovering deeper levels of the past, as Ramírez had shown in his essays on place names in Durango. It is a local kind of history, on a scale much smaller than the universalist histories that sought to juxtapose a handful of Mexican antiquities or a number of not fully explored sites with grandiose theories of the origin of American man, in tandem with the religious, mythological, linguistic, and aesthetic systems of other ancient civilizations.

Overall, Americanist antiquarianism had been the study of coincidences—mythological, linguistic, or morphological—between antiquities in the Old and the New Worlds and had operated in a selective manner, choosing to see certain objects and to ignore others according to the slant of some idea. With exceptions, this comparative strategy had served to underscore an evolutionary paradigm, placing the ancient civilizations of America as beneficiaries of Egyptian, Hindu, Chinese, or Hebrew wisdom. But, Ramírez insisted, this ignored the possibility that societies geographically separated might tend to go through certain similar technological processes and might coincidentally hit on the same solutions to various cultural problems. To find an analogy was not the same as finding an imitation; there was no evidence that Old World structures were inherited by New World cultures. "Those who do not want to grant America's unfortunate son any original thought explain the pyramids as an imitation of Egypt," complained Ramírez, as he insisted on the need for different approaches to the study of Mexico's ancient past.[92] To decenter history from a model in which the development of European culture was not only the most advanced but also the root of all other cultures meant reading Mexico's past and its present as a particular and autonomous phenomenon, which could be connected to other cultures but which absorbed or rejected them according to its own codes. Ranke wrote that "every epoch was equally close to God"—that is, no epoch could be judged in terms of another, later one; one had to seek out its phenomenology within its texts and monuments themselves.[93] Ramírez was engaged on much the same mission.

By the late 1850s, Ramírez enjoyed a modest but growing international reputation as a scholar. Paulin had invited him to study Mexican manuscripts in Paris, and Ferdinand Denis, the librarian of Sainte-Geneviève, had reviewed his studies favorably.[94] Unlike the conservators of the National Museum of Mexico who had preceded him, Ramírez participated in the international spaces where agents competed with each other to stabilize the circulation and the meanings of Mexican antiquities. In so doing, he positioned himself firmly as a scholar of his country's ancient past and helped give shape to the figure of the Mexican intellectual, being among the first in a long line that extends through such well-known contemporary figures as Octavio Paz.

Ramírez's *Descripción* was included in a much wider project of reconnaissance of Mexico by Mexicans in the midcentury, the opulent album *México y sus alrededores*, which paired up large-sized lithographs by the talented artist Casimiro Castro (1826–89) with accompanying text by some of Mexico's foremost intellectuals, such as Manuel Payno, Guillermo Prieto, and Francisco Zarco (1829–69). They had been summoned without regard for their political allegiances, in an effort to forge consensus about what places, objects, and traditions identified Mexicans (at least those from Mexico City and its environs) as Mexicans. The cathedral lit by a full moon, the luxurious Chapultepec Forest with its centuries-old *ahuehuetes* (also known as Moctezuma's cypresses), the School of Mines, the Alameda, the city's most celebrated promenades were some of the vistas that made up this first truly Mexican guidebook, whose production value and price were intended to make it the choice of both well-to-do Mexicans and foreign visitors (the album included translations of the Spanish texts into English and French). In the context of the album, Mexican antiquities were represented under the congealing narrative that endowed Mexico "both with textual tangibility and a palpable past."[95] Against the growing threat of a civil war, which haunted Mexico at the very moment Castro was producing the album, Mexico's National Museum, which ostensibly both preserved and explained the vestiges of the past, was moving toward a new role in public opinion; it was becoming a center of credentialing and knowledge, shaping and predicating the identity of the past on which the present nation was being erected.

Yet it is important not to exaggerate, retrospectively, this movement or to see in it some necessary evolution. Efforts such as those made by the circle around *México y sus alrededores* proved feeble. The reforms pushed by the liberal government starting in 1855 had had a polarizing effect on the nation. Anarchy and fragmentation won in the end, as the country plunged again into the Guerra de Reforma (1857–61). A military coup by a conservative faction forced Juárez out of the capital in January 1858; for the next three years, Mexico had two governments, one under Juárez, in Veracruz, and another under Miguel Miramón (1832–67), in Mexico City. Then on January 1, 1861, Juárez ousted Miramón from Mexico City and declared a moratorium on all the foreign debts acquired by the conservative government (specifically, 750,000 francs procured from

Jean Baptiste Jecker). This would be taken as pretext by Napoleon III—looking for strategic control of the Isthmus of Tehuantepec as a way to expand commercial ties with Asia—to land French troops in Veracruz in December of 1861, taking advantage of the civil war raging in one of Juárez's most important supporters, the United States.

Under these circumstances, the National Museum was hardly on the mind of Mexico's political authorities, who had a hard time ensuring the protection of the objects gathered there. When he visited the museum in the spring of 1856, Edward Burnett Tylor came upon the following sight:

> We were rather surprised, when we reached the gate leading into the courtyard, to be stopped by a sentry who demanded what we wanted. The lower storey had been turned into a barrack by the Government, there being a want of quarters for soldiers. As the ground floor under the cloisters is used for the heavier pieces of sculpture, the scene was somewhat curious. The soldiers had laid several of the smaller idols down on their faces, and were sitting on the comfortable seat on the small of their backs, busy playing at cards. An enterprising soldier built up a hutch with idols and sculptured stones against the statue of the great war-goddess Teoyamiqui herself and kept rabbits there. The state which the whole place was in when thus left to the tender mercies of a Mexican regiment, may be imagined by any one who knows what a dirty and destructive animal a Mexican soldier is.[96]

Tylor was not simply coloring a narrative geared toward his own political motivations. On January 7, 1860, Ramírez denounced the damages to antiquities perpetrated by a drunk sergeant of the 5th Company of Grenadiers.[97] And a year later, on January 11, 1861, he complained that troops quartered there had destroyed the wooden fence that protected museum objects.[98] Whether occupied by soldiers loyal to the liberal or to the conservative cause, it was clear that the museum and its antiquities were not safe from the vicissitudes of daily life in midcentury Mexico City. Something needed to be done to protect the country's ancient vestiges.

In 1862 Juárez charged the SMGE to draft a project for the conservation and management of antiquities, the "Proyecto de Ley Relativo a la Conservación de Monumentos Arqueológicos." The project, which benefitted from the experience of Ramírez, was published in the ninth volume of the *Boletín de la Sociedad Mexicana de Geografía y Estadística* in 1862.[99] It began with a comprehensive definition of antiquities, which encompassed, among other objects, pyramidal constructions; ruins; military defense works; tombs; statues and reliefs; ornaments and domestic utensils; weapons; tools (such as blades, trowels, scrapers, or molds); drums; silver and copper coins minted in the sixteenth century and during the War of Independence; paintings and drawings on maguey, cloth, or wood, with characters used by the Indians. Next, the project dealt directly with the management of "ancient monuments," prescribing their conservation by the country's juridical and political authorities and prohibiting their extraction, exportation out of the country, and unlicensed excavation, with permission to excavate being the exclusive domain of the Ministry of Public Works, in consultation with the National Museum. When such permits were granted, all "discoverers" had to follow scrupulous recording regimes, marking the place of the findings, the indigenous name of the place, and the disposition of the objects. Furthermore, the project specified that objects incrusted in public or private buildings were to be deposited in the National Museum, unless doing so would compromise the safety of the building. Objects found on public land belonged to the state, while those found on private land belonged to their owner. But objects found on private land could not be exported out of Mexico, and the Mexican State reserved for itself the right to purchase them at the price established by the experts.

The project presented by the Sociedad was the most comprehensive proposal regarding antiquities to date, contributing both to a long-needed definition of antiquities and to rules about their handling. However, it was presented to a government in retreat. By April of 1863, after being held back by General Ignacio Zaragoza (1829–62) in Puebla for eleven months, the French, under General Ellie Frédéric Forey, finally advanced on Mexico City. A year later, they set up a Habsburg monarchy under Emperor Maximilian. Juárez fled and set up his alternative government first in San Luis Potosí and then in Chihuahua, whence he directed the counteroffensive. While some of his contemporaries went into hiding with Juárez, Ramírez did not. He stayed behind and went on to occupy diverse political posts in the imperial administration, while holding on to the conservatorship to the National Museum for a while. Renouncing the mandarin ideal of quiet and humble study, which he had held onto for almost a decade, Ramírez irrupted again in the arena of politics, power, and influence, during particularly turbulent times. Ramírez never confided the motives that led him to this decision, but surely he knew that it was a risky one, since we do know he hesitated before taking the post.[100] Part of him must have believed that it was the only way to protect his museum from the invaders, whose "fantastic systems" and no-less-fantastical claims on Mexico's past, and on Mexico's natural and economic resources, he was only too familiar with and wary of. To his credit, he managed to thwart many of these claims and to ensure that Mexico's prized antiquities remained in the country during difficult years of the Second Empire.

6 WHOSE MUSEUM?

"Conquering Your Great Country by Science"

A few months after French troops entered Mexico City, the painter Édouard Pingret renewed his correspondence with the Louvre. Pingret, who had been waiting for seven years for a propitious moment to sell his collection to the Louvre, must have believed he could profit personally by rekindling French interest in Mexican antiquities in general. Offering his expert knowledge on the topic, Pingret wrote Count Alfred Émilien von Nieuwerkerke, general director of the Musées Nationaux, to urge him to claim for the Louvre all the antiquities at Mexico's National Museum:

> Now that the French armies have conquered Mexico, the Mexican Museum, abandoned to the dust of centuries, must belong to France; if [Mexicans] do not want to donate it, the administration of the Beaux Arts is rich enough to buy it. And if they do no want to sell or donate it, then France must take it by force. [. . .] One must imagine the vivid interest caused by the Mexican Museum in Paris and in Europe, if we suddenly announced that Mexico has honored the Emperor with that Museum in its entirety—it must contain 4000 objects. What glory [that would be] for the founder of that Museum.[1]

With his letter, Pingret included a photograph of the cathedral in Mexico City, where he circled the location of the Piedra del Sol on one of the towers, with the idea that the French should collect it, together with the rest of the antiquities in the museum.[2] Pingret's letter evoked little interest at the Louvre, so he followed up with other letters, pressing his campaign in the fall of 1863 and the first months of 1864. In February of 1864 he sent Nieuwerkerke a thirty-three-page "Notes sur les antiquités aztèques de M. Pingret," in which, besides trying to interest the director in his own collection of antiquities, Pingret insisted again that France had a golden opportunity to collect Mexico's antiquities for itself. It would be easy to obtain all these objects, he assured Nieuwerkerke, because "there is no vainer being than a Mexican: by giving him some money and a few insignia and badges, you could have from him anything you want." As for the museum of Aztec antiquities in Mexico City, "it has no value for a Mexican, who holds it for nothing."[3]

The Louvre was, once more, unimpressed. Pingret directed his next letter to Emperor Napoleon III. Part description of his own collection, with watercolor illustrations of some of his choice objects, part attempt to interest the emperor in preconquest antiquities, the 112-page "Deuxième essai de notes sur les antiquités aztèques de Monsieur Pingret" rambled cantankerously against those who Pingret thought had snubbed him.[4] High on his list of culprits was Nieuwerkerke, whom he accused of not having fulfilled his obligations as France's foremost cultural authority: rather than sitting out the Mexican invasion in his quarters at the Louvre, the count should have followed the French troops on the day of their entrance into Mexico City, in order to "see, with his own eyes," the country's antiquarian riches. Pingret was, in other words, advocating a kind of military and cultural campaign such as that led by Napoleon I in Egypt in the late 1790s. Again, there was no response. By this time, Pingret had succeeded only in confirming, among Americanist circles in Paris, that he was an unpleasant and delusional personality. But even if his extravagant project for the seizure of Mexico's cultural properties for the glory of France and their preservation from the negligence of idle Mexicans fell on deaf ears, similar arguments were being made by others.

In fact, almost at the same time as Pingret was running into a wall of silence, in February of 1864 the minister of public instruction in France, Victor Duruy (1811–94), was proposing that a scientific commission should be formed to study and collect Mexico's cultural and natural properties. In support of his project, Duruy made a Napoleonic reference that was clearly meant to please Napoleon's nephew. Under the first Napoleon, one of the intellectual glories of the empire was the Commission scientifique d'Egypt, the "colony of savants" who, following in the heels of forty thousand soldiers, "conquered Egypt in their own way."[5] The scholars had set out to "tear up the veils that had enveloped that ancient civilization during fifteen centuries," to collect facts of "practical utility" about the climate and geographic conditions of the valley of the Nile, and to produce topographical and geographical surveys needed to determine the possibility of an isthmian canal. And Duruy explained, while Europe became richer with scientific facts, ideas, and artistic forms, Egypt, "awakened from her lethargy by contact with French soldiers and savants," underwent "regeneration."[6] France could boast the honor of having "pulled those people out of their torpor."[7]

Duruy had the Egyptian campaign in mind when he insisted, "That which has been done on the Nile under Napoleon I will be done in Mexico under Napoleon III."[8] Mexico, like Egypt, concealed many "secrets" that would be uncovered through study. Duruy believed that Mexico was historically less interesting than Egypt, but there were clearly remnants of an ancient past strewn over the Mexican landscape, which required science (and European scientists) to resurrect it by solving the enigma of the origin of the American Indian races and by deciphering the unknown languages and mysterious inscriptions.[9] Additionally, botanical, meteorological, and mineralogical explorations would prove "useful for commerce and [. . .] advance the solution of a problem posed twenty years before by Napoleon I: that of piercing the American isthmus by an inter-oceanic canal."[10] Finally, anthropological studies of the mestizo would answer questions of physiological, moral, and social interest. French soldiers had accomplished the military conquest of Mexico; French scholars would conquer the country scientifically.

Napoleon approved the formation of the Commission scientifique du Mexique (CSM) on February 27, and Duruy began organizing it right away. It would consist of four different committees: natural sciences and medicine; physical and chemical sciences; linguistics and archaeology; statistics, public works, and administration. A central commission in France, made up of authorities in each of these different disciplines, was charged with providing expeditioners and correspondents in Mexico with thorough background reports of the state of research in their respective fields and with detailed instructions on the type of data and objects they were expected to collect.[11]

Duruy sought to enlist Mexican scientists as correspondents; with this purpose in mind, in a rather backhanded and tactless fashion, he invited the participation of the members of the Sociedad Mexicana de Geografía y Estadística (SMGE): "The emperor, who has not wanted a conquest by arms, has the noble ambition to finish conquering your great country by science. [. . .] Our savants will march once again behind our soldiers," to collect and organize a big assembly of studies, observations, and investigations on the soil, waters, climate, and natural productions; races and languages; and monuments in Mexico and Central America.[12] In return for French scientific generosity with Mexico, Duruy asked the SMGE for "scientific hospitality." There is no record as to what the members of the SMGE thought about being invited to participate in the scientific conquest of their own country; after all, the SMGE, organized into committees that corresponded roughly to those of the CSM, had already been studying Mexico scientifically for three decades. Some of them, ignoring the implied insult to their previous labors and looking hopefully toward the foreign invaders to create stability in their county, would have been pleased; others, more opportunistically, might have taken the occasion to cultivate European scholarly relations. In any case, on May 15 José Urbano Fonseca (1802–71), vice president of the SMGE, wrote to Duruy to say that the institution agreed to collaborate and awaited further instructions.[13] On June 4 Duruy appointed a combat engineer, Colonel Louis Toussaint Doutrelaine (1820–81), as intermediary between the central commission in France, expeditioners and correspondents in the field, and local authorities throughout Mexico.[14]

In the meantime, General François Achille Bazaine (1811–88), Forey's successor as the head of the French foreign legion in Mexico, established his own Commission scientifique, artistique et littéraire du Mexique (CSALM) in February of 1864.[15] The aim of the CSALM, as Bazaine explained in the organization's prospectus, was to "stimulate a taste" for the arts and the sciences in Mexico, to produce useful knowledge for the promotion of industry and agriculture, and to foment intellectual commerce between Mexico and France.[16] Divided into ten sections, the CSALM consisted of seventy-seven members—officials in the French army and Mexican scholars—many of whom went on to participate in the CSM as well.[17] Doutrelaine was designated de facto president of the CSALM, with wide powers of organization and supervision.[18]

Considering that the CSALM and the CSM had many goals in common and employed many of the same people, historians have tried to reconcile their autonomy with the nature of their collaborative relationship with one another.[19] Doutrelaine, playing an executive role in both, offered a convincing reflection on the CSALM as a precursor that would "prepare the terrain" for the Parisian commission to do its work: "If we are not in a condition to perform scientific work, we will at least be able to make certain simple observations, to collect materials of all kinds, and that in itself would be enough. If in the end, a commission of true scientists would come here, at least we would have prepared the way for them, and their task would be made easier. All they would have to do is coordinate, direct, and reinforce our work."[20]

In other words, the CSALM would play an ancillary role to the CSM, providing information on field conditions and raw data on a number of topics, with the idea that, once the French expeditioners began arriving, as they did by the summer of 1864, they would improve on the work begun by the CSALM and send their results to Paris, where the knowledge produced in the field would be analyzed and organized. The crowning achievement of the CSM, the three-volume *Archives de la Commission scientifique du Mexique* (1865–68), reinforces the distribution of roles between local correspondents, French expeditioners, and the central committee in Paris. Each volume consists of four sections: instructions by members of the central committee in Paris; studies by these same, based on materials received from Mexico; reports from the field; and lists and sometimes reviews of books presented to the CSM.

At the center of this large-scale operation, Doutrelaine ran the imperial peace mission with the tactics he had picked up in his military training. He scouted the terrain and his people, distributed correspondents and resources, built communication networks, solved problems when they arose, and mediated, when possible, between the personal needs and ambitions of those involved in the explorations in order to ensure the success of the entire enterprise. His 134 letters to Duruy, written over the period of two and a half years that the CSM was active in Mexico, report on the everyday workings of the commission and prove to be an invaluable source for understanding just to what extent the French commission displaced the National Museum as a collector and analyst of objects of different kinds, from antiquities to rocks, plants, and animals.[21] The success of the CSM at securing massive quantities of (sometimes massive) objects and at transporting them over large distances provides a telltale foil to the museum's limited success at accomplishing the same feat over the forty years since its foundation and makes us wonder inevitably how much richer the national collection could have been had the museum been able to count on the kind of institutional support the CSM received.

On a very basic level, Doutrelaine was in charge of moving people and things around. He accompanied expeditioners from the moment they set foot in Mexico until they returned to France, introducing them to Mexican authorities and to Mexican scholars, looking after their health and well-being, ensuring they had all the materials and instruments necessary for their work, and deploying them to the field. Thus, over the year 1865, he sent Edmond Guillemin-Tarayre (1832–90), an expeditioner for the geological and mineralogical committee who turned out to have a knack for archaeological work, to study the archaeological ruins at La Quemada, in the state of Zacatecas, and then to the Cerro de las Palmas, on the Tacubaya River, after military exercises there revealed the presence of thirty figurines of naked women and of purportedly ancient skulls.[22] In the meantime, Léon Méhédin (1828–1905), an expeditioner on the archaeological committee, went to Teotihuacan and then to Xochicalco, while geologist Auguste Dollfus (1789–1881) and mining engineer Eugène de Montserrat were sent to study the Cofre de Perote, Guanajuato, and Pachuca.[23]

Furthermore, Doutrelaine kept tabs on the progress achieved by each of the committees, including detailed periodic reports on their work, and in the process revealed his own broad understanding of many sciences and his unbridled curiosity in a large array of subjects. He praised Guillemin-Tarayre's mineralogical and archaeological surveys.[24] Meanwhile, he complained that the anthropological committee had done too little, due to the lack of commitment on the part of Alphonse Lami (1822–67) and to various technical problems: the photography workshop proved impossible to set up, there were not enough competent doctors to carry out quantitative studies, and Indians were reluctant to pose for photographs or to submit to the kinds of measurements and quantitative studies that were the hallmark of French anthropology of the time, under the influence of Jean Louis Armand de Quatrefages (1810–92), who sat on the central committee.[25] Doutrelaine hoped to recoup the failures of the anthropological contingent by bringing Guillemin-Tarayre and Emmanuelle Domenech (1825–1903), a French priest who had a good knowledge of Spanish and enjoyed trust among the Indians, onto the anthropological team.[26]

Among Doutrelaine's most important assignments was ensuring that the materials produced by expeditioners—their field notes and the objects they collected—were safely delivered to the central committee in Paris. Doutrelaine's letters reveal few details about the logistics of this end of his mandate, leaving us to speculate that he probably took advantage of the maneuvers of French troops across the Mexican territory to have the materials reach him and that, after sorting through them, he had them transported via the main route between Mexico City and Veracruz and onward by boat to France. The task was all the harder in that Mexico still lacked a railway system, so the sheer mass of stuff that was being sent had to be carted via mule.

As a case in point, we might take a look at Doutrelaine's shipment of four large boxes on September 25, 1865. A 112-kilogram box containing fossils, the mold of the so-called Stone of Tlalnepantla, jars of plants in alcohol, the ten volumes of the *Diccionario universal de historia y de geografía de México*, Clavijero's *Historia de la Antigua o Baja California*, and Echeverría y Veytia's *Texcoco en los últimos tiempos de sus antiguos reyes.* A second box, weighing 168 kilograms, contained an herbarium; a third one was packed with 27 kilograms' worth of live plants collected around Mexico City, in the Mixteca, and in the Córdoba and Orizaba region; and a forth one, weighing 44 kilograms, contained a collection of seeds.[27] A month later, Doutrelaine sent Duruy another herbarium, more live plants, and mineralogical samples gathered by Guillemin-Tarayre. No object was too big for Doutrelaine; in September of 1866 he inquired at the National Museum about obtaining the Yanhuitlán meteorite, which had arrived at the museum in October of 1864 as a gift to Emperor Maximilian.[28] But the request was denied.[29] Nor were any objects too small for his attention, though they certainly posed different challenges for shipping. Such was the case with the colony of silkworms that he hoped would reach Paris alive.[30]

Besides conveying the objects produced and collected by expeditioners and correspondents, Doutrelaine was constantly informing Duruy about the possibility of purchasing other collections for the csm. Thus, he directed Duruy's attention to Eugène Boban (1834–1908), a French industrialist who had traveled all over Mexico, amassing a wide variety of objects along the way.[31] Doutrelaine alerted Duruy that Boban was planning to sell his collection to the National Museum for 20,000 francs, though he thought Boban could be persuaded to sell it to the commission instead. With this aim in mind, he urged Boban to write up a taxonomical and analytical inventory of his pieces; over the next two years, Doutrelaine sent Duruy descriptions and drawings of Boban's antiquities, fossils, and human bone remains, which, he hoped, would prove useful for answering questions on the origins of the New World's ancient inhabitants.[32]

The work of the csm in Mexico would have been unimaginable without a large network of Mexican collaborators who intervened at different levels. Mexicans were hired to guide expeditioners to specific sites, to collect and transport specimens, to carry instruments and provisions, and to perform excavation work. For the most part, these people remain unnamed in Doutrelaine's letters.

The delegate did, however, write at length about his dealings with the Mexican correspondents of the csm. In the beginning, Doutrelaine confessed that he thought Mexicans would be of little value for the commission: "I doubt there is in the civilized world a race more indolent than that of those Spanish *metis*, who have taken as rule of behavior and as slogan the phrase [. . .] 'serious business, for tomorrow.' Add to this the fact that the Mexican is inclined to vanity, presumptuousness, self-infatuation. [. . .] Savants do not abound in Mexico and I do not think I can cite one sole man truly worthy of that name."[33]

Still, Doutrelaine was able to compile a long list of Mexican scholars and scientists worthy of note, including José Fernando Ramírez, Mexico's "most capable antiquarian"; Antonio García Cubas (1832–1912), "author of the *Atlas geográfico, estadístico e histórico de México*, the most considerable and best of what has been published here [in Mexico]"; Joaquín García Icazbalceta, "owner of precious manuscripts"; Antonio del Castillo, "a most capable geologist and mineralogist"; and Leopoldo Río de la Loza (1807–76), "one of the most able chemists in the country."[34] Doutrelaine expressed regrets that the geographer Francisco Díaz Covarrubias (1833–89); the writer Manuel Payno; and Gabino Barreda (1818–81), a doctor steeped in Auguste Comte's positivist philosophy and, according to Doutrelaine, "Mexico's only zoologist," had joined Juárez on his exile and presumably would turn down any csm invitation.[35] On November 3, 1864, Duruy named many of the scholars recommended by Doutrelaine as correspondents of the csm, taking a chance and including Barreda in the list. Not surprisingly, "Mexico's only zoologist" did not collaborate with the commission.[36] Though he admitted those Mexicans who had chosen to collaborate with the csm were "altogether superior to the rest of their compatriots," Doutrelaine did not think they were "altogether immaculate of the generic faults" that plagued all Mexicans. He "feared their moral inertia, scientific insufficiency, and presumptuousness."[37]

Doutrelaine managed, nonetheless, to have close and productive relationships with Mexican scholars, especially with those who shared his own antiquarian pursuits. Whether or not his antiquarian curiosity preceded his arrival in Mexico, Doutrelaine traveled extensively to archaeological sites, often as part of military engagements. His letters reveal a broad knowledge of Mexican antiquities, as he discusses the theories about Mexico's ancient past that were then in vogue.[38] In Mexico City he frequented Manuel Orozco y Berra (1816–89)—Emperor Maximilian's minister of public works, who, "with his habitual generosity," acquainted Doutrelaine with his studies of Teotihuacan and invited the Frenchman to examine a "curious" archaeological collection that had belonged to the Camacho brothers in Campeche.[39] Doutrelaine studied the collection and sent Duruy descriptions and four pages of drawings of the more "rare and curious" pieces: a monkey, a bat, copulating rabbits, a penis-shaped whistle, and Priapus-like figurines and phalluses in the shape of various animals.

One of Doutrelaine's most important Mexican interlocutors was José Fernando Ramírez, who held on to his curatorship at the museum throughout most of 1865 while exercising high posts in Maximilian's cabinet. In September of 1864 Ramírez gave Doutrelaine a guided tour of the museum's choicest archaeological objects and authorized the French delegate, "if not too hurriedly," to photograph them. Furthermore, Ramírez granted Doutrelaine permission to reproduce material from his private cabinet and directed the delegate's attention to other sites worthy of study—such as the ruins at Peñon de los Baños, at Chapultepec, at Iztapalapa, and at Xico (off Lake Chalco) and the pyramid at Los Remedios (three leagues southwest of the city)—while also urging Doutrelaine to organize an expedition to Teotihuacan to photograph both the two big pyramids and the smaller adjacent ones.[40]

Doutrelaine could not begin to take advantage of Ramírez's authorizations until some months later. The archaeological expeditioner of the CSM, Brasseur de Bourbourg, had run into conflicts over his excavation work at the ruins in Yucatán and had left Mexico for Central America. The CSM appointed Léon Méhédin—an artist close to Napoleon III whose photographic panoramas of the siege of Sebastopol during the Crimean War and whose molds of ruins in Italy and Egypt were much admired—to replace Brasseur.[41] Méhédin arrived in Mexico in April 1865.[42] By May he installed his workshop in the National Museum and was busy making drawings, taking photographs, and producing rubbings and molds of objects.[43] It is hard to imagine how anyone could have set up shop in the cramped quarters at the museum, but two months later, Méhédin sent to Paris an enormous box with rubbings of the museum's "principal stones," such as the Teoyamiqui and the Teoyaotlatohua, and of the Calendar Stone.[44] By August, following Ramírez's recommendation, Doutrelaine sent Méhédin to Teotihuacan.[45]

Joaquín García Icazbalceta, a hacienda owner from Morelos and a passionate historian and bibliophile, was another of Doutrelaine's Mexican collaborators; he welcomed the French delegate into his "precious library," allowing Doutrelaine to make copies of rare Spanish manuscripts, Mexican maps, and topographical plans from the second half of the sixteenth century.[46] Moreover, García Icazbalceta presented the CSM with copies of his two-volume *Colección de documentos para la historia de México* (1858–66), which contained rare sixteenth-century documents he had gathered and edited. Doutrelaine sent the central committee in Paris García Icazbalceta's book, together with copies of Orozco y Berra's topographic maps and his *Geografía de las lenguas y carta etnográfica de México* (1858)—a linguistic study of the indigenous languages spoken in Mexico, together with their ethnographic and geographic distribution—along with works by others on ethnographic and geographic matters.

In turn, Doutrelaine was anxious to reciprocate for the generosity that Mexican scholars had shown toward the commission, by securing their access to materials of interest from France. In October 1864 he presented Ramírez with Gustave Eichthal's *Études sur l'histoire primitive des races* (1845), which became the topic of a long and scathing review.[47] In his review, Ramírez systematically dismissed Eichthal's conclusions that American civilizations had an "Asiatic-Buddhist origin," with the expedition of five Buddhist monks to California in 480 AD.[48] Sometime later, in July 1865, Doutrelaine offered his Mexican collaborators more-valuable material—photographs of Mexican manuscripts at the Bibliothèque

Impériale in Paris, which Ramírez had consulted there ten years earlier.[49] The arrival of these reproductions, Doutrelaine hoped, would open the door to Ramírez's library, which, as the delegate knew, hid precious Mexican manuscripts.

As so often happens when an occupying force, animated by an imperial regard for its own superiority, comes in contact with the representatives of the occupied culture, Doutrelaine's respectful treatment of his Mexican collaborators did not always serve as an example to those in Paris, with negative consequences for the CSM's work in Mexico. The publication of a disparaging review by Aubin of works by García Icazbalceta and Orozco y Berra, among others, in the second volume of the *Archives*, constituted a low point in Franco-Mexican cooperation and put Doutrelaine at the center of a public relations crisis of sorts.[50] "I vividly regret that report, where such a large part has been given over to critique and such a minimal one to praise," wrote Doutrelaine, taking partial blame for what happened: "I should have taken the precaution to make it known to your Excellence to what excess of susceptibility Mexicans take authorial self-love (*amour propre*) and how much they can be affected, either painfully or agreeably, if these judgments are severe or flattering. M Aubin's report has been received badly among our Mexican correspondents in general, and especially so by those whose works have been analyzed in that ill-meaning *compte-rendu*."[51]

It is fair to speculate that many most likely remembered Aubin, the author of the *compte-rendu*, as the mastermind behind the cunning export of Mexican manuscripts to France in the late 1830s, which added insult to injury. Doutrelaine confessed to Duruy that he had "no desire to combat M Aubin's appreciations," considering the critiques "perfectly founded." What he regretted was that rebuke had not been balanced by "sufficient praise," to ensure Mexican cooperation with the commission; he warned that "these gentlemen will not fail to refuse, from now on, all contact with the Commission if it does not render them in return anything but critiques written in a haughty, harsh and sharp style."[52]

The incident generated by Aubin's review adds nuance to the

nature of the collaboration between the csm and its Mexican correspondents. For the latter, collaboration was an opportunity not only to pursue the study of their country's past and present at a much higher level but also, on a more personal level, to gain more renown and respect within the international circle of Americanists. After all, this group had seen the state things were in before the intervention; the *Bulletin of the Sociedad Mexicana de Geografía y Estadística*, the most important scientific journal in the country, had been practically suspended due to the internal strife prevailing in the country. Other editorial work was either being left uncompleted or unpublished during this crisis-beset period. Against this background, it is reasonable to think that Doutrelaine's Mexican collaborators—scholars like Orozco y Berra, Icazbalceta, and Pimentel—expected to see their works translated, published, and discussed fairly, side by side with those of French participants in the commission. In other words, they were probably expecting to be treated with a respect due to peers and equals in a wider intellectual and scientific community.

However, a summary glance at the three volumes of the *Archives* is enough to conclude that the Mexican collaborators of the commission were nourishing a delusion. Although the central committee in Paris periodically received books and reports by Mexican correspondents via Doutrelaine, not once was a Mexican correspondent published in what amounted to over 1,500 pages of the *Archives*. After all, the ideological justification of the intervention rested on the idea that the Mexicans were backward and needed the helpful civilizing push of the more evolved French. Given this prejudice, it was unlikely that the French would then welcome Mexican authors with open arms. Instead, the latter had the dubious honor of being reviewed by self-professed experts like Aubin or, in the best of cases, of seeing their writings being culled for raw data that served to enrich other writers' works.

The position of these Mexican scholars with respect to the csm summarizes, in effect, the place occupied by Spanish Americans since colonial times—that of suppliers of observations, notes, reports, and objects that would be evaluated, classified, organized, and systematized in centers of accumulation on the other side of the Atlantic. In the late eighteenth century, this scheme, when not treated as self-evident, was justified in terms of a patronizing Enlightenment cosmopolitanism; by the time of the French intervention, the terms of the model had hardened. It was not cosmopolitanism that was at issue. Rather, Mexico was, it was claimed, frankly underdeveloped on every level. Mexicans had to have their land, with its resources and its past, revealed and exploited for them, in order to produce, at some future time, those significant commercial, economic, and intellectual advantages that would let the ward of the higher imperial power graduate into the ranks of the higher civilizations. Even someone as sensitive as Doutrelaine, who, as we have seen, had plenty of opportunities to convince himself of the intellectual worth of his Mexican collaborators, subscribed entirely to the imperial rhetoric and argued that Mexicans should have been thankful for the work done by the csm.

Instead, Mexicans became increasingly ungrateful and less and less collaborative. Ramírez, for one, purposely delayed satisfying Doutrelaine's requests for copies of manuscripts from his personal library, while the Frenchman, on his side, was starting to despair that Ramírez would ever lend him any materials again.[53] Tension with the French was further aggravated after the arrival of Emperor Maximilian, who laid his own claims to Mexico's cultural and natural properties. His project to establish a local academy for arts and sciences, staffed mostly by Mexican scholars, gave allies of the emperor hope that the government would promote a thorough exploration program similar to that of the csm and that, under the aegis of imperial protection and renown, their own work would enjoy broader international recognition.

"An Equivocal Dialogue of Tangled Intentions"

Mexican historian Edmundo O'Gorman has referred to the circumstances that brought the younger scion of the Habsburg imperial family to Mexico as "an equivocal dialogue of tangled intentions."[54] The phrase aptly captures the complexities that made the Second Empire happen, which also brought it to its doom by the summer of 1867. When, in October of 1863, a delegation of Mexican conservatives offered him the crown, Maximilian, then thirty-one years old, was living in the Castle of Miramar in Trieste, off the Adriatic Sea, as the (more symbolic than real) head of the Austrian domains in the Veneto region. His political ambitions in the Viennese court stumped, Maximilian gravitated toward other interests, the natural sciences and the arts. An accomplished naturalist and an art collector, he transformed the Castle of Miramar into a showcase for his tastes and collections. In the garden around the castle, he planted species that he had collected on his journeys in the Mediterranean and as far off as Brazil. From Mexico, he would continue to send exotic plants for his garden in Miramar. Inside the castle, he accommodated his growing art collection, which boasted an important section of Egyptian antiquities, under the care of Simon Leo Reinisch (1832–1919), who would go on to become a renowned Egyptologist.[55]

If the Mexican delegates knew of Maximilian's liberal tendencies when they offered him the crown, they preferred to overlook them. They had settled on this relatively marginalized Habsburg because they had come to believe that only a true Habsburg would be able to counter liberal anticlericalism and put an end to the forty-year spell of civil unrest that marked Mexican independence. Maximilian cautiously conditioned his acceptance of the crown on the holding of a popular plebiscite and, less idealistically, on the promise of French support. Both conditions were quickly "fulfilled." The conservatives ran a sham plebiscite in some of the cities then under French occupation. Napoleon III pledged his military and monetary support as long as Maximilian managed to secure legitimacy, build his own imperial army, and put an end to insurgent movements around the country. A stable and peaceful Mexico would certainly be an asset to French commercial and strategic interests. Napoleon III longed to create a global French empire to compete with the English, which made the possibility of a virtual protectorate over Mexico tempting.

Maximilian accepted the crown on April 10, 1864, believing he would arrive in Mexico by popular demand, to regenerate a country that was "rich and strong by nature" and needed only science and civilization in order to "reclaim its position within the concert of American nations and its influence in determining the destiny of the continent."[56] For Maximilian this did not mean, contrary to the designs of those who had offered him the crown, restoring Mexico to the ideal of a catholic monarchy but rather continuing with some of the reforms begun by Juárez's liberal government, such as freedom of the press, religious tolerance, and the nationalization of church properties. To accomplish these reforms, Maximilian surrounded himself, at least during the first two years of his rule, with liberal moderates and sought the adherence of the local elites.[57] But the advance of these reforms, while alienating the conservative faction that had originally brought him to Mexico, did not win over the liberals, many of whom opposed the presence of a foreign monarchy in Mexico and preferred to follow Juárez into exile.

In keeping with his own scholarly pursuits, Maximilian saw science as another vehicle for regenerating Mexico. Upon accepting the crown, surely, he did not envision turning over the exploration of Mexico's cultural and natural resources to the French. Yet in June of 1864, when he arrived to claim the throne, the French, giving him little notice, had already begun the explorations. In itself, this was a sign of Maximilian's position vis-à-vis the French emperor; the French on the ground in Mexico perceived him as little more than a puppet of Napoleon III, on whom he depended for troops and money, as they made sure to remind him from the very moment of his arrival.[58] This explains Maximilian's suspicions and resentment toward the French initiatives to study Mexico and his outright refusal to support French exploration projects.

First came his snubbing of Doutrelaine by postponing delegate meetings designed to discuss the funding of the CSALM. The emperor seemed to favor instead a "pure blood Mexican Commission," lamented Doutrelaine.[59] Maximilian's gesture was not lost on Mexicans, who, taking a cue from their emperor and becoming "galvanized by the jealous overexcitement of national spirit," began to give the CSALM the cold shoulder too. As Doutrelaine complained to Duruy, "I have seen the Franco-Mexican Commission [. . .] fall into discredit among a good number of Mexicans because it has the vice, radical in their eyes, of being a French Institution. [. . .] Some no longer lend their house for meetings [of the CSALM]."[60]

Next, in November of 1864, came Maximilian's instructions to imperial commissioners throughout Mexico to "care especially for the conservation of antiquities and historical monuments and to impede at all cost the exportation of antiquities."[61] This de facto ratification of the 1862 SMGE project concerning the management of Mexican antiquities affected some of the French expeditioners directly. José Salazar Illaregui (1823–92), the imperial commissioner in Yucatán, interpreted Maximilian's instructions zealously, to the point that he forbade Brasseur de Bourbourg, the CSM archaeological expeditioner, to touch Mexican antiquities. Brasseur left Yucatán to search for ruins in Central America.[62] Sometime later, Salazar Illaregui took aim at hacienda owners in Yucatán, who "mistakenly thought they owned the ruins on their lands," and impeded them from offering the sculpture of a serpent head at Uxmal to Charles François Frédéric de Montholon (1814–86), Napoleon III's ambassador in Mexico.[63] With Salazar Illaregui in place, Doutrelaine was beginning to despair of the success of French explorations in Yucatán.

More than any other man at Maximilian's court, the French blamed Ramírez most directly for anti-French sentiment. Having abstained from voting for the monarchy, Ramírez agreed to participate in the imperial government after Empress Carlota pleaded with him to help build a strong cabinet. Ramírez was appointed minister of foreign relations in July of 1864, a post he held until March 3, 1866.[64] For his participation in the imperial government, Ramírez has gone down in official Mexican history as a traitor. The French, however, thought otherwise. The French priest Domenech, for instance, saw in Ramírez an "infiltrator" of the republican government whose intent, in accepting to join Maximilian's government, was to press the emperor to continue with the reforms begun by the exiled Juárez. As Domenech put it, "I have often heard people used to seeing that which happened in the dressing room of politics say that Juárez reigned in Mexico under Ramírez's name. I do not dare deny that assertion."[65]

For instance, the French held Ramírez directly responsible for the slow march of the negotiations for indemnifications to French citizens. The Mexican debt, accrued during Miramón's conservative government, was, after all, the only legitimate pretext France could claim for its intervention in Mexico. Even Empress Carlota, who genuinely liked and respected Ramírez, referred in her writings to the mutual animosity between Ramírez and the French ambassador Montholon, which developed into full-scale disputes between the months of July and October of 1865. For this, Carlota partially blamed Ramírez's tactics, which consisted of exercising a "truly serpentine politics" characteristic of lawyers.[66] In the long run, these altercations would cost both men their posts. Ramírez would be retired some months later in a last moment effort to make Napoleon III reconsider his decision to withdraw his support from Maximilian's empire.[67]

Having clashed in the arena of high politics, Ramírez and Montholon hardly agreed with each other on other matters. The management of Mexican antiquities was one of them. In the following passage, Domenech reported an encounter between the two men:

Little time after the arrival of the members of the scientific mission from Paris, he [Ramírez] renewed, by imperial decree, the prohibition against excavations in ancient monuments and against the export of Mexican antiquities. I went to see him [. . .]. After a long conversation, purely scientific, he accompanied me to see M. Montholon [. . .], who, making allusion to the prohibition, said to him:

"I hope, Mr. Minister, that you would not be so barbarous as to impede the excavation of monuments that you yourselves will never study and the exportation, for our museums and our emperor, who rends you such great services, of antiquities of which you have copies."

"Change the verb," responded Ramírez, "and say that I would not be so barbarous as to permit the excavation and exportation [of antiquities]."

That response made me repent for having praised the intelligence and liberality of the antiquarian-minister.[68]

It is difficult to know if this dialogue ever took place because neither Ramírez nor Montholon make reference to this encounter in their writings. Fictional or not, the passage allows us to see Ramírez as high French officials saw him. And it certainly reflects Ramírez's thought and style. As Domenech implies, Ramírez saw through the French pretense for plunder, however they disguised it; he was undoubtedly disturbed by the sheer mass of stuff that was leaving Mexico for Paris at the end of every month. So he employed a politics of indirect opposition—an opposition of inexplicable delays, local resistances, and vague promises—to ensure that antiquities and other resources did not leave the country. Several fingers pointed at Ramírez as the mastermind behind the prohibition against foreign management of antiquities in Mexico, and Doutrelaine interpreted Ramírez's unwillingness to come to Brasseur de Bourbourg's help in his conflict with the Yucatán commissioner as confirmation that Ramírez had something to do with the decree.[69]

Far from being an annex to the political and military events of the time, cultural politics in mid-1860s Mexico were a front that gave the opportunity to all parties to at least temporarily cast off their masks. When viewed against the background of French protestations that the commission, closely following on the heels of French troops, was collecting Mexico's antiquities and studying its natural resources in an effort that called itself pulling Mexico out of barbarity (even as, in actual fact, it operated to pilfer Mexican natural and cultural resources for France), Ramírez pursued a policy of reversing French justifications and laying bare the reality of French actions. Barbarity, for this Mexican intellectual, was acceding to the stronger power both the materials and the context of explanation that constituted the real wealth of Mexico. He proposed, instead, a local program of exploration. In so doing, Ramírez aligned his own antiquarian interests with those of Emperor Maximilian, who, in keeping with tendencies he had shown since his residence in

Trieste, had seen in his patronage of the arts and the sciences one way to consolidate his own imperial position.

Science at Maximilian's Court

Three months after his arrival in Mexico, Maximilian instructed Ramírez to organize a commission that would set up a state library, a state museum, and an academy of science, history, and language.[70] By April 1865 Ramírez had formed the Academia Imperial de Ciencias y Literatura (AICL).[71] Divided into three sections—the mathematical section (referring mostly to the natural sciences), the philosophical-historical section, and the philological-linguistic section—the structure of the AICL corresponded to the predominantly historical and archaeological interests of the organizer. In any case, the SMGE was already covering topics in the natural sciences. Of its thirty permanent members and thirty correspondents, many also participated in the CSM, as was the case with Río de la Loza in the mathematical section; García Icazbalceta and Ramírez in the philosophical-historical section; and Pimentel in the philological-linguistic section.[72]

Maximilian inaugurated the academy on April 10, 1865, on the first-year anniversary of his acceptance of the Mexican throne. The ceremony took place in the National Palace and began with a short speech where Maximilian spelled out some of the more important goals of the AICL: to contribute to the general well-being of the country by promoting exploration and development in agriculture, mining, and transportation and by serving as an imperial scientific council of sorts. In other words, the AICL would perform many of the same tasks assigned to the CSM, with the crucial difference that the findings would stay in Mexico. In contradistinction to Napoleon III and his ministers, who made it clear that they wanted French science to have a monopoly of cultural power in Mexico, which would in good time deliver it from its present state to civilization, Maximilian pointed out that the sciences had flourished in Mexico for a long time and only needed peace and stability in order to flourish again. Following his speech, the emperor handed out insignia to the academicians. Ramírez was named president of the academy.

Next spoke Ramírez and then José María Lacunza (1809–69), Maximilian's prime minister. Along the same lines as the emperor, Lacunza delivered a panegyric to modern science. Ramírez seized the moment to make public his reflections on Mexico's ancient past and to suggest future topics and courses of study with respect to Mexican antiquities.[73] The nineteenth century, Ramírez said, had seen the development of archaeology, which led to questions about the past of the New World. But most scholars approached ancient American monuments superficially, with an overreliance on available narrative models, which had resulted in hasty generalizations and untenable explanations. Declaring that all preconceived systems were obstacles in the path of truth, Ramírez mocked the "profane erudition" that saw vestiges of Christianity and of the Deluge in ancient American monuments and that took analogies for signs of genealogical kinship. He considered the comparison between the customs, practices, and institutions of the Old and the New Worlds to be legitimate. But he believed that comparisons had to be employed critically; American civilization was the product of neither blind imitation nor complete isolation, inasmuch as one could not discount the possibility of communications between the continents.

To avoid the pitfalls of systemic thinking, Ramírez proposed a different course of research, suggesting a working chronology for the ancient history of America and classifying areas and topics of study. He began by situating primitive man among the pyramid-shaped mounds and the humble tombs in the mountains of Nayarit. To find American man at the dawn of his intelligence, when "he took his eyes off the ground, [. . .] lifting them to the skies," Ramírez directed the antiquarian's attention to Teotihuacan.[74] Few vestiges were left over from the Toltecs, the next significant moment in the history of the continent, because most Toltec sites were destroyed at the time of the conquest. From the "true centers of an ancient and advanced civilization"—developed at Xochicalco, Papantla, Mitla, Palenque, Yucatán, and Central America—"all light and all knowledge disseminated throughout the continent [. . .] to be then eclipsed, as high civilization always has been, by the barbarity that

arrived to repair and regenerate the exhausted forces of civilization."[75] If ruins scattered across Mexico "were known to all," they
"were read by no one," lamented Ramírez.[76] Reflecting Maximilian's
political and archaeological interests, Ramírez drew his public's
attention to Yucatán as the archaeological challenge of his time.[77]

Reading the archaeological evidence in Yucatán was no easy matter, so Ramírez suggested that the material vestiges there should be
studied and deciphered much in the same way he had been studying the monuments of central Mexico, through comparison and
corroboration between different sources. He noted that there was
a "close resemblance" between hieroglyphs sculpted on the lintels
in Palenque and the glyphs represented in the *Dresden Codex* and
in the *Paris Codex*; next, he drew attention to the publication by
Brasseur de Bourbourg of Diego de Landa's manuscript that paired
up twenty-seven glyphs with twenty-seven letters of the alphabet,
which implied that the signs were phonetic. These twenty-seven
characters were the Rosetta stone of all antiquarian studies in Chiapas and Yucatán, Ramírez insisted. "If ingenuity had made the
stones of Egypt and Assyria, dumb during many centuries, speak,
why would American stones not answer when interrogated by science?" he asked.[78] They would, as long as they were being interrogated with modern, scientific methods. He concluded his speech
by urging Mexicans to accept foreign collaborators in the joint
enterprise of studying Mexico's ancient past but also by advising
them to play a central role in the exploration, as the rightful heirs
and owners of their country's monuments.

The Imperial Academy attested to the alliance between imperial
politics and imperial science. Maximilian had experienced how the
Italian discovery and celebration of its past had stirred up and unified the country. The AICL's commitment to the study of the country's past and to the exploration of its resources might generate a
comparable national project. It would bind the emperor's political
destiny to the whole of Mexican history, even as his legitimacy was
being questioned on many fronts: by the Mexicans who had brought
him in, by those who had rejected his presence in Mexico, and by
the French who had vowed their support to the empire.

Despite all the fanfare and the rhetoric that accompanied the foundation of the academy, its actual accomplishments as an institution were few, especially when compared with those of the CSM. The reasons had to do, as they often did, with lack of funds, which flowed rather to the more and more desperate project of pacifying and subduing the country. There was also a difference in the culture of specialization. Mexico's foremost scholars were at the same time, as they had been since independence, members of the political class, while French scholars were trained and employed to perform specialized tasks in semiautonomous institutions. In other words, during the particularly trying moments that characterized the Second Empire, men like Ramírez, Orozco y Berra, Lacunza, or Río de la Loza hardly had the leisure to carry on with their scientific studies. Still, members of the academy did publish some important scholarly works during 1865 and 1866, as did the SMGE. For instance, a summary look at the 657-page report by the minister of public works, Luis Robles Pezuela, gives us an idea of the diversity and sheer number of projects sponsored by his ministry during the year 1865, including the establishment of mills and factories (especially paper and textile), the layout of telegraphic cables between cities, the mapping of departments, the determination of geographical positions and altitudes of different points throughout the empire, the analysis of water sources, the collection of mining statistics, and reports by exploration commissions.[79]

Among these reports, one memoir of the expedition to Huachinango and Metlatoyuca, in the state of Puebla, is informative about how the existence of ruins of Mexico's past figured into the activity of expeditions that were set up for more immediately practical goals, such as colonization and the development of transportation and natural resources infrastructures. On July 15, 1865, Orozco y Berra appointed Ramón Almaraz—who had served on the Comisión Científica de Pachuca the year before and was writing up the memoirs of that expedition—to direct an expedition to Huachinango.[80] Orozco y Berra entrusted Almaraz with a series of tasks: to produce information on the topography, climate, and natural resources of the region comprised between Tulancingo and the navigable river Tuxpan, with an eye for the colonization of uncultivated and putatively empty plots of land (*terrenos baldíos*), and to generate archaeological data, including descriptions and plans of the ruins at Metlatoyuca.[81] Almaraz left Mexico City on July 18 in the company of William Hay, who was in charge of archaeology and photography, and Antonio García Cubas, who was responsible for the mapping aspects of the exploration. José María Velasco (1840–1912), who would later gain renown as a painter for his sweeping landscapes, joined the expedition as a naturalist.

The commission returned to Mexico City almost a month later. On August 30 Almaraz completed the memoir of the expedition, with maps, plans, and drawings.[82] The ethnographic and archaeological descriptions show the kind of assumptions that went into these expeditions. On the basis of the "good construction" of the pyramid at Metlatoyuca, Almaraz postulated an Egyptian origin for this civilization and imagined the migratory route taken by these ancient migrants from Egypt—they would have settled first in Metlatoyuca, close to the Atlantic coast, before moving on toward Teotihuacan. The statues found at Metlatoyuca were unlike central Mexican figurative sculpture, in that they respected the proportions of the body, resembled mummies, and had straight noses—sure signs, Almaraz thought, that they were made by a race different from the Aztecs (fig. 22). Who knows what Ramírez would have thought of this hypothesis, especially as it was drawn from scant evidence and hasty impressions of the kind that so plagued Americanist studies, in Ramírez's opinion.

As for contemporary Indians, Almaraz thought they fell into two groups: the Huachinangos, whose physiognomy made Almaraz suspect they were of Asian origin, and the Totonacos. About the latter, he noted that they were respectful toward civilized people and could be advantageously colonized. But Almaraz was worried about the prevalence of "ancient customs and preoccupations" among them. One incident stood out in his mind—when the Indians had to "abandon" the "idols" they had carried on their backs from the ruins of Metlatoyuca to Huachinango, whence they were to be transported on carts to the museum in Mexico City, the Indi-

22. Ramón Almaraz, sandstone figurines from the ruins of Metlatoyuca. *Memoria acerca de los terrenos de Metlatoyuca,* 1866. BNAH, Secretary of Culture-INAH-Mex-Photo Library Constantino Reyes Valerio. Reproduction authorized by the National Institute of Anthropology and History.

ans fell into deep gloominess. Almaraz reported that one of the Indians addressed his idol in Totonac—one wonders if Almaraz actually understood Totonac—in the following manner: "You are a bad god because you have allowed yourself to be carried out; I shall ask permission from the other gods to come here with all the people in the village and whip you. But, in the meantime, accept this coin promising us you will not do us any harm."[83] The rest of the Indians also deposited a coin next to the idol. It was because of superstitions like these, together with the fact the Totonacs had no industry or agriculture, that Almaraz believed it was urgent to establish colonies in these places, open up roads, and protect the indigenous race, apparently, from its savage propensities.

By September 17 an imperial decree authorized Enrique Baron de Sauvage to form an autonomous company, the Compañía Mexicana de Colonización, for the express purpose of "peopling" the "empty" terrains belonging to the districts of Huachinango, Tuxpan, and Metlatoyuca.[84] The idea of diluting indigenous populations by settling more "advanced" people among them on the best land would become popular in the Porfirian decades—in fact, there was another attempt to people the Huachinango district in 1883—and it points to the multifold nature of these expeditions, which combined scientific and commercial enterprises.

A few months after the return of the Metlatoyuca commission, Maximilian began planning an expedition on a larger scale to Yucatán. On November 14, 1865, he wrote to Manuel Siliceo, then minister of public instruction: "For my trip to Yucatán, I have given orders for a commission of scientists in all branches of science to travel with me, so that they may examine this interesting province from all angles, make collections, and finally write an illustrated oeuvre detailing the results of their scientific exploration."[85] This was the first time a Mexican head of state would visit the far-off peninsula and the first time the government would undertake a thorough study of it. Maximilian had the unique advantage of having actually been on scientific expeditions before. There was a mixture of scientific curiosity and practical politics behind the project. There was the hope that the emperor's intervention could put an end to the Caste War, a Mayan insurgency that had been afflicting the eastern side of the peninsula since 1847. On his more ambitious days, Maximilian envisioned the construction of a Central American empire, along the lines of the old Mayan ruins, as he interpreted them.[86] Such being the objectives of the imperial commission, it is no wonder that Doutrelaine began to despair that, after Brasseur de Bourbourg's fiasco, the CSM would ever be able to organize the exploration of Yucatán. The Mexican emperor would get there first, it seemed.

In the end, Maximilian never went to Yucatán. The ambitious imperial project declined into a reconnaissance party of court officials who accompanied Empress Carlota on her visit to the calmer and imperial-friendly Mérida and Campeche during November and early December of 1865, while the emperor was detained in Mexico City by an increasingly troubling domestic situation. Even so, during the brief time they spent there, the imperial party collected a relatively large number of documents on different aspects of the peninsula, from climate to agriculture, from immigration possibilities to the situation of the indigenous population, from antiquities to public instruction. In every department, the empress gathered lists with the names of the local elites who supported the imperial cause and lists of those hostile to it.[87] Carlota's visit was in itself a calculated political move to gain adepts in the far-off peninsula.

The sole representative of the "commission of scientists in all branches of science" was Ramírez. Though it is very likely that his participation in this trip corresponded with antiquarian interests, it is also possible that he might have been sent to Yucatán in order to remove him from the imperial court and put some distance between him and the indemnification commissions that were meeting in Mexico City. Ramírez's diary of the trip is rich and detailed and offers characteristically levelheaded testimony of the state of the empire. He noted, for instance, that foreign functionaries were churlish and impolite with the local population and that "foreigners in the service of the emperor caused more damage to his public image than his enemies."[88] The empress, by contrast, was gracious and accessible, even to the humblest subjects, making up in part for the abuses of officials and giving a boost to imperial public relations. In Mérida she held balls, banquets, and receptions, and the local population reciprocated. Local ladies even donned stuffy silk dresses, notwithstanding the heat and the humidity. She visited the recently founded museum there, which, she trusted, "would bear important fruit for historical research and would pay tribute to the still powerful Mayan race."[89]

Under a section titled "Popular Traditions Relative to the Ruins,"

Ramírez reported some strange beliefs associated with the empress's presence in Yucatán. Among them was the legend that under one of the pyramids at Uxmal there was a box that held a rope, which, on a specific day, would be stretched out in the air, east to west, across the peninsula. Everyone would traverse the peninsula by holding on to the rope, and whoever fell would be devoured by the snake sculpted on a monument at Uxmal. In effect, the peninsula was being traversed, but by telegraph wire, not rope. The empress's arrival in Yucatán, together with the telegraph wire stretched between Sisal and Mérida, had, in Ramírez's view, begun to undo the larger spell of superstitious belief. Carlota's presence also put an end to the rumor that her favorite food was Yucatecan human meat, which had been spread by the enemies of the empire to dampen imperial enthusiasm and to create a hostile environment.[90]

From Mérida, Ramírez went on to visit Uxmal, where he spent six days, between December 5 and 10. It was Ramírez's first and only direct experience at a Mayan site, and he followed closely in the steps of Waldeck and Stephens before. Simón Peón, the hacienda owner who had accompanied Stephens on his searches twenty-five years earlier, proved helpful and solicitous again, lending three hundred men to help clear the vegetation off the ruins so that Ramírez could take minute technical notes and measurements. Ramírez exercised caution in expressing any hypotheses about what he was shown. He took the smaller but necessary role of critic, correcting misinformation about the ruins; in particular, he praised Stephens for his explanations and found Waldeck's drawings to be "fantasist" and inexact.[91] He was especially worried about the local "spirit of destruction and barbarity" toward the vestiges, as he witnessed it on December 8, the day Carlota visited Uxmal. The curious, gathered there to see the empress, destroyed some of the objects Ramírez had set aside. Does that mean Ramírez was planning to take antiquities back with him to the museum in Mexico City? He does not say. Ramírez returned to Mexico City sometime at the beginning of January, long after the imperial retinue; he fell sick with yellow fever (*vómito prieto*) in Veracruz and arrived after a difficult convalescence.

Empty Shelves and Courtly Pageants

By the time Ramírez returned to Mexico City, the museum was in upheaval. On December 4, 1865, Maximilian had decreed the "foundation" of the Public Museum of Natural History, Archaeology, and History in the Imperial (formerly and after, National) Palace.[92] Strictly speaking, more than a founding gesture—after all, the museum had been founded forty years before—the decree signaled the emperor's commitment to the institution and his acknowledgment of its importance to the imperial court. The organization of the museum differed little from the way Icaza had envisioned it forty years before. According to imperial decree, the museum would bring together "all that is of interest to the sciences of our country" and would be divided into three sections: natural history, archaeology, and history. At the same time, the museum would host a library, with the books from the university, as well as the books and manuscripts expropriated from convents and monasteries in the wake of the liberal Juarista reforms.

In his court ceremonial of 1866—a 574-page tome that described, with great detail, all aspects of court hierarchy and ritual—Maximilian gave further instructions concerning the museum. Its director, appointed directly by the emperor, held the twenty-fourth position in a tight hierarchy at the imperial court, directly behind the president of the AICL, the president of the Academy of Beaux Arts, the director of the Imperial Library, and the Knights of the Order of Guadalupe.[93] The museum director's responsibilities included expanding the collection by maintaining close relationships with hunters and naturalists and exchanges with foreign institutions; presenting the emperor with a detailed report of the institution's activities every fifteen days; and informing him of any changes in the organization of the collection. It speaks to Maximilian's character that he believed he could impose a punctiliousness that was proper to Vienna, where it had developed over four hundred years, on a newfound court in Mexico City that had been brought into the country on the backs of a foreign army barely two years before. That he made it an official priority to keep up with changes at the museum on such a frequent basis is both astonishing and a measure of just how unprepared Maximilian, a man who was most at home collecting botanical specimens, was for the crushing tasks that awaited him.

By far the most important change entailed by these imperial measures was the decision to move the museum to the Imperial Palace. For the previous forty years, as soon as the museum was established at the university, its curators begged and pleaded for ampler and more adequate spaces to host and display the growing collection. In 1852 Ramírez had suggested, unsuccessfully, the quarters once occupied by the Royal Mint, on the northeastern side of the Palace, on the aptly named Moneda Street.[94] His proposal did not prosper at that time, but it found a welcome reception with Maximilian. First erected in 1569 and remodeled in the course of the eighteenth century, the Royal Mint, "of solid construction and sober and symmetrical layout," proudly displayed the architectural characteristics due a royal edifice: walls made of the light volcanic tezontle stone; door and window openings reinforced with gray stone from Los Remedios; the bottom floor paved with basaltic tiles; the top, with ceramic tiles.[95] By the 1860s the building was occupied by various government branches, including the Ministry of Justice, which had to be dislodged to make room for the museum. The new location of the museum would finally solve the material problem that had undermined the institution up to then, by making it possible to organize and display the national collection according to the then-current conventions of museum practice. Just as importantly, the move was an indicator of the museum's newly gained place on the urban stage, articulated by imperial residence in the Chapultepec Castle in the west, the Imperial Palace in the city center, and the avenue (then Paseo de la Emperatriz, now Reforma) that connected the two. In this context, the museum would make legible the image Maximilian intended for himself, that of a Habsburg monarch, rooted in Mexican culture, with an exalted place among the rulers of civilized nations.

To underscore that image, Maximilian sought to build the museum along the lines of European national collections. With this purpose in mind, he invited Simon Leo Reinisch, who had curated

Maximilian's art collections at Miramar, to establish a section of Egyptian antiquities, on which Reinisch was a recognized expert, in the museum in Mexico City. Reinisch spent the first months of 1866 looking to acquire Egyptian antiquities for his patron.[96] It is possible that Maximilian thought an Egyptian collection in Mexico would contribute to answering questions—or lay them to rest—about the ancient ties between the Old and New Worlds. Also, bringing Egyptian antiquities to Mexico was a political move on his part, an assertion of his cosmopolitanism and of his capacity to obtain such objects on par with the French. On a personal level, it was a gesture that connected Maximilian's past life in Italy, where he was secure in the regard of the European aristocracy in which he was bred and lived, to this new life in Mexico, with its unexpected resistances and what must have felt like a humiliating relationship with Napoleon III.

Besides ordering in Egyptian antiquities, Maximilian looked to increase the museum collection by laying claim to some symbolically charged items from Mexico's ancient and colonial past, which would give historical depth, legitimacy, and meaning to his reign as the unlikely coupling, in the same imperial figure, of Old World and New World royal lines. Accordingly, in November of 1865 he instructed Gregorio Barandiarán, his ambassador at the Austrian court, to negotiate the repatriation of a collection of letters by Cortés and of a "hieroglyphic manuscript" (the *Codex Vindobonensis Mexicanus*) held at the Imperial Library in Vienna, as well as of Moctezuma's insignia and armor at the weapons collection in the Belvedere Palace. "These objects are no more than curiosities in Vienna," wrote Maximilian, "but in Mexico, they would be appreciated as objects of utmost importance and of public value. One could not negate the great effect they would have on Indians if they knew their new emperor had brought back these insignia of sovereignty of the Indian emperors of their old country."[97] As historians have suggested, Maximilian's effort to insert himself as a legitimate heir to Mexico's ancient past was part of a conscientious indigenist policy that sought, as well, to improve the lives of contemporary Indians. In fact, Maximilian went so far as to sign pro-Indian legislation as *Huei tlatoani,* a title reserved for Mexican emperors before the Spanish conquest.⁹⁸

By February 1866 Emperor Franz Joseph sent his brother in Mexico Moctezuma's shield and Cortés's "Informe sobre la Conquista de México."⁹⁹ But it is a sad reflection of Maximilian's lack of leverage at the Viennese imperial court that he was unable to obtain any more objects; in April 1866 Barandiarán received a final rejection on his request, which meant that the hieroglyphic manuscript would remain at the Imperial Library in Vienna. Through Barandiarán, Maximilian was advised to consult copies of this manuscript, together with copies of many other Mexican hieroglyphic documents, in Kingsborough's *Mexican Antiquities,* as though he were a scholar and not an emperor, a researcher rather than *Huei tlatoani.*¹⁰⁰ Maximilian had probably hoped to display the manuscript the day the museum reopened in the Imperial Palace as both a piece of Mexican history and triumphant evidence of his connection with the European powers.

But it was hardly the only disappointment at this moment. For her part, Empress Carlota had written to the imperial minister in Brussels to ask for a bow and quiver and a feather cape that had supposedly belonged to Moctezuma, which were being held at the museum in Brussels.¹⁰¹ In May of 1866 Joseph Corio, the Mexican imperial representative in Brussels received a definitive answer: the Belgian state refused to grant the request because objects could not leave the museum in Brussels unless they were part of an exchange. The exchange never prospered.¹⁰² Surely these requests were of more than antiquarian interest; surely they operated as omens of the coming withdrawal of European support for Maximilian's Mexico adventure.

In the meantime, the task of moving the museum collections had begun. Only a couple of blocks separated the museum's old quarters at the university from its new spaces on Moneda Street, though it became clear from the beginning that this would not be an easy relocation. The collection was rich in antiquities, from heavy basalt carvings to fragile clay molds and musical instruments made of wood. Besides, by late 1864, the collection had added the

421-kilogram Yanhuitlán meteorite. For the undersecretary of public instruction, Manuel Ortiz de Montellano, writing in early December of 1865, on the eve of the museum's move, a significant source of problems were also the books held at the museum and at the university. The problem of relocation was infinitely compounded by the lack of any inventory for the objects or the books.[103]

The first phase of the move was under the direction of José Ramón Alejo Rodríguez Arangoiti (1831–82), one of Maximilian's favored architects, who had worked on monumental projects around the city and had just completed the grand reception halls at the palace.[104] The architect hired pulleys and bought wooden boxes, dozens of pounds of hemp rope, and brown paper for wrapping objects in preparation for the move. He hired assistants to stand guard at the National Palace and supervise the entry of objects.[105] Orozco y Berra was in charge of overseeing the exit of objects from the university.[106] The move began on December 18; by January 13, 1866, Rodríguez Arangoiti had transferred 46,900 volumes and a great part of the collection, at a cost of 1,138.04 pesos. Over 50,000 volumes were still at the university, however, as were the monolithic sculptures on the first floor. The architect asked for another 1,000 pesos to continue with the move.[107] No funds were discharged, and on January 23 Rodríguez Arangoiti suspended his activities.[108] Imperial splendor, at this point in the empire, was being squeezed by realpolitik. Some weeks later, Francisco Artigas, the minister of public instruction, stepped in to promise that his ministry would complete the move thriftily.[109] In early March the emperor doled out another 1,000 pesos, while more-modest amounts went to engineer Antonio Torres Torija, in charge of fixing and remodeling the spaces that would hold the incoming objects.[110]

José Fernando Ramírez—who had directed the museum, with some interruptions, since the early 1850s—was conspicuously absent from all this hustle, and it would be interesting to know why. Granted, it was work that required engineering, not antiquarian skills, but it still comes as a surprise that he had no say in the way antiquities would be organized and displayed in the museum's ample new spaces. Does this point to the distancing between the emperor and the more moderate members of the court? It does coincide with the influence of a new cabinet secretary, Augustin Fischer (1825–89), an adventurer who had turned Catholic after prospecting in California and had made his way up the ladder to become the "ominous father," turning Maximilian toward the reactionaries in Mexico.[111] Since his return from Yucatán early in 1865, Ramírez had kept a low profile in the imperial court, and on March 3 he resigned his post as minister of foreign relations.[112]

Sometime later, Dominik Bilimek (1813–84)—a rather eccentric Cistercian monk and naturalist and an avid collector of plants and insects, who accompanied the emperor on collecting trips around Mexico City—was appointed director of the natural history section at the museum, though it is unclear whether he was put in charge of the entire museum.[113] In any case, Bilimek's appointment helps explain why, in keeping with Bilimek's own interests, the natural history collection was first in place at the museum.

On July 6, 1866, on Maximilian's thirty-fourth birthday, members of the court and the Imperial Academy of Arts and Sciences gathered together to celebrate the inauguration of the Public Museum of Mexico in its new quarters on Moneda Street.[114] Present were some of the more prestigious literary and scientific figures at the time, including Ramírez, Orozco y Berra, García Cubas, and Río de la Loza. All attendants were dressed in strict formal wear: women wore silk dresses and mantilla, and men wore tailcoats, black ties, and the insignia of their respective posts. As president of the academy, Ramírez wore a heavy gold chain. Maximilian and Carlota arrived at two in the afternoon. After a round of speeches, the emperor and the empress signed the act of the museum's foundation. Then the academicians added their signatures. After this ceremony, Bilimek led a tour of the natural history section, which displayed a sizeable collection of mineralogical samples; a herbarium containing over ten thousand plants; a good number of mammals and birds; and over two thousand Coleoptera, Lepidoptera, reptiles, mollusks, and crustaceans, many of which had been collected by Bilimek personally.[115] The archaeology galleries were empty. Antiquities were still in boxes, waiting to be unpacked and organized. Some of the larger pieces had yet to be carted the couple of blocks from the old university building to their new quarters.

Maximilian was the first head of state to make the museum a center of civic ritual, which he accomplished by the simple act of gracing with his presence the inauguration of the museum in the Imperial Palace. On a very basic but crucial level, moving the collections to the palace granted the museum what curators had pleaded for since its foundation in 1825: ample quarters that would allow for better display and safekeeping of objects. In standing up against the foreign, and particularly French, accusation that the cultural and natural properties of Mexico were neither protected nor studied by Mexicans, an insinuation that justified a vast amount of foreign looting, Maximilian was sending an important message: the imperial government would not stand silently by while its usufructs and laws were trampled on. At the same time, the presence of such distinguished company of scholars showed that the museum was going to be used tactically as the face of a broader imperial political and cultural program that would create consensus and legitimacy around the image of Maximilian as a patron of the arts and the sciences and as a promoter of social and economic order and progress.

Yet symbolic flaws in the project were apparent on that day. The museum's antiquities, arguably its most emblematic objects, were not on display. This was not simply a failure of deadlines. By the time Maximilian inaugurated the museum, at the beginning of his third and last year at the head of the Mexican government, the situation of the Second Empire had become untenable. The imperial treasury was empty, and the credit markets were not eager to loan since Maximilian faced hostility both internally and externally. The Juárez-led insurgents were ominously pressing from the north; the United States, which during the Civil War had followed a policy of neutrality with regard to Maximilian, were now in a position to reassert their own influence in the hemisphere, over that of France and Austria, and began sending political and military support to the insurgents.[116] Napoleon III, facing increasing internal criticism over his American adventure and external threats from a powerful

Prussia and having seen little return on his Mexican investment, had decided to pull the French troops out of Mexico. He made public his decision in May of 1866. Only two days later, Carlota left Mexico on a diplomatic mission to Europe to ask for help. Rumors circulated that Maximilian would follow soon.

The empty rooms in the museum bore testimony to the emptiness of the Second Empire; Maximilian had failed to fashion consensus around the empire in the same way that he had failed to have the famous antiquities unpacked to celebrate what was undoubtedly an accomplishment, giving real space and status to a national museum. It comes as something of a surprise then that he went on with the inauguration at all, especially since the museum was not yet ready to open. The emperor, it seems, was digging in his heels. More than celebrating an accomplishment, Maximilian was making public an intent. He was running out of time, and his opportunities to build up legitimacy around the imperial figure were slipping away. The inauguration of the museum was an instance of what some historians have described as a "theatrical mechanism for expressing the power and dignity of the sovereign and for [making public] the adhesion of Mexican elites to the imperial project."[117] For many of Maximilian's detractors, it was no more than a misguided gesture. There were those who accused him of displacing the Ministry of Justice to make room for stuffed birds.[118] Others, like Doutrelaine, would have seen in the opening of the museum a last resort to ceremony to make up for Maximilian's lack of real power.[119]

It speaks to his genuine commitment to the museum that, despite mounting difficulties, Maximilian pushed through with the move throughout the summer and early fall of 1866. On September 15 the Ministry for Public Instruction reported that a total of 117,730 books were finally at the museum, where they were becoming a source of serious concern. Lying all around in disarray, they made all attempts at inventory a complicated task and made moving around a challenge.[120] As for the antiquities, while most of them had made the transition into the museum's new spaces, the monoliths, owing to the difficulties imposed by their weight, were still at the university. Bilimek decided that they should be left there until the emperor appointed a director of the antiquities section.[121] On November 19 Maximilian appointed Manuel Orozco y Berra to direct the museum.[122] Just a few weeks later, by early December, Reinisch, Maximilian's curator in Miramar, finally arrived in Mexico, without the Egyptian antiquities he had acquired for the purpose of an Egyptian section at the museum.[123] He was coming to claim his post as curator at the museum, as promised by the emperor, and he was not too pleasantly surprised to find out that the post had already been occupied.[124] At the same time, Reinisch had perceptively observed, there was no money to run a museum, which was hardly a priority for a tumbling empire, so that it hardly mattered who ran it or the number of that person in the hierarchy of court protocol.[125]

By the beginning of 1867, many of those who had collaborated with the intervention and the Second Empire were getting out of Mexico. On January 15 Ramírez, who had sacrificed so much for the emperor, departed for Bonn, where he died four years later. On his last interview with Maximilian, Ramírez urged the emperor to leave as well.[126] The French delegate Doutrelaine, who had been busy organizing the exodus of curiosities—including Boban's prized collection, rich in antiquities, fossils, and natural history objects— and of his team members from Mexico, sent his last letter to Duruy on February 9 and left for France a few days later.[127]

Maximilian, forced to confront the reality of his diminished state, told Bilimek that there was no money to proceed with the organization and display of objects and that, in order to protect them against the republican troops advancing on Mexico City, they should remain in their wooden boxes.[128] Maximilian relieved Bilimek of his duties at the museum and named him director of his museums in Miramar. The naturalist would return to Europe with an important collection of natural history and archaeological objects, which eventually ended up in Viennese museums.[129] Then, on February 8, on the eve of his departure for Querétaro, to fight the republican armies, Maximilian instructed Orozco y Berra to guard the museum's collections and books in a safe place. And he promised that on his return, he would "take care" of the museum.[130] Maximilian, however, was not destined to see Mexico City again. He was executed, together with his generals Miguel Miramón and Tomás Mejía, two weeks short of his thirty-fifth birthday, on June 19, 1867.

While Maximilian was making his last stand at Querétaro and becoming, before the firing squad, a romantic legend, Léon Méhédin, the expeditioner on the CSM's archaeological committee, was in Paris erecting a curious epitaph to the French intervention and the Second Empire. He was the only participant to represent Mexico at the World's Fair of 1867, and his exhibit, a 25 x 18 m replica of the two-level pyramid of Xochicalco, was causing unusual excitement among the crowds.[131] After climbing up a very steep staircase, an exercise memorably recorded by one observer who said it "was as difficult to arrive to the second level of the pyramid as it was to pronounce its name,"[132] the visitor entered into a colorful room decorated with "arabesques" and stained glass windows inspired by Mexican codices. "Natives" dressed in rough cotton trousers and sarapes greeted the public. Inside, Méhédin had organized a retrospective of his archaeological work over the past two decades. On display were photographs from Crimea, molds and replicas of Egyptian temples, rubbings of the Calendar Stone in Mexico City, molds of a monolith from Teotihuacan and of the Teoyamiqui in the museum. But the main attractions of Méhédin's exhibit, most visitors agreed, were a knife and some typical Mexican alcoholic drinks:

> One enters the sanctuary with certain emotion to [. . .] find a kitchen knife, which visitors contemplate with terror. It is worth knowing that an experienced hand, armed with this instrument, can detach the heart from the surrounding viscera all at once, to lift it up to present it [. . .] to the gods of the country.
>
> [. . .]
>
> Let us imbibe ourselves in local color and ask the guardians of this sacred place to receive us under their tent. The table is set and they serve us "chirimoya" and "mexical," the two truly national liquors. Chin-chin. Mexico is there, all whole, with its pampas and its rattlesnakes, its Redskins and its yellow fever. One gulp of it and, there is no doubting: this is the classic country of empoisonments.[133]

Méhédin's exhibit—just like Bullock's, more than forty years earlier—was a monument to barbarity. But while Bullock had been optimistic that Mexico, under England's guidance, was on its way to civilization, Méhédin's show reflects on Europe's failure to subdue the native society of Mexico even after having spent significant efforts trying to do so. One mouthful of the poisoned drink, one look at the fatal knife are enough to elide the distance between contemporary Mexico and its ancient past, that antiquity of terror, cruelty, and savagery that thrilled the crowd in Paris. Its most recent reenactment was the death of Maximilian, which was announced just as Napoleon III was inaugurating the exposition.

Though Juárez had unambiguously signaled his rejection of all foreign intervention in Mexico—and of those Mexicans, like Ramírez and Orozco y Berra, who had most intimately collaborated with it—the triumph of the liberal republic quietly absorbed certain reforms and advances of the Second Empire, most notably in preserving the new site of the museum in the heart of the capital and of the country and in maintaining the large-scale commitment to the museum project.[134] Almost miraculously, most of its objects had remained in the country despite the efficiency of the French, Belgian, and Austrian looters. By August of 1867 Juárez appointed Ramón Alcaraz (1823–86), once a member of the Academy of San Juan de Letrán and later one of Juárez's companions during his exile, as director of the museum, charging him with the task of forming a detailed inventory of everything in its collections.[135] Some months later, the Public Instruction Code of December 2, 1867, specified that museum directors, like those of the Botanical Garden, the National Library, and the National Observatory, would be named by a board, which would be in charge of revising and establishing the budget of each of these institutions.[136] The 1869 amendment to the code upheld these decisions and, additionally, specified the salary of the museum director.[137] At the same time, Juárez refounded Maximilian's Imperial Academy as the National Academy of Arts and Sciences. Together with the newly established Sociedad de Historia Natural, the academy produced studies of objects from the museum's collections. It was in collaboration with these learned societies that the museum began unpacking the boxes of antiquities that Maximilian had entrusted to Orozco y Berra's safekeeping when he left for Querétaro. It would fall to associates of the republican institutions in the coming years to write a history of the museum that would treat the fifty-year period of its neglect as a mere footnote and its beginning as a truly national museum under Maximilian as one of the family secrets of the confident Porfirian period.

EPILOGUE

The Invention of Mexican Antiquities

On September 16, 1887, the anniversary of Mexican Independence, which happened to coincide with his birthday, President Porfirio Díaz inaugurated the Galería de los Monolitos in the National Museum, in a highly publicized act. Unlike the ill-fated Maximilian, who, on his birthday twenty-one years before, had founded a museum whose objects were still in boxes, Díaz passed review on a richly stocked exhibit. A long, vaulted hall, occupying the main place in the museum's floor plan, directly across the interior patio from the entrance into the museum, the Galería de los Monolitos was touted as the first archaeological gallery in Mexico and in all of Latin America and housed over 350 stone objects, including some of Mexico's choice antiquities: a "notable" Quetzalcóatl, an "Egyptian style diorite head," "a magnificent Yucatecan so-called Chac-Mool," "the colossal sculpture of the goddess Coatlicue," "the famous Stone of Sacrifices, or [Stone] of Tízoc," "the commemorative stone of the foundation of the Templo Mayor of the Aztecs," "the acclaimed central panel of the Temple of the Cross in Palenque," and the Piedra del Sol.[1] This last monument, symbolically identified with the number one in the museum catalogue, was the latest to join the monolith collection, and its transfer from the tower of the cathedral to Moneda Street was both a technological feat and an example of cooperation between the museum and the other institutions of the Mexican state.[2] Drawing visitors' attention from the moment they entered the museum, the Piedra del Sol stood as testimony, on the one hand, to the high achievements of the ancient Mexican civilization and, on the other, to the progress of the heir of that civilization, the late nineteenth-century Mexican state, which, for the first time since the foundation of the National

Museum, had the will and the means to make the preservation, display, and appropriation of Mexico's ancient past a priority. By the late nineteenth century, the alliance between archaeology, the National Museum, the Mexican nation-state, and Mexican notions of citizenship was well underway.[3] And this confluence has been reinforced ever since by ritual acts that have chosen the museum's archaeology section as both stage and protagonist to politics.[4]

This alliance has been so tenacious that it is mostly taken for granted today, as if the state, the National Museum, and Mexican antiquities were not cultural and political constructs but ontological entities. As school children recite by heart lessons of ancient Mexican grandeur, rooted in the colossal monuments in the Mexican Hall in the National Museum of Anthropology, assumed to be the direct heir of the nineteenth-century National Museum, it is difficult to remember that both antiquities and the museum that holds and displays them have a history, dictated by small-scale events, by accidents and contingencies, in which things could have turned out differently. The fact that the National Museum and Mexican antiquities became intimately tied together in the construction of a new form of power that linked archaeology and national politics in the Porfirian period was not a clarification and expansion of the essence of the museum; it was the result of a threshold moment that exploited certain properties of the museum's history and erased others. It was, in a sense, a retrospective and politically charged act of essentializing a history that was led by no inexorable or obvious goal or dynamic. One of the main aims of this book has been to tell the story of the National Museum before Mexican antiquities became synonymous with the national collection and before the institution safeguarding them became a platform for the writing and representation of Mexicanness.

At the beginning of the history I tell here, antiquities had many uses—commercial, religious, aesthetic, and philosophical, including strictly material, as supports and foundations for buildings. And there was hardly an incontrovertible idea that they belonged in a National Museum, together with silver ores, wax figurines, and stuffed animals, with which they vied for space. Over the first half of the nineteenth century, antiquities became the objects of a new scientific discipline, the archaeology of ancient America, which took shape in intimate dialogue with the political and cultural preoccupations at the time. Among these, one of the more persistent issues was the origin of New World civilizations and their relations to the civilizations of the Old World. Inevitably, this led to a reflection shared among antiquarians and scholars of the past: contemporary nineteenth-century American Indians were not the direct descendants of the enlightened dwellers of ancient America; or if they were, their stock had degenerated beyond recognition. There was a growing sense that the vestiges of the past did not belong to present-day Indians, because the latter did not know how to properly think of them and use them. Sure, these vestiges were obtained through Indian labor, for Indians did guide explorers to ruins, bear the brunt of excavations, and transport objects on their backs. But there was a prevailing consensus that antiquities had to be rescued by modern science. Rain gods at the center of community devotion would become the objects of the rituals of reason, those of the incipient archaeological sciences. The objects would be measured, weighed, described, deciphered, with more or less success, before being placed on a shelf, next to similar objects. Descriptions and illustrations of antiquities would circulate through books, periodicals, and private correspondence, by which protocols would be generated to discriminate between the "correct" and the "wrong" ways of relating to them.

But even as it became clear that contemporary Indians did not own the past, the question of who could legitimately own and care for it still remained. The answer, invariably, coming from the custodians of European and North American museums, was that Americans south of the U.S. border, just like contemporary Egyptians and Greeks, were not worthy heirs to their past. The dire condition of the Mexican state during the first half century after independence and the equally ruinous situation of the National Museum of Mexico reinforced these claims.

By the 1850s José Fernando Ramírez began making the case that Mexicans—namely, Mexico's elites—could be entrusted with the material custodianship of Mexico's ancient past because they had by then become its intellectual heirs and curators. That is, they had begun to forge independent traditions—rooted in ancient and colonial documents and in toponymical, philological, and material studies—that produced historical truths in contradistinction to (what Ramírez shunned as) the fantastic claims of systemic and universalist histories that saw ancient America as derivative from Old World civilizations. Intellectual claims on ancient Mexico such as those expressed by Ramírez were necessary preludes to political positioning with respect to Mexican antiquities. The vestiges of Mexico's past had to be cared for exclusively by Mexicans, because those vestiges revealed something innate about the people's present, something intrinsically Mexican.

In a suggestive essay on the history of the antique, Leon Rosenstein has argued that the idea of the antique, as something to be preserved and valued, is intimately tied to "a civilization's conception of itself—of itself, in its present as compared with its past and of itself in comparison with other civilizations"; in that connection, the notion of the antique "affects how civilizations become what they are."[5] Building on Martin Heidegger's conflation of the word *Wahrung* ("safeguarding") with the related verb *bewähren* ("to prove one's worth," "to authenticate"), Rosenstein points out that "all our understanding [of the past] is a corollary of our 'caring,' of our caretaking, and especially of the past (in the face of the future). The mentality that appreciates the antique 'preserves' the world it generates [. . .] and it also 'holds' it 'true,' thereby authenticating, maintaining, saving, standing by, and in a sense 'approving' it."[6] By the late nineteenth century, when the Mexican state made it its mission to preserve and "care for" Mexico's antiques, this gesture was an extension of the ambition to authenticate a certain idea of the Mexican nation as determined by and continuous with that past. Justo Sierra (1848–1912), President Díaz's influential minister of public instruction, expressed a common sentiment when, in anticipation of the one-hundred-year anniversary of Mexican Independence, he urged his colleagues at the Ministry of Finance to allocate more funds for the care of antiquities: "For you, who are men of affairs and finances, this thing called archaeology is no more than a trivial and paltry thing, of little importance; but for us, it is the only thing that distinguishes Mexico's personality before the scientific world; everything else exists elsewhere and is already being done [studied] by foreigners."[7]

Since Sierra spoke these words, more than a century ago, the identification of Mexico's distinct personality trait with the country's antiquities and the emergence of the powerful binomial state-archaeology have had two important effects. On the one hand, there has been a concerted effort to silence and obscure all other meanings and uses of these objects. As preconquest antiquities arrive in the National Museum, they are disciplined and disenchanted. Their ties with the local communities that used them, broken.[8] They are supposed to take their places in the museum side by side like objects, to form a national collection that belongs, abstractly, to all Mexicans and is entrusted with the serious task of educating them in the rituals of citizenship. At the same time, the relevance acquired by Mexican antiquities, especially since the late nineteenth century, has displaced all other objects from the museum, those, as Sierra would have insisted, that could be found and studied anywhere else. After a ninety-year coexistence between antiquities and objects of natural history, in 1906 Sierra decreed their separation. A Natural History Museum was established by 1913 on Chopo Street, in a glass-and-steel structure imported from Germany. The Museum of Archaeology, History, and Ethnography remained in the National Palace until 1964, when, reiterating its commitment to state archaeology, the Mexican government endowed it with one of the more emblematic buildings of Mexican modernism, where it is still housed today as the National Museum of Anthropology. Ironically, in that same year, 1964, the natural history collection was dismembered, with many of its specimens being thrown out. Some natural history collection objects from the twentieth century joined the biological collections at the Universidad Nacional Autónoma de México, while others were brought together to form a new, mostly forgotten, Museum of Natural History, whose sad stuffed bears entertain only school children. The Mexican state has selectively decided to look after the country's ancient past and, to a lesser extent, its colonial and postindependence history, leaving its natural properties for others to study and care for.

Today, the meanings of Mexico's cultural and natural properties have been called increasingly into question from different angles. As archaeological sites become feature parks under private management or are being reclaimed by local communities, as the distinctions between natural and cultural patrimonies have become increasingly blurred, the values with which the Mexican state has imbued Mexico's ancient past and the National Museum of Anthropology as the custodian of that past have become subject to debate.[9] As we align ourselves on different sides of these debates, it is worth remembering a time when Mexico's natural and cultural properties were semiotically malleable and that now, as then, they can be used to forge new stories.

NOTES

Introduction

1. For an overview of the political and social upheaval during Mexico's postindependence years, see Fowler, *Mexico in the Age of Proposals*.
2. Brantz Mayer, *Mexico, as It Was and as It Is*, 100.
3. These questions were hardly unique to the National Museum of Mexico. For specific case studies, see, for instance, Alberti, *Nature and Culture*; Gosden, Larson, and Petch, *Knowing Things*; Podgorny and Lopes, *El desierto en una vitrina*. For a compilation of case studies of Latin American museums and collections in the nineteenth century, see Achim and Podgorny, *Museos al detalle*.
4. On the history of collecting during the Enlightenment, see especially Constantino Ortiz, "Coleccionismo de naturaleza en la Nueva España del siglo XVIII"; Bleichmar and Mancall, *Collecting across Cultures*; and González Claverán, *La expedición científica de Malaspina en Nueva España*. The bibliography is vast for Mexico's national patrimony in the last decades of the nineteenth century; see especially Garrigan, *Collecting Mexico*; Rutsch, "Natural History, National Museum, and Anthropology in Mexico"; and Tenorio Trillo, *Mexico at the World's Fairs*.
5. The term was coined by Josefina Zoraida Vázquez in her review on the historiography of the decades following the War of Independence, "Los años olvidados." Since Vázquez's review almost thirty years ago, the "forgotten years" have attracted a good deal of scholarship, especially by political and constitutional historians.
6. Anna, *Forging Mexico*.
7. The expression "linearity of a singular narrative" is Raymond Craib's ("Nationalist Metaphysics," 68). See also Bernal, *Historia de la arqueología en México*; Díaz-Andreu, *A World of Nineteenth-Century Archaeology*; Florescano, "La creación del Museo Nacional de Antropología"; Rico Mansard, *Exhibir para educar*.
8. Bennet, *Birth of the Museum*; Benedict Anderson, *Imagined Communities*; Carol Duncan, *Civilizing Rituals*, especially "The Museum as Ritual."
9. The past decade has seen an important revision of the history of Latin American museums and the increasing insistence on dense case

histories. See Gänger, *Relics of the Past* and "Of Butterflies, Chinese Shoes, and Antiquities"; Podgorny and Lopes, *El desierto en una vitrina*; Sanhueza, "El Gabinete de Historia Natural de Santiago de Chile"; Lopes, "Minerales y fósiles."

10. Since the 1980s this sort of archaeological positivism has been subjected to a more critical gaze. See, for instance, Morales Moreno, "Ancestros y ciudadanos" and "En torno a la museología mexicana."

11. For more on reassessments of the museum's natural history collection, see Vega y Ortega, "La riqueza del Gabinete de Historia natural del Museo Nacional de México." For more reconstructions of Mexican antiquarianism, see Fauvet-Berthelot and López Luján, "Édouard Pingret, un coleccionista europeo de mediados del siglo XIX" and "La Piedra del Sol, ¿en París?"; Fauvet-Bethelot, López Luján, and Guimarães, "Six personnages en quête d'objets"; López Luján, "La historia póstuma de la Piedra de Tízoc" and "La Isla de Sacrificios." For more on reviews of legislation, see Cotton, "La concepción jurídica del Museo Nacional." For accounts of the museum during the Second Empire, see Acevedo, "El legado artístico de un imperio efímero"; Arciniega Ávila, "La galería de las Sibilas"; Azuela and Vega y Ortega, "El Museo Público de Historia Natural Arqueologia e Historia (1865–1867)"; Opriessnig, "Política cultural en el Segundo Imperio de Maximiliano."

12. Gosden, Larson, and Petch, *Knowing Things*. The project led by Gosden produced at the same time a comprehensive website of the objects and collecting practices associated with Pitt Rivers, *Rethinking Pitt-Rivers*, http://web.prm.ox.ac.uk/rpr/.

13. Gosden, Larson, and Petch, *Knowing Things*, 23.

14. Aguirre, *Informal Empire* and "William Bullock"; Evans, *Romancing the Mayas*; Penny, *Objects of Culture*.

15. In a recent article, García and Podgorny have called attention to the scholarly bias that has made English pubs and marketplaces—but not Latin American museums, cafés, and salons—into spaces for the production and exchange of natural knowledge ("Los pilotos del Río Negro"). See also Podgorny, "Terebrátulas y piedras de águila en el Río de la Plata"; Gänger, "Many Natures of Antiquity."

16. Colla, *Conflicted Antiquities*; Reid, *Whose Pharaohs?*

17. On sixteenth-century attitudes toward preconquest objects, see Gruzinski and Bernand, *De l'idolâtrie*. For a review of the legislation concerning the management of antiquities between the Spanish conquest

and early twentieth-century Mexico, see Lombardo de Ruiz and Solís Vicarte, *Antecedentes de las leyes sobre Monumentos Históricos*, 29–30.

18. For 1790s descriptions of antiquities around Mexico City, see León y Gama, *Descripción histórica y cronológica de las dos piedras*; Dupaix, "Descripción de monumentos antiguos mexicanos," Fondo Reservado, BNAH. For a study of Dupaix's manuscript, see López Luján, "El capitán Dupaix y su álbum arqueológico de 1794."

19. On Sigüenza y Góngora's antiquarianism, see More, *Baroque Sovereignty*, 110–57.

20. For an introduction to the Museo Boturini and its tribulations, see Cañizares-Esguerra, *How to Write the History of the New World*, 130–54.

21. Alcina Franch, *Arqueólogos o anticuarios*.

22. Villaseñor Espinosa, Introduction, 23.

23. Alzate y Ramírez, *Descripción de las antigüedades de Xochicalco*.

24. Alcina Franch, *Arqueólogos o anticuarios*, 90–123.

25. In the context of these debates, Borunda wrote the "Clave general de jeroglíficos americanos," while León y Gama published the *Descripción histórica y cronológica de las dos piedras*. For a more detailed account of these debates, see Achim, "La literatura anticuaria en la Nueva España."

26. Achim, "La literatura anticuaria," 550–51.

27. Joseph Antonio Ca to José de Iturrigaray, May 2, 1804, AGN, Instituciones coloniales, Gobierno Vireinal, Reales cedulas originales y duplicados, vol. 193, file 31. All translations, including this one, are my own, unless otherwise specified.

28. For studies on Dupaix, see Alcina Franch, *Arqueólogos o anticuarios* and "Guillermo Dupaix y los orígenes de la arqueologia en Mexico"; Estrada de Gerlero, "La labor anticuaria novohispana en la época de Carlos IV" and "La Real Expedición Anticuaria de Guillermo Dupaix"; de Pedro Robles, "La Real Expedición Anticuaria de México."

29. Webb, "Appropriating the Stones."

30. Garrigan, *Collecting Mexico*, 88.

1. Genealogies

1. On Alamán, see Rafael, *Noticias biográficas del Exmo Sr D. Lucas Alamán*; Méndez Reyes, *El hispanismo de Lucas Alamán*; and especially Valadés, *Alamán, estadista e historiador*. Unless otherwise noted, the account of Alamán's early years I give here is largely based on his own autobiographical sketch, "Épocas de los principales sucesos de mi vida," August 28, 1843, manuscript 236, Lucas Alamán Papers, 1598–

1853, Benson Latin American Collection, University of Texas Libraries, University of Texas at Austin; and on the work by Valadés.

2. Méndez Reyes, *El hispanismo de Lucas Alamán*, 87.

3. Alamán, quoted by Simpson, *Many Mexicos*, 213.

4. Humboldt, *Essai politique sur le royaume de la Nouvelle-Espagne*, 2:173.

5. Humboldt, *Essai politique sur le royaume de la Nouvelle-Espagne*, 2:179.

6. Humboldt, *Essai politique sur le royaume de la Nouvelle-Espagne*, 2:138.

7. Bakewell, "Mining," 245.

8. Moreno de los Arcos, *Linneo en México*.

9. Deans-Smith, *Matters of Taste*.

10. *Gazeta de México*, August 24, 1790, 152–54.

11. Constantino Ortiz and Pimentel, "Cómo inventariar el (Nuevo) Mundo."

12. For a detailed study of Longinos's cabinet, see Constantino Ortiz, "Coleccionismo de naturaleza."

13. Humboldt, *Essai politique sur le royaume de la Nouvelle-Espagne*, 2:121.

14. Humboldt, *Essai politique sur le royaume de la Nouvelle-Espagne*, 2:123.

15. Humboldt, *Essai politique sur le royaume de la Nouvelle-Espagne*, 2:119.

16. Humboldt, *Essai politique sur le royaume de la Nouvelle-Espagne*, 2:146.

17. Iturrigaray to Dupaix, June 3, 1808, G317, Guillermo Dupaix Papers, 1804–1820, Benson Latin American Collection, University of Texas Libraries, University of Texas at Austin.

18. Hénaut, "Preface."

19. Disraeli, "Memoir," 24.

20. Lawson, *Frontier Naturalist*.

21. Rafael, *Noticias biográficas del Exmo Sr D. Lucas Alamán*, 20.

22. Valadés, *Alamán, estadista e historiador*, 108–11.

23. Disraeli, "Memoir," 36.

24. *El Águila Mexicana*, May 6, 1823, cited by Valadés, *Alamán, estadista e historiador*, 142.

25. For detailed studies of these events, see Fowler, *Mexico in the Age of Proposals*; Ávila and Jáuregui, "La disolución de la monarquía hispánica."

26. Alamán, "Circular sobre la formacion de un plan general de instrucción y educación pública," May 1, 1823, AGN, GSS, box 49, file 16.

27. Bustamante to Alamán, June 4, 1823, AGN, GSS, box 49, file 16.

28. Fausto de Elhuyar, "Nota de los dibujos de antigüedades de México que existen en poder del albacea de la testamentaria del capitán Guillermo Dupaix," G369, Guillermo Dupaix Papers, 1804–1820, Benson Latin American Collection, General Libraries, University of Texas at Austin.

29. Alamán, marginal note on Bustamante's June 4, 1823, letter to Alamán, June 5, 1823, AGN, GSS, box 49, file 16.

30. Cervantes to Alamán, June 20, 1823, AGN, GSS, box 49, file 16.

31. Cervantes to Alamán, July 31, 1823, AGN, GSS, box 49, file 16.

32. I have not been able to find out more about the Conservatorio, which is mentioned in passing by Castillo Ledón, *El Museo Nacional*, 9.

33. Alamán to Cubas, August 11, 1823, AGN Gobernación, Ministerio de Relaciones, vol. 46, files 8–9.

34. Cubas to Alamán, August 18, 1823, AGN, Gobernación, Ministerio de Relaciones, vol. 46, file 9.

35. Alamán, *Memoria* (1823).

36. Alamán, *Memoria* (1823), 15.

37. Alamán, *Memoria* (1823), 21.

38. Alamán, *Memoria* (1823), 39.

39. Alamán, *Memoria* (1823), 34. For instance, in his *México considerado como nación independiente y libre*, diplomat and entrepreneur Tadeo Ortiz de Ayala insisted on the necessity of establishing a system of "compact, reasonable and liberal educaion" as a way to uphold "liberty, newly reconquered from under the foreign and domestic yoke" (112).

40. Alamán, *Memoria* (1823), 34.

41. Alamán, *Memoria* (1823), 34.

42. Fernández de Lizardi, *Obras XIII*.

43. Bustamante, *Mañanas de la Alameda de México*.

44. Alamán, "Quinta Disertación."

45. Alamán, "Quinta Disertación," 59–60.

46. For a detailed biography of William Bullock, see Costeloe, *William Bullock* and "William Bullock and the Mexican Connection." For studies of Bullock as an entrepreneur and exhibit curator, see Aguirre, *Informal Empire* and "William Bullock"; Leask, *Curiosity and the Aesthetics of Travel Writing*; Pascoe, *Hummingbird Cabinet*.

47. Pilbeam, *Madame Tussaud and the History of Waxworks*, 13.

48. Aguirre, *William Bullock*, 225.

49. Pascoe, *Hummingbird Cabinet*, 98–99.

50. Bullock, *Companion to Mr. Bullock's London Museum and Pantherion*, 1–2.

51. Bullock, *Six Months' Residence* (1824), title page.

52. I base my following description of Bullock's exhibit on *A Descriptive Catalogue of the Exhibition Entitled Ancient and Modern Mexico*.

53. Bullock, *Descriptive Catalogue*, 8.

54. Bullock, *Six Months' Residence* (1825), v.

55. Bullock, *Six Months' Residence* (1825), 334.

56. Bullock, *Six Months' Residence* (1825), 340.

57. Bullock, *Six Months' Residence* (1825), 341–42.

58. Bullock, *Six Months' Residence* (1825), 342.

59. Bullock, *Six Months' Residence* (1825), 342.

60. Matos Moctezuma and López Luján, *Escultura monumental mexica*.

61. Bullock, *Six Months' Residence* (1825), 335.

62. Bullock, *Six Months' Residence* (1825), 337.

63. Bullock, *Six Months' Residence* (1825), 329.

64. Costeloe, *William Bullock*, 60.

65. Costeloe, *William Bullock*, 65.

66. Anonymous, "Mr. Bullock's Travels and Acquisitions in Mexico," *Literary Gazette and Journal of Belles Lettres*, January 3, 1825, 8.

67. Anonymous, "Mr. Bullock's Travels and Acquisitions in Mexico," *Literary Gazette and Journal of Belles Lettres*, January 10, 1825, 25.

68. Anonymous, "Some Observations," 186.

69. Alamán, *Memoria* (1825), 15.

70. Alamán, *Memoria* (1825), 33.

71. Alamán, *Memoria* (1825), 34.

72. Alamán, *Memoria* (1825), 35.

73. Alamán, *Memoria* (1825), 35.

74. Alamán, *Memoria* (1825), 35.

75. During the nineteenth century, the official name of the museum kept changing. It was called Museo Nacional Mexicano from 1826–31; Establecimiento Científico Mexicano from 1831–34; Museo Mexicano from 1834–52; Museo Nacional, Archivo, Biblioteca y Jardín Botánico from 1852–65; Museo Público de Historia Natural, Arqueología e Historia from 1865–67; and Museo Nacional from 1867–1909. For the sake of coherence, throughout this book I will be referring to it as the National Museum.

76. Alamán to the dean of the university, March 18, 1825, AGN, GSS, box 82, file 20.

77. Mier y Terán, order, February 15, 1825, AGN, GSS, box 71, file 3.

78. Miguel Barragán to Alamán, March 1, 1825, AGN, GSS, box 71, file 3. For a history of collecting in the Isla de Sacrificios, see Nuttall and Batres, *Isla de Sacrificios*; López Luján, "Isla de Sacrificios."

79. Cotton, "Concepción jurídica," 30.

80. Alamán, "Quinta Disertación," 58.

81. During the year 1825, the museum's records contain a large number

of transactions between Cubas and various artisans. See AGN, GSS, box 82, file 20.

82. Inventory, March 20, 1825, AGN, GSS, box 82, file 20.

83. Bill signed by Andrés Estrada, May 1, 1825, AGN, GSS, box 82, file 20.

84. Cubas, list of donations, May 9, 1825, AGN, GSS, box 82, file 20.

85. Cubas, inventory, July 17, 1825, AGN, GSS, box 82, file 20.

86. Cubas, inventory, July 17, 1825, AGN, GSS, box 82, file 20.

87. Carlos María de Bustamante to Cubas, August 1, 1825, AGN, GSS, box 82, file 20.

88. Correspondence between Cervantes and Alamán, January 1825, AGN, GSS, box 71, file 6.

89. Correspondence between Alamán and Oseguera, March–April, 1825, AGN, GSS, box 82, file 20.

90. In a letter dated March 12, the city council of Tlaxcala informed Alamán that the Italian traveler Giacomo Beltrami had demanded a codex showing Cortés's entrance into Tlaxcala. Beltrami had grounded his petition in his ambition to write a book on America's geography and natural history. The city council, backed by Alamán, rejected Beltrami's petition. See correspondence between Alamán and the Ayuntamiento of Tlaxcala, March 12 and March 19, 1825, AGN, GSS, box 82, file 20.

91. Disraeli, "Memoir," 9.

2. Measures of Worth

1. Icaza to Camacho, December 6, 1825, AGN, GSS, box 82, file 20.

2. Icaza and Cubas, "Inventario de los monumentos de antigüedad que actualmente componen la colección perteneciente al Museo Nacional Mexicano," AGN, GSS, box 82, file 20, 56r–71r.

3. Icaza, letter to Camacho accompanying the "Inventario," December 29, 1825, AGN, GSS, box 82, file 20, 122r–123v.

4. Icaza to the Camacho, December 31, 1825, AGN, GSS, box 82, file 20, 124r–v.

5. Cited by Burrus, "Clavigero and the Lost Sigüenza y Góngora Manuscripts," 70.

6. Icaza to Camacho, January 14, 1826, AGN, GSS, box 82, file 20.

7. Bustamante's dedicatory to Lucas Alamán, in León y Gama, *Descripción histórica y cronológica de las dos piedras*, iii.

8. Icaza to Camacho, March 10, 1826, AGN, GSS, box 82, file 20 ("El conservador del Museo sobre que se dieran providencias para evitar la extracción que se está haciendo de antigüedades mexicanas"), 116v.

9. For a history of this purchase, see Fauvet-Berthelot, López Luján, and Guimarães, "Six personnages."
10. Icaza to Camacho, March 10, 1826, AGN, GSS, box 82, file 20 ("El conservador del Museo sobre que se dieran providencias para evitar la extracción que se está haciendo de antiqüedades mexicanas"), 116r–117v.
11. Icaza to Camacho, March 10, 1826, AGN, GSS, box 82, file 20 ("El conservador del Museo sobre que se dieran providencias para evitar la extracción que se está haciendo de antiqüedades mexicanas"), 117r.
12. Icaza, "Proyecto de reglamento para el Museo Nacional," AGN, GSS, box 82, file 20.
13. These included the Colegio Mayor de Santa María y Todos los Santos (1829), the jail in the National Palace (1831), the Colegio Máximo de San Pedro y San Pablo (1831), and the building of the ex-Inquisition (1831–32). After Icaza's death, the search for space continued. See Rico Mansard, "El Museo Nacional de México."
14. Icaza to Camacho, June 15, 1826, AGN, GSS, box 82, file 20, 129v–135v.
15. Icaza to Camacho, June 15, 1826, AGN, GSS, box 82, file 20, 133r.
16. Beaufoy, *Mexican Illustrations, Founded upon Facts*, 199.
17. Camacho, "Circular a los gobiernos de los estados invitándolos a que proporcionen por los medios que caben en su autoridad los objetos con que debe enriquecerse el establecimiento," October 6, 1826, AGN, GSS, box 98, file 9, 58r–60v.
18. Ramos Arizpe, "Circular a los prelados diocesanos," October 6, 1826, AGN, GSS, box 98, file 9, 61r–v.
19. Icaza, "El conservador acusando recibo de las piezas que donó para el establecimiento D. Pablo de la Llave y que le fueran entregadas en esta Secretaría," AGN, GSS, box 118, file 3, 4r–5v.
20. "El ministro de hacienda que se le diga si será conveniente aplicar a este establecimiento las cuatro piedras de plata virgin que ofrece remitir el Comisionario General de Chihuahua," April 15–June 20, 1828, AGN, GSS, box 109, file 5, 2r–8v.
21. AGN, GSS, box 109, file 9. For a detailed study of natural history collecting by the museum during the 1830s, see Vega y Ortega, "La riqueza del Gabinete de Historia natural del Museo Nacional de México."
22. Riesgo, "Nota de las curiosidades y cosas naturales procedentes de la Alta California por el comisario general de Occidente que remite para el Museo Nacional," AGN, GSS, box 118, file 3, 38r–42v.
23. López to Camacho, February 16, 1827, AGN, GSS, box 98, file 9, 83r–v.

24. López to Camacho, February 16, 1827, AGN, GSS, box 98, file 9, 83r–v.
25. Rugeley, *Rebellion Now and Forever*, 72.
26. González Angulo to Icaza, May 8, 1929, AGN, GSS, box 109, file 5, 27r–30v.
27. See AGN, GSS, box 98, file 9, 26r–28r, for inventory.
28. Icaza to the Ministry of the Treasury, July 22, 1827, AGN, GSS, box 109, file 5, 20r–22v. The skeleton was later identified to have belonged to a mammoth.
29. Camacho to Zavala, August 30, 1827, AGN, GSS, box 109, file 5, 25r–v.
30. Icaza to the Ministry of the Treasury, July 22, 1827, AGN, GSS, box 109, file 5, 34r–v.
31. Icaza to the Ministry of the Treasury, February 5, 1828, AGN, GSS, box 109, file 5, 28r–v.
32. Ministry of the Treasury to Icaza, March 1, 1828, AGN, GSS, box 109, file 5, 33r–v.
33. Espinosa de los Monteros, *Memoria del Ministerio de Relaciones Interiores y Exteriores de la República Mexicana*, 19.
34. For specific studies, see, among others, Alberti, *Nature and Culture*; Gänger, *Relics of the Past*; Gosden, Larson, and Petch, *Knowing Things*; Podgorny and Lopes, *El desierto en una vitrina*; Achim and Podgorny, *Museos al detalle*.
35. Eco, *From the Tree to the Labyrinth*.
36. Rosa Isidica, *El sol*, November 4, 1827, cited by Morales Moreno, *Orígenes de la museología mexicana*, 240–41.
37. The announcement appeared as a broadsheet and was reprinted in the facsmilar edition of Icaza and Gondra's *Colección de las antigüedades mexicanas que existen en el Museo Nacional*, 1927, no page number.
38. Estrada de Gerlero, "En defensa de América," 23–34; Estrada de Gerlero, "Litografía y Museo Nacional," 153–67.
39. Darby Smith, *Recollections of Two Distinguished Persons*, 80.
40. Waldeck kept detailed diaries (unpublished) of his life in Mexico, and they constitute today valuable references to collecting and antiquarianism in the late 1820s to the early 1830s. His diaries are divided between the Newberry Library in Chicago ("Journal 1826–1829," Newberry Library, Manuscript, Ayer 1261) and the British Library in London ("Baron de Waldeck Diaries," Add MS 73163–73164, concerning the years 1821–25 and "Journal, in French, of Baron Jean Frédéric Maximilien de Waldeck, 14 oct., 1829–21 aug. 1837," Add MS 41684). In this and the next chapter, I will be referring to Waldeck's diaries by date. There are various studies on Waldeck's

experiences in Mexico. See Baudez, *Waldeck, peintre*; Brunhouse, *In Search of the Mayas*; Perera, "De viajeros y coleccionistas de antigüedades"; Diener, "El diario del artista viajero Jean Frédérick Waldeck." For a comprehensive study on Waldeck's art, see Pasztory, *Jean-Frédéric Waldeck*.

41. Waldeck, *Voyage pittoresque et archéologique*, xx.
42. Waldeck, "Proyecto para explorar Chiapas y Yucatán para estudiar antigüedades mexicanas," October 4, 1831, BNAH, Fondo Reservado, ser. IA, file 1, doc. 5.
43. López Luján, personal communication with the author, concerning why Icaza would have favored Waldeck over contemporary Mexican artists. See also López Luján, "First Steps on a Long Journey."
44. Pasztory, *Jean-Frédérique Waldeck*, x.
45. Estrada de Gerlero, "Defensa de América," 30.
46. Estrada de Gerlero, "Litografía y Museo Nacional," 159.
47. Cited by Castillo Ledón, "Advertencia," xviii.
48. Especially relevant in this context was the *Description d'Égypte*, the multivolume collaborative work on Egyptian antiquities that was produced in the wake of Napoleon's Egyptian expedition in the late eighteenth century.
49. For a detailed description of Franck's album, see Warden, "Rapport fait à la Société de géographie." For a recent study of Franck's drawings and their role in the production of knowledge about Mexico's preconquest past, see Achim, "Colecciones de papel."
50. Maximilien Franck to Auguste de Forbin, director of the Louvre, February 27, 1832, AMN, A6-1831-1840.
51. The album is catalogued as Maximilien Franck, "Drawings; six hundred and sixteen drawings on eighty-one sheets of mainly Mexican antiquities, accompanied by a twenty-page descriptive manuscript catalogue written in French," British Museum, Am2006.
52. For a detailed account of Waldeck's activities in the late 1820s and early 1830s, see Achim, "Maleta de doble fondo y colecciones de antigüedades."
53. Icaza, "El Sr. Conservador participando las propuestas de cambio que han hecho al Establecimiento de objetos propios de él los Señores Poinsett y Baradere," April 7, 1829, AGN, GSS, box 109, file 5, 48r–49v.
54. Lombardo de Ruiz and Solís Vicarte, *Antecedentes de las leyes sobre Monumentos Históricos*, 31.
55. Quoted by Aguirre, *Informal Empire*, 30–31.

56. Bernecker, *Contrabando*; Mayo, "Consuls and Silver Contraband."

57. Boban, "Notes biographiques sur M. J. M. A. Aubin," 14. Aubin went as far as to erase incriminating details and dates from some of the manuscripts, showing some confidence in the power of his memory. However, once in Paris, he found the task of reconstructing them more difficult, perhaps, than he had imagined and would spend the rest of his life trying to reassemble them.

58. Icaza to Alamán, January 13, 1831, AGN, GL, box 102, file 16.

59. "Ley. Formación de un establecimiento científico que comprenda antigüedades, productos de industria, historia natural y jardón botánico," in Arrillaga, *Recopilación de leyes*, 496–98. A history of the Botanical Garden in the nineteenth century is long overdue, and the relationship (legal, financial, and intellectual) between the museum and the garden remains to be reconstructed.

60. For a detailed description of how the board functioned, see Vega y Ortega, "El asociacionismo y la Junta Directiva del Museo Nacional de México, 1830–1840."

61. Castillo Ledón, *El Museo Nacional*, Apéndice 1.

3. Collecting the Ruins of Palenque

1. Morelet, *Voyage dans l'Amérique Centrale*, 266, 276.

2. The imperial program of antiquarian study was the subject of Alcina Franch, *Arqueólogos o anticuarios*. The history of archaeological exploration at Palenque has been variously recounted by recent historians. See Brunhouse, *In Search of the Mayas*, and especially Podgorny, "Silent and Alone."

3. Vázquez Olivera, "Chiapas entre Centroamérica y México."

4. Secretaría de guerra y marina to the secretaría de relaciones, April 24, 1826, AGN, GSS, box 98, file 7, 91r–93v.

5. Secretaría de guerra y marina to the secretaría de relaciones, April 24, 1826, AGN, GSS, box 98, file 7, 91r–93v.

6. Icaza and Cubas, "Inventario de los monumentos de antigüedad que actualmente componen la colección perteneciente al Museo Nacional Mexicano," AGN, GSS, box 82, file 20, 73v–76v.

7. For a detailed study of the so-called Prix Palenque, see Prévost Urkidi, "Historiographie de l'américanisme." Prévost Urkidi focuses on the Société's management of the prize but leaves out the discussion of the competition for the prize as played out in the field.

8. Icaza, "Traslado de propuestas de Henrique Barader [*sic*] para hacer

conservaciones y recoger objetos de antigüedades e historia natural que merecen conservarse en [el Museo Nacional]," November 5, 1828, AGN, GSS, box 109, file 5, 39r–42v.

9. Icaza, "El Sr. Conservador participando las propuestas de cambio que han hecho al Establecimiento de objetos propios de él los Señores Poinsett y Baradere," April 7, 1829, AGN, GSS, box 109, file 5, 48v.

10. For a more detailed account of this exchange, see Achim, "Art of the Deal."

11. There is little biographical information available on Henri Baradère, decidedly a picturesque and controversial figure. For a detailed study of his passage through Mexico, see Edison, "Colonial Prospecting in Independent Mexico."

12. Dubouchet, *Le Guazacoalco*.

13. W. Anderson, *Mermaids, Mummies, and Mastodons*; Asma, *Stuffed Animals and Pickled Heads*; Prince, *Stuffing Birds, Pressing Plants, Shaping Knowledge*.

14. Lesson, "Manuel de taxidermie à l'usage des marins," 49. For a review of the methods and writings on taxidermy published in the early nineteenth century, see Faber, "Development of Taxidermy and the History of Ornithology"; Morris, "Historical Review of Bird Taxidermy in Britain"; and Wonders, *Habitat Dioramas*. See also Alberti, "Constructing Nature behind Glass."

15. See my discussion of Rosa Isidica's review of the museum in chapter 2.

16. Constantino Ortiz, "Coleccionismo de naturaleza en la Nueva España del siglo XVIII"; Constantino Ortiz and Lafuente, "Hidden Logistics of Longinos's Novohispanic Cabinet."

17. See especially AGN, GL, box 102 (1, 2, 3). See also Vega y Ortega, "La riqueza del Gabinete de Historia natural del Museo Nacional de México."

18. Icaza, "Traslado de propuestas de Henrique Barader," 39r–42v.

19. Icaza, "Traslado de propuestas de Henrique Barader," 40r.

20. Icaza, "Traslado de propuestas de Henrique Barader," 40r.

21. Baradère to the Société de géographie, June 4, 1829, BNF Richelieu, Cartes et Plans, Société de géographie, colis 19, bis 3253.

22. Warden, "Rapport fait á la Société royale des antiquaires de France."

23. Warden, "Rapport fait á la Société royale des antiquaires de France," 47.

24. Prévost Urkidi, "Historiographie de l'américanisme," 131.

25. Cochelet to the Société de géographie, October 30, 1830, BNF Richelieu, Cartes et Plans, Société de géographie, colis 19, bis 3329.

26. Cochelet to the Société de géographie, December 31, 1831, BNF Richelieu, Cartes et Plans, Société de géographie, colis 19, bis 3373.

27. Waldeck, "Proyecto para explorar Chiapas y Yucatán para estudiar anti-güedades mexicanas," October 4, 1831, BNAH, Fondo Reservado, ser. IA, file I, doc. 5.

28. Alamán, "Circular donde se da a conocer que el dibujante anticuario Dn. J. F. Waldeck ha presentado al E. S. Presidente un plan para realizar una expedición científica a Yucatán y Chiapas," October 12, 1831, BNAH, Fondo Reservado, ser. 4A, file 24.

29. Icaza to Alamán, January 13, 1831, AGN, GL, box 102, file 16.

30. Cochelet to the Société de géographie, August 8, 1832, BNF Richelieu, Cartes et Plans, Société de géographie, colis 19, bis 3382. Cochelet wrote that he had high hopes the savant world would finally obtain positive information on those mysterious ruins.

31. Prévost Urkidi, "Historiographie de l'américanisme," 140.

32. Waldeck to Gutiérrez, May 14, 1832, Newberry Library, Ayer 1269, folder 19.

33. Waldeck to Icaza, May 15, 1832, BNAH, Fondo Reservado, ser. 3A, file 28, doc. 4.

34. Secretaría de relaciones interiores y exteriores to Gutiérrez, AGN, GL, box 102, file 39.

35. Waldeck to Corroy, December 5, 1832, "Onze lettres du nouveau Champollion Mexicain," BNF Richelieu, Cartes et plans, Société de géographie, colis 7, bis 2146; Waldeck to Corroy, January 27, 1833, "Onze lettres du nouveau Champollion Mexicain"; Waldeck to Corroy, February 21, 1833, "Onze lettres du nouveau Champollion Mexicain."

36. Waldeck to Corroy, March 20, 1833, "Onze lettres du nouveau Champollion Mexicain."

37. Waldeck to Corroy, March 9, 1833, "Onze lettres du nouveau Champollion Mexicain."

38. Waldeck to Corroy, July 8, 1833, "Onze lettres du nouveau Champollion Mexicain."

39. Waldeck to Corroy, March 20, 1833, "Onze lettres du nouveau Champollion Mexicain."

40. Waldeck to Corroy. March 20, 1833, "Onze lettres du nouveau Champollion Mexicain."

41. Corroy was publishing in the *Knickerbocker*. See Podgorny, "Silent and Alone."

42. Waldeck to Juan Cayetano Portugal, September 30, 1834, AGN, GL, box 102 (2), file 33.

43. Waldeck to Gutiérrez, governor of the state of Chiapas, April 17, 1833, AGN, GL, box 102 (2), file 33.

44. Gutiérrez to the secretary of internal and external relations, June 5, 1833, AGN, GL, box 102 (2), file 33.

45. Waldeck, *Voyage pittoresque et archéologique*, 17.

46. There is a flurry of letters, starting in November of 1834 and through the following year, by various officials in Mexico City demanding reports on Waldeck's activities at the ruins. AGN, GL, box 102 (2), file 33.

47. Corroy to the Ministry of Internal and External Relations, June 22, 1835, AGN, GL, box 102 (2), file 33.

48. Barragán to Corroy, July 24, 1835, AGN, GL, box 102 (2), file 33.

49. Toro to the Ministry of Internal and External Relations, May 8, 1836, AGN, GL, box 102 (2), file 33.

50. Waldeck, *Voyage pittoresque et archéologique*, 75–76.

51. Waldeck, *Voyage pittoresque et archéologique*, 76.

52. Waldeck, *Voyage pittoresque et archéologique*, 17.

53. Menéndez Rodríguez, "Las formas del cisne," 16.

54. Angrand, "Rapport de M. L. Angrand à S. Exc. M. le Ministre de l'Instruction Publique," v–xi.

55. Waldeck, *Voyage pittoresque et archéologique*, 76.

56. Tinker, *Les écrits de langue française en Louisiane au XIXe siècle*, 374.

57. Perdreauville, "Viaje a las antigüedades de Xochicalco."

58. Isidro Icaza to the Ministry of Internal and External Relations, February 24, 1833, AGN, GL, box 102 (2), file 27.

59. *Boletín del Insituto Nacional de Geografía y Estadística de la República Mexicana*, "Prólogo."

60. "Varios individuos proponiendo la creación de una sociedad que investigue las ruinas de Palenque," AGN, GL, box 102 (2), file 34.

61. Corroy to the Administrative Board of the Museum, August 10, 1833, AGN, GL, box 102 (2), file 33.

62. Larrainzar, *Estudios sobre la historia de América*, 148.

63. Lenoir, "Formation d'une Société historique mexicaine." Interestingly, negative references to Waldeck, which appeared in the original proposal in Spanish, were eliminated from the French publication.

64. Warden et al., "Le Prix Palenque."

65. I borrow the expression from Podgorny, "Silent and Alone," 530.

66. Interestingly, Prévost Urkidi ("Historiographie de l'américanisme") believes Edmé Jomard was most closely responsible for this decision, which marked the rejection of linguistic and philological studies of ancient America in favor of archaeological and ethnographic research. This choice would determine the essence of French "scientific" Americanism.

67. Société de géographie, "Process verbal de la séance générale du 5 avril," 253.
68. Sellen, "Fraternal Curiosity."
69. Norman, *Rambles by Land and Water*, vi–vii. In 1843 Norman had published a book on his travels in Yucatán, *Rambles in Yucatán*.
70. St.-Priest, "Carta escrita al Excmo Sr. Gobernador de este departamento," 238.
71. St.-Priest, "Carta escrita al Excmo Sr. Gobernador de este departamento," 241.
72. Burkhardt, "Leopard in the Garden."
73. This argument was made by Elliott Colla in *Conflicted Antiquities*.
74. See Aguirre, *Informal Empire*; Mackenthum, "Imperial Archaeology."

4. Modes of Display

1. Several visitors have left accounts of their visits to the museum housed in the building of the university: Lyon, *Journal of a Residence and Tour of the Republic of Mexico*; Hardy, *Travels in the Interior of Mexico*; Ward, *Mexico in 1827*; Ampère, *Promenade en Amérique*; Fossey, *Le Mexique*; Arroniz, *Manual del viajero en México*.
2. Calderón de la Barca, *Life in Mexico*, 281.
3. Brantz Mayer, *Mexico, as It Was and as It Is*, 82.
4. Gualdi lived in Mexico City during the decade of the 1840s; in 1841 he published his *Monumentos de México tomados del natural*, which included views of the cathedral and its interior, the School of Mines, the interior of the university, and the Church of Guadalupe.
5. Brantz Mayer, *Mexico, as It Was and as It Is*, 83.
6. Brantz Mayer, *Mexico, as It Was and as It Is*, 83.
7. Brantz Mayer, *Mexico, as It Was and as It Is*, 88.
8. Brantz Mayer, *Mexico, as It Was and as It Is*, 89.
9. Brantz Mayer, *Mexico, as It Was and as It Is*, 90.
10. Brantz Mayer, *Mexico, as It Was and as It Is*, 90.
11. Brantz Mayer, *Mexico, as It Was and as It Is*, 91.
12. The fortification, built by Antonio Olivo, had been purchased by the government on behalf of the museum for 300 pesos in June of 1836. (Gómez de la Cortina, "Letter to the Ministry of Justice and Ecclesiastical Affairs," June 6, 1836, AGN, GL 102, box 2, file 35.)
13. Brantz Mayer, *Mexico, as It Was and as It Is*, 91.
14. Brantz Mayer, *Mexico, as It Was and as It Is*, 84.
15. Brantz Mayer, *Mexico, as It Was and as It Is*, 100.

16. Brantz Mayer, *Mexico, as It Was and as It Is*, 91.

17. Brantz Mayer, *Mexico, as It Was and as It Is*, 96.

18. Brantz Mayer, *Mexico, as It Was and as It Is*, 106. Here Mayer might have been referring to the codices taken to England by William Bullock, although those had been apparently returned.

19. Brantz Mayer, *Mexico, as It Was and as It Is*, 107.

20. See, among others, Bennet, *Birth of the Museum*; for Mexico, see Rico Mansard, *Exhibir para educar*.

21. Brantz Mayer, *Mexico, as It Was and as It Is*, 107.

22. Brantz Mayer, *Mexico, as It Was and as It Is*, 108.

23. AGN, GSS, box 360, file 9.

24. The expression is Brading's, *First America*, 642–43.

25. Cruz Soto, "Los periódicos del primer periodo de vida independiente," 66.

26. There are a number of recent studies on the development of the nineteenth-century Mexican press. Especially useful are Martínez, *La expression nacional*; Ruíz Castañeda, *Revistas literarias del siglo XIX*; Pérez Salas, *Costumbrismo y litografía*; and Suárez de la Torre and Castro, *Empresa y cultura en tinta y papel*, which contains a number of case studies on different aspects of nineteenth-century printing.

27. Pérez Salas, *Costumbrismo y litografía*, 172.

28. Villaseñor y Villaseñor, *Ignacio Cumplido*, 14. For a short introduction to Cumplido's life and works, see also Avilés, *Ignacio Cumplido*; Pérez Salas, "Cumplido, un empresario a cabalidad."

29. For an introductory study to *El Mosaico mexicano*, see Ruíz Castañeda, *El Mosaico mexicano, o Colección de amenidades curiosas e instructivas*.

30. Prieto, *Memoria de mis tiempos*, 154.

31. *El Mosaico mexicano*, "Advertencia preliminar," 3.

32. Garone Gravier, "Nineteenth-Century Mexican Graphic Design."

33. For an introductory study to *El Museo mexicano*, see Alonso Sánchez, "Una empresa educativa y cultural."

34. *El Ateneo Mexicano*, "Anales del Ateneo," 48.

35. *El Museo mexicano*, "Introducción."

36. For a different approximation to *El Museo mexicano* as a museum, see Mejía, "Nación, coleccionismo y tecnologías visuales en el viaje a Veracruz de Manuel Payno."

37. Pérez Salas has described the turn to Mexico's ancient past as a tendency by Mexican intellectuals to accept the ancient as one's own and engage in the search and rescue of Mexico's cultural roots in its indigenous past, in much the same way that European romantics strad-

dled the prevailing ideology of progress by embracing the medieval as
something other than a rupture separating the modern from the classical (*Costumbrismo y litografía*, 186).

38. Gondra, "Arqueología," 411.
39. Tornel, "Arqueología," 35.
40. Gondra, "Antigüedades mexicanas," 375.
41. Gondra, "Antigüedades mexicanas," 375.
42. Gondra, "Antigüedades mexicanas," 380.
43. Gondra, "Antigüedades mexicanas," 373.
44. Gondra, "Antigüedades mexicanas," 380.
45. L.E., "Monumentos antiguos de México."
46. Gondra, "Antigüedades mexicanas," 374.
47. Lewuillon, "Archaeological Illustrations."
48. Schnapp, *La conquête du passé*, 185–87.
49. For a detailed reconstruction of early Mormon readings of preconquest civilizations, see Evans, *Romancing the Mayas*, especially "Joseph
Smith and the Archaeology of Revelation."
50. Farcy, "Discours préliminaire," xi.
51. Farcy, "Discours préliminaire," xi.
52. Gondra, "Arqueología," 411.
53. Anonymous, "La frenología."
54. Anonymous, "Razas americanas," 200.
55. Anonymous, "Diferencias de las especies humanas."
56. Anonymous, "De la estatura humana y principalmente de los llamados
gigantes."
57. For a study of the intersection of antiquarianism and anthropometrics
as related to the origin of American civilization, see Achim, "Skulls
and Idols."
58. Nineteenth-century Mexican history offers numerous examples of
land surveying and prospecting missions that provided opportunities
for the collection of antiquities. The same rationale was often used to
reclaim land and preconquest antiquities from American Indian communities, who, according to the logic of nineteenth-century modernity,
did not know how to use them. See, for instance, Garay y Garay's expedition to the Isthmus of Tehuantepec, recounted in *Survey of the Isthmus of Tehuantepec*.
59. Prescott, *History of the Conquest of Mexico*, 1:7.
60. Prescott, *History of the Conquest of Mexico*, 1:6.
61. Prescott, *History of the Conquest of Mexico*, 1:85.

62. Prescott, *History of the Conquest of Mexico*, 1:86.

63. Prescott, *History of the Conquest of Mexico*, 1:59.

64. Prescott, *History of the Conquest of Mexico*, 1:108.

65. Prescott, *History of the Conquest of Mexico*, 1:35.

66. Prescott, *History of the Conquest of Mexico*, 1:79.

67. Prescott, *History of the Conquest of Mexico*, 1:58.

68. Prescott, "Appendix. Part I: Origin of Mexican Civilization," in *History of the Conquest of Mexico*, 2:377–410.

69. For the following account of the reception of Prescott's book in Mexico, I draw on Costeloe's "Prescott's *History of the Conquest*."

70. Littman, "John Lloyd Stephens," 535.

71. Sierra O'Reilly, "La historia de la conquista de México," 200.

72. Lucas Alamán, "Nota b," in Prescott, *Historia de la conquista de Méjico*, 1:15.

73. Alamán, "Nota a," in Prescott, *Historia de la conquista de Méjico*, 1:37.

74. Ignacio Cumplido, "Advertencia del editor," in Prescott, *Historia de la Conquista de México*, 2:ii.

75. Echeverría y Veytia's *Historia antigua de México* was eventually published in Mexico in 1836; Robertson's *History of America* was published in 1777; Cavo's *Historia civil y política de México* was published in Mexico between 1836 and 1838; and a Spanish translation of Clavigero's *Storia antica del Messico* (1780–81) was published in Mexico in 1844.

76. Ramírez, "Notas y esclarecimientos," in Prescott, *Historia de la Conquista de México*, 2:xv.

77. Others of Prescott's errors addressed by Ramírez included the assertion that there were mines in Mexico at the time of the conquest (Ramírez's note 5); the failure to recognize Cortés's mercenary spirit (note 6); claims that Cortés did not order his fleet destroyed (note 8); and clarifications on colonial currency and historical topography (notes 8 and 10).

78. Ramírez, "Notas y esclarecimientos," 25.

79. Gondra, in Prescott, *Historia de la Conquista de México*, 3:25.

80. Gondra, in Prescott, *Historia de la Conquista de México*, 3:19.

81. Gondra, in Prescott, *Historia de la Conquista de México*, 3:x.

82. Jaksic, *Hispanic World and American Intellectual Life*, 154.

83. Jaksic, *Hispanic World and American Intellectual Life*, 155.

84. Varios Mexicanos, *Consideraciones sobre la situación política y social de la República Mexicana en el año 1847*, 42.

85. Prieto, *Mi Guerra del 47*, 55. See also Ramírez to Luis G. Cuevas, sec-

retary of internal and external relations, April 27, 1849, AGN, box 360, files 13 and 14.

5. José Fernando Ramírez

1. Ampère, *Promenade en Amérique*, vol. 2, chap. 17.
2. Ampère, *Promenade en Amérique*, 2:284.
3. Ampère, *Promenade en Amérique*, 2:285.
4. Gondra, "Inventario o noticia de los aumentos que ha tenido el Museo Nacional, desde el año de 1844 hasta el de 1848," August 30, 1848, AHMN, vol. I, sec. 8.
5. See Anonymous, *Remate al mejor postor del Museo de Curiosidades naturales y artísticas.*
6. Ampère, *Promenade en Amérique*, 2:287.
7. Ampère, *Promenade en Amérique*, 2:287.
8. Ampère, *Promenade en Amérique*, 2:291.
9. Gondra to Arista, March 11, 1852, AGN, GSS, box 411, file 18. His resignation and a pension were approved on April 16.
10. Tornel to Fonseca, minister of justice and ecclesiastical affairs, April 26, 1852, AGN, GSS, box 411, file 18.
11. Arista to Ramírez, June 4, 1852, AGN, GSS, box 411, file 18.
12. Cited by González Obregón, "Vida y obras de Don José Fernando Ramírez," 90. Chavero published many of Ramírez's manuscripts in the *Anales del Museo Nacional* in the last decades of the nineteenth century.
13. There is no definitive biography of Ramírez. For a useful review of his life and work, see González Obregón, "Vida y obras de Don José Fernando Ramírez." Ramírez's *Obras históricas* is a five-volume anthology of writings, which was edited by Ernesto de la Torre Villar and includes summaries of Ramírez's life and work. In recent years, studies on different aspects of Ramírez's intellectual endeavors have been published: Rivas Mata and Gutiérrez L., *Libros y exilio*; Flores Olea, "José Fernando Ramírez"; and Krauze, *La presencia del pasado.*
14. On February 16, 1837, after the Texan secession, Parral would be incorporated to the new state of Chihuahua.
15. Ramos-Escandón, *Industrialización, género y trabajo femenino*; Bernecker, *De agiotistas y empresarios.* Ramírez provides a detailed description of the factory in his "Fábrica de Tejidos El Tunal."
16. Krauze, "Un héroe de la historiografía."
17. Ramírez, "Carta a Carlos María de Bustamante," in Rivas Mata and Gutiérrez L., *Libros y exilio*, 99–104.

18. A vara is about 0.84 meters.

19. Ramírez to Gondra, in Rivas Mata and Gutiérrez L., *Libros y exilio*, 110–31.

20. Ramírez to Gondra, in Rivas Mata and Gutiérrez L., *Libros y exilio*, 126.

21. Ramírez to Gondra, in Rivas Mata and Gutiérrez L., *Libros y exilio*, 125.

22. Ramírez to Gondra, in Rivas Mata and Gutiérrez L., *Libros y exilio*, 125.

23. Ramírez to Gondra, in Rivas Mata and Gutiérrez L., *Libros y exilio*, 125.

24. Ramírez, "Cuadro histórico-geroglífico de la peregrinación de las tribus Aztecas."

25. Ramírez to Gondra, in Rivas Mata and Gutiérrez L., *Libros y exilio*, 130.

26. Among the most important articles penned by Ramírez for the *Boletín* is "Noticias históricas y estadísticas de Durango." For an overview of his contributions to the *Diccionario*, see Pi-Suñer Llorens, *México en el Diccionario universal de historia y geografía*. Most of Ramírez's work remained unpublished for a long time, and some of his essays are still awaiting publication. For a guide to his manuscripts in the BNAH, see Sepúlveda y Herrera, *Catálogo de diarios de José Fernando Ramírez*.

27. Arroyo to Ramírez, March 4, 1853, AGN, GSS, vol. 423, file 3.

28. Oseguera to Ramírez, December 31, 1852, in Rivas Mata and Gutiérrez L., *Libros y exilio*, 251.

29. See letters from Mora to Ramírez, November 28, 1852, and April 29, 1853, in Rivas Mata and Gutiérrez L., *Libros y exilio*, 244–47, 260–64.

30. Mora to Ramírez, May 28, 1853, in Rivas Mata and Gutiérrez L., *Libros y exilio*, 267–72.

31. Mora to Ramírez, April 29, 1853, in Rivas Mata and Gutiérrez L., *Libros y exilio*, 260–64.

32. Oseguera to Ramírez, April 30, 1853, in Rivas Mata and Gutiérrez L., *Libros y exilio*, 265–66.

33. For a guide to Ramírez's library at the time of his death, see Puttick and Simpson Gallery, *Bibliotheca Mexicana*.

34. Ramírez to Bustamante, November 18, 1852, AHMN, vol. 1, sec. 13.

35. Pedrozo to Ramírez, June 15, 1853, AHMN, vol. 1, sec. 16.

36. "Se repone a Manuel G. Pedrozo en su empleo de preparador de aves del Museo Nacional," AHSRE, file H/139 (S-7) "855"/16.

37. Pedrozo to Ramírez, January 11, 1861, AHMN, vol. 1, sec. 31.

38. See Prieto, "La corte de Santa Anna," in *Memoria de mis tiempos*, chap. 3.

39. Fowler, *Santa Anna of Mexico*, 297.

40. Ramírez to Icazbalceta, February 3, 1855, in Rivas Mata and Gutiérrez L., *Libros y exilio*, 176.

41. Ramírez to Díez de Bonilla, November 16, 1854, Coleccion Padilla, folder 1853–55, doc. 83.

42. Ramírez does not mention his visit, although he is quoted in the catalogue of the Uhde collection for having supposedly affirmed that "America herself did not offer so great a collection of Aztec antiquities" as Uhde's did (Müller, Squier, and Thomsen, *Catalogue des objets formant le Musée Aztéco-Mexicain*, 6). I discussed Uhde's collection briefly in chapter 2.

43. Hernández de León Portilla, "Visita de José Fernando Ramírez a Alejandro de Humboldt," 303.

44. Hernández de León Portilla, "Visita de José Fernando Ramírez a Alejandro de Humboldt," 304.

45. It would be translated into Spanish and published as "De los nombres de los lugares aztecas."

46. Hernández de León Portilla, "Visita de José Fernando Ramírez a Alejandro de Humboldt," 307.

47. Hernández de León Portilla, "Visita de José Fernando Ramírez a Alejandro de Humboldt," 309.

48. Hernández de León Portilla, "Visita de José Fernando Ramírez a Alejandro de Humboldt," 310.

49. Ramírez to Paulin, December 27, 1855, BNF, Manuscrits mexicains, 360.

50. Longpérier, *Notice des monuments desposés dans la Salle des Antiquités Américaines*, 2.

51. Longpérier, *Notice des monuments desposés dans la Salle des Antiquités Américaines*, 3.

52. Longpérier, *Notice des monuments desposés dans la Salle des Antiquités Américaines*, 10.

53. Boban, "Notes biographiques sur M. J. M. A. Aubin," 25–26.

54. Boban, "Notes biographiques sur M. J. M. A. Aubin," 40.

55. Ramírez to Paulin, December 27, 1855, BNF, Manuscrits Mexicains, 360.

56. Ramírez to Paulin, December 27, 1855, BNF, Manuscrits Mexicains, 360.

57. Ramírez recounted his chase in the draft of an unfinished letter that he apparently did not send to Paulin ("Noticia de los manuscritos mexicanos que se conservan en la Biblioteca Imperial de Paris," December 27, 1855, BNAH, Fondo Reservado, Colección Gómez de Orozco, G.O., 142, doc. 1).

58. Anonymous, "Manuscrits mexicains à Paris."

59. Ramírez, unfinished letter to Paulin, "Noticia de los manuscritos mexicanos que se conservan en la Biblioteca Imperial de Paris,"

December 27, 1855, BNAH, Fondo Reservado, Colección Gómez de Orozco, G.O., 142, doc. 1.

60. Ramírez does not name the culprit, though he could have been referring to Baradère's *Antiquités mexicaines* or to Waldeck's *Voyage pittoresque et archéologique*.

61. Ramírez would lead a tireless campaign to rescue these books and manuscripts. See, for instance, his request to pick up books from the Convent of Jesús María, June 11, 1861, AHMN, vol. 1, sec. 30.

62. Ramírez to Comonfort, Colección Padilla Ramírez, folder 1853–1855, doc. 61. There is no date associated with this text, which appears to be a fragmented copy of his letter, but we can safely assume it was written sometime during the first half of 1856.

63. For a study of *México y sus alrededores*, see Roberto Mayer, "Nacimiento y desarrollo del álbum México y sus alrededores."

64. Ramírez, *Descripción*, 1.

65. Pingret, "Antiquités mexicaines."

66. For a study of Pingret, particularly in his relation to Mexico, see Ortiz Macedo, *Édouard Pingret*.

67. *El Siglo XIX*, January 12, 1851, cited in Rodríguez Prampolini, *La crítica de arte en México en el siglo XIX*, 302.

68. "Exposición en la Academia de San Carlos," *El Daguerrotipo*, January 4, 1851, in Rodríguez Prampolini, *La crítica de arte en México en el siglo XIX*, 296.

69. Pingret, "Notes sur les antiquités aztèques," February 14, 1864, AMN, A-5, 1864.

70. Pingret, "Notes sur les antiquités aztèques," February 14, 1864, AMN, A-5, 1864.

71. Pingret, "Notes sur les antiquités aztèques," February 14, 1864, AMN, A-5, 1864.

72. Pingret, "Notes sur les antiquités aztèques," February 14, 1864, AMN, A-5, 1864. For a study of Pingret's collection of Mexican antiquities, see Fauvet-Berthelot and López Luján, "Édouard Pingret."

73. Pingret, "Notes sur les antiquités aztèques," February 14, 1864, AMN, A-5, 1864.

74. Pingret, "Antiquités mexicaines," 176–78.

75. Pingret, "Antiquités mexicaines," 176–78.

76. Pingret, "Antiquités mexicaines," 178.

77. Tylor, *Anáhuac*, 230.

78. Tylor, *Anáhuac*, 230.

79. Tylor, *Anáhuac*, 229.

80. Ramírez, *Descripción*, 2.

81. Ramírez, *Descripción*, 2.

82. For instance, regarding the upright statue in the center of the illustration, Ramírez told his readers that the darkened face was not a defect of the lithography; the statue was stained, covered in a one-milimeter-thick layer of incense smoke. "How many years must have passed," mused Ramírez, "for this 'scab' to have formed on a statue placed outside, exposed as it was to the inclemency of weather and blasted by continuous winds? Its cult must have been extraordinary." Ramírez, *Descripción*, 4.

83. For a thorough study of the potentials of lists and case studies as technologies for knowledge production, see Hess and Mendelsohn, "Case and Series."

84. Ramírez, *Descripción*, 5.

85. At the time of Bullock's visit, "the upper surface only was exposed to view, which seemed to have been done designedly, to impress upon the populace an abhorrence of the horrible and sanguinary rites that had once been performed on this very altar. [. . .] I have seen the Indians themselves, as they pass, throw stones at it; and I once saw a boy jump upon it, clench his fist, stamp with his foot, and use other gesticulations of the greatest abhorrence" (Bullock, *Six Months' Residence and Travels in Mexico*, 335).

86. Ramírez, *Descripción*, 5.

87. Ramírez, *Descripción*, 5.

88. Ramírez, *Descripción*, 5.

89. Ramírez, *Descripción*, 7.

90. The concept is Daston's from "Sciences of the Archive."

91. Ramírez, "Noticias históricas y estadísticas de Durango," 13.

92. Ramírez, "Noticias históricas y estadísticas de Durango," 14.

93. Ranke, "On Progress in History," 21.

94. Denis, "Paléographie mexicaine."

95. Craib, "Nationalist Metaphysics," 35. Craib's analysis refers to Antonio García Cubas's 1857 *Carta general de la República Mexicana*, where the geographer represented, in an upper right-hand cartouche, images of Palenque, the pyramid at Papantla, Mitla, and Uxmal, affirming, at once, the country's "historical longevity" and "sedentarist past." But I believe that the argument can be extrapolated to make sense of the inclusion of a plate with Mexican antiquities in an album of vistas of central Mexico, as was the case with *México y sus alrededores*.

96. Tylor, *Anáhuac*, 222.

97. Ramírez, mariginal notes in museum log book, January 7, 1860, AHMN, vol. 1, sec. 25.

98. Ramírez, mariginal notes in museum log book, January 11, 1861, AHMN, vol. 1, sec. 32.

99. Ramírez, Romero, and Fonseca, "Proyecto de Ley Relativo a la Conservación de Monumentos Arqueológicos."

100. Ramírez described his hesitations and his interview with Carlota in his "Memorias para servir a la historia del Segundo Imperio," 530.

6. Whose Museum?

1. Pingret to Count Nieuwerkerke, September 12, 1863, AMN, A-5 1863.

2. Fauvet-Berthelot and López Luján, "La Piedra del Sol."

3. Pingret to Count Nieuwerkerke, September 12, 1863, AMN, A-5 1863.

4. Pingret, "Deuxième essai des notes sur les antiquités aztèques de Monsieur Pingret," MQB, MQB-70-2001-33-1.

5. Duruy, "Rapport à l'Empereur," February 27, 1864, in Ministère de l'Instruction publique, *Archives de la Commission scientifique du Mexique*, 1:1.

6. Duruy, "Rapport à l'Empereur," February 27, 1864, in Ministère de l'Instruction publique, *Archives de la Commission scientifique du Mexique*, 1:2.

7. Duruy, "Rapport à l'Empereur," February 27, 1864, in Ministère de l'Instruction publique, *Archives de la Commission scientifique du Mexique*, 1:3.

8. Duruy, "Rapport à l'Empereur," February 27, 1864, in Ministère de l'Instruction publique, *Archives de la Commission scientifique du Mexique*, 1:3.

9. Duruy, "Rapport à l'Empereur," February 27, 1864, in Ministère de l'Instruction publique, *Archives de la Commission scientifique du Mexique*, 1:3.

10. Duruy, "Rapport à l'Empereur," February 27, 1864, in Ministère de l'Instruction publique, *Archives de la Commission scientifique du Mexique*, 1:5.

11. Napoleon III, "Décret," in Ministère de l'Instruction publique, *Archives de la Commission scientifique du Mexique*, 1:8–9.

12. Duruy, "Lettre de S. Exc. M le Ministre de l'Instruction publique à M le Président de la Société méxicaine de géographie et de statistique," February 8, 1864, in Ministère de l'Instruction publique, *Archives de la Commission scientifique du Mexique*, 1:14.

13. Fonseca, "Lettre de M le Vice-Président de la Société mexicaine de géographie et de statistique à S. E. M. le Ministre de l'Instruction Publique," May 15, 1864, in Ministère de l'Instruction publique, *Archives de la Commission scientifique du Mexique*, 1:15–16.

14. Duruy, "Décret," June 4, 1864, in Ministère de l'Instruction publique, *Archives de la Commission scientifique du Mexique*, 1:9–10.
15. Prévost Urkidi, "La Commission scientifique du Mexique."
16. Anonymous, *Comisión Científica, Literaria y Artística de México*.
17. The ten sections were zoology; geology and mineralogy; physics and chemistry; mathematics and mechanics; astronomy, geography, hydrography, and meteorology; veterinary medicine and medicine; statistics, agriculture, and industry; history and literature; ethnology, linguistics, and archaeology; beaux arts, painting, sculpture, architecture, engraving, and photography.
18. Prévost Urkidi, "La Commission scientifique du Mexique," 2.
19. See especially Prévost Urkidi, "La Commission scientifique du Mexique"; Soberanis, "Sabios, militares y empresarios."
20. Doutrelaine, quoted by Prévost Urkidi, "La Commission scientifique du Mexique," 3.
21. That correspondence has been recently edited by Le Goff and Prévost Urkidi, *Homme de guerre, homme de science?*
22. Doutrelaine, Dépêche 71, November 8, 1865, in Le Goff and Prévost Urkidi, *Homme de guerre, homme de science?*; Doutrelaine, Dépêche 76, December 9, 1865, in Le Goff and Prévost Urkidi, *Homme de guerre, homme de science?*
23. For a detailed discussion of the work done by the archaeological commission, see Riviale, "La science marche au pas cadence."
24. Doutrelaine, Dépêche 35, May 9, 1865, in Le Goff and Prévost Urkidi, *Homme de guerre, homme de science?*
25. Doutrelaine, Dépêche 42, July 2, 1865, in Le Goff and Prévost Urkidi, *Homme de guerre, homme de science?*
26. Doutrelaine, Dépêche 45, July 25, 1865, in Le Goff and Prévost Urkidi, *Homme de guerre, homme de science?*
27. Doutrelaine, Dépêche 63, October 1, 1865, in Le Goff and Prévost Urkidi, *Homme de guerre, homme de science?*
28. See AHMN, vol. 1, doc. 59, 122–29. This entry contains also a historical memoir and a chemical analysis of the meteorite: Castillo and Río de la Loza, *Masa de hierro meteórico de Yanhuitlán*.
29. Doutrelaine, Dépêche 112, September 1, 1866, in Le Goff and Prévost Urkidi, *Homme de guerre, homme de science?*
30. Doutrelaine, Dépêche 83, January 25, 1866, in Le Goff and Prévost Urkidi, *Homme de guerre, homme de science?*
31. On Boban, see Riviale, "Eugène Boban."

32. Doutrelaine to Duruy, October 7, 1863, in Le Goff and Prévost Urkidi, *Homme de guerre, homme de science?*

33. Doutrelaine, Dépêche 1, August 8, 1864, in Le Goff and Prévost Urkidi, *Homme de guerre, homme de science?*

34. Doutrelaine, Dépêche 1, August 8, 1864, in Le Goff and Prévost Urkidi, *Homme de guerre, homme de science?*

35. Doutrelaine, Dépêche 1, August 8, 1864, in Le Goff and Prévost Urkidi, *Homme de guerre, homme de science?*

36. Duruy, "Arrête," November 3, 1864, in Ministère de l'Instruction publique, *Archives de la Commission scientifique du Mexique*, 1:17–18.

37. Doutrelaine, Dépêche 1, August 8, 1864, in Le Goff and Prévost Urkidi, *Homme de guerre, homme de science?* In due fairness, Doutrelaine had serious misgivings about the French cadres in Mexico as well; in the same letter, Doutrelaine wrote that most of them had very little technical background and had arrived in Mexico to get rich.

38. For his observations on the ruins at Mitla, see Doutrelaine, Dépêche 40, July 1, 1865, in Le Goff and Prévost Urkidi, *Homme de guerre, homme de science?*

39. Doutrelaine, Dépêche 51, August 18, 1865, in Le Goff and Prévost Urkidi, *Homme de guerre, homme de science?* For a detailed study of the Camacho brothers' collection and of Doutrelaine's interpretations of the collection, see Sellen, "Fraternal Curiosity."

40. Doutrelaine, Dépêche 4, September 4, 1864, in Le Goff and Prévost Urkidi, *Homme de guerre, homme de science?*

41. For a study of Léon Méhédin, see Gerber, Nicaise, and Robichon, *Un aventurier du Second Empire.*

42. Doutrelaine, Dépêche 32, April 10, 1865, in Le Goff and Prévost Urkidi, *Homme de guerre, homme de science?*

43. Doutrelaine, Dépêche 37, May 10, 1865, in Le Goff and Prévost Urkidi, *Homme de guerre, homme de science?*

44. Doutrelaine, Dépêche 43, July 2, 1865, in Le Goff and Prévost Urkidi, *Homme de guerre, homme de science?*

45. Doutrelaine, Dépêche 51, August 18, 1865, in Le Goff and Prévost Urkidi, *Homme de guerre, homme de science?*

46. Doutrelaine, Dépêche 48, August 5, 1865, in Le Goff and Prévost Urkidi, *Homme de guerre, homme de science?*

47. Doutrelaine, Dépêche 14, October 7, 1864, in Le Goff and Prévost Urkidi, *Homme de guerre, homme de science?*

48. Ramírez, "Carta de J. F. Ramírez al señor coronel Doutrelaine," BNAH,

Fondo Reservado, CA 201, doc. 2, pp. 43–210. Like many of Ramírez's writings, this review remained unpublished.

49. Doutrelaine, Dépêche 43, July 4, 1865, in Le Goff and Pévost Urkidi, *Homme de guerre, homme de science?*

50. Joseph Marius Alexis Aubin, "Rapport de M. A. Aubin sur diverses communications" and "Rapport de M. Aubin," in Ministère de l'instruction publique, *Archives de la Commission scientifique du Mexique* 2:12–18 and 2:164–70, respectively.

51. Doutrelaine, Dépêche 85, January 1, 1865, in Le Goff and Pévost Urkidi, *Homme de guerre, homme de science?*

52. Doutrelaine, Dépêche 85, January 1, 1865, in Le Goff and Pévost Urkidi, *Homme de guerre, homme de science?*

53. Doutrelaine, Dépêche 104, June 8, 1866, in Le Goff and Pévost Urkidi, *Homme de guerre, homme de science?*

54. O'Gorman, *La supervivencia política novohispana*, 79.

55. For more details on Maximilian's education and life before his arrival in Mexico, see Ratz, *Tras las huellas de un desconocido*.

56. Franz von Hauslab, one of Maximilian's tutors, quoted in Ratz, *Tras las huellas de un desconocido*, 4. Ratz suggests that Maximilian shared von Hauslab's diagnostic of Mexico.

57. Ratz, *Tras las huellas de un desconocido*, 24.

58. Kolonitz, *Un viaje a México en 1864*, 43.

59. Doutrelaine, Dépêche 1, August 8, 1864, in Le Goff and Pévost Urkidi, *Homme de guerre, homme de science?*

60. Doutrelaine, Dépêche 1, August 8, 1864, in Le Goff and Pévost Urkidi, *Homme de guerre, homme de science?*

61. "Instrucción para los prefectos políticos," *La Razón de México*, November 4, 1864.

62. Brasseur went on to condemn the policy in his "Rapport sur les ruines de Mayapan et d'Uxmal au Yucatán (Mexique)," published in the second volume of the *Archives de la Commission scientifique du Mexique*: "Salazar had perverted the emperor's decree [. . .] Maximilian had prohibited exportation, but Salazar prohibited excavations, even touching [of antiquities] by foreigners. He had forgotten that in Yucatán one did not build anything but with the stones taken from the old monuments [and he] ignored that if certain Mexican antiquities were known, it was due to foreign explorers who alone have given them their value and know how to appreciate them" (245).

63. "Documentos sobre Yucatán," in Weckmann, *Carlota de Bélgica*, 341.

64. Ratz, *Tras las huellas de un desconocido*, 155–56.

65. Domenech, *Le Mexique tel qu'il est*, 213.

66. Carlota to Maximilian, July 29, 1865, in Weckmann, *Carlota de Bélgica*, 185–89.

67. Carlota, "Mémoire remis par moi à l'Empereur Napoléon à St. Cloud," August 11, 1866, in Weckmann, *Carlota de Bélgica*, 181.

68. Domenech, *Le Mexique tel qu'il est*, 214.

69. Doutrelaine, Dépêche 43, July 2, 1865, in Le Goff and Pévost Urkidi, *Homme de guerre, homme de science?*

70. The instructions were published in the *Periódico oficial de México*, August 3, 1864.

71. The AICL has received little scholarly attention. An exception is Soberanis's "La Academia Imperial de Ciencias y Literatura."

72. The description was published in the periodical *El Pájaro verde*, April 12, 1865.

73. Ramírez, speech for the inauguration of the AICLM, April 10, 1865, in Anonymous, *Acta de Instalación de la Academia Imperial de Ciencias y Literatura de México.*

74. Ramírez, speech for the inauguration of the AICLM, April 10, 1865, in Anonymous, *Acta de Instalación de la Academia Imperial de Ciencias y Literatura de México*, 13–14.

75. Ramírez, speech for the inauguration of the AICLM, April 10, 1865, in Anonymous, *Acta de Instalación de la Academia Imperial de Ciencias y Literatura de México*, 15.

76. Ramírez, speech for the inauguration of the AICLM, April 10, 1865, in Anonymous, *Acta de Instalación de la Academia Imperial de Ciencias y Literatura de México*, 15.

77. Anders, "Yucatán, die 'Indios Barbaros' und Kaiser Maximilian von Mexiko."

78. Ramírez, speech for the inauguration of the AICLM, April 10, 1865, in Anonymous, *Acta de Instalación de la Academia Imperial de Ciencias y Literatura de México*, 15.

79. Robles Pezuela, *Memoria presentada a S.M. el Emperador.*

80. Almaraz, *Memoria de los trabajos ejecutados por la Comsión Científica de Pachuca.*

81. Announcement published in *El Pájaro verde*, July 15, 1865.

82. Almaraz, *Memoria acerca de los terrenos de Metlatoyuca.*

83. Almaraz, *Memoria acerca de los terrenos de Metlatoyuca*, 19.

84. Announcement published in *El Pájaro verde*, September 17, 1866.

85. Maximilian to Siliceo, November 1865, quoted by Arciniega Ávila, "La galería de las Sibilas," 41.

86. In fact, Maximilian seemed to have envisioned a scenario where the United States, Mexico, and Brazil would carve out the Western Hemisphere between themselves. Renouncing the Mexican lands in the north in an attempt to appease the United States, Maximilian hoped he would make Yucatán into the nucleus of his own Central American Empire, which would border the Brazilian Empire to the south ("Documentos sobre Yucatán," in Weckmann, *Carlota de Bélgica*, 340–50).

87. "Documentos sobre Yucatán," in Weckmann, *Carlota de Bélgica*, 340–81.

88. Ramírez, "Viaje a Yucatán," 602.

89. Carlota to Maximilian, in Weckmann, *Carlota de Bélgica*, 127–28.

90. Ramírez, "Viaje a Yucatán," 645.

91. Ramírez, "Viaje a Yucatán," 617.

92. Announcement published in *El Pájaro verde*, December 5, 1865.

93. Comisión Científica, Literaria y Artística de México, *Reglamento para los servicios de honor y ceremonial de la corte*, sec. 7, 111 and 195. See also Pani, "El proyecto de estado de Maximiliano."

94. Rico Mansard, "El Museo Nacional de México," 60.

95. Rivera Cambas, *México pintoresco, artístico y monumental*, 2:175–81.

96. For a detailed account on Reinisch's passage through Mexico, see Anders, "Simon Leo Reinisch."

97. Opriessnig, "Política cultural en el Segundo Imperio," 327.

98. Erika Pani, "'Verdaderas figuras de Cooper' o 'pobres inditos infelices'?," 577.

99. Opriessnig, "Política cultural en el Segundo Imperio," 328.

100. Opriessnig, "Política cultural en el Segundo Imperio," 332–34.

101. Carlota to Joseph Corio, imperial representative in Brussels, August 8, 1865, in Weckmann, *Carlota de Bélgica*, 150–52. Opriessnig clarifies that the cape was not Moctezuma's as many believed at the time but was originally from a Tupinamba tribe in Brazil ("Política cultural en el Segundo Imperio," 338).

102. Opriessnig, "Política cultural en el Segundo Imperio," 335–38.

103. Montellano to Maximilian, December 6, 1865, AGN, Segundo Imperio, vol. 38, file 48, p. 13.

104. On Rodríguez Arangoiti, see Arciniega Ávila, "La galería de las Sibilas."

105. Rodríguez Arangoiti kept detailed records of the move in his "Memoria de los gastos erogados [. . .] en la traslación del Museo y Biblioteca," AGN, Segundo Imperio, vol. 49, file 36, pp. 4–5.

106. Maximilian to his civil cabinet, letter no. 25, December 15, 1865, AGN, Segundo Imperio, vol. 37, file 11, p. 7.

107. Rodríguez Arangoiti, "Memoria de los gastos erogados," AGN, Segundo Imperio, vol. 49, file 36, p. 4r.

108. Artigas to the emperor, January 22, 1866, AGN, Segundo Imperio, vol. 49, file 36, p. 17.

109. Artigas to the emperor, February 6, 1866, AGN, Segundo Imperio, vol. 49, file. 36, pp. 17–23.

110. Maximilian to Artigas, March 8, 1866, AGN, Segundo Imperio, vol. 49, file 36, p. 29; Ministry of Public Instruction, "Copia del libro diario del Ministerio de Instruccion Pública y Cultos," March and April 1866, AGN, Segundo Imperio, vol. 24, file 7.

111. Ratz, *Tras las huellas de un desconocido*, 141.

112. Rivera, *Anales Mexicanos*, 237.

113. Ratz, *Correspondencia inédita entre Maximiliano y Carlota*, 275, 281, 287. Although Bilimek was not officially put in charge of the natural history section at the museum until May 1, 1866, he started receiving remuneration for his naturalist work at the museum as early as May of the previous year (AGN, Segundo Imperio, box 24, file 7).

114. The inauguration of the museum has been described by Noriega, "Ceremonia de apertura del Museo Nacional," 3.

115. Azuela, Vega y Ortega, and Nieto García, "Un edificio científico para el imperio de Maximiliano," 120.

116. During the winter of 1865–66, the United States supplied Juárez with thirty thousand muskets and stationed U.S. troops on the north side of the Río Grande (Wheelan, *Terrible Swift Sword*).

117. Pani, "El proyecto de estado de Maximiliano," 438; for a detailed study of the mechanisms of legitimation and state building by Maximilian, see Robert H. Duncan, "Political Legitimation and Maximilian's Second Empire."

118. As reported by Ramírez in his "Memorias para servir a la historia del Segundo Imperio," 571.

119. Doutrelaine's diagnostic of Maximilian's situation during the last year of his rule is demolishing: "If I cruelly say the emperor is worth nothing in Mexico, that he has absolutely no power, no influence, no credit, I would only be telling an incontestable truth. The poor Sire is respected by the Mexicans no more and no less than Soliveau by the frogs in the fable. Though he bestows on them his kind smiles and his graceful greetings, and wears leather vests and dons on a som-

brero, though he fills up the official journal with decrees, decisions, letters to his ministers and scribblings of all kinds, he has not the least authority and never will have it. He is a truly otiose (fainéant) king; certainly, he has chosen badly the moment to resurrect this Merovingian type" (Doutrelaine to Vaillant, March 27, 1866, in Le Goff and Prévost Urkidi, *Homme de guerre, homme de science?*).

120. Bejarano to the emperor, August 24, 1866, AGN, Segundo Imperio, vol. 49, file 36, pp. 39–45.

121. Bejarano to the emperor, September 16, 1866, AGN, Segundo Imperio, vol. 48, file 46, p. 4.

122. Juan Barquera (undersecretary of public instruction) to Orozco y Berra, November 19, 1865, AGN, Segundo Imperio, vol. 24, file 44.

123. Reinisch, *Tagebuchaufzeichnungen*, 43.

124. Anders, "Simon Leo Reinisch," 20.

125. Reinisch, *Tagebuchaufzeichnungen*, 57.

126. Ramírez, "Memorias para servir a la historia del Segundo Imperio," 571.

127. Doutrelaine, Dépêche 117, September 6, 1866, in Le Goff and Prévost Urkidi, *Homme de guerre, homme de science?*

128. Maximilian to Bilimek, January 25, 1867, quoted by Arciniega Ávila, "La galería de las Sibilas," 52.

129. Basch, *Recuerdos de México*, 153.

130. Maximilian to Orozco y Berra, February 8, 1867, quoted by Arciniega Ávila, "La galería de las Sibilas," 53.

131. For a study of Méhédin's participation in the fair, see Demuelenaere-Douyère, "Le Mexique s'expose à Paris."

132. Jacques, "Le Temple de Xochicalco." The following description of Méhédin's pyramid is based on this chronicle.

133. Jacques, "Le Temple de Xochicalco," 277.

134. Unlike Ramírez, Orozco y Berra was pardoned after serving a prison term of one year, after which he went on to work for the republican government.

135. Castillo Ledón, *El Museo Nacional*, 23.

136. Juárez, *Ley orgánica de la Instrucción Pública*, capítulo 5.

137. Juárez, *Ley orgánica de Instrucción Pública en el Distrito Federal*, capítulo 3.

Epilogue

1. Galindo y Villa, *Breve noticia histórico-descriptiva del Museo Nacional de México*, 10. Other antiquities, together with the objects of history and natural history, were displayed in adjoining rooms.

2. Jesús Sánchez, the museum's director between 1883 and 1889, asked the secretary of war and navy for help to move the Piedra del Sol. The secretary lent the museum pulleys and contributed technical advice as well (Sánchez, letters to secretary of war and navy, August 1885, AHMN, vol. 7, file 15, and vol. 8, file 1).

3. The literature on the late nineteenth-century forging of this alliance is vast. See, among others, Tenorio Trillo, *Mexico at the World's Fairs*; Garrigan, *Collecting Mexico*; Bueno, "Forjando Patrimonio"; Kelly, "Waking the Gods."

4. The latest of such acts has been a state dinner in April 16, 2009, organized by ex-president Felipe Calderón for the U.S. president Barack Obama in the Sala Mexica of the Museo Nacional de Antropología. See Otero, "Obama en México."

5. Rosenstein, *Antiques*, 190.

6. Rosenstein, *Antiques*, 191.

7. Justo Sierra to Roberto Núñez, vice secretary of finance, May 18, 1909, in Sierra, *Epistolario y papeles privados*, 289–90.

8. This break is not always as complete as museum authorities would expect. In a recent film, *La piedra ausente*, Jesse Lerner and Sandra Rozental have documented the rich social life of the Tlaloc monolith in the midst of the Coatlinchan community before and after the statue was moved to the National Museum of Anthropology in 1964.

9. Breglia, *Monumental Ambivalence*; Ferry, *Not Ours Alone*. See also the collection of recent articles on the idea of Mexican patrimony by Escalante Gonzalbo, *La construcción de la idea de nuestro patrimonio histórico y cultural*.

BIBLIOGRAPHY

Archival Sources

Archives de Musées Nationales, France (AMN)

Archivo del Histórico de la Secretaría de Relaciones Exteriores Genaro
Estrada (AHSRE)

Archivo General de la Nación, Mexico (AGN)
Gobernación Legajos (GL)
Gobernación Sin Sección (GSS)

Archivo Histórico del Distrito Federal (AHDF)

Archivo Histórico del Museo Nacional (AHMN)

Biblioteca Nacional de Antropología e Historia (BNAH)

Bibliothèque Nationale, France (BNF)

British Museum Library (BM)
Drawings of Maximilien Franck: "Drawings; six hundred and sixteen drawings on eighty-one sheets of mainly Mexican antiquities,
accompanied by a twenty-page descriptive manuscript catalogue
written in French."

Colección Padilla, Mexico
José Fernando Ramírez Papers

Musée du Quay Branly, France (MQB)
Édouard Pingret Papers

Newberry Library
Edward E. Ayer Manuscript Collection, Jean-Frédéric Waldeck Papers

University of Texas Libraries, University of Texas at Austin
Benson Latin American Collection

Published Sources

Acevedo, Esther. "El legado artístico de un imperio efímero: Maximiliano
en México, 1864–1867." In *Testimonios artísticos de un episodio fugaz,
1864–1867*, edited by Esther Acevedo and Ana Laura Cué, 33–61. Mexico City: Museo Nacional de Arte, 1995.

Achim, Miruna. "The Art of the Deal, 1828: How Isidro Icaza Traded Pre-
Columbian Antiquities to Henri Baradère for Mounted Birds and Built

a National Museum in Mexico in the Process." *West 86th* 18, no. 2 (September 2011): 214–31.

———. "Colecciones de papel: Hacia una ciencia del pasado de México." In *Piedra, papel, tijera*, edited by Laura Cházaro, Nuria Valverde, and Miruna Achim. Mexico City: Universidad Autónoma Metropolitana, Cuajimalpa, forthcoming.

———. "La literatura anticuaria en la Nueva España." In *Historia de la literatura mexicana*, edited by Nancy Vogeley and Manuel Ramos Medina, 549–69. Mexico City: Editorial Siglo XXI, 2011.

———. "Maleta de doble fondo y colecciones de antigüedades, Ciudad de México, ca 1830." In Achim and Podgorny, *Museos al detalle*, 99–126.

———. "Skulls and Idols: Anthropometrics, Antiquity Collections, and the Origin of American Man, 1810–1850." In *Nature and Antiquities: The Making of Archaeology in the Americas*, edited by Philip Kohl, Irina Podgorny, and Stefanie Gänger, 23–46. Tucson: University of Arizona Press, 2014.

Achim, Miruna, and Irina Podgorny. *Museos al detalle: Colecciones, antigüedades e historia natural*. Buenos Aires: Colección Prohistoria, 2013.

Aguilar Ochoa, Arturo. "Los inicios de la litografía en México: El periodo oscuro (1827–1837)." *Anales del Instituto de Investigaciones Estéticas* 90 (2007): 66–100.

Aguirre, Robert. *Informal Empire: Mexico and Central America in Victorian Culture*. Minneapolis: University of Minnesota Press, 2005.

———. "William Bullock (1780–1844): British Museum Curator and Showman in Mexico." In *The Human Tradition in the Atlantic World, 1500–1850*, edited by Karen Racine and Beatriz Mamigonian, 223–36. Plymouth: Rowman and Littlefield, 2010.

Alamán, Lucas. *Memoria presentada a las dos cámaras del Congreso General de la Federación, por el secretario de Estado y del despacho de Relaciones Exteriores e Interiores*. Mexico City: Imprenta del Supremo Gobierno de los Estados Unidos Mexicanos, en Palacio, 1825.

———. *Memoria que el Secretario de Estado y Despacho de Relaciones Exteriores e Interiores presenta al Soberano Congreso Constituyente*. Mexico City: Imprenta del Supremo Gobierno de los Estados Unidos Mexicanos, en Palacio, 1823.

———. *The Present State of Mexico*. Notes by Benjamin Disraeli. London: John Murray, 1825.

———. "Quinta Disertación: Noticias particulares concernientes a D. Fernando Cortés." In *Disertaciones sobre la historia de la República megicana*, edited by Lucas Alamán, 2:1–62. Mexico City: Imprenta de J. M. Lara, 1844–49.

Alberti, Samuel J. M. M. "Constructing Nature behind Glass." *Museum and Society* 6, no. 2 (2008): 73–97.

———. *Nature and Culture: Objects, Disciplines, and the Manchester Museum.* London: Palgrave Macmillan, 2009.

Alcina Franch, José. *Arqueólogos o anticuarios: Historia antigua de la arqueología en la América Española.* Barcelona: El Serbal, 1995.

———. "Guillermo Dupaix y los orígenes de la arqueologia en México." *Estudios de historia novohispana* 10, no. 10 (1991): 325–46.

Almaraz, Ramón. *Memoria acerca de los terrenos de Metlatoyuca.* Mexico City: Imprenta Imperial, 1866.

———. *Memoria de los trabajos ejecutados por la Comsión Científica de Pachuca en el año de 1864.* Mexico City: Imprenta de Andrade y Escalante, 1865.

Alonso Sánchez, Magdalena. "Una empresa educativa y cultural de Ignacio Cumplido, *El Museo mexicano,* 1843–1846." In Suárez de la Torre and Castro, *Empresa y cultura en tinta y papel,* 553–60.

Alzate y Ramírez, José Antonio. *Descripción de las antigüedades de Xochicalco.* Mexico City: Zúñiga y Ontiveros, 1791.

Ampère, Jean Jacques. *Promenade en Amérique: États-Unis, Cuba, Mexique.* 2 vols. Paris: Michel Levy Frères, 1860.

Anders, Ferdinand. "Simon Leo Reinisch—Sein Lebensweg: Der 'Vater de Ägyptologie und Afrikanistik in Wien' als Pionier der Mexikanistik." In *Simon Leo Reinisch—Werk und Erbe,* edited by Hans Günther Mukarovsky, 9–36. Vienna: Osterreichischen Akademie der Wissenschaften, 1987.

———. "Yucatán, die 'Indios Barbaros' und Kaiser Maximilian von Mexiko: Utopie und Realität im 'Segundo Imperio Mexicano.'" *Archiv für Völkerkunde* 33 (1979): 44–60.

Anders, Ferdinand, Margarete Pfister-Burkhalter, and Christian F. Feest. *Lukas Vischer (1780–1840), Künstler, Reisender, Sammler: Ein Beitrag zur Ethnographie der Vereinigten Staaten von Amerika sowie zur Archäologie und Volkskunde Mexikos.* Hanover: Kommissionsverlag Münstermann-Druck, 1967.

Anderson, Benedict. *Imagined Communities: Reflections on the Origins and Spread of Nationalism.* London: Verso, 2003 [1983].

Anderson, William T., ed. *Mermaids, Mummies, and Mastodons: The Emergence of the American Museum.* Washington DC: American Associations of Museums, 1992.

Angrand, Léonce. "Rapport de M. L. Angrand à S. Exc. M. le Ministre de l'Instruction Publique." In *Recherches sur les ruines de Palenque et sur les origins de la civilization du Mexique*, edited by Charles Étienne Brasseur de Bourbourg, v–xi. Paris: Arthus Bertrand, 1866.

Anna, Timothy. *Forging Mexico, 1821–1835.* Lincoln: University of Nebraska Press, 1998.

Anonymous. *Acta de Instalación de la Academia Imperial de Ciencias y Literatura de México.* Mexico City: Imprenta de Andrade y Escalante, 1866.

———. "De la estatura humana y principalmente de los llamados gigantes." *El Mosaico mexicano* 3 (1840): 21–24.

———. "Diferencias de las especies humanas calculadas sobre la línea facial." *El Mosaico mexicano* 3 (1840): 449–55.

———. "La frenología." *El Mosaico mexicano* 1 (1836): 326–28.

———. "Manuscrits mexicains à Paris." *Bulletin des Sciences Historiques, Antiquités, Philologie*, no. 14 (1830): 278–80.

———. *Noticias biográficas del Exmo Sr. D. Lucas Alamán.* In *Diccionario universal de historia y geografía*. Vol. 1. Mexico City: Rafael, 1853.

———. "Razas americanas." *El Mosaico mexicano* 2 (1837): 198–203.

———. *Reglamento para los servicios de honor y ceremonial de la corte.* Mexico City: Imprenta de J. M. Lara, 1866.

———. *Remate al mejor postor del Museo de Curiosidades Naturales y Artísticas que fue del difunto Sr. D. Mariano Sánchez Mora, ex-conde de Peñasco.* Mexico City: Ignacio Cumplido, 1846.

———. "Some Observations Caused by the Introduction by Mr. Bullock into England of Various Rare and Curious Specimens of Mexican Antiquity." *Classical Journal* 29 (1824): 186.

Arciniega Ávila, Hugo. "La galería de las Sibilas: El Museo Público de Historia Natural, Arqueología e Historia de México." *Boletín de Monumentos Históricos* 14 (2008): 35–64.

Arrillaga, José Basilio. *Recopilación de leyes, decretos, bandos, reglamentos, circulares y providencias de los supremos poderes y otras autoridades de la República Mexicana.* Mexico City: Imprenta de J. M. Fernández de Lara, 1831.

Arroniz, Marcos. *Manual del viajero en Méjico.* Paris: Librería de Rosa y Bouret, 1858.

Asma, Stephen T. *Stuffed Animals and Pickled Heads: The Culture and Evolution of Natural History Museums.* Oxford: Oxford University Press, 2001.

Aveleyra Arroyo de Anda, Luis. *Cueva de la Candelaria.* Mexico City: Instituto Nacional de Antropología e Historia, 1956.

Ávila, Alfredo, and Luis Jáuregui. "La disolución de la monarquía hispánica y el proceso de independencia." In *Nueva historia general de México*. Mexico City: Colegio de México, 2010.

Avilés, Jaime. *Ignacio Cumplido, un impresor del siglo XIX*. Mexico City: Instituto Mora, 1992.

Azuela, Luz Fernanda, and Rodrigo A. Vega y Ortega. "El Museo Público de Historia Natural Arqueologia e Historia (1865–1867)." In *La geografía y las ciencias naturales en el siglo XIX mexicano*, edited by Luz Fernanda Azuela Bernal and Rodrigo A. Vega y Ortega, 103–20. Mexico City: Universidad Nacional Autónoma de México, 2011.

Azuela, Luz Fernanda, Rodrigo A. Vega y Ortega, and Raúl C. Nieto García. "Un edificio científico para el imperio de Maximiliano: El Museo Público de Historia Natural, Arqueología e Historia." In *Geografía e historia natural: Hacia una historia comparada*, coordinated by Celina A. Lértora Mendoza, 101–24. Buenos Aires: Ediciones FEPAI, 2008.

Bakewell, Peter. "Mining." In *Colonial Spanish America*, edited by Leslie Bethell, 203–49. Cambridge: Cambridge University Press, 1987.

Bankmann, Ulf, and Gerhard Baer. *Ancient Mexican Ceramics from the Lukas Vischer Collection, Ethnographic Museum Basel*. Basel, Switzerland: Friedrich Reinhardt, 1996.

Basch, Samuel. *Recuerdos de México: Memorias del médico ordinario del Emperador Maximiliano (1866 a 1867)*. Mexico City: Nabor Chávez, 1870.

Baudez, Claude François. *Waldeck, peintre, le premier explorateur des ruines mayas*. Paris: Hatan, 1993.

Beaufoy, Mark. *Mexican Illustrations, Founded upon Facts*. London: Carpenter and Son, 1828.

Bennet, Tony. *The Birth of the Museum: History, Theory, Politics*. New York: Routledge, 1995.

Bernal, Ignacio. *Historia de la arqueología en México*. Mexico City: Porrúa, 1979.

Bernecker, Walther. *Contrabando: Ilegalidad y corrupción en el México del siglo XIX*. Mexico City: Universidad Iberoamericana, 1994.

———. *De agiotistas y empresarios: En torno de la temprana industrialización mexicana (siglo XIX)*. Mexico City: Universidad Iberoamericana, 1992.

Bleichmar, Daniela, and Peter C. Mancall, eds. *Collecting across Cultures: Material Exchanges in the Early Atlantic World*. Philadelphia: University of Pennsylvania Press, 2011.

Boban, Eugène. "Notes biographiques sur M. J. M. A. Aubin." In *Documents pour servir à l'histoire du Mexique: Catalogue raisonné de la col-*

lection de M. E.-Eugène Goupil, edited by Eugène Boban, 21–30. Paris: Ernest Leroux, 1891.

Boletín del Insituto Nacional de Geografía y Estadística de la República Mexicana. "Prólogo." No. 1 (1839): 1–5.

Brading, David. *The First America: The Spanish Monarchy, Creole Patriots, and the Liberal State, 1492–1867.* Cambridge: Cambridge University Press, 1993.

Breglia, Lisa. *Monumental Ambivalence: The Politics of Heritage.* Austin: University of Texas Press, 2006.

Brunhouse, Robert. *In Search of the Mayas: The First Archaeologists.* Albuquerque: University of New Mexico Press, 1973.

Bueno, Christina. "Forjando Patrimonio: The Making of the Archaeological Patrimony in Porfirian Mexico." *Hispanic American Historical Review* 90, no. 2 (2010): 215–45.

Bullock, William. *A Companion to Mr. Bullock's London Museum and Pantherion.* London, 1812.

———. *A Descriptive Catalogue of the Exhibition Entitled Ancient and Modern Mexico.* London, 1825.

———. *Six Months' Residence and Travels in Mexico.* Rev. ed. London: John Murray, 1825. First edition published in 1824.

Burkhardt, Richard W., Jr. "The Leopard in the Garden: Life in Close Quarters at the Muséum d'Historie Naturelle." *Isis* 98, no. 4 (2007): 675–94.

Burrus, Ernest J. "Clavigero and the Lost Sigüenza y Góngora Manuscripts." *Estudios de cultura Náhuatl* 1 (1959): 59–90.

Buschmann, Johann Karl Eduard. "De los nombres de los lugares aztecas." *Boletín de la Sociedad Mexicana de Geografía y Estadística* 8 (1858).

Bustamante, Carlos María de. "Al Exmo Sr. Don Lucas Alamán." In Antonio de León y Gama, *Descripción histórica y cronológica de las dos piedras*, edited by Carlos María de Bustamante, i–iv. Mexico City: Imprenta del Ciudadano Alejandro Valdés, 1832.

———. *Mañanas de la Alameda de México.* Mexico City: La Testamentaria de Valdés, 1835.

Calderón de la Barca, Fanny. *Life in Mexico.* Los Angeles: University of California Press, 1982.

Cañizares-Esguerra, Jorge. *How to Write the History of the New World: Histories, Epistemologies, and Identities in the Eighteenth-Century Atlantic World.* Stanford: Stanford University Press, 2001.

Castillo, Antonio del, and Leopoldo Río de la Loza, *Masa de hierro meteórico de Yanhuitlán.* Mexico City: A. Boix, 1865.

Castillo Ledón, Luis. "Advertencia." In Icaza and Gondra, *Colección de anti-güedades que existían en el Museo Nacional*, v–xxvi.

———. *El Museo Nacional de Arqueología, Historia y Etnografía*. Mexico City: Talleres Gráficos del Museo Nacional de Arqueología, Historia y Etnografía, 1924.

Clark de Lara, Belém, and Elisa Speckman Guerra. *La república de las letras: Asomos a la cultura escrita del México decimonónico*. Mexico City: Universidad Nacional Autónoma de México, 2005.

Colla, Elliott. *Conflicted Antiquities: Egyptology, Egyptomania, Egyptian Modernity*. Durham NC: Duke University Press, 2007.

Comisión Científica, Literaria y Artística de México. *Reglamento provisional*. Mexico City: Imprenta de Andrade y Escalanate, 1864.

Constantino Ortiz, María Eugenia. "Coleccionismo de naturaleza en la Nueva España del siglo XVIII: Actores, meetodos, prácticas, debates y escrituras." PhD diss., Cinvestav, 2014.

Constantino Ortiz, María Eugenia, and Antonio Lafuente. "The Hidden Logistics of Longinos's Novohispanic Cabinet." *Nuncius* 27, no. 2 (2012): 348–70.

Constantino Ortiz, María Eugenia, and Juan Pimentel. "Cómo inventariar el (Nuevo) Mundo: Las instrucciones como instrumentos para inventariar y coleccionar objetos naturales." In *Piedra, papel, tijera*, edited by Laura Cházaro, Nuria Valverde, and Miruna Achim. Mexico City: Universidad Autónoma Metropolitana, Cuajimalpa, forthcoming.

Costeloe, Michael. "Prescott's *History of the Conquest* and Calderón de la Barca's *Life in Mexico*: Mexican Reaction, 1843–1844." *Americas* 47, no. 3 (1991): 337–48.

———. "William Bullock and the Mexican Connection." *Mexican Studies/Estudios Mexicanos* 22, no. 2 (2006): 275–309.

———. *William Bullock: Connoisseur and Virtuoso of the Egyptian Hall: Piccadilly to Mexico (1773–1849)*. Bristol: HIPLAM, 2008.

Cotton, Bolfy. "La concepción jurídica del Museo Nacional, una visión interdisciplinaria." *Boletín de Monumentos Históricos* 14 (2008): 25–34.

Craib, Raymond. "A Nationalist Metaphysics: State Fixations, National Maps, and the Geo-historical Imagination in Nineteenth-Century Mexico." *Hispanic American Historical Review* 82, no. 1 (2002): 33–68.

Crane, Susan. *Collecting and Historical Consciousness in Early Nineteenth-Century Germany*. Ithaca NY: Cornell University Press, 2000.

Cruz, Soto. "Los periódicos del primer periodo de vida independiente (1821–1836)." In Clark de Lara and Speckman Guerra, *La república de las letras*, 57–76.

Darby Smith, Mary R. *Recollections of Two Distinguished Persons: La Marquise de Boissy and the Count de Waldeck.* Philadelphia PA: J. B. Lippincott, 1878.

Daston, Lorraine. "The Sciences of the Archive." *Osiris* 27, no. 1 (2012): 156–87.

Deans-Smith, Susan. *Matters of Taste: The Politics of Culture in Mexico and the Royal Academy of San Carlos (1781–1821).* Stanford: Stanford University, forthcoming.

Delbourgo, James, and Staffan Müller-Wille. "Listmania: How Lists Can Open Up Possibilities for Research in the History of Science." *Isis* 103, no. 4 (2012): 710–15.

Demuelenaere-Douyère, Christiane. "Le Mexique s'expose à Paris: Xochicalco, Méhédin et l'exposition universelle de 1867." *Revue: Histoire(s) de l'Amérique latine* 3 (2009): 1–12.

Denis, Ferdinand. "Paléographie mexicaine: Documents publiés par M. Ramírez, de Mexico." *Revue Américaine et Orientale* 5 (1861): 70–73.

Díaz-Andreu, Margarita. *A World of Nineteenth-Century Archaeology: Nationalism, Colonialism, and the Past.* Oxford: Oxford University Press, 2007.

Diener, Pablo. "El diario del artista viajero Jean Frédérick Waldeck, 1825–1837." *Jahrbuch für Geschichte Lateinamerikas* 47 (2010): 105–25.

Disraeli, Benjamin. "Memoir." In *The Present State of Mexico, as Detailed in a Report Presented to the General Congress by the Secretary of State for the Home Department and Foreign Affairs at the Opening of the Session in 1825, by Lucas Alamán.* London: John Murray, 1825.

Domenech, Emmanuel. *Le Mexique tel qu'il est: La verité sur son climat, ses habitants et son gouvernement.* Paris: E. Dentu, 1867.

Dubouchet, Charles. *Le Guazacoalco, colonie de MM. Laisné de Villvêque et Giordan, ou les horreurs dèvoilées de cette colonie.* Paris: B. Nale, 1830.

Duncan, Carol. *Civilizing Rituals: Inside Public Art Museums.* London: Routledge, 1995.

Duncan, Robert H. "Political Legitimation and Maximilian's Second Empire in Mexico, 1864–1867." *Mexican Studies / Estudios Mexicanos* 12, no. 1 (1996): 27–66.

Dupaix, Guillermo. *Antiquités mexicaines: Relation des trois expeditions du colonel Dupaix, ordonnées en 1805, 1806 et 1807 pour la recherche des antiquités du pays, notamment celles de Mitla et de Palenque.* Edited by Henri Baradère. 2 vols. Paris: Bureau des antiquités mexicaines / Imprimerie de J. Didot l'aîné, 1834–38.

Echanove Trujillo, Carlos A. *Dos héroes de la arqueología maya: Frederick de Waldeck y Teobert Maler*. Mérida: Ediciones de la Universidad de Yucatán, 1974.

Eco, Umberto. *From the Tree to the Labyrinth: Historical Studies on the Sign and Interpretation*. Translated by Anthony Oldcorn. Cambridge MA: Harvard University Press, 2014.

Edison, Paul N. "Colonial Prospecting in Independent Mexico: Abbé Baradére's *Antiquités mexicaines* (1834–1836)." *Proceedings of the Western Society for French History* 32 (1998): 195–214.

El Ateneo Mexicano. "Anales del Ateneo." 1 (1844): 48.

El Mosaico mexicano. "Advertencia preliminar." 2 (1837): 3.

El Museo mexicano. "Introducción." 1 (1843): 3–4.

Escalante Gonzalbo, Pablo, ed. *La construcción de la idea de nuestro patrimonio histórico y cultural*. Mexico City: Universidad Nacional Autónoma de México, 2010.

Espinosa de los Monteros, Juan José. *Memoria del Ministerio de Relaciones Interiores y Exteriores de la República Mexicana*. Mexico City: Imprenta del Supremo Gobierno de los Estados Unidos Mexicanos, en Palacio, 1828.

Estrada de Gerlero, Elena Isabel. "En defensa de América: La difusion litográfica de las antigüedades mexicanas en el siglo XIX." In *México en el mundo de las colecciones de arte: México moderno*, edited by María Luisa Sabau García, 5:23–36. Mexico City: Editorial Azabache, 1994.

———. "La labor anticuaria novohispana en la época de Carlos IV: Guillermo Dupaix, precursor de la historia del arte prehispánico." In *Arte, historia e identidad en América: Dos visiones comparativas*, edited by Gustavo Curiel et al., 1:191–205. Mexico City: Universidad Nacional Autónoma de México, 1994.

———. "La Real Expedición Anticuaria de Guillermo Dupaix." In *México en el mundo de las colecciones de arte*, edited by María Luisa Sabau García, 4:168–81. Mexico City: Editorial Azabache, 1994.

———. "Litografía y Museo Nacional como armas del nacionalismo." In *Los pinceles de la Historia: De la patria criolla a la nación mexicana, 1750–1860*, edited by Esther Acevedo, Jaime Cuadriello, and Fausto Ramírez, 153–67. Mexico City: Instituto Nacional de Bellas Artes, 2000.

Étienne, Noémie, ed. "La restauration des oeuvres d'art en Europe entre 1789 et 1815: Practiques, transferts, enjeux." Special issue, *Conservation, Exposition, Restauration d'Objets d'Art* (2012). Accessed November 16, 2014. http://ceroart.revues.org/2314.

Evans, Tripp. *Romancing the Mayas: Mexican Antiquity in the American Imagination, 1820–1915*. Austin: University of Texas Press, 2004.

Faber, Paul L. "The Development of Taxidermy and the History of Ornithology." *Isis* 68 (1977): 550–66.

Farcy, Charles. "Discours préliminaire." In Dupaix, *Antiquités mexicaines*, v–xii.

Fauvet-Berthelot, Marie-France, and Leonardo López Luján. "Édouard Pingret, un coleccionista europeo de mediados del siglo XIX." *Arqueología mexicana*, no. 114 (2012): 68–75.

———. "La Piedra del Sol, ¿en París?" *Arqueología mexicana*, no. 107 (2011): 16–21.

Fauvet-Berthelot, Marie France, Leonardo López Luján, and Susana Guimarães. "Six personnages en quête d'objets: Histoire de la collection archéologique de la Real Expedicion Anticuaria en Nouvelle-Espagne." *Gradhiva* 6, no. 1 (2007): 104–26.

Fernández de Lizardi, Joaquín. *Obras XIII: Folletos (1824–1827)*. Mexico City: Universidad Nacional Autónoma de México, 1995.

Ferry, Elizabeth Emma. *Not Ours Alone: Patrimony, Value, and Collectivity in Contemporary Mexico*. New York: Columbia University Press, 2005.

Florescano, Enrique. "La creación del Museo Nacional de Antropología y sus fines científicos, educativos y politicos." In *El patrimonio cultural de México*, 145–64. Mexico City: Fondo de Cultura Económica, 1993.

Flores Olea, Aurora. "José Fernando Ramírez." In *Historiografía mexicana: En busca de un discurso integrador de la nación, 1848–1884*, edited by Antonia Pi-Suñer, 313–38. Mexico City: Universidad Nacional Autónoma de México, 1996.

Fossey, Mathieu de. *Le Mexique*. Paris: H. Plon, 1857.

Fowler, Will. *Mexico in the Age of Proposals, 1821–1853*. Westport CT: Greenwood Press, 1998.

———. *Santa Anna of Mexico*. Lincoln: University of Nebraska Press, 2009.

Galindo y Villa, Jesús. *Breve noticia histórico-descriptiva del Museo Nacional de México*. Mexico City: Imprenta del Museo Nacional, 1896.

Gänger, Stefanie. "The Many Natures of Antiquity: Ana María Centeno and Her Cabinet of Curiosities, Peru, ca. 1832–1874." In *Nature and Antiquities: The Making of Archaeology in the Americas*, edited by Philip Kohl, Irina Podgorny, and Stefanie Gänger, 110–24. Tucson: University of Arizona Press, 2014.

———. "Of Butterflies, Chinese Shoes, and Antiquities: The History of Peru's National Museum, 1826–1881." *Jahrbuch für Geschichte Lateinamerikas* 51 (2014): 283–301.

———. *Relics of the Past: The Collecting and Study of Pre-Columbian Antiquities in Peru and Chile, 1837–1911*. Oxford: Oxford University Press, 2014.

Garay y Garay, José. *Survey of the Isthmus of Tehuantepec*. London: Ackermann, 1844.

García, Susana V., and Irina Podgorny. "Los pilotos del Río Negro y las escorias de la Patagonia." In Achim and Podgorny, *Museos al detalle*, 127–56.

Garone Gravier, Marina. "Nineteenth-Century Mexican Graphic Design: The Case of Ignacio Cumplido." *Design Issues* 18, no. 4 (2002): 45–63.

Garrigan, Shelley. *Collecting Mexico: Museums, Monuments, and the Creation of National Identity*. Minneapolis: University of Minnesota Press, 2012.

Gautier, Hypolite. *Les curiosités de L'Exposition universelle*. Paris: Charles Delagrave, 1867.

Gerber, Frédéric, Christian Nicaise, and Christian Robichon. *Un aventurier du Second Empire: Léon Méhédin, 1828–1905*. Rouen, France: Bibliothèque municipal de Rouen, 1992.

Gondra, Isidro. "Antigüedades mexicanas." *El Ateneo Mexicano* 1 (1844): 374–82.

———. "Arqueología." *El Mosaico mexicano* 2 (1837): 411–18.

González Claverán, Virginia. *La expedición científica de Malaspina en Nueva España (1789–1794)*. Mexico City: Colegio de México, 1988.

González Obregón, Luis. "Vida y obras de Don José Fernando Ramírez." *Memorias de la Sociedad José Antonio Alzate* 16 (1901): 47–90.

Gosden, Chris, Frances Larson, and Alison Petch. *Knowing Things: Exploring the Collections at the Pitt Rivers Museum*. Oxford: Oxford University Press, 2008.

Gruzinski, Serge, and Camen Bernand. *De l'idolâtrie: Une archéologie des sciences religieuses*. Paris: Seuil, 1988.

Hardy, William. *Travels in the Interior of Mexico in 1825, 1826, 1827, and 1828*. London: Henry Colburn and Richard Bentley, 1829.

Hénaut, Léonie. "Preface: Restauration, spoliations et controversies." In Étienne, "La restauration des oeuvres d'art en Europe entre 1789 et 1815." http://ceroart.revues.org/2423.

Hernández de León Portilla, Ascensión. "Visita de José Fernando Ramírez a Alejandro de Humboldt, Potsdam, 14 junio, 1855." *Estudios de Cultura Náhuatl* 24 (1994): 297–313.

Hess, Volker, and Andrew Mendelsohn. "Case and Series: Medical Knowledge and Paper Technology, 1600–1900." *History of Science* 48 (2010): 287–314.

Humboldt, Alexander von. *Essai politique sur le royaume de la Nouvelle-Espagne*. Paris: Chez F. Schoell, 1805.

———. *Vues des cordilleres et monuments des peuples indigènes de l'Amérique*. París: Librairie Grecque, Latine, Allemande, 1816.

Icaza, Isidro, and Isidro Rafael Gondra. *Colección de las antigüedades mexicanas que escisten en el Museo Nacional*. Mexico City: Pedro Robert, 1827.

———. *Colección de las antigüedades mexicanas que existían en el Museo Nacional*. Facsimilar Edition. Mexico City: Talleres gráficos del Museo Nacional de Arqueología, Historia y Etnografía, 1927.

Jacques, L. G. "Le Temple de Xochicalco." In *L'album de l'Exposition illustrée: Histoire pittoresque de l'Exposition universelle de 1867*. Paris: G. Richard, 1867.

Jaksic, Iván. *The Hispanic World and American Intellectual Life, 1820–1880*. London: Palgrave Macmillan, 2012.

Jenkins, David. "Object Lessons and Museum Displays: Museum Exhibitions and the Making of American Anthropology." *Comparative Studies in Society and History* 36, no. 2 (1994): 242–70.

Juárez, Benito. *Ley orgánica de la Instrucción Pública en el Distrito Federal, publicada en el* Diario oficial de la Federación *el día 2 de diciembre de 1867*. Accessed March 22, 2015. http://www.sep.gob.mx/work/models/sep1/Resource/3f9a47cc-efd9-4724-83e4-0bb4884af388/ley_02121867.pdf.

———. *Ley orgánica de Instrucción Pública en el Distrito Federal, publicada en el* Diario oficial de la Federación *el día 15 de mayo de 1869*. Accessed March 22, 2015. http://www.biblioteca.tv/artman2/publish/1869_156/Ley_Org_nica_de_la_Instrucci_n_P_blica_en_el_Distrito_Federal_printer.shtml.

Kelly, Larissa Kennedy. "Waking the Gods: Archaeology and State Power in Porfirian Mexico." PhD diss., University of California, Berkeley, 2011.

Kingsborough [Edward King]. *Antiquities of Mexico, Comprising Facsimiles of Ancient Mexican Paintings and Hieroglyphics*. 9 vols. London: James Moyse, 1831–48.

Kolonitz, Paula. *Un viaje a México en 1864*. Mexico City: Fondo de Cultura Económica, 1984.

Krauze, Enrique. *La presencia del pasado*. Mexico City: Banamex, 2006.

———. "Un héroe de la historiografía." *Letras Libres*, no. 77 (May 2005): 14–19.

Larrainzar, Manuel. *Estudios sobre la historia de América, sus ruinas y antigüedades*. Mexico City: Imprenta de Villanueva, Villageliu y Comp., 1875.

Lawson, Russel. *Frontier Naturalist: Jean Louis Berlandier and the Explora-*

tion of Northern Mexico and Texas. Albuquerque: University of New
Mexico Press, 2012.

L.E. "Monumentos antiguos de México." *El Museo mexicano*, no. 1 (1843):
156–57.

Leask, Nigel. *Curiosity and the Aesthetics of Travel Writing, 1770–1840.*
Oxford: Oxford University Press, 2002.

Le Goff, Armelle, and Nadia Prévost Urkidi. *Homme de guerre, homme
de science? Le colonel Doutrelaine au Mexique; Edition critique de ses
dépêches (1864–1867).* Paris: Editions du Comité des travaux historiques et scientifiques, 2011.

Lenoir, Alexandre. "Formation d'une Société historique mexicaine." *Journal de l'Institut Historique* 4 (February–July 1836): 162–67.

León y Gama, Antonio de. *Descripción histórica y cronológica de las dos piedras
descubiertas en 1790 durante la reconstrucción de la Plaza Principal en México.*
Mexico City: Imprenta de Don Felipe de Zúñiga y Ontiveros, 1792.

Lerner, Jesse, and Sandra Rozental. *La piedra ausente.* Mexico City: Conaculta, 2013. 81 min.

Lesson, René-Primevère. "Manuel de taxidermie à l'usage des marins."
Annales maritimes et coloniales. Paris: Imprimerie Royale, 1819.

Lewuillon, Serge. "Archaeological Illustrations: A New Development in
19th Century Science." *Antiquity* 76, no. 291 (2002): 223–34.

Littman, Helene. "John Lloyd Stephens." In *American National Biography*,
supplement 2, edited by Mark C. Carnes, 535. Oxford: Oxford University Press, 2005.

Lombardo de Ruiz, Sonia, and Ruth Solís Vicarte. *Antecedentes de las leyes
sobre Monumentos Históricos (1536–1910).* Mexico City: Instituto Nacional de Antropología e Historia, 1984.

Longpérier, Adrien de. *Notice des monuments desposés dans la Salle des
Antiquités Américaines (Mexique et Pérou) au Musée du Louvre.* Paris:
Vinchon, Imprimeur des Musées Nationaux, 1850.

Lopes, Maria Margaret. "Minerales y fósiles para escudriñar el país, abarro-
tar las vitrinas y educar a la gente." In Achim and Podgorny, *Museos al
detalle*, 179–200.

López Luján, Leonardo. "El capitán Dupaix y su álbum arqueológico de
1794." *Arqueología mexicana*, no. 109 (2011): 71–81.

———. "The First Steps on a Long Journey: Archaeological Illustration in
Eighteenth-Century New Spain." In *Past Presented: Archaeological Illus-
trations and the Ancient Americas*, edited by Joanne Pillsbury, 68–105.
Washington DC: Dumbarton Oaks, 2012.

———. "La historia póstuma de la Piedra de Tízoc." *Arqueología mexicana*, no. 102 (2010): 60–69.

———. "La Isla de Sacrificios en los albores del México independiente." *Arqueología mexicana*, no. 124 (2013): 80–87.

Lyon, George Francis. *Journal of a Residence and Tour of the Republic of Mexico in 1826*. London: John Murray, 1828.

Mackenthum, Gesa. "Imperial Archaeology: The American Isthmus as Contested Scientific Contact Zone." In *Surveying the American Tropics: A Literary Geography from New York to Rio*, edited by Maria Cristina Fumagalli, Peter Hulme, Owen Robinson, and Lesley Wylie, 101–30. Liverpool: Liverpool University Press, 2013.

Mansion, Hyppolite. *Précis historique sur la colonie française au Goazacoalcos*. London: Davidson and Sons, 1831.

Martínez, José Luis. *La expression nacional*. Mexico City: Oasis, 1984.

Matos Moctezuma, Eduardo, and Leonardo López Luján. *Escultura monumental mexica*. Mexico City: Fondo de Cultura Económica, 2010.

Mayer, Brantz. *Mexico, as It Was and as It Is*. Philadelphia: G. B. Zieber, 1843.

Mayer, Roberto L. "Nacimiento y desarrollo del álbum México y sus alrededores." In *Casimiro Castro y su taller*, 135–57. Mexico City: Banamex, 1996.

Mayo, John. "Consuls and Silver Contraband on Mexico's West Coast in the Era of Santa Anna." *Journal of Latin American Studies* 19 (1987): 389–411.

Mejía, Edgar. "Nación, coleccionismo y tecnologías visuales en el viaje a Veracruz de Manuel Payno." *Literatura mexicana* 23, no. 3 (2012): 5–29.

Méndez Reyes, Salvador. *El hispanismo de Lucas Alamán (1792–1853)*. Toluca: Universidad Autónoma del Estado de México, 1996.

Menéndez Rodríguez, Hernán. "Las formas del cisne." In *Viaje pintoresco y arqueologico a la provincial de Yucatán*, by Frédéric Waldeck, 3–25. Mexico City: CONACULTA, 1996.

Ministère de l'Instruction publique. *Archives de la Commission scientifique du Mexique*. 3 vols. Paris: Imprimerie impériale, 1865–67.

Morales Moreno, Luis Gerardo. "Ancestros y ciudadanos: El Museo Nacional de México, 1790–1925." PhD diss., Universidad Iberoamericana, 1998.

———. "En torno a la museología mexicana: La crítica de las imágenes fundantes." *Curare, espacio crítico para las artes* 22 (2003): 35–46.

———. *Orígenes de la museología mexicana: Fuentes para el estudio histórico del Museo Nacional, 1780–1940*. Mexico City: Universidad Iberoamericana, 1994.

More, Anna. *Baroque Sovereignty: Carlos de Sigüenza y Góngora and the Creole Archive of Colonial Mexico.* Philadelphia: University of Pennsylvania Press, 2013.

Morelet, Arthur. *Voyage dans l'Amérique Centrale, l'île de Cuba et le Yucatán.* Paris: Gide et J. Baudry, 1857.

Moreno de los Arcos, Roberto. *Linneo en México: Las controversias sobre el sistema binario sexual, 1788–1798.* Mexico City: Universidad Nacional Autónoma de México, 1989.

Morris, Pat. "A Historical Review of Bird Taxidermy in Britain." *Archives of Natural History* 20 (1993): 241–55.

Müller J. G., E. G. Squier, and C. J. Thomsen. *Catalogue des objets formant le Musée Aztéco-Mexicain de feu M. Charles Uhde a Handschuhsheim, pres Heidelberg.* Paris: Martinet, 1857.

Nebel, Carl. *Voyage pittoresque et archéologique dans la partie la plus intéressante du Mexique.* Paris: Moench, 1836.

Noriega, Pedro C. "Ceremonia de apertura del Museo Nacional por el emperador y su esposa." *La Sociedad,* July 7, 1866, 3.

Norman, Benjamin Moore. *Rambles by Land and Water.* New York: Paine and Burgess, 1845.

———. *Rambles in Yucatán, or Notes of Travel through the Peninsula, including a Visit to the Remarkable Ruins of Chi-Chen, Kabah, Yazi, and Uxmal.* Philadelphia PA: Carey and Hart, 1843.

Nuttall, Zelia, and Leopoldo Batres, *La Isla de Sacrificios.* Mexico City: Tipografía Económica, 1910.

O'Gorman, Edmundo. *Documentos para la historia de la litografía en México.* Mexico City: Universidad Nacional Autónoma de México, 1955.

———. *La supervivencia política novohispana: Reflexiones sobre el monarquismo mexicano.* Mexico City: Fundación Cultural Condumex, S.A. / Centro de Estudios de Historia de México, 1969.

Opriessnig, Chrsitian. "Política cultural en el Segundo Imperio de Maximiliano." In *Encuentro de liberalismos,* edited by Patricia Galeana, 323–39. Mexico City: Universidad Nacional Autónoma de México, 2004.

Ortiz de Ayala, Tadeo. *México considerado como nación independiente y libre.* Bordeaux, France: Imprenta de Carlos Lawalle Sobrino, 1832.

Ortiz Macedo, Luís. *Édouard Pingret: Un pintor romantico que retrató el México del mediar del siglo XIX.* Mexico City: Fomento Cultural Banamex, 1989.

Otero, Silvia. "Obama en México." *El Universal,* April 16, 2009. http://archivo.eluniversal.com.mx/notas/591567.html.

Pani, Erika. "El proyecto de estado de Maximiliano a través de la vida cortesana y del ceremonial público." *Historia mexicana* 45, no. 2 (1995): 423–60.

———. "'Verdaderas figuras de Cooper' o 'pobres inditos infelices'? La política indigenista de Maximiliano." *Historia mexicana* 48, no. 3 (1998): 571–604.

Pascoe, Judith. *The Hummingbird Cabinet: A Rare and Curious History of Romantic Collectors.* Ithaca NY: Cornell University Press, 2006.

Pasztory, Esther. *Jean-Frédéric Waldeck, Artist of Exotic Mexico.* Albuquerque: University of New Mexico Press, 2010.

Pearce, Susan. "William Bullock: Collections and Exhibitions at the Egyptian Hall, London, 1816–25." *Journal of the History of Collections* 20, no. 1 (2008): 17–35.

Pedro Robles, Antonio E. de. "La Real Expedición Anticuaria de México (1805–1808), y la representación del imaginario indianista del siglo XIX." *Anales del Museo de América* 17 (2009): 42–63.

Penny, H. Glenn. *Objects of Culture: Ethnology and Ethnographic Museums in Imperial Germany.* Chapel Hill: University of North Carolina Press, 2002.

Perdreauville, René de. "Viaje a las antigüedades de Xochicalco, verificado de orden del gobierno supremo de México, en marzo de 1835." *Revista mexicana: Periódico científico y literario* 1 (1835): 539–50.

Perera, Miguel Ángel. "De viajeros y coleccionistas de antigüedades: Jean Frédéric Waldeck en México; Historia, origen y naturaleza del hombre americano en los albores de la modernidad." PhD thesis, El Colegio de Michoacán, 2008.

Pérez Salas, María Esther. *Costumbrismo y litografía en México: Un nuevo modo de ver.* Mexico City: Universidad Nacional Autónoma de México, 2005.

———. "Cumplido, un empresario a cabalidad." In Suárez de la Torre and Castro, *Empresa y cultura en tinta y papel,* 145–56.

Pilbeam, Pamela. *Madame Tussaud and the History of Waxworks.* London: Continuum, 2006.

Pingret, Édouard. "Antiquités mexicaines." *L'Illustration* 28 (September 13, 1856): 176–78.

Pi-Suñer Llorens, Antonia. *México en el* Diccionario universal de historia y geografía. Mexico City: Universidad Nacional Autónoma de México, 2004.

Podgorny, Irina. "'Silent and Alone': How the Ruins of Palenque Were

Taught to Speak the Language of Archaeology." In *Comparative Archaeologies: A Sociological View of the Science of the Past*, edited by Ludomir R. Lozny, 527–54. New York: Springer, 2011.

———. "Terebrátulas y piedras de águila en el Río de la Plata: Entre las palabras y las cosas alrededor de 1810." In Achim and Podgorny, *Museos al detalle*, 77–98.

Podgorny, Irina, and Maria Margaret Lopes. *El desierto en una vitrina*. Mexico City: Limusa, 2008.

Prescott, William H. *Historia de la conquista de México*. Translated by Joaquín Navarro. 3 vols. Mexico City: Igancio Cumplido, 1844–46.

———. *Historia de la conquista de Méjico, con un bosquejo preliminar de la civilización de los antiguos mejicanos y la vida del conquistador Hernán Cortés*. Translated by José María González de la Vega. 2 vols. Mexico City: Vicente García Torres, 1844.

———. *History of the Conquest of Mexico, with a Preliminary View of Ancient Mexican Civilization, and the Life of the Conquerer, Hernán Cortés*. 2 vols. New York: Harper and Brothers, 1843.

Prévost Urkidi, Nadia. "Historiographie de l'américanisme au XIXe siècle: Le prix Palenque (1826–1839) ou le choix archéologique de Jomard." *Journal de la Société des Américanistes* 95, no. 2 (2009): 117–49.

———. "La Commission scientifique du Mexique: Un exemple de collaboration scientifique entre l'élite savante française et mexicaine?" *Revue d'Histoire des Sciences Humaines* 19 (2008): 107–16.

———. "Las actividades científicas durante el Segundo Imperio en México, vistas a través de la Sociedad Mexicana de Geografía y Estadística." In *Encuentro de liberalismos*, edited by Patricia Galena, 502–33. Mexico City: Universidad Nacional Autónoma de México, 2004.

Prieto, Guillermo. *Memoria de mis tiempos*. Mexico City: Editorial Patria, 1969 [1906].

———. *Mi Guerra del 47*. Mexico City: Universidad Nacional Autónoma de México, 2006.

Prince, Sue Anne, ed. *Stuffing Birds, Pressing Plants, Shaping Knowledge: Natural History in North America, 1730–1860*. Philadelphia: American Philosophical Society, 2003.

Puttick and Simpson Gallery. *Bibliotheca Mexicana, or A Catalogue of the Rare Books and Important Manuscripts Relating to Mexico and Other Parts of Spanish America, Formed by the Late Señor Don José Fernando Ramírez, . . . days of sale . . . July [7–9, 12–13, 1880]*. London: G. Norman and Son, 1880.

Rafael, Rafael de. *Noticias biográficas del Exmo Sr D. Lucas Alamán.* Mexico City: Rafael, 1853.

Ramírez, José Fernando. "Antigüedades mexicanas que existen en el Museo Nacional de México." In *México y sus alrededores,* 36–44. Mexico City: Decaen, 1857.

———. "Cuadro histórico-geroglífico de la peregrinación de las tribus Aztecas que poblaron el valle de México." In *Atlas geográfico, estadístico e histórico de la República Mexicana,* by Antonio García Cubas. Mexico City: Imprenta de Mariano Fernández de Lara, 1858.

———. *Descripción de algunos objetos del Museo Nacional de antigüedades de México.* Mexico City: Imprenta de Andrade y Escalante, 1857.

———. "Fábrica de Tejidos El Tunal o sean Apuntes para la historia de la industria mexicana." *El Museo mexicano* 1 (1843): 121–28.

———. "Memorias para servir a la historia del Segundo Imperio." In *Obras históricas,* 3:173–594.

———. "Noticias históricas y estadísticas de Durango." *Boletín de la Sociedad Mexicana de Geografía y Estadística* 5 (1857): 6–116.

———. *Obras históricas.* Edited by Ernesto de la Torre Villar. 5 vols. Mexico City: Universidad Nacional Autónoma de México, 2001.

———. "Viaje a Yucatán." In *Obras históricas,* 3:595–652.

Ramírez, José Fernando, José Guadalupe Romero, and José Urbano Fonseca. "Proyecto de Ley Relativo a la Conservación de Monumentos Arqueológicos." *Boletín de la Sociedad Mexicana de Geografía y Estadística* 9 (1862): 197–99.

Ramos-Escandón, Carmen. *Industrialización, género y trabajo femenino en el sector textil mexicano.* Mexico City: Centro de Investigación y Estudios Superiores en Antropología Social, 2005.

Ranke, Leopold von. "On Progress in History (From the First Lecture to King Maximilian II of Bavaria, 'On the Epochs of Modern History, 1854')." In *The Theory and Practice of History,* edited by Georg G. Iggers, 20–23. London: Routledge, 2011.

Ratz, Konrad. *Correspondencia inédita entre Maximiliano y Carlota.* Mexico City: Fondo de Cultura Económica, 2003.

———. *Tras las huellas de un desconocido.* Mexico City: Siglo XXI Editores, 2008.

Reid, Donald Malcolm. *Whose Pharaohs? Archaeology, Museums, and Egyptian National Identity from Napoleon to World War I.* Berkeley: University of California Press, 2002.

Reinisch, Simon Leo. *Tagebuchaufzeichnungen von Simon Leo Reinisch Reise nach Mexiko 1867*. Transcribed by Ferdinand Anders. Vienna: Nationalbibliothek, 1971.

Rico Mansard, Luisa Fernanda. "El Museo Nacional de México: Una lucha por los espacios." *Boletín de Monumentos Históricos* 14 (2008): 55–67.

———. *Exhibir para educar: Objetos, colecciones y museos de la ciudad de México (1790–1910)*. Mexico City: Ediciones Pomares / Universidad Nacional Autónoma de México, 2004.

Río de la Loza, Leopoldo. *Descripción del aerolito de Yanhuitlán*. Mexico City: Imprenta de Andrade y Escalante, 1865.

Rivas Mata, Emma, and Edgar O. Gutiérrez L., eds. *Libros y exilio: Epistolario de José Fernando Ramírez con Joaquín García Icazbalceta*. Mexico City: Instituto Nacional de Antropología e Historia, 2011.

Rivera, Agustín. *Anales Mexicanos: La Reforma y el Segundo Imperio*. Guadalajara: Escuela de Artes y Oficios, 1897.

Rivera Cambas, Manuel. *México pintoresco, artístico y monumental*. Vol. 2. Mexico City: Imprenta de la Reforma, 1880.

Riviale, Pascal. "Eugène Boban ou les aventures d'un antiquaire au pays des américanistes." *Journal de la Société des Américanistes* 87 (2001): 351–62.

———. "La science marche au pas cadencé: Les recherches archéologiques et anthropologiques durant l'intervention française au Mexique (1862–1867)." *Journal de la Société des Américanistes* 85 (1999): 307–41.

Robles Pezuela, Luis. *Memoria presentada a S.M. el emperador por el Ministerio de Fomento Luis Robles Pezuela de los trabajos ejecutados en su ramo el año de 1865*. Mexico City: Imprenta de Andrade y Escalante, 1866.

Rodríguez Prampolini, Ida. *La crítica de arte en México en el siglo XIX*. Mexico City: Universidad Nacional Autónoma de México, 1964.

Rosenstein, Leon. *Antiques: The History of an Idea*. Ithaca NY: Cornell University, 2009.

Rugeley, Terry. *Rebellion Now and Forever: Mayas, Hispanics, and Caste War Violence in Yucatán, 1800–1880*. Stanford: Stanford University Press, 2009.

Ruíz Castañeda, María del Carmen. *El Mosaico mexicano, o Colección de amenidades curiosas e instructivas*. In Suárez de la Torre and Castro, *Empresa y cultura en tinta y papel*, 529–36.

———. *Revistas literarias del siglo XIX*. Mexico City: Universidad Nacional Autónoma de México, 1987.

Rutsch, Mechthild. "Natural History, National Museum, and Anthropology in Mexico: Some Reference Points in the Forging and Re-Forging of National Identity." *Perspectivas latinoamericanas* 1 (2004): 89–122.

Sahagún, Bernardino de. *Historia general de las cosas de la Nueva España.* Edited by Carlos María de Bustamante and José Servando Teresa de Mier. Mexico City: Imprenta del Ciudadano Alejandro Valdés, 1830.

Sanhueza, Carlos. "El Gabinete de Historia Natural de Santiago de Chile (1823–1853)." In Achim and Podgorny, *Museos al detalle,* 201–18.

Schnapp, Alain. *La conquête du passé: Aux origins de l'archaeologie.* Paris: Carré, 1993.

Sellen, Adam. "Fraternal Curiosity: The Camacho Museum, Campeche, Mexico." In *Nature and Antiquities: The Making of Archaeology in the Americas,* edited by Philip Kohl, Irina Podgorny, and Stefanie Gänger, 91–109. Tucson: University of Arizona Press, 2014.

Sepúlveda y Herrera, María Teresa. *Catálogo de diarios de José Fernando Ramírez.* Mexico City: Instituto Nacional de Antropología e Historia, 1994.

Sierra, Justo. *Epistolario y papeles privados.* Vol. 14 of *Obras Completas.* Mexico City: Universidad Nacional Autónoma de México, 1984.

Sierra O'Reilly, Justo. "La historia de la conquista de México." *Registro yucateco,* 1844, 200.

Simpson, Lesley Byrd. *Many Mexicos.* Berkeley: University of California Press, 1966.

Smith, Murphy D. *A Museum: The History of the Cabinet of Curiosities of the American Philosophical Society.* Philadelphia PA: American Philosophical Society, 1996.

Soberanis, Arturo. "La Academia Imperial de Ciencias y Literatura: Sabios y militares durante el Segundo Imperio Mexicano." In *La definicion del Estado mexicano, 1857–1867,* edited by Patricia Galeana, 353–90. Mexico City: Archivo General de la Nación, 1999.

———. "Sabios, militares y empresarios: Sansimonismo y exploración científica." In *México-Francia: Memoria de una sensibilidad común. Siglos XIX–XX,* edited by Javier Pérez-Siller and Chantal Cramaussel, 243–70. Puebla: Benemérita Universidad Autónoma de Puebla / El Colegio de San Luis, 1998.

Société de géographie. "Process verbal de la séance générale du 5 avril." *Bulletin de la Société de Géographie* 11, no. 1 (1839): 253.

St.-Priest. "Carta escrita al Excmo Sr. Gobernador de este departamento." *Registro yucateco,* March 1845, 238–41.

Suárez de la Torre, Laura, and Miguel Angel Castro, eds. *Empresa y cul-*

tura en tinta y papel (1800–1860). Mexico City: Universidad Nacional Autónoma de México, 2001.

Tenorio Trillo, Mauricio. *Mexico at the World's Fairs: Crafting a Modern Nation*. Berkeley: University of California Press, 1996.

Tinker, Edward Larocque. *Les écrits de langue française en Louisiane au XIXe siècle: Essais biographiques et bibliographiques*. Paris: H. Champion, 1933.

Tornel, José María. "Arqueología: Un Viejo Mundo en el Nuevo." *El Museo mexicano* 2 (1843): 33–38.

Tylor, Edward Burnett. *Anáhuac, or Mexico and the Mexicans, Ancient and Modern*. London: Longman, Green, and Roberts, 1861.

Valadés, José C. *Alamán, estadista e historiador*. Mexico City: Antigua Librería Robredo, José Porrúa e Hijos, 1938.

Varios Mexicanos. *Consideraciones sobre la situación política y social de la República Mexicana en el año 1847*. Mexico City: Valdés y Redondas Impresores, 1848.

Vázquez, Josefina Zoraida. "Los años olvidados." *Mexican Studies / Estudios mexicanos* 5, no. 12 (1989): 313–26.

Vázquez Olivera, Mario. "Chiapas entre Centroamérica y México, 1821–1826." In *El establecimiento del Federalismo en México, 1808–1827*, edited by Josefina Zoraida Vázquez, 582–608. Mexico City: El Colegio de México, 2003.

Vega y Ortega, Rodrigo A. "El asociacionismo y la Junta Directiva del Museo Nacional de México, 1830–1840." *Temas americanistas* 27 (2011): 74–98.

———. "La riqueza del Gabinete de Historia natural del Museo Nacional de México: La década de 1830." *Nuevo mundo / Mundos nuevos*, November 2011. Accessed January 31, 2015. http://nuevomundo.revues.org /62086?lang=es.

Villaseñor Espinosa, Roberto. Introduction to *Atlas de las antigüedadees mexicanas halladas en el curso de los tres viajes de la Real Expedición*. By Guillermo Dupaix. Mexico City: Ediciones San Ángel, 1978.

Villaseñor y Villaseñor, Ramiro. *Ignacio Cumplido, impresor tapatío*. Guadalajara: Gobierno de Jalisco, 1987.

Waldeck, Jean-Fréderic. *Voyage pittoresque et archéologique dans la province d'Yucatán (Amérique Centrale), pendant les années 1834 et 1836*. Paris: Bellizard Dufour, 1838.

Ward, Henry George. *Mexico in 1827*. London: Colburn, 1828.

Warden, David Bailie. "Rapport fait à la Société de géographie, dans la séance du vendredi 4 mars, sur la collection des dessins d'antiquités mexicaines executes, par M. Franck." *Bulletin de la Société de Géographie*, no. 15 (1831), 116–28.

———. "Rapport fait á la Société royale des antiquaires de France (séance du 29 juin, 1829)." *Bulletin de la Société de Géographie*, no. 11 (1829): 43–49.

Warden, David Balie, Edmé Jomard, Philippe de Renaudière, and Charles Walckenaer. "Le Prix Palenque." *Bulletin de la Societé de Géographie*, no. 25 (1836): 252–88.

Webb, Timothy. "Appropriating the Stones: The 'Elgin Marbles' and the English National Taste." In *Claiming the Stones / Naming the Bones: Cultural Property and the Negotiation of National and Ethnic Identity*, edited by Elazar Barkan and Ronald Bush, 51–96. Los Angeles: Getty Research Institute, 2002.

Weckmann, Luis. *Carlota de Bélgica: Correspondencia y escritos sobre México en los Archivos Europeos (1861–1868)*. Mexico City: Porrúa, 1989.

Wheelan, Joseph. *Terrible Swift Sword: The Life of Philip H. Sheridan*. Philadelphia PA: Da Capo Press, 2012.

Wonders, Karen. *Habitat Dioramas: Illusions of Wilderness in Museums of Natural History*. Uppsala, Sweden: Acta Universitatis Upsaliensis, 1993.

INDEX

Page numbers in italics refer to illustrations.

antiquarian studies (*cont.*)
scholars of, 184–91; and focus on Mexican studies, 160–62; foreign dominance in, 118, 143, 145, 179; government role in, 145; increasing visibility of, 144–46; and José Fernando Ramírez, 176–91, 203–4, 231–32; NMM's role in, 126, 128; politics in, 119–20; portrayal of, in publications, 142–46; and pseudosciences, 149; references for, 143–44; during the Spanish colonial era, 10–14. *See also* New World civilizations

Antiquités mexicaines (Baradère), 123, 143–44, 147–48

antiquities: addressed in Lucas Alamán's report, 33; changing views on, 252–53; classification of, 185–86; exportation of, 44–45, 59–60, 91–93, 107, 115, 208, 227–30, 283n62; following independence, 44–46; forgeries of, 197–99; increasing visibility of, 144–46; José Fernando Ramírez's methods of describing, 200–204; legislation covering, 42, 45–46, 208; Maximilian's instructions on, 227–30; mixed commodification of, 10–15, 32, 60, 68, 90, 127–28; and national identity, 1, 60, 252, 254–55; and ownership debates, 14, 68, 113–14, 147, 149–50, 253–54; and political power, 113–14, 127–28, 252; represented in *México y sus alrededores*, 206; smuggling of, 91–93; during the Span-

ish colonial era, 10–14, 61; and transportation logistics, 50–51, 102, 109, 110, 217–18; in William Bullock's Egyptian Hall, 39–40. *See also* collecting practices

antiquities collection (NMM): art albums featuring, 139; during Benito Juárez's term, 250; in the *Colección*, 70–71, 76–85; fake antiquities at, 197–98; featured in publications, 139; illustrated in William Prescott's *History*, 162–67; inventories of, 56–57, 192; under Isidro Gondra, 172–73; Isidro Icaza's proposed policy for, 62; Maximilien Franck's illustrations of, 87–90; from Palenque, 97–98; during the Second Empire, 244–45, 246–47; visitor descriptions of, 133–34, 136–38. *See also* collections (NMM)

Antiquities of Mexico (Kingsborough), 123, 143–44, 150–51, 159, 178

archaeology: and alliance with Mexican state, 15, 252; and politics, 128; and pseudosciences, 148–49; shaping of, in Mexico, 146, 253. *See also* antiquarian studies

archives, 6, 31–32, 35–36, 46, 58, 191

Archives de la Commission scientifique du Mexique, 215, 223

Archivo General de la Nación (AGN), 6

Archivo General y Público de la Nación, 31

Archivo Histórico del Museo Nacional (AHMN), 6

Arista, Mariano, 172, 174, 182, 193

Arizpe, Miguel Ramos, 65

Carlos IV, King, 48

Carlota, Empress, 227, 228, 237–38, 242, 244, 246

Castañeda, Luciano: collection of, 71, 103, 123; criticism of illustrations of, 72; defense of illustrations of, 144; and expedition to Palenque, 96, 97–98; in the Royal Antiquarian Expeditions, 13, 25, 76, 96, 97–98; and selling antiquities, 60; at Texcoco, 51; and William Bullock, 40

Caste War, 125, 236

Castillo, Antonio del, 219

Castle of Miramar, 225

Castro, Casimiro, 206

cathedral (Mexico City), 40, 41–42

Catherwood, Frederick, 124, 143; *Incidents of Travel*, 143, 154

Cavo, Andrés, 58

centralism, 28, 53, 66, 68, 114, 119–20, 127–28

Cervantes, Vicente, 23, 30–31, 40

Chavero, Alfredo, 174, 275n12

Chiapas (state), 97. *See also* Palenque (ruins)

Chichimecs, 151, 164

chromolithography, 140

civilizations (New World). *See* New World civilizations

civilizations (Old World). *See* Old World civilizations

Coatzacoalcos (French colony), 100

Cochelet, Adrian, 105, 269n30

Codex Vindobonensis Mexicanus, 241–42

codices: in the Aubin collection, 187; *Codex Vindobonensis Mexicanus*, 241–42; *Dresden Codex*, 187–88; and hieroglyphic writing, 159; Jean-Frédéric Waldeck's illustrations of, 78, 79; NMM's collections of, 136; *Paris Codex*, 187–88; in William Bullock's exhibits, 39

Colección de antigüedades, 16, 70–85, 138–39; first issue of, 72–81; illustrations in, 73, 77, 79, 80, 83, 84; reviews of, 81–82; second issue of, 82–85; suspension of, 85; third issue of, 82, 85; written descriptions in, 78–79

Colección de documentos (García Icazbalceta), 221

collecting practices: hindering NMM, 51–52, 92; inherited by NMM, 53–54; in Latin America, 9–10; and need for regulations, 45–46, 48; and ownership debates, 273n58; during the Spanish colonial era, 10–14

collections (NMM): in the *Colección*, 81; colonial period portrayed in, 134–35; diverse nature of, 2, 68–69; and Egyptian antiquities, 241; fortification model in, 134–35, 271n12; under Ignacio Cubas, 49–50; illustrated in William Prescott's *History*, 162–67; impact of politics on, 65–68; inventories of, 56–57, 192, 249; under Isidro Gondra, 172–73; under Isidro Icaza, 62, 64, 68–69; from Isla de Sacrificios, 47–48; management of, 7; monuments in, 12–13, 160–62, 251–52; and Peñasco collection, 172; and removal of objects protocol, 85–86; during

Cushing, Caleb, 168

El sol, 69

employees (NMM), 55, 59, 62–63, 64, 93, 239, 249

Enlightenment, 11–12, 23, 159

Espinosa de los Monteros, Juan José, 68

Études sur l'histoire primitive des races (Eichthal), 221

excavation permits, 208

exhibitions: *Ancient and Modern Mexico*, 71; at the 1867 World's Fair, 248–49; images of, *38, 39*; at NMM, 69; of William Bullock, 36–40

expeditions: ability of NMM to mount, 17, 99, 102; and CSALM, 214–16, 226–27, 281n17; and CSM, 213–24, 227, 229; government approval for, 105; to Huachinango, 233–36; impact of, on private collecting, 24–25; and infrastructure development, 233–34; to the Isthmus of Tehuantepec, 49; and local politics, 124–25, 127; to Palenque by Francisco Corroy, 112–13, 115; to Palenque by Henri Baradère, 100–105; to Palenque by Jean-Frédéric Waldeck, 106–17; to Palenque by Mexican government, 115; to Palenque by René de Perdreauville, 117–22; to Palenque by Spanish Empire, 96; role of NMM in, 17, 96, 99; during the Spanish colonial era, 11–13; to Xochicalco, 117–18; to Yucatan by Maximilian, 236–38. *See also* Royal Antiquarian Expeditions

exportation: Jean-Frédéric Waldeck accused of, 115; legislation on, 44–45, 91, 107, 208; Maximilian's instructions on, 227–30, 283n62; as problem, 44–45, 59–60, 107; and smuggling, 91–93

Fagoaga, Francisco, 115

fake antiquities, 197–99

Farcy, Charles, 143–44

federalism, 28, 53, 66, 68, 114, 119–20, 127–28

Fernández de Lizardi, José Joaquín, 24, 34

Fischer, Augustin, 244

Fonseca, Urbano, 214

Forey, Ellie Frédéric, 208

forgeries, 197–99

Fortia d'Urban, Agricol-Joseph, 181; *Description de la Chine*, 181

France: and Mexican political instability, 207; and Mexico's Second Empire, 245–46; and Pastry War, 116; scientific expeditions of, 212–14, 226

Franck, Maximilien, 86–90, 93, 185

Franz Joseph, Emperor, 242

funding: attempts to increase, 57, 61, 63, 64, 67–68, 94, 145; for Henri Baradère's Palenque expedition, 102; impact of, on acquisitions, 181; for Jean-Frédéric Waldeck's Palenque expedition, 106–7; legislation regarding, 249; for move to Imperial Palace, 243; in the Porfirian Era, 254–55; for René de Perdreauville's Palenque expedition, 120

168; illustrations in translations of, 162–67; José Fernando Ramírez's notes on, 157–62, 178, 274n77; Lucas Alamán's objections to, 155–56; preconquest civilizations covered in, 150–53; and prejudices against Mexican peoples, 158–59, 167; publication of, 153; reasons for translations of, 153–55; sources for, 150–51; success of, 153, 154, 168

Hospital de Jesús, 35

Hospital de los Naturales, 31

Huachinango (ruins), 233–36

Huitzíhuitl, Emperor, 72, 73, 82

Huitzilopochtli, 162

human sacrifice, 39, 151–52, 158–59, 195–96

Humboldt, Alexander von, 22, 24, 41, 159, 184–85, 192, 202; *Vues des cordillères*, 13, 41

Hygeia OH, 43

Icaza, Isidro Ignacio: acquisition of antiquities by, 65–68, 97–98; ambitions of, 68–70; background of, 55; and the *Colección*, 70–72, 82, 138–39; collection removal protocols of, 85–86; deal of, with Henri Baradère, 99–105; death of, 94; and foreign collectors, 59–60, 92–93, 107, 144; inventorying museum's collection, 56–57; legal protocols proposed by, 61–64; and the León y Gama collection, 58–59; as museum conservator, 16, 55–65, 67–71, 82, 85–86, 90, 92–94

Imperial Palace, 240, 244–45

Incidents of Travel (Stephens and Catherwood), 143, 154

indigenous American peoples: connections of, to ancient peoples, 41, 78, 148–49, 234–36, 253; mistreatment of, 171, 273n58; in ownership debates, 14, 147; in the Porfirian Era, 236; under the Second Empire, 241–42; William Prescott's theories on, 152

industrialization, 175

Instituto de Geografía y Estadística, 118–19

Isidica, Rosa, 69

Isla de Sacrificios, 28, 47–48, 81, 136

Islas, Saturnino, 67

Isthmus of Tehuantepec, 49

Iturbide, Agustín de, 28, 29, 31, 55

Iturrigaray, José de, 25

Jecker, Jean Baptiste, 207

Jomard, Edmé-François, 113, 270n66

Journal de L'Institut Historique, 122

Juárez, Benito, 182, 191, 206–7, 208, 209, 226, 245, 249–50, 286n116

Junta de Antigüedades, 25, 31

Kingsborough, Edward King: *Antiquities of Mexico*, 123, 143–44, 150–51, 159, 178; on origins of preconquest peoples, 147, 148, 190; and the Palenque Prize, 124; supporting Jean-Frédérick Waldeck, 112, 116, 117

Kircher, Athanasius, 11

knowledge production: in Jean-Frédérick Waldeck's illustrations, 78, 81; museums' role in, 2, 8, 206; and national identity, 118; scholarly biases in, 258n15

Lacunza, José María, 231
Lami, Alphonse, 217
Landa, Diego de, 232
La piedra ausente, 288n8
Larrainzar, Manuel, 121
legislation: on the Botanical Garden, 93–94; concerning antiquities management, 61, 208; concerning foreign collecting, 42, 45–46; concerning funding, 249; on exportation, 44–45, 91, 107, 208; proposed by Isidro Icaza, 61–64; ratifying NMM, 93–94
León y Gama, Antonio de, 12, 58–59, 202; *Descripción histórica y cronológica de las dos piedras*, 59
Lerner, Jesse, 288n8
Lesson, René-Primevère, 101
Ley Lerdo, 191
liberalism, 3, 4, 120, 206, 225, 226, 249
L'Illustration, 193, 194–97
Linnaean taxonomy system, 23
literary associations, 138, 140–42
lithography, 29, 71, 140, 146
local communities, 51, 108–10, 127, 255
Longinos Martínez, José, 24
Longpérier, Adrien de, 185–86, 194
López, José Tiburcio, 66–67
Louvre, 87, 180–81, 185–86, 193–94, 211–12

Lyceum of Natural History, 113

Mañanas de la Alameda de México (Bustamante), 76
Marina, Doña, 135
Massé, Agustín, 140
Maximilian, Emperor, 19–20; administration of, 209, 225–27, 239, 245–46; and the AICL, 230–32, 249; Central American empire vision of, 285n86; death of, 249; and José Fernando Ramírez, 176; Louis Toussaint Doutrelaine's diagnostic of, 286n119; and the NMM, 239–42, 244–45, 251; policies of, on antiquities, 283n62; scholarly interests of, 224, 225, 226–27, 229–30, 236
Mayer, Brantz, 131–38, 173; *Mexico, as It Was and as It Is*, 132
Méhédin, Léon, 216, 220–21, 248–49
Mejía, Tomás, 248
Metlatoyuca (ruins), 233–36
Mexican Antiquities (Kingsborough), 123, 143–44, 150–51, 159, 178
Mexico: independence of, from Spain, 28; infrastructure needs of, 33, 46; postindependence, 171–72; and Texas, 17, 122, 138, 168; travel books on, 37; treaties of, with United States, 52–53; and war with France, 116; and war with United States, 17, 138, 168–69, 175
Mexico, as It Was and as It Is (Mayer), 132
México y sus alrededores, 192, 205–6

Michelena, José, 42
mineralogical collection (NMM),
65–66
mining industry, 23, 28, 33, 43,
44, 136
Miramar, Castle of, 225
Miramón, Miguel, 206, 228, 248
missionaries, 10, 151, 155–56
Mociño, José Mariano, 24
Modern and Ancient Mexico, 37–40
monolith collection (NMM), 12–13,
160–62, 251–52
Montholon, Charles François
Frédéric de, 227, 228–29
Montserrat, Eugène de, 216
*Monumentos de México tomados del
natural* (Gualdi), 271n4
Monuments anciens du Mexique
(Brasseur de Beaubourg), 117
Mora, Francisco Serapio, 180–81
Morelet, Arthur, 95
Muséum d'histoire naturelle, 95
Museum of Archaeology, History,
and Ethnography, 255
Museum of Natural History, 255
museums: in the Americas, 1, 9;
emergence of, 26; exhibition
experience of, 137; and national
identity, 4–5, 252; on owner-
ship debates, 253; and universal
knowledge objective, 69
musical instruments, Aztec, *166*, *167*

Napoleon I, 13–14, 26, 36, 58, 193,
212–13
Napoleon III, 19, 207, 212–13, 225,
226, 228, 230, 241, 245–46, 249
national identity, 1, 4–5, 60, 252,
254–55

nationalism, 35, 139–42, 149–50
National Museum of Anthropology,
6, 252, 255. *See also* National
Museum of Mexico (NMM)
National Museum of Mexico
(NMM): archives of, 6; artists
working for, 86–90, 139; during
Benito Juárez's term, 249–50;
and the *Colección*, 70–85; crisis
of meaning for, 2–3, 129; and
the CSM, 216, 220–22; deal of,
with Henri Baradère, 99–105;
disorganization of, 131, 136–37,
173; donations to, 50, 57–58, 63–
64, 102; educational role of, 1,
137–38; European views of, 105,
149–50; founding of, 1, 15, 21,
47–48; funding issues of, 2, 47,
57, 61, 63, 64, 67–68, 94, 138,
145; government commitment
to, 55–56, 57–58, 145; historiography of, 3–7; under Ignacio
Cubas, 49–51; images of interior of, *133*; impact of politics on,
16, 53–54, 207, 252; impact of
William Prescott's *History* on,
166–68; and inadequate infrastructure, 59; and inauguration
at the Imperial Palace, 244–45,
246; inventories of, 7, 56–57,
192, 249; under Isidro Icaza, 16,
55–72, 82, 85–86, 90, 92–94,
99–105, 107; and Jean-Frédérick
Waldeck's Palenque expedition,
107, 113, 115–16; under José Fernando Ramírez, 18–19, 174, 176,
180–82, 191–93, 209; lack of
institutional support for, 6, 61,
216; and lack of space, 1–2, 49,

National Museum of Mexico (*cont.*)
63, 69, 131, 173, 240, 264n13; legislation regarding, 93–94, 208;
and León y Gama's collections,
58–59; Lucas Alamán's impact
on, 51–52, 53; Lucas Alamán's
vision for, 30–32, 33–34, 46–47;
move of, from the National Palace, 255; move of, to the Imperial Palace, 240, 242–45, 246;
neglect of, 1–2, 3; official names
of, 262n75; operating hours of,
63, 64; operating protocols of,
7, 85–86, 102; and Palenque
expeditions, 17, 96, 99; personnel of, 55, 57, 59, 62–63, 64, 93,
239, 249; during the Porfirian
Era, 2–3, 251–52; print industry's
impact on, 17–18, 138–39, 142,
150; proposed legal protocols for,
61–64; publications of, 70–71, 85,
86, 138–39, 141–42; publicity for,
70, 86, 103; relational study of,
8–10; relations of, with foreign
collectors, 92–93, 99, 102–5, 115–
16, 126–29; and René de Perdreauville's Palenque expedition,
117–22; reputation of, 63–64, 118,
129, 149–50; role of, in public
opinion, 206; during the Second
Empire, 19–20, 239–47; sources
covering, 6–7; Spanish colonial
era's impact on, 15–16; state contributions to, 65–68; Teoyamiqui
statue at, 41; ties of, to Sociedad
de Anticuarios de Palenque, 120–
22; troops quartered at, 207; at
the university, 48–49; during the
U.S.-Mexican War, 169; visitor

descriptions of, 131–38, 271n1. *See
also* antiquities collection (NMM);
collections (NMM); natural history
collection (NMM)
National Palace, 20, 50–51, 239,
240, 255
natural history: mixed commodification of, 32, 101, 256; and
Palenque expeditions, 121;
during the Spanish colonial era,
11–12, 101; and taxidermy, 101–2
natural history collection (NMM):
under Ignacio Cubas, 49; under
Isidro Gondra, 172; under José
Fernando Ramírez, 181–82;
and mineralogical specimens,
65–66; policies for, 62, 101–2;
during the Second Empire, 244,
286n113; separated from NMM,
255–56; visitor descriptions of,
134, 136
Natural History Museum, 255
Navarro, Joaquín, 156
Nebel, Carl, 86, 105–6, 202; *Voyage pittoresque et archéologique*,
86, 105
Negrete, Celestino, 29
New World civilizations: in Americanist antiquarianism, 204–5; as
arising independently, 18, 152–
53; and art comparisons with
Old World, 81; and connections
to contemporary Indians, 148–
49, 152, 253; covered in William Prescott's *History*, 150–53;
and debated ties to Old World,
14, 38–39, 82–85, 97, 147, 231,
234; as equal to Old World, 143;
hypothesized origins of, 78, 147–

49; José Fernando Ramírez's hypotheses on, 177–78; Mormon readings of, 147; and national identity, 120; proposed research strategies for, 231–32
Nietzsche, Friedrich, 5
Nieuwerkerke, Émilien de, 180–81, 211–12
NMM. *See* National Museum of Mexico (NMM)
Norman, Benjamin Moore, 124, 271n69
Notes on Mexico (Poinsett), 32

Ocampo, Melchor, 182
O'Donojú, Juan, 28
O'Gorman, Edmundo, 224
Old World civilizations: in Americanist antiquarianism, 204–5; and art comparisons with New World, 81; and debated ties to New World, 14, 38–39, 82–85, 97, 147, 231, 234; as equal to New World, 143; and imperial political power, 128; as unconnected to New World, 18, 152–53; used in reconstruction of Mexican past, 76, 81
Olivo, Antonio, 271n12
Orbegoso, Juan de, 153
Ordoñez y Aguiar, Ramón de, 96, 97; *Historia de la creación*, 96, 97
Orozco y Berra, Manuel, 220, 221, 222, 233, 243, 247, 249, 287n134; *Geografía de las lenguas y carta etnográfica de México*, 221
Ortiz de Ayala, Tadeo, 261n39
Ortiz de Montellano, Manuel, 243
Oseguera, Andrés, 180, 181

Oteiza, Joaquín, 94

Palenque (ruins): and Adoration of the Cross relief, 108–9; Arthur Morelet's travels to, 95; condition of, 95, 108; Francisco Corroy's expedition to, 112–13, 115; Henri Baradère's expedition to, 100–105; Jean-Frédéric Waldeck's expedition to, 106–17; Juan Pablo Anaya's expedition to, 97; NMM's role at, 17, 126–29; and ownership debates, 109; and politics, 120, 126–28; René de Perdreauville's expedition to, 117–22; Royal Antiquarian expeditions to, 13, 97–98; scholarly interest in, 98–99, 105, 112, 123–24, 128; and the Sociedad de Anticuarios de Palenque, 118–19; Spanish exploration of, 12, 96
Palenque (village), 108–10
Palenque Prize, 96, 98–99, 103, 105, 106, 107, 112, 122–24, 270n66
Panes y Abellán, Diego, 163
Pantherion, 36
Paris Codex, 187–88
Pastry War (1838–39), 116
Pasztory, Esther, 76
Paulin, M., 187, 205
Payno, Manuel, 140, 206, 219
Peau de chagrin (Balzac), 100
Pedrozo, Manuel, 182
Peón, Simón, 238
Perdreauville, René de, 117–22; *Revista mexicana*, 118
personnel (NMM), 55, 57, 59, 62–63, 64, 93, 239, 249

phrenology, 148–49

Pichardo, José Antonio, 58

Piedra de los Sacrificios, 201–3, 279n85

Piedra del Sol, 251–52, 288n2. *See also* Calendar Stone

Pingret, Édouard, 193–99; José Fernando Ramírez's response to, 199–205; letter of, to Count Nieuwerkerke, 211–12

Pitt Rivers Museum, 7–8

Podgorny, Irina, 258n15

Poinsett, Joel R., 32, 52–53, 86–87, 90; *Notes on Mexico*, 32

politics: and antiquities, 33–34, 114, 119–20, 192, 252; and centralist-federalist debates, 53, 68, 114, 119–20, 127–28; and forgetting, 5; history of, 3–4; impact of, on NMM, 16, 53–54, 126–29; José Ramírez in, 175; Lucas Alamán in, 27–28, 33–34; and political instability, 29, 33–34, 125, 172, 182, 191, 206–7, 208–9; during the Second Empire, 232–33, 237. *See also* government (federal)

Polk, James, 168

Ponce de León, José Cayetano, 39

Ponz, Antonio, 25–26; *Viage de España o Cartas*, 25–26

Porfirian Era, 2–4, 174, 252

positivism, 178, 187

Prescott, William H., 150–53. *See also History of the Conquest of Mexico* (Prescott)

The Present State of Mexico (Disraeli), 33

Prévost Urkidi, Nadia, 270n66

Prieto, Guillermo, 140, 206

print industry: antiquarian studies depicted in, 142–46; editors dominating, 139–40; expansion of, 139; impact of, on NMM, 17–18, 138–39, 142, 150; and literary associations, 140–42

private collections. *See* collections (private)

Prix Palenque, 96, 98–99, 103, 105, 106, 107, 112, 122–24, 270n66

Promenade en Amérique (Ampère), 171–73

pseudosciences, 148–49

Quetzalcóatl, 27, 86, 162, 164, 251

Quintana Roo, Andrés de, 153

racial studies, 148–49

Ramírez, Ignacio, 140

Ramírez, José Fernando, 18–19; and the AICL, 230–32; antiquarian interests of, 176–82; background of, 174–76; under Benito Juárez, 249; bibliophilia of, 178–81; and critique of romantic history, 189; and the CSM, 219, 220–22, 224; death of, 176, 247; exile of, 182–83; hieroglyphic decipherments of, 160–62; impact of, on NMM, 174; international scholarly network of, 205; as minister of internal and foreign affairs, 173; as museum conservator, 168, 173–74, 176, 191–93, 194, 240; notes of, on William Prescott's *History*, 156–62, 178, 274n77; on ownership debate, 253–54; response of, to

Édouard Pingret's article, 199–205; and review of Gustave Eichthal's *Études*, 221; during the Second Empire, 209, 227–32, 237–38, 239–40, 243–44, 247; on troops in NMM, 207; writings of, 275n13, 276n26

Ramírez, Lino, 182

Ranke, Leopold von, 205

Registro trimestre, 139

Registro yucateco, 154

regulations. *See* legislation

Reinisch, Simon Leo, 225, 240–41, 247

Revista mexicana (Perdreauville), 118

Riaño, Juan Antonio de, 21–22

Riesgo, Juan Manuel, 66

Río de la Loza, Leopoldo, 219, 230

Robert, Pedro, 71, 82

Robertson, William, 150; *History of America*, 150, 274n75

Robinson, Peter F., 36

Robles Pezuela, Luis, 233

Rodríguez, Pablo, 172

Rodríguez Arangoiti, José Ramón Alejo, 243

Rosenstein, Leon, 254

Royal Academy of San Carlos, 22, 23–24

Royal Antiquarian Expeditions, 13, 25, 61, 76, 96, 103

Royal Mint, 240

Royal Society, 112, 125

Royal University: antiquities chair at, 12; Coatlicue monument buried at, 13, 41; conservatism at, 49; images of, 133; NMM housed in, 2, 47, 48–49, 131, 132; visitor description of, 132

Rozental, Sandra, 288n8

Sad Indian (Indio Triste) statue, 50, 134

Sahagún, Bernardino de, 10

Salas, Pérez, 272n37

Salazar, Hipólito, 156

Salazar Illaregui, José, 227, 283n62

Salinas, Carlos, 5

Sánchez, Jesús, 288n2

Sánchez, José Vicente, 58–59

Sánchez Mora, José Mariano (Conde de Peñasco), 78, 86, 172

Santa Anna, Antonio López de, 109, 112, 120, 139, 172, 182, 191

Schnapp, Alain, 146

School of Mines, 6, 22, 23, 24, 30, 40, 138

School of Surgery, 30

Scott, Winfield, 168

Second Empire, 19–20, 174, 176, 209, 224–26, 239–40, 245–46

security watchmen (NMM personnel), 59, 62

Selva Nevada, Marquesa de la, 69, 79

Sessé, Martín, 24

Sierra O'Reilly, Justo, 154, 254–55

Siglo XIX (Cumplido), 153

Sigüenza y Góngora, Carlos de, 11, 58

Siliceo, Manuel, 236

Six Months' Residence and Travels in Mexico (Bullock), 37, 190

SMGE. *See* Sociedad Mexicana de Geografía y Estadística (SMGE)

Sociedad de Anticuarios de Palenque, 119–22

Sociedad de Historia Natural, 249–50

Sociedad del Museo Mexicano, 94

To order or obtain more information on these or other University of Nebraska Press titles, visit nebraskapress.unl.edu.

www.ingramcontent.com/pod-product-compliance
Lightning Source LLC
Chambersburg PA
CBHW020335270326
41926CB00007B/185

9 781496 203373